MW01621223

JAMES LONDON

A Reference Guide To Locations

Gary Giblin

For Lisa...

Designed by Dave Worrall
Cover designed by Jeff Marshall
Typeset in Times New Roman and Bookman Medium. Designed in Adobe PageMaker

ISBN 0-9713133-0-X Library of Congress Catalog Number TXu 965-399

Printed and bound in England

This edition first published November 2001 by
Daleon Enterprises
PO Box 152, Dunellen, NJ 08812, USA

Actor Christopher Lee, who wrote the Tribute to Ian Fleming,
and film director Peter Hunt, who wrote the Foreword for the book.

KEY

Ian Fleming Locale: a location such as a home, office, restaurant or hotel associated with James Bond's creator

Literary Locale: a location described or referred to in one or more of Ian Fleming's James Bond novels, stories, manuscripts or treatments. This includes fictional locations, such as Hugo Drax's London Home, as well as real-life places and institutions such as Regent's Park and the Bank of England.

Film Locale: a location used in or associated with one or more of the Eon Productions James Bond films. This includes locations used "as is", such as the College of Arms and the Ministry of Defence; "disguised" locations such as RAF Northolt (which doubled as Bluegrass Field, Kentucky in *Goldfinger*); and "associated locations" (offices, shops, cinemas, recording studios, etc.) with connections to one or more of the films.

Spy Locale: a location associated with the real-life world of espionage or police work, such as MI6, the Russian Embassy or Scotland Yard

Disguised Locale: a location, generally from the films, that doubles as something else, e.g., Somerset House, which appears as a St. Petersburg Square in the film *GoldenEye* and the MOD in *Tomorrow Never Dies*

"Trespassers Will Be Eaten" Locale: a private home or other site that is off limits to visitors, such as Turner's House or MI6

"Shaken *and* Stirred" Locale: a highly recommended site of special interest or significance (see the list below)

The word **ex** appears before the name of a location to indicate "former site of" or, if the building itself is gone, "site of the former"

DIRECTIONS:	UNDERGROUND LINES:	
N: North	BA: Bakerloo	JU: Jubilee
S: South	CE: Central	ME: Metropolitan
E: East	CI: Circle	NO: Northern
W: West	DI: District	PI: Piccadilly
R: Right	EL: East London	VI: Victoria
L: Left	HC: Hammersmith & City	WC: Waterloo & City
		DL: Docklands

All film and book titles are italicized. In cases where there may be confusion as to whether a film or novel is intended, the abbreviation F (for Film) and B (for Book) is used immediately before the title.

Place names printed in boldface type within the text, e.g., **Bond Street** (13:9), have entries of their own. The two-part number in parentheses immediately following the name indicates the entry itself; in this case, 13:9, Bond Street, is the 9th entry under Mayfair, which is the 13th section of the book. The Index also lists locations by entry numbers, not page numbers. Relatively obscure locations are listed as "Quick Ones, en route" at the end of the relevant section; in the text they are followed by a Q, e.g., (5:Q). References to locations in the forthcoming volume *James Bond's Britain* are followed by (JBB). For a **Fleming/Bond Chronology**, keyed to entries in this book, see Appendix Five.

A Note on Terminology: I have used the names "Secret Service", "MI6", "SIS" and "Secret Intelligence Service" interchangeably throughout this book, whether referring to the actual British intelligence-gathering agency or to the fictional versions of this organization. For the history and usage of these terms, both in real life and reel life, see **MI6 (1926-1967)** (27:22).

A Cautionary Note: In addition to the many places that you can actually visit, I have also listed, purely for reference, a number of locations that are not open to the public. Among these are business headquarters, military installations, government offices and private homes. The addresses of the businesses, military and government facilities are all in the telephone directory, of course, but the sites themselves are still closed to the public. The addresses of private homes have also been derived from public sources, namely the following previously published works: Andrew Lycett's *Ian Fleming: The Man Behind James Bond* and John Pearson's *The Life of Ian Fleming*; Pearson's *James Bond: The Authorized Biography*; Roy Berkeley's *A Spy's London*; Nigel West's *MI6* and *MI5*; York Membery's *Pierce Brosnan*; Paul Donovan's *Roger Moore*; John Hunter's *Great Scot*; Michael Feeney Callan's *Sean Connery*; and Alan Barnes' and Marcus Hearn's *Kiss Kiss Bang Bang! The Unofficial James Bond Film Companion*. However, I cannot overemphasize the need to respect the privacy of those who now live or work in these buildings, many of whom have no idea that Ian Fleming or Sean Connery once slept under their roof. These locations have been marked with a "Trespassers Will Be Eaten" skull and crossbones to remind you of this fact. The location and description of the present MI6 headquarters may be found in numerous travel guides, architecture guides and books on modern intelligence-gathering, including the government's own handbook, *Central Intelligence Machinery*, published by Her Majesty's Stationery Office.

Finally, an obvious caveat: things change. Since I began this book in January 1998, a number of people and places associated with James Bond's Britain have "passed from the scene". Apart from the tragic loss of John Stears and Desmond Llewelyn, mentioned below, buildings have been pulled down, businesses have closed or relocated, corporate names have been changed and people have retired or moved on to new jobs. I have done my best to keep up with all the changes and to incorporate them into this manuscript. Nevertheless, I can guarantee you that *James Bond's London* is bound to differ, if only slightly (I hope), from James Bond's London. Keep this in mind as you look for your favorite locations and please feel free to forward any updates to the publisher.

Ian Fleming's former home at 22b Ebury Street.
Note the English Heritage plaque upper left.

ACKNOWLEDGMENTS

As this project grew from small to "not so small", many people on both sides of the Atlantic freely gave of their time, expertise and inspiration. Some provided basic factual information about the locations, some contributed reminiscences about people, places and events from the world of Bond and still others did actual legwork, helping me research locations that might otherwise have remained "lost". To them I extend my most sincere thanks.

Nicholas Barker, Editor, the Book Collector, London; David Barlow and the former Whitehall Radio operators Glynn Burhouse, Brian Parkes and Henry Matthews, all in England; John Beasley, Editor, Peckham Society Newsletter, Peckham, London; Peter Beatty, Senior Administrator, Press Office, Sotheby's, London; Mary Bee, Director, Portal Gallery, London; Eleanor Blake, Royal College of Art, London; Charlie Bodycomb, Supervising Armourer, Bapty & Co., London; Squadron Leader John Boston, Business Development Manager, RAF Northolt, London; Alison Burton, Air Studios, London; Edna Clark, the College of Arms, London; Andy Clifton, Public Relations Manager, Ladbroke Racing Ltd, Harrow, Middlesex; Pat Cooper, the Book Collector, London; Elizabeth Corey, City of Westminster Archives, London; Marjory Cornelius, England; Tim Cottingham, Webmaster, Aston Martin Picture Gallery, at: www.astonmartins.com; Clare Crawford, PR Coordinator, Alfred Dunhill, London; Jacqueline Domenech, Associate PR Executive, David Morris International Ltd, London; Patrick Douglas-Millican and the staff of Turnbull & Asser, London; Mark Farley, Managing Director, and the staff of Farley and H.J. Spiller Hire, London; Andrew Fletcher, General Manager, Bapty & Co., London; Frances Fox, Swaine Adeney Brigg, London; Dan Franklin, Jonathan Cape Publishers, London; Timothy Glazier, Press Officer, Geo F. Trumper, London; Harriet Goodall, Assistant to Manager, Drama Centre London; Joanna Gormanley, SBC Warburg, London; Mari Carmen Benitez Gutierrez, Personnel Training Manager, Family Leisure, London; Zena Hatton, London; Douglas Hayward, Chairman, Douglas Hayward Ltd, London; Jean Hudson, Assistant Secretary, Boodle's, London; Beatrice "Bunty" Johnson, London Press Club, London; Iain Johnstone, London; Malcolm Lander, Webmaster, Unofficial RAF Northolt Page; Shaun Lawlor, Building Interiors Group Manager, The Buying Agency, Cabinet Office, London; The Staff of Les Ambassadeurs Club, London; Donald F. Leopold, Vice President, Member Services, AAA, Cincinnati, Ohio; Amanda Lewis, Marketing Manager, Entertainment Team, London; Jonathan Lipman, Production Director, Angels & Bermans, London; Squadron Leader Robert Livingston RAF (Retired), RAF Northolt, London; Silke Lohmann, Press Office Assistant, Sotheby's, London; Fergus MacDermot, Japanese Embassy, London; Dimitro Major, Chairman, Major's Ltd., London; Mohamed Manjra, Vallance Lodge & Co Ltd, London; Mike Marsh, Ministry of Health, London; David Moore, Technical Services Manager, West Ferry Printers, London; Tim Moore, Webmaster, 007Bond, Baildon, West Yorkshire, at: http://x-stream.fortunecity.com/ millenium/155; Robert Noel, Lancaster Herald, College of Arms, London; Canon John Oates, St. Bride's Church, the City of London; Stephen Potter, Library Manager, Southwark Local Studies Library, London; Michael Quinn and the staff of Church's, London; Eugene Rae, Archivist, Royal College of Art, London; Anthony Richards, Archivist, Imperial War Museum, London; Gerry O'Riordan, Manager, Snake Ranch Studio, London; Shane O'Riordan, Press Officer, Robert Fleming Holdings Company, London; Robert Park, Swaine Adeney Brigg, London; H. E. Paston-Bedingfeld, York Herald, College of Arms, London; Vagn Pedersen, Assistant Librarian, Civil Aviation Authority, Gatwick Airport, West Sussex; Graham Rye, President, James Bond 007 International Fan Club & Archive, Addlestone, Surrey; Hugh Scrope, Company Secretary (Retired), Vickers, East Sussex; PC John Seal, Thames Division, Metropolitan Police Service, London; David Shilling, London; Joel Silver, Curator of Books, Lilly Library, Indiana University, Bloomington, Indiana; A. Kenneth Snowman and the staff of Wartski, London; Adrian Stephenson, Queen Anne Press, Harpenden, Herts.; Georgina Sullivan, Press and Public Relations Manager, The Ritz, London; Janet Taylor, Marketing Manager, Lock & Co., London; Saundra Taylor, Curator of Manuscripts, Lilly Library, Indiana University, Bloomington, Indiana; Mark Thomson, Press Officer, HM Customs and Excise, London; David G. Thursby, Advertising and Marketing Manager, Scotch House, London; Peter Trinder, Head of Security, Foreign & Commonwealth Office, London; John M. Veale, Hoare & Company, London; Robin Walker, De Beers, London; Helena Walsh, Lilly Library, Indiana University, Bloomington, Indiana; Pam Whiffin, Blue Plaques Administrator, English Heritage, London; David M. Williams, Managing Director, Anderson & Sheppard, London; Iain Wright, Archivist, HM Customs and Excise, London

I would also like to acknowledge Eon Productions, Danjaq, LLC and Pinewood Studios, whose very kind assistance during the hectic production period of *The World Is Not Enough* not only enhanced this book but literally made *James Bond's London* and the forthcoming *James Bond's Britain* possible. In particular, I would like to thank Vice-President of Marketing John Parkinson; Unit Manager Iris Rose (who also gets a big hug!); Line Producer Anthony Waye; former Production Controller Reg Barkshire; former Marketing Director Charles (Jerry) Juroe; Miniature Supervisor John Richardson; First Assistant Editor Simon Cozens; Costume Designer Lindy Hemming; Production Buyer Ron Quelch; Supervising Art Director Neil Lamont and last, but certainly not least, Neil's father, Production Designer Peter Lamont. The Oscar-winning art director not only provided exhaustive answers to all of my questions, but also contributed a number of wonderful behind-the-scenes stories about the 16 Bond films on which he has worked, starting with *Goldfinger* in 1964 and continuing through *The World Is Not Enough*. Peter was never, ever too busy to take my phone calls, whether working on the mammoth *TWINE* production itself or preparing for a much-deserved holiday abroad. He is a kind, courteous, generous man (not to mention one hell of a production designer!) and I simply cannot thank him enough for his help on this book.

Finally, I must extend a special thanks to Chris Gardner for his many and varied contributions to this project, from its genesis in January 1998 through its completion three years later; to Robert Goodman, Guide Director, Big Bus Company, London, for his enthusiastic "guidance" (he is, quite simply, a living encyclopedia of the British capital) and for his witty repartee and all-round good fellowship; to Randy Gregory for his aeronautical expertise; to Kate (Fleming) Grimond, Merrimoles, Oxfordshire, for her gracious assistance and encouragement; to Jamie Healy, Marketing Assistant, Brighton & Hove Council, for researching the Brighton area locations (his sleuthing skills are second to none); to Peter Janson-Smith, Chairman, Ian Fleming (Glidrose) Publications, London, for his helpful suggestions; to Andrew Lycett, for his expertise, insight and advice on the *implicit* subject of this book; to Earl Messer for his earnest counsel; to David O'Reilly of the London Film Commission, for his invaluable updates during the early days of the *TWINE* production; to Tony Phipps, for locating and photographing the Harefield Quarry site; to Dr. Susan Shapiro, Assistant Professor of Classics, Xavier University, Cincinnati, for translating and identifying the source of Fleming's epitaph; to Steve Wichrowski, for diligently researching and photographing several of the Greater London locations; to David Williams, for his indispensable help in documenting and describing the *TWINE* boat chase; to Nigel West, the world's foremost expert on British Intelligence (at www.nigelwest.com), for his comments on the espionage entries; to Doug Redenius and Dave Reinhardt of the Ian Fleming Foundation, for providing a copy of the Ian Fleming-Raymond Chandler BBC radio program; to Brenda (Mrs. John) Stears, for her warm and generous support; to the cinematic Bond veterans Syd Cain, Allan Cameron, Marjory Cornelius, Joe Fitt, J. W. "Corkey" Fornof, John Glen, Bill Hill, Bert Luxford, Peter Murton and Arthur Wooster, for kindly sharing so many of their experiences with me; to the two very special gentlemen, Peter Hunt and Christopher Lee, for penning the book's opening remarks (needless to say, I am an unabashed admirer of these legendary artists); to my publishers Lee Pfeiffer, Ron Plesniarski and Dave Worrall, for setting the standard and paving the way; and, lastly, to my wife, Lisa, whose contributions to this book, and to my life, are literally incalculable...

Two Special Acknowledgments: During the preparation of this manuscript, I was saddened to learn of the deaths of two legendary Bond veterans: special effects designer John Stears and actor Desmond Llewelyn. John Stears, as many of this book's readers know, won Oscars for his visionary work on both *Thunderball* and *Star Wars*, blockbuster entries in two of the most important and influential series in film history. His contributions to the Bond legend cannot, of course, be overstated. He was there at the beginning, blowing up the masterful model of Crab Key in *Dr. No*, customizing the "most famous car in the world" for *Goldfinger* and designing those Oscar-winning effects for *Thunderball*. What many readers may not know is that John Stears also generously encouraged and supported those of us who write about the wonderful films on which he worked. I first phoned John about *James Bond's London* in the summer of 1998 and, having known him only slightly, was somewhat surprised (though certainly pleased) at his immediate enthusiasm for this project. He took the time and trouble to give serious, detailed answers to my questions, and when he was unsure of the answer, would search through his files and then call me back with the new information. And if he *still* didn't know the answer, he and Brenda (his beloved wife and partner) would put the question to their friends and colleagues to see if *they* might be able to help solve the mystery. Thoughtful, considerate and highly modest, John Stears was a gentleman in the true sense of the word, one whose warmth and humor will be greatly missed by all who knew him.

The same, of course, can be said of Desmond Llewelyn, whose tragic death the week before Christmas 1999 stunned his family, friends and co-workers, not to mention legions of fans throughout the world. Desmond graciously contributed to countless Bond-related projects over the years, including, I am pleased to say, this book and another Bond project on which I worked in 1996. And like John Stears, Peter Lamont and so many other Bond veterans, Desmond always seemed to go above and beyond the call of duty... way beyond. He would, as a matter of course, pick up his out-of-town (or out-of-country) visitors at the train station, treat them to lunch in the local pub, entertain them in his home and even take them on tours of historic English locales! Imagine standing on the spot where William the Conqueror landed in 1066, arm in arm with "Q", as a carload of sightseers do double takes and shake their heads in disbelief... Could it be him? No, it couldn't be! Yes, it is! Desmond was, undeniably, a superstar in his 80s, a vital part of a legendary film series. But he was not awed by his own celebrity and certainly didn't expect anyone else to be. To those who knew him well or to those just getting to know him, he was simply "Desmond": a warm, wonderful grandfather whose broad smile and twinkling eyes always made you feel like a cherished member of the family. As cliché as it may sound, to know Desmond Llewelyn was to love him, on-screen and off. *Ffarwel fy annwyl ffrind...*

Top: Author Gary Giblin with the late Desmond Llewelyn at his home in Bexhill-on-Sea, 1996. *Above (left):* Production Designer Peter Lamont. *Right:* SFX genius John Stears.

The premiere of Peter Hunt's "On Her Majesty's Secret Service", held at The Odeon Leicester Square (*see Page 104*)

FOREWORD

When I was first asked to write a Foreword to this fascinating book, my reaction was one of mixed pleasure and hesitancy. Pleasure because just leafing through its pages steeped me in nostalgic memories of happy, if frequently frantic days with friends and colleagues, some, alas, since departed; and hesitancy because my personal contribution to the Bond films was restricted to the original six, starting with the first, *Dr. No* in 1962, and culminating in *On Her Majesty's Secret Service*, which I directed in 1969.

It was thinking about these dates that finally allowed me to overcome my hesitancy. Because it seemed to me (and probably to most who were closely concerned with those early films) that Bond himself was symbolic of the Sixties, that period when Britain was at long last emerging from the fog of grey austerity that had engulfed her following the thunderstorms of war.

When Ian Fleming first introduced James Bond in his novel *Casino Royale* in 1953, the lights of London and other British towns and cities were still frequently blacked out, although by the demands of rationing, rather than the fear of an air attack. And this rationing affected not only electricity, bacon and butter, but such luxuries as hand-made Balkan cigarettes and vodka martinis, whether shaken or stirred. Yet Fleming, with his memories of happier days, was able to pierce through this drabness and look forward to a brighter and more exciting future.

Looking back now, I realize that the team that first presented James Bond to cinema audiences (producers Broccoli and Saltzman, screenwriter Dick Maibaum, director Terence Young, cameraman Ted Moore and myself) was almost entirely made up of "over-thirties". We had, therefore, all been on nodding terms with danger and the prospect of imminent annihilation, whether as children of the Blitz or, in my case, as a member of the armed forces. I suppose many of us might be considered "oldies", but, in fact, it was our own experience of those times that helped us identify so closely with Fleming's creation. And I shall always be glad that he lived long enough to see his vision brought so vividly to life on the screen, and that I was privileged to contribute to the birth and early years of the "007 Phenomenon".

As I read this beautifully researched book, it occurred to me that Gary has done more than just assemble a list of locations. He has actually evoked a bygone time and place. The Sixties were perhaps the last days when charm, sophistication, elegance and courtesy still had a place in contemporary life. And it is interesting that those early Bond films of the Sixties are as popular as ever today. Of course, Bond himself, probably best represented by those Sixties films, still adheres to these old values. True, he kills people (though only "baddies", and only when left no other option!), but he almost always dispatches them with a valedictory or perhaps even an apologetic word. And his attitude toward women, be they delectable or deadly, is always tinged with a kind of old-world courtesy, whether his ultimate intention be seduction or extinction. However dangerous to know, Bond is always the gentleman and there is no room for brutality in his love-making or for vulgarity or obscenity in his manner or speech. He represents the triumph of good over evil, a true descendant of the Knights of Old. And, besides, even Sir Galahad accumulated a respectable number of notches on his sword.

So, a walk through the many interesting locations Gary has described provides an excursion not only for the imagination, but also for the reliving of past, more glamorous days. And it is an added bonus that the Bond films, from the Sixties to the present-day, are not only frequently shown on television all over the world, but are also available on video, giving the reader of *James Bond's London* the opportunity to refresh his or her memory before setting out on a journey of discovery.

And who knows? You and I might come across each other in the shadow of the College of Arms or across the bar in El Vino's and, catching each other's eye, share together a moment of escape into an infinitely more exciting world of espionage, elegance and high adventure...

Peter Hunt

IAN FLEMING: A TRIBUTE

As most of you are doubtless aware, I played the title role in the 1974 James Bond film *The Man With The Golden Gun*. What you may not know is that Bond's creator, Ian Fleming, was my cousin, or, more precisely, he was my step-cousin: his maternal uncle Harcourt was my stepfather. I really didn't get to know Ian until after World War II, although, as I learned many years later, my sister Xandra knew him at the Admiralty, where they had both worked in Naval Intelligence during the war. The first time I actually met him was when he had a house in Victoria Square, which is a lovely, rather secluded little square not far from Victoria Station in London. He was then working for *The Sunday Times* and had already married Ann, the former Lady Rothermere. Then, some time later, I had gone down to Royal St George's at Sandwich and suddenly there was Ian in the bar saying, "Oh, hello, how are you? Haven't seen you for a long time. We really must play golf together." So we began to play together quite often and from that time on, almost all my associations with Ian were on the golf course. On one occasion, after having read *Goldfinger*, I remember saying to him "How clever of you to do this," because hole by hole he had described the entire course of Royal St George's, which he called Royal St Mark's. Anyone who was a member or who had ever played there would have recognized it immediately. On another occasion he told me that they were going to make a picture called *Dr. No* and he wanted me to play the title role. It might have been that he'd seen me as a Chinese villain in *The Terror of the Tongs* or because of my height, because Dr. No is described as an Asian who is enormously tall. In any case, he said, "I believe you know the director, Terence Young." Indeed I did: Terence Young directed me in my first film, *Corridor of Mirrors*, as well as several others. He said, "I think you'd be ideal for Dr. No and I'll mention it to Terence." I thought it would have been wonderful to play such a part, especially since Ian was then alive to see it. However, by the time Ian got round to mentioning this to Terence, they had already cast Joseph Wiseman, who is one of America's finest actors. Of course, when I did finally get the chance to play in a Bond movie, sadly, Ian was gone. The last time I saw him was at the golf club and he said to me, "You know, one of my great ambitions is going to be realized next year." I asked him what it was and he said, "I'm going to be Captain of Royal St George's." That meant more to him, it seems, than almost anything else. And, of course, before it could happen, he had a heart attack and died in the ambulance on the way to Canterbury Hospital.

It is sometimes remarked that Ian's death was all the more tragic because it occurred prior to the "Bond explosion" in 1965-66. But, I believe that Ian fully realized what he had created, ever since President Kennedy's "endorsement" in 1961. There was, of course, a lot of Ian in Bond, as everybody knows. He was very high up in the Intelligence world, which occasionally we would chat about, since I, too, had been in Intelligence during the war. He therefore placed this character within the British intelligence network, taking the initial "C" from the real head of MI6 and changing it to "M", apparently after the real-life Admiral Messervy, then making Bond a commander in the Navy because he had been a commander in the Navy and so on. But "007", or rather, the "00" prefix, the "licence to kill", was his own very clever invention, because no such thing ever existed in British intelligence or American intelligence, for that matter. And, of course, Ian also knew a great deal about wine and food, had a pretty good knowledge of firearms and in his capacity as journalist was able to find out a great deal about the secret agencies, some of which was public knowledge, some of which was pretty close to being public knowledge. He also made the character of Bond enormously attractive to the opposite sex, as he was himself. Women found Ian immensely appealing. He was very amusing, very entertaining and physically very attractive. There's no question about that. So, he created this wonderful character and then placed him in those wonderful stories. For he was a great storyteller. And before Ian there hadn't been many stories where the food and the drink and the weaponry and the women and the baddies were all described in such precise, specific and accurate detail. Another interesting thing about his stories is that virtually all the male characters had names which existed in real life: Drax, Goldfinger, Blofeld and most certainly there was a man called Scaramanga. He was at Eton with Ian, who disliked him intensely and so put him in the book. It's a Greek name, in fact, and if you go to the merchant dockyards in the Port of Athens you will see that they are called "Scaramanga". I know this for a fact because I've been there myself. The names of the women, of course, are a different matter. You have to be pretty daring to call one of your leading ladies "Pussy Galore", although I suppose there were probably some people who didn't get it. But, then, that was Ian's sense of humor.

Finally, to touch upon one of the themes in this book, I should mention that Ian was also a great patriot and his novels very much reflect this fact. One might say that Bond represented all that was best in British tradition. He was cool, calm, unflappable, ready to do anything his country demanded of him, all of which reflected Ian's own feelings. So, I am very pleased to see a book about James Bond's London, which is something that has never been done before. On one level, of course, Bond's London encompasses things like Bond's flat, his housekeeper, his Turkish cigarettes from Grosvenor Street, his supercharged Bentley (about which I know nothing!) and of course the Admiralty and Naval Intelligence. Underscoring all this, however, is the theme of Britain and the Empire, which Ian and many people of my generation believed in, myself included. I therefore hope that when you read this book, you will come away with a better understanding of both my cousin, Ian Fleming, and the Britain in which he so strongly believed.

Christopher Lee

History in the making: Ian Fleming signs his contract with Eon Productions, as producers Albert R. Broccoli and Harry Saltzman, and the then relatively unknown Sean Connery look on.

Photo: Courtesy, The Lily Library, Indiana University, Bloomington, Indiana, USA

INTRODUCTION

"I feel that the only man behind James Bond was Ian Fleming."
Albert R. Broccoli, September 15, 1965

This project evolved from a short guide to James Bond's London that I prepared for Lee Pfeiffer's "Let's Bond in Britain Tour 1997". Having visited the British capital several times, and done a bit of research on the subject, I was aware of a number of London sites used in the Bond films, as well as other locations, such as Ian Fleming's homes, that might be of interest to wandering 007 fans. The result was a list of some 20 locations, which, along with accompanying photos and a map, was to provide a fun way both to explore the British capital and follow in the footsteps of James Bond. After the trip, Lee suggested that an expanded version of the Guide might make a worthwhile book and so, *voilà,* here it is! Of course, it wasn't *really* that simple. First there was the question of which locations to include and which to omit. Obviously, things like Ian Fleming's Birthplace, Bond's Chelsea Home, and the "St Petersburg-on-the-Thames" locations from *GoldenEye* were all musts. But what about Ian Fleming's barber or the place where the author got his tailored suits? Eventually I realized that what I might think was worthwhile and what others might consider worthwhile would probably never coincide. So, I resolved to include every Bond and Fleming-related location that I could possibly uncover. Then, somewhere along the way, trying to determine where to draw the geographical line (did Pinewood Studios count as Greater London, for example), I decided to go for broke and compile a list of locations from James Bond's *Britain*. So now, three years and several thousand frequent flier miles later, here it is: a comprehensive, two-part reference guide to nearly 500 locations and institutions associated with the life of Ian Fleming; described or mentioned in his James Bond novels; and depicted in or connected with the Eon Productions/United Artists' films from *Dr. No* to *The World Is Not Enough*. The first part, *James Bond's London*, covers over 270 locations in the British capital; the second part, which will be published in 2003, covers some 200 additional locations throughout England, Scotland, Wales and Ireland.

You will notice that I have omitted non-Fleming and non-Eon locations, i.e., those depicted in the novels of Messrs. Amis, Gardner and Benson, as well as the films *Casino Royale* and *Never Say Never Again*. My reasons for this were both practical and subjective. First, to include locations from these works would have made for a book at least twice the size of the present one and that kind of project was simply beyond my resources. Second, I happen to believe that, regardless of whatever merits they may possess, the non-Eon films are not "true" Bond films; they do not command (or merit) the interest and devotion accorded the United Artists' series. With apologies to Fleming's literary successors, I believe the same holds true for the novels. Ian Fleming is the creator of James Bond, plain and simple. What he said, or wrote, is gospel; anything else is apocryphal.

With further apologies to the legendary creators of the films *Dr. No*, *From Russia With Love*, et al., I also believe that the so-called "Cinematic Bond" was already there, in print, before anyone else ever typed a word in collaboration with or adaptation of Ian Fleming. The blueprint for the series isn't *Goldfinger* the film, it's *Goldfinger* the novel, from the pre-credit adventure in Mexico and the "three-girl formula", to the Aston Martin with modifications and the tough, stylish and, yes, even wisecracking character of James Bond himself. Did the films elaborate upon, intensify, exaggerate, and even perfect some of the characteristics of Fleming's fictional world? Of course. For a time, they also came dangerously close to becoming overblown parodies of themselves, the salvation coming about only with a return to the Flemingesque in *For Your Eyes Only*. Today, the best Bond films are generally considered to be the early Connery ones. You know, *From Russia With Love, Goldfinger*, or, among true diehards, the masterful *On Her Majesty's Secret Service*. Is it simply a coincidence that these films also happen to be the most faithful to their literary sources? I don't believe so. And neither, apparently, did producer Cubby Broccoli. In a September 1965 interview with Fleming biographer John Pearson, Cubby acknowledged the contributions of his production team (Terence Young, Richard Maibaum, Ken Adam, Peter Hunt and Ted Moore) but then added: "All the same, I feel that the only man behind James Bond was Ian Fleming." For this reason, then, I have devoted a significant amount of this book to the life of Bond's creator and to the events in his life that seem to bear upon the origins of James Bond.

I have also devoted a great deal of space to locations described or merely mentioned in Fleming's James Bond adventures: the novels, the short stories and even the 1959 screen treatment *James Bond of the Secret Service* (see Appendix Two). Many of these locales, although familiar to the author's original British audience, will be unknown to modern readers, especially non-Britons. For example, Fleming mentions Ladbroke's, the off-track betting shop chain, in the novel *Moonraker*, but does not elaborate. You and I either know what this means or we don't. Of course, most Britons will recognize the name, since there are Ladbroke's shops all over the country. But even many Britons might wonder what was so important about Blades, the exclusive St James's Club, having "a direct line to Ladbroke's". Read the entry on Ladbroke's (13:17) to find out why this would have mattered in 1954.

A second, and perhaps more fundamental, reason for mentioning the many literary locales is to elucidate what I believe to have been Fleming's "hidden agenda", "greater purpose", "ulterior motive", call it what you will. For Bond's creator, as Christopher Lee notes in his Tribute, was a patriot, and he demonstrates his pride in British history, customs and accomplishments in virtually everything he wrote. Thus, well-known hotels, restaurants, museums, theatres, auction houses, jewelers, golf courses, public schools, train stations, bus routes, news agencies, tobacco manufacturers and more turn up with remarkable frequency in the pages of his novels. Most obvious in this regard are the adventures set in England, either wholly (*Moonraker*, "The Property of a Lady") or in part (*Goldfinger, Diamonds Are Forever* and *Thunderball*, among others). Yet even when the action takes place overseas, Fleming name-drops so many homegrown locales and institutions that Britain is seldom far from the reader's consciousness. At the end of Bond's ordeal in *Doctor No*, for example, an injured and exhausted 007 sits in the Governor's office in Kingston, daydreaming about the people and pigeons in Trafalgar Square. A similar nostalgic episode occurs in *Goldfinger*, as Bond faces death at the hands of the villain (or, rather, at the teeth of his circular saw) in a Swiss factory. In other novels, an "outsider" may be called upon to wax poetic about the land of Shakespeare and Robin Hood, as the Italian Domino Vitali does in Chapter 15 of *Thunderball* and as the French-Canadian Vivienne Michel does in Chapter 3 of *The Spy Who Loved Me*. These and countless other examples (the roster of Blofeld's British and Irish targets in *OHMSS*, for example) reinforce the notion that Britain is important, that Britain matters.

True, it may not always *look* that way. Even Fleming realized that. So, the relatively pure and unadulterated nationalism of his earlier novels, in which Britain stands at the forefront of world affairs (*Moonraker* comes most readily to mind), eventually gives way to a somewhat more realistic picture in the later novels. Here, the author acknowledges that Britain's power and influence have declined and even allows Bond to sound off about the nation's troubles ("We don't show teeth any more - only gums," he laments in Chapter 19 of *From Russia, With Love*). Of course, outsiders cannot get away with inflammatory remarks like these, no matter how close to the truth they may be. Thus, when the American Milton Krest boasts that the only thing England is good for is old buildings and the Queen or when the Japanese Tiger Tanaka suggests that Britain has self-destructed since World War II, Bond is there to defend his country's honor. "I propose to... display not only the superiority of Great Britain, and particularly Scotland, over Japan, but also the superiority of our Queen over your Emperor" he avers at the start of *You Only Live Twice*. He is, as the neurologist Sir James Molony understates of him in Chapter 2 of the same novel, "a patriotic sort of chap". And if he cannot rebut the charges in word, then he will certainly do so in deed. For it is always Bond who saves the day, always the British agent who must slay the dragon, to evoke an image from several novels, including *Goldfinger, You Only Live Twice* and *The Spy Who Loved Me*. The latter is especially notable in this context as it presents an extended paean to both Britain and Bond, courtesy of its first-person narrator, Vivienne Michel. Viv had attended a prestigious girls' school in England, where she was teased for being foreign, then suffered two heart-breaking affairs in London, one of which ended in an abortion. At first she blamed London for her misfortunes, but once back in Québec she realized that it was her provincial, French-Canadian upbringing that had "ill-equipped [her] for the great world outside!" Later, as she is about to be murdered in a sleazy upstate New York motel, Viv puts her English experiences (some sweet, some sad) into perspective and identifies her present situation (symbolic of America as a whole?) as "the true jungle of the world, with its real monsters". When Bond arrives in the nick of time, she tells her readers: "[m]y heart leaped. He was English!" Thus, Bond not only saves her life, he also helps restore her faith in England by "just being 'British'".

Of course, Bond isn't merely British; he is the very personification of Britain herself. Fleming clearly articulates this theme in Chapter 4 of *From Russia, With Love*, where the heads of the Soviet secret services plot an act of terrorism against a Western intelligence agency. They successively consider and eliminate the nations of Continental Europe, as well as the United States, which tries to do everything with money, but generally accomplishes very little. So which nation would present the most effective target? Why, the one whose national identity is wrapped up in the myth of

Scotland Yard, Sherlock Holmes and *the Secret Service.* And the man who best represents the myth of the Secret Service is not M, its chief, because he is unknown to the public. Rather, it is the man whose death will help to destroy this very English myth, the man who is a hero both to his organization and to his country, the only man, indeed, who seems both willing and able to stand up to the Soviet bullies. The message is loud and clear: James Bond is not just a secret agent who happens to be English, or rather, British (since his father was a Scot); James Bond is Britain itself, or at least Britain as it once was and as it could and should be again. And what is certainly true of Fleming's creation is largely true of the cinematic character, as well. Bond may occasionally suffer the villain's disparaging remarks about his "pitiful little island", as in *Diamonds Are Forever*, or jibes about his role as "Her Majesty's loyal terrier", as in *GoldenEye*. He may be reminded that Britain sometimes puts pragmatism before principle, as in *GoldenEye*, or security before sentiment as in *The World Is Not Enough*. He may even have to rely upon the assistance of American, Japanese, Chinese or Russian counterparts to accomplish his objectives. But when it comes to salvaging America's space program, defending its gold supply, preventing World War III or saving the entire world from annihilation, the credit inevitably goes to the one man who has been keeping the *British* end up since 1953. It is, therefore, no accident, no mere stunt or technique (to keep readers grounded in "reality"), that Fleming evokes so many British places and institutions throughout his novels. It is quite simply his purpose-to remind the reader that there is no place like home. And while the cinematic slant may be a bit more Anglo-*American*, it is still Britain, or at least one particular Briton, that matters.

So, in addition to being reference and travel guides, these books are intended as a celebration of the history and culture of Britain itself. Where Fleming and the filmmakers use British landmarks as backdrops for James Bond's investigations, we can use James Bond as the backdrop for an investigation of British landmarks. Through the landmarks and locations associated with the life of Fleming himself, we can evoke the world of Edwardian England, where every man, not to mention schoolboy, knew, and more importantly, *did* his duty; the days when London staggered from the onslaught of Hitler's bombs, but never fell; the time when members of a certain class (do they still exist?) lived and worked in the City during the week, but retreated to their country homes at the weekend. Through the books, and only through the books (at least for most of us), we can enter the all-male world of Clubland London, where those same members of a certain class would gather in their private clubs for fine dining, a little bridge and a great deal of gossiping. Through the films we can admire the courage of a beautiful gambler at the exclusive Les Ambassadeurs Club or attend a black tie dinner with the Governor of the Bank of England. Through both the books and films we can golf on the most exclusive links in Britain; attend tension-filled auctions at world-famous Sotheby's; and traverse the hallowed halls of the Heralds' College, content in our knowledge that most of us will never have to bother about the care and maintenance of a personal coat of arms. In short, through these locations, we can truly come away with a better understanding of the history and culture of the great British nation: a nation that just happened to produce a writer named Fleming and a legend named Bond....

These, then, are the reasons I have sought to include so many of the locales, firms and institutions mentioned or depicted in Bond's adventures. There is no doubt that I have unintentionally omitted some locations, either from the novels, the films, or both. Nor is there any doubt that I have included locations that some readers might consider trivial or unimportant. I apologize in advance for both these faults and sincerely look forward to your feedback on improving future editions of this book, as well as the forthcoming *James Bond's Britain*.

That said, I will tell you how I came up with the list of locations. First, I re-read every Fleming novel and short story, making notes on all the British locales mentioned. I re-read the most important Fleming biographies, John Pearson's *The Life of Ian Fleming*, Donald McCormick's *17F* and Andrew Lycett's *Ian Fleming: The Man Behind James Bond.* I reasoned that if a house, office, shop, club or restaurant was important enough to be mentioned in one of these books (and most are mentioned in all of them) then it had to be included in this guide. I also reviewed the extensive collection of Fleming materials at the Lilly Library at Indiana University, Bloomington. The collection includes nearly all of Fleming's original typewritten manuscripts, an impressive selection of his personal correspondence and the original notes and interviews compiled by John Pearson for his biography of Fleming. Then, I re-watched the Eon films (research involves a lot of "re-doing" things), looking for all the scenes that had been shot in Britain, including those which are supposed to be somewhere else (like the Hamburg hotel parking garage chase in *Tomorrow Never Dies*, which, was actually shot in London). In identifying these "disguised locations", I consulted a number of books on the making of the Bond films (see Bibliography) and interviewed several of the filmmakers themselves (see Acknowledgments).

Then there was the actual "road trip" itself: James Bond's Britain or bust! For this facet of the research, I was fortunate to have the help of my friend (and former boss) Chris Gardner. Chris not only agreed to take many of the photographs for the book, but also to help me organize what was to be a very busy few weeks in Britain. What's more, he proved a dab hand at driving on the other side of the road, something I myself would have attempted, had I ever bothered to learn how to drive a standard transmission car. (And renting an automatic in Britain is not really a viable option when traveling on a limited budget.) In any case, armed with the location list, maps, cameras and reference photos, we set out for the first of the locations....

Weeks later, with blisters upon blisters on both feet, I sat back and reflected on what we had done, where we had gone and what we could share with Bond fans around the world. First, I am pleased to report that the majority of the locations we sought, we found, even the relatively obscure ones. From the Mayfair house where Ian Fleming was born in 1908 to the Kent golf club at which he spent his last day on earth. From the Chelsea home of James Bond to the Kingsdown base of Hugo Drax in the novel *Moonraker*. From the Thames-side buildings that doubled for MI6 in *Dr. No* to the church (actually *churches*) where Natalya meets Boris in *GoldenEye*. We had "penetrated" the Malaysia Tourist office that doubled as MI6 in *The Living Daylights*; we had hiked to the Scottish glen where the helicopter chase was staged in *From Russia With Love*. We had even found a piece of the helicopter itself, which, as the locals fondly recall, was blown up and never removed. They have been scavenging pieces of it for over 35 years.

Naturally, there were some disappointments. Many places had limited access or none at all, thus precluding more extensive coverage and better pictures. The Ministry of Defence, for example, allows photographs of the exterior, but entrance to the building itself is prohibited. And, obviously, over the course of three or four decades, many shops will have closed, many offices will have moved and many buildings will have succumbed to the wrecking ball, even in historic Britain. One of the biggest disappointments in that regard was discovering that the beautiful riverside mansion Thames Lawn, the *Quarterdeck* of *On Her Majesty's Secret Service*, had recently been torn down and replaced with another house.

However, the disappointments were more than outweighed by the successes, many of them quite unexpected. One that caught us completely off guard was gaining access to 10 Downing Street in order to replicate the shot of the PM's residence in *For Your Eyes Only*. It seems that everybody's a Bond fan, even the police officers guarding the Prime Minister! Then there were those once-in-a-lifetime experiences that this Fleming fan will always cherish: the chance to explore the author's Old Mitre Court Office near Fleet Street; personal tours of both the Old Admiralty Building, where Fleming worked for Naval Intelligence during World War II, and Boodle's, the exclusive gentleman's club to which Fleming belonged in the 1940s and '50s; and, most memorable of all, lunch at the Garrick Club (see B *The Man with the Golden Gun*) as the guest of Mr. Kenneth Snowman, one of the few real-life characters to appear in a Bond story *as himself*. Now 80, the Fabergé expert still fondly recalls his friendship with Ian Fleming and his own delight in being included in the story "The Property of a Lady". He is an utterly charming, thoroughly modest gentleman, whose kindness to a stranger from the States seemed truly boundless.

Of course, I can't promise you lunch at the Garrick or even the chance to stumble over all the office furniture stored in the Old Admiralty. But I can promise you that the next time you read a Fleming novel, watch one of the films or actually tour London itself, it will be with a slightly different perspective. If, for example, you have never visited the National Gallery in Trafalgar Square, now, intrigued by the Bond connection, perhaps you will be tempted to do so. And if you *have* visited the prestigious gallery, and never known of its Bond connection, well, now you will have one more reason to savor its treasures. Of course, it's all up to you: you can sit back and relax *or* you can hop up out of that armchair, jump on a plane, catch a train, grab a cab and explore James Bond's London for yourself. Either way, I hope you enjoy this book.

Gary Giblin

August 2001

USING THIS BOOK

This book is divided into two parts: **Central London** and **Greater London**. The Central London section is itself divided into 27 districts (also known as areas or neighborhoods), which are arranged alphabetically from Bayswater to Westminster/Whitehall. You should note that London's districts are somewhat vaguely defined, as opposed to the strictly-drawn *boroughs* that comprise Greater London, so that what one writer may locate in Belgravia another writer might locate in Victoria, and so forth. You should also note that the city of London (note the lowercase "c") actually has a "double center": the first is the City of London (with a capital "C"), which contains the business and financial district known, fittingly enough, as the City; the second is the City of Westminster, the borough containing both **Parliament** (27:18) and **Buckingham Palace** (16:27). Also within the latter is the *district* of Westminster, which includes the government buildings in Whitehall, but not Buckingham Palace. Admittedly, it's all a bit confusing, but at least you'll know why the street signs in west central London say "City of Westminster". The City and Westminster *districts* are at the top of the "must-see" list, along with those of Mayfair and St James's. Take the suggested **Walking Tour** of at least one of these districts (5:0, 14:0, 17:0 and 28:0) for the best of both Bondian and British heritage if you don't have time for anything else.

The Greater London section contains 30 districts, most with but a single location. These sites are often several miles from the center of London and, in at least one case, **Beckton Gas Works** (29:1), a good hour by train and foot. Still, the Underground does more or less service every site included in this section, so if you choose to go, at least you'll have cheap transportation. Bus service is also available to most of these locations and while much slower than the tube, it does provide a far more scenic journey. For best results, purchase a Travelcard valid for all six Greater London zones; this allows you to travel by Underground, bus, Docklands Light Railway and some British Rail lines.

007 THINGS TO ENHANCE YOUR VISIT TO JAMES BOND'S LONDON:

1. **Spot the Warrants:** Many businesses sport beautiful coats of arms above or near their entrances. Look closely and you will notice that the coats of arms belong to one of four members of the Royal Family: the Queen, the Queen Mother, the Prince of Wales or the Duke of Edinburgh. Displaying such arms means that the firm in question has a Royal Warrant from that particular member of the royal family, in other words, that the firm supplies some good or service to, say, the Queen or her Mum. Warrants may be issued after a firm has supplied such items for at least five years; the honor lasts for ten years, after which time it is subject to review. Many of the Bond locales you will visit are the proud holders of one or more such warrants, for example, **Swaine Adeney** (16:14), the makers of Bond's attaché case and the Queen's riding whips and gloves. So, during your walks, see who can spot the most warrants or, indeed, which firms have the most warrants. When you spot a three- or four-warrant holder, be sure to pop in and ask for a business card as a souvenir. The various methods of getting three or four coats of arms on a single card are truly amazing.

2. **Pop into the Pubs:** In the course of your travels, you will pass many pubs and taverns that are not listed in this book, for example, King's Head and Eight Bells pub in Cheyne Walk. This particular pub happens to be located next door to Ian Fleming's Carlyle Mansions home (4:8) in Chelsea. Now, Bond's creator was a man who enjoyed a drink or two in the company of a few good friends, so the odds are probably fairly good that Fleming stopped in here from time to time during his stay in Chelsea. In his honor, and in keeping with the venerable British tradition of popping into the local pub for a pint, you may wish to add a few stops like the King's Head and Eight Bells pub to your Bondian itinerary. The provision is that any pub you visit has to be near at least one Fleming/Bond location. You can make a game out of this by trying to identify the pub that is physically closest to a Fleming/Bond location. (**The Marquis of Granby** (27:27) in Westminster doesn't count since it is a pub!) I can think of a couple apart from the King's Head that are at most a few yards away from their respective Bond sites, but I'll leave their identification to you. A variation is to identify the location with the greatest number of pubs in the immediate vicinity.

3. **Don't Follow the Sun:** As Britons know all too well, but as some Americans may not, the weather in London (and in the whole of the country, come to that) is a bit unpredictable. I have seen the sun shine for days on end in the autumn or winter, only to spend untold hours in the summer waiting for old Sol to put in an appearance. This on again/

off again relationship with the sun is, of course, very frustrating for us tourists, who would naturally prefer to visit all those great British locales with the aid of a little clement weather. We would also like the chance to take some reasonably decent photographs, using both the right film and the right camera settings. Unfortunately, the London sun (as opposed to the London *Sun*) can be frustratingly uncooperative. For example, I spent several minutes one warm July day setting up a shot of one of Ian Fleming's London homes, only to have the sun disappear at the last minute. Fine. I decided to forgo the shot entirely as I had already taken a number of photos the previous March. I walked across the small square and before I had reached nearby Buckingham Palace Road, the sun was out again. Fine. I walked back across the square, set up the shot again and, of course, you know what happened. And again I attempted to leave the square, and again the sun returned. This time I literally ran back to my spot and even as I pushed the camera button, the sun vanished. So, my suggestion is to assume the worst in English weather, whenever you go, and then be content with an occasional pleasant surprise. The point is, don't let the sun get you down. And in the end, you may take some comfort from the grass-is-always-greener irony of English weather as expressed in *Doctor No*. At the beginning of the novel, Bond is pleased to escape a harsh London March for the warmer climes of the Caribbean. By the time he's finished with Doctor No, a battered and bruised 007 is wishing he were back home in London, a truly magnificent city under fair skies or gray.

4. **Don't Drive to Distraction:** Britain is blessed with a marvelous public transportation system, at least compared to anything one might find in the States. You can pretty much get anywhere any time using the Tube, British Rail or a bus, and that includes the vast majority of locations described in this book. Occasionally, however, you may wish to take a taxi or hire a car. So, for all the Yanks reading this, here are the tips: make your reservation as far in advance as possible. On more than one occasion, we were met with a profound look of astonishment and the incredulous: "What? You want to rent a car *today*?!" "Uh, yes. We do. We are Americans, and we expect everything *now*." Well, in Britain things are done a little differently and the impatience for which Americans are famous will get you nowhere fast, *literally*. You will also find that hiring a standard transmission automobile will cost you far less than an automatic (although it's still expensive), so make sure that at least one person in your group can drive a stick. Once you're on the road, of course, everything is simple: just sit on the right, drive on the left and, oh yes, forget about shifting with your right hand. This kind of driving forces you to become ambidextrous in a hurry. In fact, the biggest adjustment for an American probably isn't driving, or even shifting, on the left, but rather the bank loan he has to secure in order to pay for the petrol. Yes, gasoline is just a bit more expensive in Britain than the U.S., say about three times! So plan your auto excursions accordingly, allowing for the maximum number of locations with the minimum amount of driving. Fortunately, in a country as small as Britain, that is a relatively easy task.

5. **Room Without a View (to a Kill or otherwise):** Staying in London, as in most major cities, can be very expensive. Even an *extremely* small double room in a moderately-priced hotel can cost you £100 ($160) or more per night. Now, some of you may well wish to sample Room Service at **The Ritz** (16:1) and that's certainly a suitably Bondian thing to do. My approach, however, is to skimp on the accommodation, and thereby allow myself both a longer stay and a greater cash reserve for souvenirs and shopping (see below). This means looking for rooms outside the very heart of London, a bit off the typical tourist's beaten path. The Earl's Court area, near Chelsea, for example, is far enough away from the city's center to offer some reasonably-priced accommodations, while still being located no more than a short Tube ride away from **Parliament** (27:18) or the **Bank of England** (5:12). You will save even more money if you are willing to share "the convenience", since Britain, unlike America, offers plenty of cheap hotel rooms *without* bathrooms. I tried this approach on one London trip when I was feeling both socially adventurous and particularly cheap. After two weeks I was hardly the worse for wear for such a sacrifice and the money I saved allowed me to indulge in a little "fine dining" à la James Bond. Of course, most Americans traveling to Bond's Britain, especially couples, will probably want a bathroom right there in the room. If so, be sure to specify that you require an "en suite" bathroom when making your reservation. This has nothing to do with a hotel suite in the American sense; it simply means that you will get a room with a loo...

6. **Dress To Kill (your Wallet):** James Bond is undoubtedly one of the best-dressed heroes to ever grace a movie screen. Indeed, his wardrobe is an integral part of his character, a point amply illustrated in *"Dressed To Kill: James Bond The Suited Hero* (Flammarion).. It is therefore incumbent upon all you men following in 007's footsteps to make at least one sartorial purchase during your visit to James Bond's Britain. It may be a tie from **Turnbull & Asser** (16:10), a pair of Chetwynd brogues from **Church's** (13:10) or, going all out, a suit from either **Brioni** (see 13:40) or one of the traditional **Savile Row** (13:12) tailors. And while you're at it, don't forget **Burberry's** (19:4) for your trenchcoat, **Alfred Dunhill** (16:12) for your cuff links and lighter and **Swaine Adeney** (16:14) for your attaché case.

True, this lot will set you back thousands, but, remember, nothing is too good for 007 or all us James Bond wannabes. And don't think for a moment that you ladies are off the hook: **Harrods** (10:2), jewelry stores (13:18; 13:19; 13:20) and more await you in *James Bond's London.*

7. **Cop a 'Tude on the Tube:** During those wonderfully long Underground rides, when you are compressed against the doors of the car by multitudes of indefatigable travelers of alternate hygiene requirements, just cock an eyebrow and smile knowingly to yourself: James Bond himself traveled by Tube, in the novel *Goldfinger*, and to a meeting at the **Bank of England** (5:12) no less. Say no more!

30 SHAKEN AND STIRRED LOCATIONS 

A subjective list of landmark locations from the lives of Ian Fleming and James Bond

1. Ian Fleming's Ebury Street Home 2:1
2. ex Office of Jonathan Cape Publishers 3:6
3. Ian Fleming's Office (and El Vino) 5:2
4. College of Arms 5:11
5. Bank of England 5:12
6. The Ivy 6:4
7. Regent's Park 12:2
8. Ian Fleming's Birthplace 13:1
9. Bond Street 13:9
10. Sotheby's 13:11
11. Savile Row 13:12
12. ex Offices of Eon Productions 13:31-13:34
13. The Dorchester 13:36
14. The Ritz 17:2
15. "Blades" (and the St James's Clubs) 16:6
16. Turnbull & Asser 16:10
17. Alfred Dunhill (and the St James's shops) 16:12
18. ex Scott's Restaurant 19:6
19. Odeon Leicester Square 19:9
20. Somerset House 23:5
21. The Savoy 23:8
22. River Thames and *TWINE* Boat Chase Route 24:1
23. MI6 24:2
24. Ian Fleming's Victoria Square Home 25:1
25. ex War Office 27:6
26. ex Admiralty 27:10
27. ex HQ of MI6 (and Home of the Secret Service Chief) 27:22
28. North Car Park, Brent Cross 39:1
29. West India Docks/Millwall Docks 41:1 and 41:2
30. Tobacco Dock 52:1

Ian Fleming's birthplace
(see Page 59)

TRIVIA CHALLENGE

Sprinkled throughout *James Bond's London* are 50 trivia questions from the novels, films and life of Ian Fleming. I warn you now, most of them are not easy, although a careful read of this book may reveal an answer or two. Each question is worth two points; a few can earn you one or more bonus points. The answers and how to rate your BBQ (*Bond's Britain Quotient*) will be found at the end of the book, just before the Appendices.

CENTRAL LONDON

London is James Bond's city: he lives here, works here, dines here, gambles here and even does a bit of romancing here, all in gloriously high style. In all this, he takes after his creator, Ian Lancaster Fleming: banker, stockbroker, journalist, spy and, of course, best-selling author. Fleming was born in London in 1908 and maintained some kind of residence here (leased flat, hotel room, house) until the day he died. Literary Bond lived in the fashionable, even trendy, district of Chelsea (4:2), worked in an office building near (or in) **Regent's Park** (12:2), lunched at **Scott's** (19:6) restaurant in **Piccadilly Circus** (19:1), smoked hand-made cigarettes from **Morland's** (13:8) of Grosvenor Street, partied in Park Lane and clubbed at **Crockford's** (16:23) of Carlton House Terrace. In fact, London locations figure more or less prominently in every one of Fleming's Bond novels and in five of the nine short stories. On-screen, the British capital has figured to a greater or lesser extent in every Eon film save one (hint: think Japanese). From these films we know that Bond often works in **Whitehall** (27:0), with occasional assignments in **Belgrave Square** (2:3), **Trafalgar Square** (27:1) and, most recently, Vauxhall Cross; that he shops at **Harrods** (10:2); gambles at **Les Ambassadeurs Club** (13:38); dines at the **Bank of England** (5:12); and bones up on heraldry at the **College of Arms** (5:11). He has even been known to commandeer a high-tech speedboat from **MI6** (24:2), chase a lethal lovely down the **River Thames** (24:1) and watch her incinerate herself over the **Millennium Dome** (35:1), all in the line of duty, of course. Therefore, if you want to follow in the footsteps of the world's greatest superspy, Central London is definitely the place to go. And, to throw immodesty right out the window, *James Bond's London* is definitely the place to start!

1. BAYSWATER

Once fashionable residential district now noted for its many budget bed & breakfasts

1:1

Cathedral of St Sophia
Moscow Road, W2

Doubles as: Church of Our Lady of Smolensk, St. Petersburg, Russia (interior) in *GoldenEye*

The next time you watch *GoldenEye*, remind yourself that *none* of the principal actors (Pierce Brosnan, Izabella Scorupco, Joe Don Baker, et al.) actually went on location to Russia. All of their "Russian" scenes were actually shot in England, either at Leavesden Studio (see *JBB*) or in and around London. Case in point: the scene at the "Church of Our Lady of Smolensk", where a frightened Natalya meets the traitorous Boris Grishenko. The interiors were filmed inside this ornate *Greek* Orthodox cathedral, which was constructed in 1877. Of course, it's supposed to be a Russian church, but filming is not permitted inside Russian Orthodox churches, hence the Hellenic substitution. The exterior shot, showing Natalya approaching the church, was actually filmed at **The Chapel, Brompton Cemetery** [26:1], in West Brompton. In fact, Eon Productions had originally planned to film these sequences in and around St Petersburg. However, as production designer Peter Lamont recalled, once the decision had been made to stage

the elaborate (and highly destructive!) tank chase at Leavesden, the question arose as to whether the first unit needed to go to Russia at all. "Martin [Campbell, the director] asked me if I thought I could find all the locations here in England and I said, 'Yes'. So that's how we came up with **Epsom Downs** (*JBB*) for the 'dull, international terminal' [where Bond meets Wade] and **Drapers' Hall** (5:19) for the meeting of the Russian Defence Council." Additional "St. Petersburg-on-the-Thames" locations included the **Langham Hilton** (12:6) (Bond's hotel), **St Pancras Station** (17:1) (Natalya's arrival) and **Somerset House** (23:5) (Wade's car repair). Actual Russian footage appears only in a handful of establishing shots (Bond's plane landing, Wade's car crossing the bridge and the Winter Palace exterior) and in the small section of the tank chase staged along the River Moyka. Lamont's technique of dressing English locales to look like exotic foreign ones proved so successful (and practical), that Eon employed it extensively in both *Tomorrow Never Dies* and *The World Is Not Enough*.

Station: Bayswater (CI; DI) From the station go W in Moscow Road. The cathedral is ahead on the right.

Trivia Challenge 1: A ridiculously easy one to start off with: who accompanies Boris to the church for his rendezvous with Natalya?

2. BELGRAVIA

Exclusive west-central residential district, considered one of the most desirable areas in London

2:1

Ian Fleming's Home
22B Ebury Street, SW1

Located on the southeastern fringe of Belgravia, the former Pimlico Literary Institute was designed by architect J. P. Gandy-Deering and completed in 1830. Its Doric columns and pediment suggest a kind of temple or chapel and, indeed, the building served as such in the 19th century. After the Strict Baptists moved out, No. 22 was used as a school, a nightclub and even a furniture store. In the 1930s, it was converted into four flats, one of which was leased by Sir Oswald Mosley, the head of the British Union of Fascists. In October 1936, Ian Fleming decided that Mosley's flat, No. 22B, was the perfect place to set up a "bachelor quarters" away from his domineering mother Eve, who was then living in Cheyne Walk, Chelsea (see **Turner's House** [4:9]). The young stockbroker undertook a number of renovations to his new abode, including the installation of a toilet in the alcove that had once contained the church's altar. Fleming happily entertained his many lady friends here, as well as the members of his informal dining/bridging/golfing club *Le Cercle*, until the threat of German bombs forced his evacuation to safer quarters in 1940 (see the **ex Carlton Hotel** [16:21]). After the war, Fleming briefly occupied flats in Marylebone (12:7), Mayfair (13:27) and Chelsea (4:8) before finally setting upon the Victoria Square house (25:1) that would be his last London residence. Indeed, it was the Victoria Square home that Ian's brother Peter petitioned the Greater London Council to commemorate with its prestigious "blue plaque" in 1966. To merit this award, a proposed recipient must be judged eminent by his or her peers; or have made an important positive contribution to human welfare or happiness; *or* have a name that the well-informed passer-by immediately recognizes; *or* deserve national recognition. Judged by any of these criteria, Ian Fleming seemed a sure bet. However, in 1966, an honoree also had to have been dead at least 10 years and as Ian had scarcely been dead two years, his nomination was rejected. In 1983, as the twentieth anniversary of Ian's death approached (the criterion had been changed to 20 years in 1969), Peter's son Nicholas renewed the application. (Peter Fleming himself died in 1971.) Seven more years were to pass before English Heritage, the new custodians of the blue plaque scheme, "short-listed" the suggestion and another three before the London Advisory Committee officially endorsed the nomination. The commissioners then approached the owner of the Victoria Square property for permission to erect the plaque, but were refused. English Heritage then sought, and eventually obtained, permission to erect the plaque here in Ebury Street, although by this time, sadly, Nicholas Fleming, too, had passed away. Finally, on April 15, 1996, with members of the Ian Fleming Foundation, Peter's daughters Lucy Williams and Kate Grimond and actor Desmond Llewelyn in attendance, English Heritage erected the prestigious plaque at No. 22B. It reads simply: "IAN FLEMING 1908-1964 Creator of James Bond lived here".

Station: Victoria (VI; CI; DI) Go L out of the Station, cross Buckingham Palace Road to Lower Belgrave Street and follow this to Ebury Street; turn L into Ebury and look for the house ahead on the R.

2:2

St Paul's Church,
Knightsbridge, Wilton Place, SW1

Ian Fleming's parents were married at this beautiful 19th-century church, the site of many fashionable weddings, on February 18, 1906. Twenty-three-year-old Valentine Fleming, son of one of the most prominent bankers in the City of London was a kindly, cautious, honorable gentleman, who would go on to serve his country in the House of Commons and on the battlefields of France. Twenty-one-year-old Evelyn St Croix Rose was a flamboyant, strong-willed, self-absorbed beauty, whose need to manipulate and control those around her would cause lasting pain to Ian and his siblings. Their marriage, however, was by all accounts a happy one, producing four sons in rapid succession: Peter (a successful author years before his now legendary younger brother) in 1907, Ian in 1908, Richard in 1911 and Michael in 1913. Tragically, Major Val was killed by a German bomb on May 20, 1917, barely a week before Ian's ninth birthday. His ***Times*** (5:7) obituary was written by his friend and fellow MP Winston Churchill, a signed copy of which Ian kept on display for the rest of his life. St Paul's was also the setting for actor Desmond Llewelyn's memorial service, which was held on March 27, 2000. Speakers included Roger Moore, Llewelyn's friend and frequent co-star, Eon marketing vice-president John Parkinson, actor Christopher Lee and current Moneypenny, Samantha Bond. Also in attendance: Barbara and Dana Broccoli, Shirley Eaton, Peter Lamont, Lewis Gilbert and David Arnold. For more on the legendary actor see **Radley College** (*JBB*).

Station: Knightsbridge (PI) Take the Sloan Street South Exit R into Knightsbridge, walk to Wilton Place and turn R. The church is ahead on the L. Continue to Wilton Crescent, then turn R and R again into Motcomb Street, to see the impressive, late-Regency warehouse known as the Pantechnicon. Ian Fleming stored his famous collection of rare and important books here during the 1950s and '60s. For more on his avocation see **ex Dulan's** (13:21) and **ex Elkin Matthews** (13:7).

2:3

Belgrave Square SW1

Designed by Thomas Cubitt and built during the second quarter of the 19th century, Belgrave Square was and is one of the most fashionable and expensive residential areas in London. In fact, its very name is synonymous with "high society," for which reason it was ironically invoked in the film *On Her Majesty's Secret Service.* There, in a Swiss barn, James Bond and Tracy discuss where they would like to live as man and wife. She suggests Tunbridge Wells (see **Proposed Home of Mr and Mrs James Bond** [*JBB*]), presumably with tongue in cheek, while he wonders about Belgrave Square. She then suggests the Via Veneto in Rome, and he counters with Paris, which would be convenient for the French resort Le Touquet. Bond ultimately wonders how much they're asking for the barn, to which Tracy responds with a hearty laugh. Yet, given the fact that Bond had just vowed to quit his job, how can she be sure he wasn't serious?

Stations: Knightsbridge (PI) See above; **or Hyde Park Corner (PI)** Take Exit 3 R into Grosvenor Place then go R into Grosvenor Crescent, which leads to Belgrave Square.

Trivia Challenge 2: Which tiny European country does Tracy also suggest as a possible home?

2:4

Residence of the Argentine Ambassador 49 Belgrave Square, SW1

Doubles as: Whitehall (exterior) in *Thunderball*

According to the shooting script for *Thunderball*, the conference room scene, in which all the Double-0 Agents have assembled to hear the ransom demand from SPECTRE, takes place in the **Home Office** (27:15), which in 1965 was located in Whitehall. The finished film, on the other hand, suggests that the conference takes place at Universal Exports itself, which, in the film *Dr. No*, was located on the south bank of the **Thames** (24:1) (see **Queensborough House/Hampton House** [11:2]). Here, however, the venue has been changed to elegant Belgrave Square. How do we know this? Because the building that you see through the conference room window (over M's shoulder) is none other than the residence of the Argentine Ambassador at No. 49 Belgrave Square, a stylish stucco villa built for Sidney Herbert, Florence Nightingale's patron, in 1847. Universal Exports itself, then, would have been located across the street, more or less on the site of No. 1 Belgrave Square. However, to obtain the view of No. 49 that is shown in the film, you actually have to stand in the middle of the street. *Thunderball* art director Peter Murton couldn't recall how or why this mansion was chosen for the background of the conference room scene, although he suggested that the Eon crew may have been drawn here by producer Kevin McClory, whose own London home was in nearby Belgrave Place. In fact it was at McClory's home, No. 7, that Ian Fleming, writer Jack Whittingham and McClory himself worked on the screen treatments for the proposed Xanadu Productions film project of 1959-1960. As is well known, the film never materialized, but a novel called *Thunderball* did (see Appendix Two). As a result of legal action taken in 1961-1963, Ian Fleming agreed to assign the screen rights to the novel to Mr. McClory, for which reason he is credited as producer of the film *Thunderball.* For more on this story, see the **Royal Courts of Justice** (8:1).

Stations: Knightsbridge (PI) See above; or **Hyde Park Corner (PI)** exit R into Grosvenor Place then turn R into Grosvenor Crescent, which leads to Belgrave Square. Turn around and look back at the house in the wedge formed by Grosvenor Crescent and Halkin Street, opposite No.1 Belgrave Square.

Trivia Challenge 3: How many Double-0 agents are gathered in the conference room?

3. BLOOMSBURY

Cultural and intellectual hub of London centered around the British Museum

3:1

ex Kemsley House/Thomson House 200 Gray's Inn Road, WC1

Talk about the ideal job in post-war Britain: £4,500 salary (£115,00 in today's money), £500 for expenses, a guaranteed two-month holiday and an impressive-sounding title: "Foreign Manager (not Editor) of the Kemsley Newspapers". Ian Fleming occupied a paneled office on the second floor (US: third floor) of Kemsley House, where he presided over a network of foreign correspondents dubbed the "Mercury Service", much as M would preside over his Double-0 operatives in all those novels to come. His patron and boss in this dream-come-true job was James Gomer Berry, the first Lord Kemsley. Fleming had known Lord Kemsley since before the war, when the two had played bridge at **The Dorchester** (13:36). Now, Fleming seemed to have the world by the tail, going on to become the leading columnist (under the pseudonym *Atticus*) of Lord Kemsley's flagship paper, *The Sunday Times*, in November 1953. During his tenure here in Gray's Inn Road, Fleming also became a *publisher*, through his purchase of the *Book Collector* (see **ex Shenval Press Ltd** [19:11]) and his directorship of Lord Kemsley's **Queen Anne Press** (3:2). He remained the foreign manager until Kemsley sold his newspaper chain to Canadian tycoon Roy Thomson (later Baron Thomson of Fleet) in 1959. Ian then acquired his own office and secretary in Old Mitre Court (5:2), although at Thomson's invitation he continued to attend the Tuesday morning meetings of *The Sunday Times* editorial board. (Indeed, it was at one such meeting that Ian suffered his first heart attack, in April 1961). Thomson House, as the building was renamed, remained the headquarters of *The Sunday Times* until 1984. In that year, both *The Sunday Times* and *The Times*, which Thomson had also acquired, relocated to 9 Pennington Street, E1 (see **ex HQ of The Times**, [5:7]). The present building is home to Independent Television News.

Station: Chancery Lane (CE) Take Exit 1 into Gray's Inn Road and continue past the intersection with Theobald's Road to the L and Clerkenwell to the R; the site is just ahead on the R.

3:2

ex Office of the Queen Anne Press Ltd 9 Great James Street, WC1

Lord Kemsley, owner of *The Sunday Times* (and Ian Fleming's boss [see above]), set up the small but prestigious Queen Anne Press in 1952. The directors were Kemsley himself, his son, Lionel Berry, and the *Book Collector* trio of John Hayward, Percy Muir and Ian Fleming (see **ex Shenval Press Ltd** [19:11]). Fleming, et al. held the inaugural meeting of the editorial board at Frascati's restaurant on Wednesday, October 8th. One of their very first efforts was Evelyn Waugh's *The Holy Places*, which the author later claimed had been thoroughly botched by Kemsley's press. In 1954, Kemsley offered to sell the QAP to Fleming, but the two men could never agree on a price. Nevertheless, Fleming remained a director of the prestigious little imprint until his death in 1964. The QAP was subsequently acquired by the British Printing Corporation and later still by the infamous media mogul Robert Maxwell. Today, the Queen Anne Press is owned by Adrian Stephenson, a charming gentleman who bought the imprint in 1992, the year of its fortieth anniversary. It is based in Mackerye End, Harpenden, Hertfordshire, some 30 miles north of London.

Station: Chancery Lane (CE) Take Exit 1 into Gray's Road, continue to Theobald's Road, where you will turn L; look for Great James Street to the R.

3:3

ex Registered Office of Glidrose Productions Ltd 4 Bloomsbury Square, WC1

Ian Fleming acquired the defunct Glidrose theatrical agency in October/November 1952 as a tax shelter for income he expected to earn when his first novel was published the following year. He assigned all literary rights in the novel to Glidrose, and installed himself and his wife, Ann, as the company's directors. Film, serialization and, later, television rights were settled in a series of trusts set up for the Flemings' son Caspar. The company was officially based here at No. 4 Bloomsbury Square, which was actually the "West End" office of Ian's accountant, **Vallance Lodge** (51:1). Later, the author transferred Glidrose to his own office at 4 Old Mitre Court, Fleet Street (5:2). In March 1964, Fleming sought to ease his tax burden even further by selling 51% of Glidrose to Booker McConnell Ltd, a large agro-industrial company owned by his Old Etonian friend and **Huntercombe** (*JBB*) golfing partner Sir Jock Campbell. At the time of the author's death, in August 1964, 30 million copies of the Bond books had been sold; two years later, at the height of Bond mania in 1966, that figure had already doubled. Booker continued to reap the rewards of Fleming's creation until 1996, when Ian's nieces, Lucy Williams and Kate Grimond, in conjunction with the Robert Fleming Holdings Company (see 5:16), bought out the majority shareholders. Glidrose Publications, as it was renamed in 1972, remained in the Booker Entertainment offices at 141 Sloane Street, SW1, until 1998. Today, from its new Kensington offices, Ian Fleming (Glidrose) Publications, Ltd can boast of having sold over 75 million copies of Fleming's James Bond thrillers in nearly 40 languages.

Station: Holborn (CE; PI) Go W in High Holborn, R into Southampton Place, then L into Bloomsbury Way, where you will see No. 4. Fleming also located *The Spy Who Loved Me* heroine Vivienne Michel's furnished flat here in Bloomsbury Square, although he did not specify the number.

3:4

ex De Bry (de Paris)
64 New Oxford Street, WC1

According to Chapter 11 of *From Russia, With Love*, Bond's very strong coffee (which he brews in an American *Chemex* percolator) comes from the exclusive De Bry of New Oxford Street. As with so many of his other habits and preferences, this one, too, Bond acquired from his creator. Unfortunately, as with **Morland's** (13:8) of Grosvenor Street, the Paris-based chocolate-makers and purveyors of fine coffee went out of business years ago. Today, HR Higgins, 79 Duke Street, W1, and Algerian Coffee Stores, 52 Old Compton Street, W1, would be the best (and most fashionable) places to shop for Fleming's favorite Jamaican Blue Mountain coffee. For more Bondian shopping venues see Appendix One.

Station: Tottenham Court Road (CE; NO) Take Exit 3 into New Oxford Street and go L. The shop was ahead on the L, just before Bloomsbury Street.

3:5

British Museum
Great Russell Street, WC1

Founded on this site in 1755, the British Museum today occupies a neoclassical structure designed by Sir Robert Smirke and built in four stages between 1823 and 1847. It houses unrivaled collections of Egyptian antiquities (including the famous Rosetta Stone), Western Asiatic antiquities, Greek and Roman antiquities, Oriental antiquities and rare coins and medals. The latter department, along with **Spinks** (16:19), advised the Secret Service that Mr. Big's coins were indeed part of Bloody Morgan's treasure, according to Chapter 2 of *Live and Let Die*. In *James Bond of the Secret Service* (see Appendix Two), **Scotland Yard** (27:16) calls in the British Museum's expert on Medieval Italian to help decipher the Sicilian dialect that Henrico Largo uses during his tapped telephone conversations. Also, according to "The Hildebrand Rarity", it is the British Museum, not the Smithsonian, as originally intended, that will end up with the unique member of the squirrelfish family commemorated in the story's title. Finally, in "The Property of a Lady", the British Museum, among other parties, expresses interest in the valuable Fabergé globe which has mysteriously turned up for sale at **Sotheby's** (13:11). Notwithstanding the Bondian connections, no trip to London would be complete without a visit to this extraordinary establishment.

Stations: Russell Square (PI) The museum is located on the opposite side of Russell Square from the station; or from **Tottenham Court Road** (CE; NO) take Exit 3 and go R into Tottenham Court Road and then R into Great Russell Street. The museum is ahead on the L. Hours: Mon-Sat 10am-5pm; Sun noon-6pm

The former offices of Jonathan Cape Publishers.

3:6
ex Office of Jonathan Cape Publishers
30 Bedford Square, WC1

From 1925 until 1990, Ian Fleming's British publishing company was located in a plain brick house on the western side of the finest surviving Georgian Square in London. Fleming had been introduced to Jonathan Cape by their mutual friend, author William Plomer, who was one of Mr. Cape's literary advisers. Cape had already published Peter Fleming's early books and seemed quite taken with the author's younger brother. Thus, when Ian finally emerged with the *Casino Royale* manuscript in the spring of 1952 (see **The Ivy** [6:4]), it was to Plomer and Cape that he turned. With the exception of James M. Cain's *The Postman Always Rings Twice*, Cape had never before published a thriller; his readers, including Plomer, convinced him to make an exception in Fleming's case. Cape himself, then in his 70s, did not care for *Casino Royale* (and read none of its sequels), but he formally accepted the novel in September 1952. He and Fleming then proceeded to squabble over royalties, the size of the first printing, advertising, the publication date and even the design of the dust jacket. Somehow, they worked it all out amicably enough and *Casino Royale* was published on April 13, 1953. Mr Cape died in 1960, but his company continued to publish Ian Fleming offerings through 1966, including the posthumous collection *Octopussy* and *The Living Daylights*. At the time of Fleming's death, the phenomenally best-selling James Bond books accounted for nearly every penny of Cape's profits. The publisher is today located at 20 Vauxhall Bridge Road, in southwest London.

Station: Tottenham Court Road (CE; NO) Take Exit 3 R into Tottenham Court Road, turn R into Bedford Avenue then L into Adeline Place, which takes you into the Square. No. 30 is ahead to the L.

> **Eyes Only, 007:** The *Tomorrow Never Dies* premiere party was held in the garden in the center of Bedford Square on the night of December 9, 1997.

3:7
ex J. Rose
19 Ridgmount Place, WC1

Credit for the creation of Scaramanga's famous Golden Gun, composed of a cigarette lighter, a cigarette case, a Waterman pen and a cuff link, has traditionally gone to the famous Colibri lighter company, whose distinctive logo appears at the end of *The Man With The Golden Gun*. I first suspected that there might be more to the story when I discovered a number of prototype gold pens and cuff links in the Eon Productions archives. Some time later, special effects designer John Stears told me about *his* work on the Golden Gun project, thereby confirming the fact that someone besides Colibri had been involved in the creation of this incomparable prop. Thanks to production designer Peter Lamont, production buyer Ron Quelch and unit manager Iris Rose, the "untold story" can now be told. Apparently, Colibri, then based in 69 Warren Street, W1, was commissioned to manufacture a working model of the Golden Gun, which actor Christopher Lee could assemble and disassemble in close-up shots of the prop itself. Lamont, who served as art director on the film, actually made the preliminary sketches and a balsa wood mock-up of the Gun to aid Colibri in their design. According to him, Colibri's work was supposed to be done on a "product placement" basis, i.e., the gun would be provided free in exchange for an endorsement in the film. Unfortunately, what Colibri delivered did not function as it was supposed to, nor did it have the sleek, polished look the filmmakers were seeking. What's more, Lamont recalls, the Golden Gun came with a bill for £5,000! *That* aspect of the deal was subsequently resolved by producer Cubby Broccoli. In the meantime, Lamont and Quelch (rhymes with "Welsh") had to come up with a new gun and fast. So they turned to J. Rose, a professional silversmith that catered to London's jewelry trade. Using Colibri's Molectric 88 lighter as their starting point, Rose's craftsman then manufactured one Component or Gimmick Gun, which came apart, and two Solid Guns, which did not. One of the Solid Guns was designed to fire blanks; the other did nothing. All three guns were made of silver and plated in gold. The Component Gun, also called "Gun No. 1", was earmarked for the scene in which Scaramanga casually assembles the weapon before shooting Hai Fat ("Oh, that's no problem.") and for the scene in which the villain takes aim at Bond over the dinner table. Although both sequences would be shot at **Pinewood Studios** (*JBB*), the Component Gun was nevertheless taken on location to Thailand. A short "instructional film" was therefore made at the studio in order to demonstrate the proper assembly and disassembly of the gun. The performer: none other than Ron Quelch. "The gun had to go together in a certain order, which Rose explained to me. So we made this film of me assembling the gun and shipped it out to the location," Quelch told me. Christopher Lee apparently never saw this film because when the time came to shoot the scene between Scaramanga and Hai Fat, the actor approached Peter Lamont for advice on how to assemble the gun. As they chatted, Lamont casually manipulated the components then abruptly pointed the assembled gun at Lee and said, "Bang! You're dead." Lee was shocked and asked how Lamont had learned to assemble the prop so smoothly. "I take it home at night and practice while I watch TV," was the art director's cheeky reply. So Lee borrowed the gun for the night, practiced the assembly and, of course, performed the job perfectly for Guy Hamilton's cameras the following day. Even so, the actor recalled that assembling the gun was "damn difficult...especially when I was looking at somebody and supposedly putting it together without glancing down, which was impossible!" That John Stears and his associate Bert Luxford worked on the Golden Gun is also clear, although in Luxford's case it may have been on the earlier Colibri prop, which, again, everyone at Eon agrees was problematic. Stears, of course, rigged the barrel of one of the Solid Guns (which were used for most of the filming) with a small explosive squib so that Scaramanga could dispatch his victims with appropriate verisimilitude. Unfortunately, one of the Solid Guns was stolen from an exhibition at New York's Waldorf Astoria hotel in 1975 and has never resurfaced. Iris Rose notes that as Eon's insurance claim was paid long ago, if the gun ever does turn up it will belong to the insurance company! The Component Gun is the one that has gone out on all subsequent tours, including the Museum of Modern Art Exhibit in New York (1987) and the World of 007 Tour in Britain and Germany (1997-98). Although it's now "a bit wobbly", according to Iris, the gun still goes together and comes apart more or less as Lamont and the manufacturers intended over 25 years ago. *See Photo above.*

Station: Goodge Street (NO) Exit into Chenies Street and walk toward Gower Street. Just before Gower, look for Ridgmount Street on the R. Turn here and then turn R again into Ridgmount Place.

> **Trivia Challenge 4:** How many people does Scaramanga actually kill in the film itself?

3:8

Royal Academy of Dramatic Art 62-64 Gower Street, WC1

England's oldest and most prestigious drama school was founded by actor-producer Sir Herbert Beerbohm Tree in 1904. The following year, Sir Herbert moved his Academy of Dramatic Art to a Georgian house in Gower Street, where it has remained ever since. George V granted the school a royal charter of incorporation in 1920, hence *Royal* Academy of Dramatic Art. Among RADA's many illustrious students was a certain Roger George Moore of South London, who entered the academy in October 1944. Here, he met future Bond co-stars Lois Hooker (who changed her name to Maxwell while at RADA) and Jill Bennett (who played Jacoba Brink in *For Your Eyes Only*). Unfortunately, Roger left the school in 1945 and so presumably did not meet a beautiful Italian student named Domino Vitali, née Petacchi. Precisely when Domino studied acting at RADA is not stated in Chapter 11 of *Thunderball*. However, as she was born in late 1929 or early 1930, we can safely assume that it was around 1946 or 1947. Future Bond performers Bernard Lee, Robert Shaw, Diana Rigg, Julian Glover, Timothy Dalton, Sean Bean, Serena Gordon and Jonathan Pryce also attended the prestigious school.

Station: Goodge Street (NO) Cross Tottenham Court Road to Chenies Street and follow this to Gower Street. Turn L at Gower and look for the school across the street.

Eyes Only, 007: Director Alfred Hitchcock used the exterior of the building in his underrated 1950 suspense yarn *Stage Fright*, his last British film until *Frenzy*, in 1972.

Quick Ones...

London School of Hygiene and Tropical Medicine Keppel Street, WC1 (at Gower)

According to Chapter 2 of *Doctor No*, "[i]t was a bright chap at the School of Tropical Medicine who finally identified the poison which had nearly killed Bond at the end of *From Russia, With Love*. (Unlike her cinematic counterpart, the novel's Rosa Klebb actually scored a direct hit with her lethal shoe.) Turns out it was *fugu* poison, "from the sex organs of the Japanese globe-fish." Fortunately, it has much the same effect (paralysis of the central nervous system) as curare, which is what the doctor who first treated Bond had assumed the poison to be. **Station: Goodge (NO)**

British Medical Association BMA House Tavistock Square, WC1

In Chapter 21 of *OHMSS*, Leathers, the Head of the Secret Service's Scientific Section, tells M that the BMA frowns upon the practitioners of hypnosis, even though there is plenty of evidence in support of the practice. Thus, according to Leathers, Blofeld's techniques for "curing" the Piz Gloria girls could be "completely efficacious." Founded in 1832, the BMA today represents some 80% of British doctors and plays an important role in shaping the policy of the National Health Service. Its impressive London headquarters was designed by Sir Edwin Lutyens and completed in 1923.
Station: Euston Square (ME)

4. CHELSEA

Stylish (and expensive) area of west central London, famous for its many artists and "Bohemian" types

4:1

Sloane Square SW1

Bond passes through this fashionable west London square, which connects the King's Road to Sloane Street, on his daily drive to **Universal Export** (12:3) in **Regent's Park** (12:2) (see **James Bond's Route** [4:3]). He generally manages this drive without incident (we assume), but on one particular Monday evening in May 1954, something unusual occurs. According to Chapter 3 of *Moonraker*, Bond enters Sloane Square from the King's Road and is intrigued by a flashing electric sign on a building across the square (on the eastern side). He pulls over to the curb, gets out of the Bentley and walks across the street for a better look. The sign turns out to be an advertisement that "SUMMER SHELL IS HERE". However, what Bond had originally seen, when the sign was partially hidden by one of the buildings in the square, was a rather more ominous message: "HELL IS HERE...HELL IS HERE...HELL IS HERE." This is one of the most striking passages in Fleming's oeuvre, cleverly foreshadowing the potential atomic nightmare to come. Unfortunately, the author doesn't specify the precise location of the sign. Presumably, it would have been mounted on one of the buildings behind, and therefore partially obstructed by, the Royal Court Theatre, then newly rebuilt, and/or the tube station.

Station: Sloane Square (CI; DI) Cross the square to the King's Road for the view back toward the theatre and the potential site of the ominous sign.

Eyes Only, 007: If you follow Lower Sloane Street out of the square and down to the river, you will see Chelsea Bridge, which James Bond crosses at high speed in Chapter 19 of *Moonraker*. See **the *Moonraker* Car Chase Route** (*JBB*) for more on this dramatic passage.

4:2

James Bond's Home
Wellington Square, SW3

Fleming first mentions James Bond's "Chelsea flat" in the novel *Casino Royale*, but apart from the district in which it is located, offers no further details. In the third novel, *Moonraker*, he tells us that Bond's is a small ground floor (US: first floor) flat in a converted Regency house off the King's Road; that Bond parks his car under the plane trees in the little square; and that there is a book-lined sitting room with a broad window. In *From Russia, With Love*, he repeats that Bond lives in a "plane-treed square off the King's Road" and adds that the sitting room contains a *bay* window. In *Doctor No*, he mentions that the tube trains shake the ground beneath Bond's cool, dark bedroom, presumably a reference to the Circle and District Lines, which run from nearby **Sloane Square** (4:1) to the South Kensington station. In *Thunderball*, he reminds us that Bond's is a *little* Chelsea Square and, given the description of Bond's drive to HQ, suggests that it is fairly near Sloane Square. The King's Road locale that best fits all these criteria is tiny Wellington Square, a picturesque setting that dates from the 1830s and is lined on both sides with magnificent plane trees (a ubiquitous London hybrid, *Platanus* X *hispanica*, that resists air pollution and sheds its bark in winter). Fleming biographer John Pearson opted for a Wellington Square address in his fictional *James Bond: The Authorized Biography*, published in 1973. The house he selected was No. 30, for no particular reason that I can discern. Like any other address in the square, No. 30 is an aesthetically pleasing stucco terrace house, built in the late Regency period and possessing the requisite steps mentioned in both *From Russia, With Love* and *On Her Majesty's Secret Service*. The one drawback is the window: it is not a bay one. In fact, none of the Wellington Square houses has a bay window, so presumably Fleming (and Pearson) simply took a little artistic license with the home of the world's greatest spy. (Adding a bay window to a stylish home in Chelsea is nothing compared to relocating an entire ten-story building from **St James's Park** [27:21] to **Regent's Park** [12:2]; see MI6 [27:223] for more on *that*.) Sharp-eyed buffs long ago noted that No. 38 *Markham* Square, just down the road from Wellington Square, does have a bay window. In fact, Markham was the square chosen to illustrate Bond's Chelsea home in the NBC television documentary *The Incredible World of James Bond*, which debuted in November 1965. However, Markham is not the "little Chelsea square" that Fleming consistently described, nor is it lined with plane trees. Nor, to be a bit more subjective about it, is it nearly as attractive as the truly elegant Wellington Square across the street. Thus, Pearson's choice of squares (if not the actual house itself) appears to be spot on. Indeed, the Wellington Square address has caught on with the editors of both general and specialist London guidebooks, appearing for example in Roy Berkeley's well-researched and highly recommended *A Spy's London*. Oddly, some sources (*The London Encyclopaedia*, for example) locate Bond's home in Royal Avenue, an open-ended street, not a proper square, just east of Wellington Square. I can see little justification for this locale, apart from its plane trees, but any evidence in support of its claim is welcome.

In the films, the exterior of Bond's house has been shown only once, albeit briefly, in *Live and Let Die*. No

number is indicated, nor is there any other suggestion as to its whereabouts. I asked *LALD* production designer Syd Cain if he had actually envisioned Bond in the Chelsea locale. "Well, no, nothing in particular inspired me," the veteran film artist told me. "I mean, in reading the script, the most important thing was the closet [where Miss Caruso hides] and the bedroom. Apart from that, it could have been Chelsea, Fulham or anywhere, really." Still, with a little imagination, you can almost see the **Pinewood Studios** (JBB) set as the last house on the western side of Wellington Square, although, unfortunately, the windows above the respective doors do not match.

Station: Sloane Square (CE; DI) Cross Sloane Square, walk down the King's Road past Walpole Street and then turn L into Wellington Square. Markham is just down from this, on the other side of the road. A. A. Milne, creator of Winnie the Pooh, lived in two rooms at No. 8 Wellington Square from 1904 to 1906. (He also lived and wrote at 11 [now 13] Mallord Street, Chelsea, from the 1920s until 1940.) The unnamed garage in which James Bond kept his vintage Bentley, according to Chapter 2 of *Live and Let Die*, was presumably the King's Road Garage, at No. 85. The site is just down from Wellington (and Markham) Square and is today occupied by a Marks and Spencer store.

Eyes Only, 007: According to the prop driving license and Avis rental agreement prepared for the film *Tomorrow Never Dies*, James Bond lives at No. 61 Horseferry Road, a quasi-governmental area in Westminster, near **Parliament** (27:18). This should come as quite a surprise to Fleming fans, as well as to the local government of the City of Westminster: there is no 61 Horseferry Road!

4:3

James Bond's Route to Universal Export From Wellington Square, SW3 to Regent's Park, NW1

Fleming describes portions of James Bond's daily drive in several adventures, although no one story contains the entire route. However, an examination of the descriptions in *Live and Let Die, Moonraker, Thunderball,* and *On Her Majesty's Secret Service*, combined with a bit of background in the layout of London streets in the 1950s, yields the following reconstruction: Starting from Wellington Square (see facing page), Bond would have turned right into the King's Road and continued into **Sloane Square** (4:1), where he turned left into Sloane Street itself. At the top of Sloane Street, he crossed Knightsbridge and entered **Hyde Park** (9:1). There, he would have turned right into The Ring road and continued around the eastern edge of the park, parallel to Park Lane. With some "fancy driving" he could make the Marble Arch exit in three minutes flat. After exiting the park, he would have veered left around Marble Arch itself and into Edgware Road for the "slow around the houses" (presumably via Seymour Street) into **Baker Street** (12:1) and thence into **Regent's Park** (12:2). The drive took him 10 to 15 minutes, depending on the time of day. Today, the equivalent drive takes between 15 and 20 minutes in average traffic conditions, and there are a few differences. First, even as Fleming was writing OHMSS (Bond's last drive "through" Hyde Park), Park Lane was being converted into a duel carriageway (US: divided highway). The new thoroughfare actually replaced the eastern part of the old Hyde Park ring road, so a portion of your drive will have to be along Park Lane. Second, Baker Street is now one way south, so from Seymour Street, you, and Bond, will have to turn L into Portman, which becomes Gloucester Place and runs parallel to Baker Street. Precisely what Bond did in getting from Baker Street to HQ is a little vague, but continuing up Gloucester Place into Outer Circle and alighting soon after that should get you fairly close to the old neighborhood, if only that blasted nine- (or ten-) story building were there (see **Universal Export** [12:3]). Along the way, you will pass the decidedly un-Bondian King's Road Safeway and McDonald's restaurant, the trendy shops of Sloane Street and Knightsbridge, the fashionable hotels of Park Lane and finally, on the return, the congestion of the shops and fast food restaurants of Baker Street, not to mention the Sherlock Holmes museum across from No. 221B (for which, see [12:1]).

Station: Sloane Square (CI; DI) Proceed to Wellington Square, as above, and then hail a taxi.

4:4

"Chelsea Clarion Office" King's Road (?), SW3

For three years, Vivienne Michel worked for this "glorified parish magazine" with an "Empire Loyalist" bent, according to Chapter 4 of her memoir, *The Spy Who Loved Me*. Although once a broken-down paper, the *Chelsea Clarion* (which Fleming had originally called the *South Kensington Gazette*, and then the *Chelsea Gazette*) became a prominent and well-respected local journal under its owner and editor, a Welshman named Len Holbrook, formerly of the ***Express*** (5:4). According to the British Newspaper Library, there never was a local paper called the *Chelsea Clarion*. However, there was and is a prominent periodical called the *Chelsea News*, which in Viv's day was based at 123 King's Road.

Station: Sloane Square (CI; VI) Walk down the King's Road, past Wellington and Markham Squares and look for No. 123 on the S side of the street. It is within a few blocks of Viv's Old Church Street home.

4:5

ex Chelsea Register Office
250 King's Road, SW3

Two days after Christmas 1980, actors Pierce Brosnan and Cassandra Harris (née Sandra Waites) were married here at the Chelsea Register Office, the setting for many society and celebrity weddings. Pierce, then 27, was a struggling actor, some two years away from television success in America. Australian-born Cassandra, then 39, was in the midst of shooting *For Your Eyes Only*, in which she portrayed the faux Austrian Countess Lisl Von Schlaf. The two had met at a party in the summer of 1978 and Pierce was apparently smitten at first sight. Their marriage proved to be a true love story, surviving a go-for-broke move to California, the rise and fall of *Remington Steele*, the loss of the Bond role in 1986 and, most tragically, Cassandra's much-publicized battle with cancer in the late 1980s. The actress struggled valiantly to see in both Christmas 1991 and the couple's 11th anniversary, finally succumbing to the disease on December 28th. Less than two and a half years later, Cassandra's dream for her husband came true when Pierce was announced as the fifth James Bond.

Station: Sloane Square (CI; VI) Walk down the King's Road, past the above locations and look for the former Register Office to the R, just past Sydney Street. The office was closed in 1981 and the registers transferred across the street to Chelsea's Old Town Hall (see Quick Ones).

> **Trivia Challenge 5:** Name the films in which James Bond attends (or interrupts!) a wedding party.

4:6

Vivienne Michel's Flat, et al.
Old Church Street, SW3

According to Chapter 2 of her memoir, *The Spy Who Loved Me*, 17-year-old Vivienne Michel took up residence with her friend Susan Duff in a tiny three-room flat in Old Church Street, just off the King's Road. (In the original manuscript, Fleming locates the pair in "Oakham Street", presumably an error for Oakley Street, which, like Church Street, connects the King's Road to Cheyne Walk.) They apparently lived on the first floor (US: second floor) and were just across the way from "the Popotte", a place for which Viv did not care. As far as I can determine, there was no such restaurant near the corner of the King's Road and Old Church Street in the 1950s. There was, however, a La Popote (the correct French spelling), at 3 Walton Street, just off Brompton Road and not too far from **Harrods** (10:2). While certainly within walking distance of Old Church Street, La Popote was hardly across the way. Viv and Susan were also conveniently close to a pub which Fleming doesn't name, but which would have likely been the Cadogan Arms at 298 King's Road. And, of course, Viv was also just down the road from the Wellington Square home of the spy who would eventually love her (see [4:2]), but, of course, she didn't know that at the time.

Station: Sloane Square (CI; VI) Cross **Sloane Square** (4:1), walk down the King's Road past Wellington Square and continue on for several blocks to Old Church Street. Fleming did not say whether the girls lived north or south of the King's Road, but, given their proximity to the pub, it may well have been the north. An obvious choice, of which Fleming would have likely been aware (his half-sister Amaryllis lived at 137 Old Church Street), was Carlyle House, at No. 103.

4:7

Chelsea Old Church (formally All Saints, Chelsea)
Old Church Street, SW3 (at Cheyne Walk)

Founded in the 12th century and largely destroyed by German bombs during World War II, Chelsea Old Church was faithfully restored with the aid of old prints and paintings. Its most famous parishioner was the statesman and humanist Sir Thomas More, Henry VIII's unfortunate chancellor (executed for refusing to acknowledge the king as head of the Church of England). Henry himself married Wife Number 3, Jane Seymour, here in 1536. More to the point, All Saints was also the church attended by Ian Fleming when he lived here in Chelsea (see the next two entries). Indeed, it was here, on October 29, 1952, that Ian and Ann Fleming's baby son was christened Caspar Robert, with a middle name in honor of his paternal great-grandfather and a first name inspired by fictional characters (including Casper Milquetoast) that had amused the author. Officiating at the evening ceremony was the Reverend C. E. Leighton Thomson. In attendance were the baby's godparents Noël Coward, Cecil Beaton and Peter Fleming, Ian's brother. Another godparent, Lady Clarissa Eden, wife of Prime Minister Anthony Eden, was unable to attend; Peter's wife, actress Celia Johnson, stood proxy for Mrs. Eden.

Station: Sloane Square (CI; VI) See **Vivienne Michel's Flat** (4:6); turn L into Old Church Street and follow it to the end. The church is on the L.

4:8

Ian Fleming's Home 24 Carlyle Mansions Cheyne Walk, SW3

Ian moved into a fifth floor (US: sixth floor) corner flat here in August 1950, barely a half mile from **Turner's House** (4:9), his mother's former home. In a letter to Eve dated May 11, 1950, he refers to this move from 21 Hays Mews, Mayfair (see [13:27]) as a return "to childhood surroundings in Cheyne Walk!" The building itself, again in Ian's words, was "an old-fashioned and gloomy Victorian block, but very solidly built and with nice rooms." He was particularly keen on the "terrific views up and down the river and across London," although he fretted about how much it would cost to paint and decorate the place. In connection with the latter, his mother, then staying in Cannes, sent him a "handsome contribution", for which he thanked her in a letter dated June 15. Ian was so confident about Carlyle Mansions that he took a five-year lease on No. 24, boasting to his mother that "if anything happened, I should have absolutely no difficulty in getting rid of it." The "anything" that happened was, of course, his marriage to Ann, who moved into Carlyle Mansions with her daughter Fionn in March 1952. Ann never particularly warmed to the place and within a year, the family had sold the lease and moved to No. 16 Victoria Square (see [25:1]), just a stone's throw or so from **Buckingham Palace** (16:27). *Note:* right next door to Carlyle Mansions was-and is-the historic King's Head and Eight Bells pub, a 16th-century establishment that the author no doubt visited from time to time. Be sure to pop in for a swift half in Ian's honor.

Station: Sloane Square (CI; DI) Proceed from Wellington Square (see **James Bond's Home** [4:2]) down King's Road; turn L into Oakley Street; follow it toward Albert Bridge, just before which, you will turn R into Cheyne Walk. The building is ahead on the R. No. 24 is in the top left-hand corner as you face the building. The pub, a favorite of writers and show biz celebrities, is open Mon-Sat noon-11pm and Sun noon-3pm and 7pm-10:30pm.

4:9

Turner's House 118 Cheyne Walk, SW10

Selling **Pitt House** (37:1) in 1923, Eve Fleming acquired three small workers cottages here in Cheyne (pronounced "Chain-ee") Walk and converted them into a single dwelling. She named the result Turner's House, after the romantic landscape painter J.M.W. Turner, who had spent his last years at No. 119 and, indeed, had died here in 1851. She redecorated Turner's large studio at the back of the building in rather lavish gold canvas wallpaper, adorning its walls with several portraits of herself. She then established a sort of "Bohemian salon" in Turner's House, where artists like her friend (and lover) Augustus John could socialize with patrons like her friend Winston Churchill. Ian visited his mother here throughout the 1920s and actually moved in with her in the summer of 1931. He remained at Turner's House, with Eve, until 1936, when he finally acquired his own residence, at No. 22B Ebury Street (see [2:1]). See also **Grey's Court** (*JBB*) for more on the Flemings' '30s-era living arrangements.

Station: Sloane Square (CE; DI) Make Turner's House the next to last stop on your Chelsea walk, after visiting **Ian Fleming's Home** (4:8) at Carlyle Mansions. Go W in Cheyne Walk past the Battersea Bridge; the small house is just ahead on the R. The station closest to this, the far western end of Cheyne Walk, is actually **Fulham Broadway**, on the District Line. Not far from here, just off the King's Road, is Shalcomb Street, where, in the basement of No. 12, Sean Connery lived in 1955-56, following his two-year *South Pacific* Tour (see **Scala Theatre** [7:2] and the **Theatre Royal Drury Lane** [6:2]).

Eyes Only, 007: Just down from Turner's House, at 90 Lots Road, is the Snake Ranch Studio. This is where the "Country Band" recorded the backing for Minnie Driver's rendition of "Stand By Your Man" in *GoldenEye*. No actual filming was done here, although at least one fan web site has described this as the location of the scene in which Bond meets Zukovsky. That scene, Pierce Brosnan's first as Bond, was, of course, shot at the **Eon Studios** (*JBB*) at Leavesden Aerodrome, Hertfordshire, on January 16, 1995.

Quick Ones...

Draycott Hotel
24-26 Cadogan Gardens, SW3

While his official introduction as James Bond occurred at the lavish **Regent Hotel** (12:9) in Marylebone (*see photo below*), actor Pierce Brosnan actually retreated to a suite in the low-key Draycott to gather his thoughts and reflect on the career move he had just made. Brosnan's stay here was brief, however, for the day after his June 8, 1994 press conference, the bearded star was off to Papua New Guinea to film *Robinson Crusoe*.
Station: Sloane Square (CI; DI)

Chelsea Kitchen
98 King's Road, SW3

A Chelsea institution for over two decades, this cheerful but cheap restaurant was a favorite haunt of Pierce Brosnan and his late wife Cassandra Harris (Lisl in *For Your Eyes Only*) prior to their move to America in the early '80s. According to Garth Pearce, author of *The Making of GoldenEye*, Brosnan breakfasted here on June 9, 1994, the morning after his debut press conference as James Bond at the **Regent Hotel** (12:9) in Marylebone.
Station: Sloane Square (CI; DI)

ex HQ of the Chelsea Council
Chelsea Old Town Hall
King's Road, SW3

In Chapter 4 of *The Spy Who Loved Me*, local reporter Vivienne Michel tells us that her boss, Len Holbrook (see the ***Chelsea Clarion*** [4:4]) had a tip-off on the [Chelsea] Council from whom he obtained confidential information about newsworthy events in the borough. Formed in 1900, the Chelsea Borough Council, or local administrative body, was headquartered here in the district's Old Town Hall. In 1965, the Metropolitan Borough of Chelsea and the Royal Metropolitan Borough of Kensington merged to form the Royal Borough of Kensington and Chelsea, whose council is headquartered in the Town Hall, Kensington.
Station: Sloane Square (CI; VI)

5. THE CITY

The financial and commercial center of London, virtually deserted on the weekends

5:0

The City Walking Tour
EC2, EC3, EC4

Start: **Fleet Street;** ***Finish:*** **The Tower of London**

London's financial center is intimately connected with both James Bond's creator and James Bond himself. Ian Fleming's grandfather Robert established his merchant bank here in the early 20th century, Ian worked here on and off throughout his life and, of course, Bond visited the City in several novels and films. You may even recall that a certain Max Zorin is "the talk of the City and the Bourse", according to M in the film *A View To A Kill*. The tour of selected City sites (each has its own entry, with tube and directions, below) begins in Fleet Street, the traditional home of London's major newspapers.

Above: St Paul's Cathedral as seen in *OHMSS* (*see page 39*).
Below: M's Motorcade Route from *Tomorrow Never Dies* (*see page 38*).

5:1

Inner Temple Garden
Inner Temple
Victoria Embankment, EC4

Post-premiere parties are an established tradition in the film world, a tradition to which the Bond filmmakers have adhered since the very beginning. In the 1960s and '70s these celebrity-studded affairs were generally held at exclusive Mayfair venues such as **Les Ambassadeurs Club** (13:38) or the **Playboy Club** (13:35). However, since the '80s, the locations have been a little less "Hollywood" and a little more "London". Take for example, the after-picture bash for *A View To A Kill*, which was held on the night of June 12, 1985. Roger Moore's swansong Bond saw the regular Eon family, in addition to newcomers Patrick Macnee, Grace Jones and Duran Duran, partying under a large, decorative marquee (or, for American readers, a field-tent used for social functions) in the impressive Inner Temple Garden. The Inner Temple itself is one of the four Central London law societies, known as the Inns of Court, to one of which every English barrister must belong. (The other societies are the Middle Temple, adjacent to the Inner Temple, and Lincoln's Inn and Gray's Inn, Holborn.) The Inner Temple's neo-Georgian hall dates from 1955, the 19th-century Gothic building having been destroyed by German bombs in 1941. This handsome setting, garden and hall, proved so popular among the Bond family that the post-premiere parties for both *The Living Daylights* (June 29, 1987) and *Licence To Kill* (June 13, 1989) were held here as well. I asked former Eon production controller Reg Barkshire if he noticed any difference between the Roger Moore-era parties and those for the Timothy Dalton pictures. "Well, Tim was certainly a quieter temperament than Roger. Not exactly withdrawn, but perhaps not as relaxed as Roger. At the studio, for example, whenever you saw Tim, he would be looking at a script, rehearsing his lines, absolutely oblivious to what was going on elsewhere. Roger, on the other hand, would always look over whenever he saw me and say, "Look out, here comes Moneybags!" Doug Redenius, Vice-President of the Ian Fleming Foundation, attended both Dalton parties, the first of which commemorated the 25th anniversary of James Bond in the cinema. "It was an intimate, highly controlled affair, where you could easily approach the celebrities and sit down for a casual chat," Doug recalled. Celebrity guests that year included veteran Bond performers Patrick Macnee, Britt Ekland and Jane Seymour, as well as Patrick Swayze, then starring in the blockbuster *Dirty Dancing*. The *Licence To Kill* party two years later would be the last premiere bash for nearly six and a half years, as the James Bond franchise went through one its darkest periods. When Bond returned in the 1995 blockbuster *GoldenEye*, so did the parties, with London's famous **Imperial War Museum** (11:Q) in Lambeth providing the backdrop. For more Bond premiere party settings, see **Les Ambassadeurs Club** (13:38), the **ex London Playboy Club** (13:35), the **Café Royal** (19:2), the **Royal Garden Hotel** (9:4) and the **Roof Gardens** (9:3).

Station: Temple (CI; DI) Exit the station, turn L, ascend the steps and then turn R into Temple Place. Turn L at Milford Lane then veer R into the path and steps that lead to the Middle Temple, which will be on your right. Take a look at this magnificent 16th-century banqueting room, itself the venue for a royal premiere (that of Shakespeare's *Twelfth Night*, in the presence of Queen Elizabeth I, on February 2, 1601), before crossing over into the Inner Temple itself.

5:2

Ian Fleming's Office
4 Old Mitre Court, EC4

When *The Sunday Times* was sold in 1959, Ian Fleming lost his position as foreign manager (see **ex Kemsley House/Thomson House** [3:1]) and was therefore out on his own for the first time in his professional life. As an established fiction writer, on the verge, it seemed, of transferring his hero to the motion picture screen, Fleming obviously needed some kind of office, and, through his friend Rennie Hoare, found one here in Mitre Court Chambers, a building owned by Hoare's Bank. Ian subleased two rooms on the fourth floor (US: fifth floor), the entirety of which was occupied by Dr. Hugh Richards, a GP on retainer to the bank. In addition to working here, Fleming also seems to have spent the night here from time to time, possibly to avoid facing another one of his wife's dinner parties. Dr. Richards died in 1994 and the Bank undertook an extensive renovation of the fourth floor in 1999. The former office of James Bond's creator is today occupied by a barrister's chambers.

Station: Blackfriars (CI) Go R in New Bridge Street and L into Fleet Street. Four streets down, and just past El Vino's, turn L into Mitre Court. No. 4 is ahead on the R. Fleming's office was on the top floor, the second and third windows over from the left. Be sure to stop by El Vino's itself; this famous Fleet Street wine bar was one of Fleming's favorite watering holes.

5:3

ex HQ of Reuters Ltd
Victoria Embankment, EC4
(at Carmelite Street)

Ian Fleming worked for the renowned Reuters news agency as a sub-editor and occasional reporter from October 1931 until October 1933. From his table on the first floor (US: second floor) of Reuters' large, red brick headquarters, Ian undertook a variety of "stimulating" duties including the updating of more than 500 of the agency's obituaries. In April 1933, he was sent to Moscow to cover the espionage trial of six engineers of the Metropolitan-Vickers Electrical Company (see **ex Vickers Ltd** [27:28]). When there were no hard facts to report, Ian simply invented colorful, even melodramatic stories for the folks back home ("Tonight, thousands of enemies of the Soviet State are skulking in cellars, gnashing their teeth" was the way he led off one particularly lurid piece). Such dispatches, along with his more objective coverage of the sensational show trial itself, met with great favor in London and, of course, Fleming himself received a valuable education in the ways of "Redland". Still, come autumn, he would turn his back on journalism in order to "get rich quick" with the bank of **Cull & Company** (5:Q). Years later, Fleming would acknowledge his former employer in such novels as *The Spy Who Loved Me* and *OHMSS*, but by then, Reuters had moved to its present location (see [5:5]).

Station: Blackfriars (CI) Walk S toward the river, take the steps to the embankment walk and proceed W along the **Thames** (24:1). Return to street level and look for Carmelite Street across the embankment. Reuters was located in the corner building E of Carmelite Street. Alternatively, as a side trip on the **City Walking Tour**, you may turn R into Whitefriars Street from Fleet Street and cross Tudor Street to Carmelite. Follow this to the Embankment.

5:4

ex HQ of the Daily Express
121-128 Fleet Street, EC4 (at Shoe Lane)

Founded in 1900, the *Daily Express* is one of several mass-circulation "popular papers", or tabloids, which are to be distinguished from "quality papers" such as *The Times* or the *Daily Telegraph*. The *Daily Express* moved into this distinctive black vitrolite and chrome Art Deco structure in 1932, making every other Fleet Street building seem staid by comparison. The *Express* remained here until 1989, when, along with most of the rest of the Fleet Street journals, the paper moved across the river. (cf. the **Financial Times** and **The Times** [5:7]. Novice reporter Ian Fleming achieved his first by-line in the *Daily Express.*The time was April 1933 and Fleming had been sent by the **Reuters** (see left) to cover the espionage trial of six British engineers in Moscow. When the Soviets denied the *Express's* special correspondent an entry visa, Ian, who happened to be in the right place at the right time, stepped into the breach. As a result, it was *his* article on the opening of the trial that appeared on the front page of the *Express* the following day. This would be Fleming's last by-line until after the war, when he became foreign manager of the Kemsley Group (see **ex Kemsley House/Thomson House** [3:1]). Author Fleming would go on to mention both the *Daily Express* and its sister publication the *Sunday Express* in several James Bond novels, including *Moonraker, Diamonds Are Forever, The Spy Who Loved Me* and *OHMSS.* In the first, we learn that the *Sunday Express* is running the life story of the "national hero" Sir Hugo Drax and Bond himself reads a copy of the *Express* at **Drax's Plant** (*JBB*). In *Diamonds*, Bond playfully tells his secretary, Loelia Ponsonby, that for all he cares, she can send the files he is supposed to read over to the *Daily Express*. He then teasingly asks if *Express* reporter Sefton Delmer isn't a boyfriend of hers. Delmer, of course, was a real-life journalist and former intelligence officer, as well as a friend of Fleming's. In *Spy*, Vivienne Michel works for a former *Express* reporter named Len Holbrook, now the editor of the ***Chelsea Clarion*** (4:4). And in *OHMSS*, Sir Hilary Bond reads a copy of the *Daily Express* from last page to first during his helicopter ride to Piz Gloria. (In the film itself, it is Shaun Campbell, not Bond, who reads the paper [see below].)

In July 1958, the *Daily Express* began a series of comic strip adaptations of the Bond novels (the first, appropriately, being *Casino Royale*), which continued through the mid-1960s. Fleming also offered them the chance to serialize *The Spy Who Loved Me* in 1962, but the editorial board turned him down. Mind you, they were very upset when Fleming's short story "The Living Daylights" appeared in the rival *Sunday Times* magazine on February 9 of that same year. This, it seems, indicated a "change of allegiance" and so the *Express* promptly cancelled the comic strip, which was then in the thick of the *Thunderball* adventure. Fleming wrote to his friend Lord Beaverbrook, the powerful owner of the Express Group, begging for forgiveness. He offered the excuse that *The Sunday Times*, of whose "editorial board" he was still a member, had been hounding him to contribute an article or story and, besides, given the *Express's* rejection of *Spy*, how could he have known that they still expected first crack at a Bond story? Beaverbrook, closer to Ann than to her husband, relented, insisting in a letter of August 12, 1962 that Ian should "forget all about it." The two made up and James Bond reemerged in the pages of the *Express* in 1964. Meanwhile, in August 1961, the first Bond film was in preproduction and the starring role had yet to be cast. The *Daily Express* conducted a poll of its readers and among the top three favorites was Scottish actor Sean Connery. Having impressed producers Cubby Broccoli and Harry Saltzman as well (see [13:31]), Connery was duly signed and announced as Bond that November. On the last day of the following month, the *Sunday Express* published the now-infamous interview, in which Connery told reporter Susan Barnes that he didn't "think there's anything very wrong with hitting a woman." Although appalling when taken out of context, the remark seems to have been calculated to bait a gullible young writer, one whose sensibilities were suitably "shocked" by the actor's forthright comments on sex and sadism.

Finally, as mentioned above, Shaun Campbell, MI6's man in Switzerland, reads a copy of the *Daily Express* in F *On Her Majesty's Secret Service*. Campbell's scene is set in a Swiss train station and occurs immediately after the **College of Arms** (5:11) sequence, which concludes with Bond's line that if Sir Hilary Bray's client *is* Blofeld, "I'd like to get him away from Switzerland". It has long been known that the original *OHMSS* script contained a longer version of the College of Arms sequence, in which Bond discovers that Sir Hilary's office has been bugged and that the culprit is Bray's assistant Phidian. According to director Peter Hunt, Bond was then to have chased Phidian across the College's roof and thence to an underground rail line, where the agent would have met his demise (see also **St Paul's Cathedral** [5:10]). Precisely what would have happened to Phidian (and how MI6 would have concealed his death from Blofeld) must remain "top secret", since Eon could conceivably resurrect the sequence for a future film. However, if you scan the headlines on the front page of Campbell's newspaper, you may just discover a tantalizing clue as to the elaborate (and highly ingenious) sequence the filmmakers originally intended.

Station: Blackfriars (CI) Go R in New Bridge Street and L into Fleet Street. The building is just ahead on the N side of the street. SciFi film buffs may recognize the stylish structure from the cult classic *The Day the Earth Caught Fire*, featuring a pre-Rumpole Leo McKern as an *Express* reporter.

Trivia Challenge 6:
In which film does Bond himself read the *Daily Express*?

5:5

HQ of Reuters Ltd and the Press Association 85 Fleet Street, EC4

Ian Fleming worked for Reuters, the famous international news agency, in the 1930s, so it's no surprise that he acknowledged the organization in several James Bond stories. In his very first novel, for example, he tells us that Fawcett, Bond's control for the *Casino Royale* assignment, spends his time sifting photographs submitted by the great agencies, including Reuter-Photo. In Chapter 5 of *The Spy Who Loved Me*, narrator Vivienne Michel tells us that her employer and future lover Kurt Rainer runs the London office of a West German news agency organized and financed "rather on the lines of Reuters." In the penultimate chapter of *OHMSS*, Bond, having destroyed Piz Gloria and saved Britain from Biological Warfare, reads a copy of *Die Welt* (he is in Munich, about to marry Tracy) and discovers an article with the headline "In England, Polio Scare". The "brief Reuter dispatch" was "date-lined the day before from London". That dispatch would have emanated from No. 85 Fleet Street, the impressive L-shaped building into which the agency moved in 1935. (Fleming left the agency in 1933.) The last commercial structure designed by the renowned "imperial" architect Sir Edwin Lutyens, Reuters' steel-framed head office is clad in Portland stone and commands attention for, among other things, its concave-fronted roof pavilion surmounted by a distinctive drum. The company itself, started by Paul Julius Reuter in 1849, is today one of the largest electronic publishers in the world.

Reuters shares the Lutyens building with the Press Association, a large national news agency for the UK and Ireland, founded in 1867. Of the "Polio Scare" story mentioned above, Fleming actually states that it would have been "put out to the world...through the Press Association to Reuter." And in Chapter 2 of *The Man with the Golden Gun*, M tells the Chief of Staff to put out a communiqué to the Press Association announcing the return of Commander James Bond, who was believed to have been killed on a mission to Japan the previous year. He also directs the COS to send a "D" Notice [*sic*] to the editors, requesting that they do not add their own speculation or comment, nor try to trace Commander Bond's whereabouts. The D(efence)-notice is an actual censorship tool still employed by the British Government. It consists of a formal letter sent in confidence to mass media editors, advising them that a particular item of classified information should not be disclosed. Failure to observe the D-notice can result in prosecution under the Official Secrets Act, although the system is theoretically one of "voluntary" censorship on the part of the media. A famous recent example was the D-notice issued to the British media in May 1999, when a former MI6 officer threatened to disclose the names of more than a hundred top intelligence officers to Internet sites throughout the world.

Station: Blackfriars (CI) Go R in New Bridge Street and L into Fleet Street. The building is just ahead on the S side of the street, opposite the **ex *Daily Express*** (5:4).

5:6

ex Press Club
St Bride's Passage, EC4 (off Fleet Street)

Founded in 1882 and first housed at 63 Fleet Street, the Press Club counted the City's most distinguished journalists among its members. One of those who enjoyed the club's largely social gatherings was Ian Fleming, for many years the foreign manager of the Kemsley newspapers (see [3:1]). Another notable member was Vivienne Michel, heroine/narrator of *The Spy Who Loved Me*. She tells us in Chapter 5 that her new boss, Kurt Rainer of the VWZ news agency, checked up on her through her friends at the Press Club. At that time (late 1950s), the club was based in St Bride's Passage, behind the church. It moved to the International Press Centre, 76 Shoe Lane, in 1973 and declared bankruptcy in 1986. Sixteen former members then founded a successor organization, the London Press Club, which is today based in the St Bride Institute, very near the original location.

Station: Blackfriars (CI) Go R in New Bridge Street, then L into Bride Lane, a small alleyway. At the bend, take the steps up to St Bride's Passage; the two-story Press Club was on the R, just behind the church.

5:7

ex HQ of The Times
Printing House Square
Queen Victoria Street, EC4

One of the greatest newspapers in the world was established here on January 1, 1785. Its publisher, John Walter, called it *The Daily Universal Register.* Three years later to the day, the paper acquired its present name, as well as the first version of its famous masthead, a stylized reproduction of the Royal Coat of Arms. By the middle of the following century, *The Times* had become Britain's preeminent national journal, popularly known as the "Thunderer." Its most famous building, a large Victorian fortress erected in 1874, would last until 1962, when a new headquarters was opened on the same site. Lord Thomson of Fleet acquired *The Times* in 1966 and eight years later transferred the paper to a purpose-built headquarters in Gray's Inn Road, adjacent to that of *The Sunday Times* (see **ex Kemsley House/Thomson House** [3:1]). Controversial media mogul Rupert Murdoch acquired Times Newspapers, Ltd in 1981 and subsequently moved the entire operation to its present headquarters at 9 Pennington Street, E1. Murdoch, of course, is a possible inspiration for *Tomorrow Never Dies* villain Elliot Carver, right down to his well-publicized efforts to break into China's vast TV market.

The Times' Bondian connections began in March 1939, when stockbroker (or **Foreign Office** (27:15) spy?) Ian Fleming traveled to Moscow for the paper. There, as a special correspondent, Fleming covered a series of important trade talks between British and Soviet government officials. Upon his return to London, Fleming submitted a long, impressionistic analysis of the Soviet armed forces, which *The Times* declined to print. (He later submitted the report to the Foreign Office, where his cautionary view of the potential Soviet ally, in what everyone knew would soon be a major war, met with greater favor.) There were apparently no hard feelings, however, as the author frequently endorsed *The Times* in his James Bond novels. In Chapter 13 of *Moonraker*, for example, Bond reads a copy of *The Times* at **Drax's Plant** (*JBB*), while in Chapter 11 of *From Russia, With Love*, we learn that *The Times* is the only paper that Bond ever reads. This is not strictly true (cf., for example, Chapter 6 of *Diamonds Are Forever*, where Bond reads the *Evening Standard*), but we get the idea. In Chapter 7 of *Goldfinger*, *The Times*' front-page "Agony Column", a section of classified personal advertisements, is suggested as a possible communication medium among SMERSH agents. Additional references occur in "The Hildebrand Rarity", *Thunderball* and *On Her Majesty's Secret Service*. In fact, in the original manuscript of the latter novel, Fleming indirectly refers to the Printing House Square location, telling us that the **College of Arms** (5:11) is in the fringe of the City "not many doors from *The Times*." In the finished book, he has Bond carry a folded copy of the paper as part of his Hilary Bray disguise; and, then, later, has an acquaintance of the real Sir Hilary express shock at having missed Bray's "obituary" in *The Times*. (Bond claims to be a first cousin who has inherited the title upon the death of the "other" Hilary Bray.) In *The Man with the Golden Gun*, M actually "barricade[s] himself behind *The Times*" (a marvelous Fleming pun), pretending to read it over his meagre luncheon. For his penultimate novel, *You Only Live Twice*, Fleming hit upon the idea of having James Bond's obituary appear beneath the newspaper's famous masthead. (Bond had already contemplated his **Times** obituary in Chapter 26 of *OHMSS.*) Through his brother Peter, who had worked for the paper, Ian eventually secured permission to include the signature coat of arms, although as *The Times* rightly pointed out, the arms actually belonged to the Queen, and not to the paper itself. Ian's publisher, Michael Howard of **Jonathan Cape** (3:6), was still not happy. He believed that the whole idea of M publicizing the death of a secret agent through such an obituary was simply unrealistic. Fleming, however, insisted that it should remain in the novel, saying that, "the main thing is that the whole obituary idea is a bit of a lark to which I am much attached." Of course, he was right, and *The Times* "Obit", with its tongue-in-cheek reference to "a series of popular books" written about James Bond "by a personal friend and former colleague", went on to become one of the most famous and often-cited chapters in the whole of Fleming's oeuvre.

Blackfriars (CI; DI) The site is directly across Queen Victoria Street from the north side of the station.

5:8

Central Criminal Court (The Old Bailey) Old Bailey, EC4

Britain's leading criminal court occupies an imposing granite structure erected on the site of Newgate Prison in 1900-1907. Familiar to Britons and Americans alike from countless appearances in films and television series (e.g., *Rumpole of the Bailey*), the Central Criminal Court serves Greater London as well as portions of Essex, Kent and Surrey (see the **ex Bucket of Blood** [*JBB*] for one of the court's most celebrated trials). According to Chapter 3 of *You Only Live Twice*, James Bond actually gave evidence here at the Old Bailey during the trial of Secret Service Agent Prenderghast on charges of treason. This affair was so serious that M had actually tendered his resignation (which, of course, was not accepted). Work at HQ was held up for at least a month because of the trial, at the end of which Prenderghast was sentenced to thirty years' imprisonment (forty, in the original manuscript). Fleming presumably based this incident on the sensational Old Bailey trial of George Blake, an MI6 agent who, in 1961, was found guilty of treason under the Official Secrets Act (he had been spying for Russia since 1950) and sentenced to an unprecedented 42 years' imprisonment. In 1966, Blake escaped from Wormwood Scrubs prison and fled to Moscow, where he remains to this day.

Station: St Paul's (CE) Take the St Paul's exit, go L at the top of the stairs into Newgate Street and look for the Old Bailey ahead on the L. **Hours:** Mon-Fri, when Courts are in session, from 10:30am-1pm and 2pm-4:30pm

> **Eyes Only, 007:** Fleming namedrops the famous London prison into Chapter 2 of *Thunderball*, where Bond's pimply-faced taxi driver derides the Shrublands clinic as "Wormwood Scrubs".

5:9

Aldersgate Street and M's Motorcade Route EC2

James Bond generally receives his briefing from M in the London headquarters of the Secret Service. Occasionally, however, M likes to get out of the office and so Bond may end up being briefed on a submarine, at the **Diamond Corporation** (8:2) or even in his own Chelsea flat. In *Tomorrow Never Dies*, the setting for the obligatory scene is M's Daimler, with Robinson and Moneypenny in tow. The group is first shown turning right into Poultry (with the imposing Royal Exchange behind them), from which, presumably, they will be making their way *south* toward Vauxhall Cross. Instead, they end up driving *north* on Aldersgate, *above* the traffic circus, then *east* on London Wall, both of which are several blocks *northwest* of where the group originally started. The whole thing makes a bit more sense once you know that the actors and crew spent a quiet Sunday afternoon riding around in circles to the northeast of **St Paul's Cathedral** (5:10). The actual route, which you can easily retrace on foot, begins in St Martin's-le-Grand, opposite the St Paul's Underground Station, proceeds north into Aldersgate, turns right into London Wall, then right into Moorgate, veers left into Prince's Street, turns right into Poultry (where we first see them in the film), continues into Cheapside, then turns right into St Martin's-le-Grand, where the whole thing starts all over again. Of course, it is still unclear why the MI6 gang were joyriding through the *City*, when they were supposedly coming from a briefing in Whitehall. Perhaps M's driver charges by the mile!

Station: Barbican (CI; HC; ME) From the station, walk S in Aldersgate toward the traffic circus at London Wall. Pass the Theodore Goddard building at No. 150 then turn around and look back up Aldersgate for the view of M's escorted Daimler that appears just after the shots in front of the Royal Exchange. Then walk S to London Wall, turn L and walk as far as Wood Street. You should recognize the area, including the short tunnel beneath the Museum of London, as the backdrop for the shots of M, in close-up, briefing Bond. For the entire route, start at **St Paul's (CE)**, exit the station and cross into St Martin's-le-Grand, continuing on as outlined above.

Trivia Challenge 7: During their ride, M tells Bond that the PM would have her head if...what?

5:10

St Paul's Cathedral
Ludgate Hill, EC4

Designed by the Baroque genius Sir Christopher Wren, this truly awe-inspiring cathedral (the fourth on this site), was begun in 1675 and completed in 1711. It is medieval in plan (a Latin cross with side chapels), but Renaissance in external appearance, including the great dome, clearly inspired by that of the Vatican. Along with the clock tower of the **Houses of Parliament** (27:18), the dome of St Paul's is, arguably, the most famous landmark in London. Among the many notable Britons entombed in the cathedral crypt are Sir Christopher himself, the Duke of Wellington and Lord Nelson, who rests directly beneath the dome. Bondwise, the massive building dominates the establishing shot of the **College of Arms** (5:11) in *On Her Majesty's Secret Service*. The cathedral's exterior was also to be included as the backdrop to a scene in which Bond, having twigged that Phidian (Sir Hilary's assistant) actually works for Blofeld, chases the man across the roof of the College, past St Paul's and thence to the dimly lit Post Office Railway, an automated underground line linking London's major sorting offices. According to director Peter Hunt, the idea of such a chase quite appealed to him, but, in the end, the scene was dropped to save both time and money. (Contrary to previous reports, the scene was never filmed, merely storyboarded, according to both Hunt and *OHMSS* set decorator Peter Lamont.) Candid photos of George Lazenby running and jumping in front of St Paul's suggest what might have been—as does a headline in Shaun Campbell's copy of the *Daily Express* (see [5:4])!

Stations: St Paul's (CE) Take the St Paul's exit, turn to the L and walk back past the station entrance to the cathedral. **Open for sightseeing:** Mon-Sat 8:30am-4pm (admission charge)

Eyes Only, 007: Look fast and you may just spot St Paul's dome in—*The Man With The Golden Gun*! It's part of the backdrop in Scaramanga's fun house, visible over Bond's shoulder when he runs into the glass wall.

5:11

College of Arms
Queen Victoria Street, EC4

The Corporation of Kings, Heralds and Pursuivants of Arms, popularly known as the College of Arms or Heralds' College, researches claims to existing coats of arms and, on behalf of the Sovereign, grants new coats of arms to worthy applicants (those whose life or work has been of benefit to the community). The Head of the College is the Earl Marshal, traditionally the Duke of Norfolk, who supervises the day-to-day work of the Officers of Arms, approves the granting of all coats of arms, and settles rival claims to coats of arms. In addition, the Earl Marshal also organizes coronations, funerals and other great ceremonies of State, for which reason his throne contains the cushion on which Elizabeth II sat for her coronation in 1953. That throne is located in the impressive Earl Marshal's Court, the principal and finest room of the college and the first one you enter when you walk through the front door. It was this two-story paneled room, with its gallery, throne and cushion, that director Peter Hunt and production designer Syd Cain meticulously recreated for the film *On Her Majesty's Secret Service*. After parking his car in front of the actual building, Bond enters the filmmakers' version of the Earl Marshal's Court. He is then briefed by a Pursuivant (or "follower") called Sable Basilisk, who, in the film, is conflated with Sir Hilary Bray, a separate character in the novel (and one whose name Fleming pinched from a stockbroker friend). Ian himself had been briefed by Robin Mirrlees, the Rouge Dragon, from whom he was thrilled to learn of the real Bond family motto: "The World Is Not Enough". In the novel, however, he employed two new Pursuivants, *Griffon Or* and *Sable Basilisk*, i.e., the golden griffon and the black basilisk. To save you a trip to the dictionary: a griffon (more correctly, *griffin*) is a mythical beast with the head, forepart and wings of an eagle, and the body, hind legs and tail of a lion; a basilisk is a mythical snake whose breath is fatal to all plant and animal life. Is it just me or does the "black basilisk" suggest comparisons with a certain villain and his threat of biological warfare? For more on the Bond family motto, see **Bond Street** (13:9) and **ex Seat of Sir Thomas Bond** (46:1).

Above: Director Peter Hunt (left) and actor George Baker (right) conduct York Herald Dr. Conrad Swan (gesturing) and his assistant, Mr. George, on a tour of the College of Arms set at Pinewood Studios.

Station: St Paul's (CE) Take the St Paul's exit, turn L at the top of the stairs and walk back past the station entrance toward the cathedral. Follow St Paul's Churchyard around to the R so that you pass in front of the cathedral, then continue on around the building to the L. Now, to the R, look for the City Information Centre at the corner of Godliman Street. Turn R here and continue on to Queen Victoria Street. The College is on the L, at the corner of Godliman and Queen Victoria. **Hours:** Mon-Fri 10am-4pm

Trivia Challenge 8: In the film, what is Sir Hilary's fee for researching Blofeld's claim to the de Bleauchamp title?

5:12

The Bank of England Threadneedle Street, EC2

This august institution, where James Bond received an important briefing in both the novel and film *Goldfinger* and which Alec Trevelyan planned to rob in the film *GoldenEye*, has advised the British government on financial matters since the 17th century. Today, it is roughly equivalent to the Federal Reserve System in the United States, overlapping with the US Treasury Department in creating paper currency. Its principal tasks are to maintain the integrity and value of Britain's currency, ensure the stability of the financial system and promote the efficiency and competitiveness of that system. It also stores the bulk of Britain's gold reserves, presently calculated to be 573 metric tons and valued at £3.4 billion ($5,440,000,000). (The United States possesses the largest official reserve of gold: 8,140 metric tons, valued at $80,160,000,000.) The Bank of England is governed by a Court of Directors, at the head of which sits the Gover-

Left:
The College of Arms has changed very little since *OHMSS* was filmed here in 1969.
Below Left:
The Bank of England set from *Goldfinger*, built at Pinewood Studios in 1964.

nor, who is appointed by the sovereign for a five-year term. The Directors meet weekly in the Court Room, a large and richly-appointed 18th-century setting, every bit as elegant as the "board room" designed by Ken Adam for the film. The Bank itself resides in an impressive "imperially classical" building, the exterior of which, unfortunately, was not shown in the finished film. However, those with a sharp eye, can spot the Bank in the second shot of M's Daimler careening out into Poultry in front of the Royal Exchange in the film *Tomorrow Never Dies*. M then briefs Bond on Elliot Carver but, as noted above, has somehow managed to end up traveling north in **Aldersgate** (5:9) instead of along the Embankment toward Westminster.

Station: Bank (CE; NO; WC; DL) Take Exit 2 L into Threadneedle Street and follow this to Bartholomew Lane, where you will turn L for the Museum. When you do, remember that you're literally walking in Bond's footsteps—he exited the Bank's main entrance (which you will pass on the L) and walked along to the Tube after his briefing here in Chapter 7 of *Goldfinger*.

Eyes Only, 007: At the Bank's museum you can ogle and even touch actual gold bars, weighing 400 troy ounces (27 lbs. 7 oz.) and worth about £72,000 (over $115,000) apiece. They are cool, smooth and really quite beautiful, even more impressive than the well-executed props from *Goldfinger*. And while you cannot take one home as a souvenir, you *can* pick up a free piece of gold-bearing ore in a handy BOE commemorative bag. Please—only one to a customer.

Trivia Challenge 9: In which novel does the Bank of England step into to halt a run on the British pound?

5:13

Mansion House
Mansion House Place, EC4

The official residence of the Lord Mayor of London is a Palladian Revival masterpiece constructed between 1739 and 1752. It is famous for the lavish banquets given by the Lord Mayor in the Banqueting Room, (generally known as the Egyptian Hall), one of which Assistant Commissioner Vallance enjoys in Chapter 19 of *Moonraker*. Enjoys, that is, until Bond interrupts the **Scotland Yard** (27:16) official with an urgent phone call about the missing Gala Brand.

Station: Bank (CE; NO; WC; DL) Exit 8 brings you up beside Mansion House.

Trivia Challenge 10: In which Bond film can you spot the front of Mansion House?

5:14

ex Glyn, Mills & Co.
(now the Royal Bank of Scotland)
67 Lombard Street, EC3 (at Birchin Lane)

Upon his discharge from His Majesty's Service in November 1945, Commander Ian Fleming had yet to find a fixed abode. He therefore gave his address as "care of Glyn Mills Bank, Lombard Street", where he had an account. Never one to waste a real-life name, Fleming later appropriated "Glyn, Mills" for the use of communist mole Maria Freudenstein in "The Property of a Lady". Interestingly, Glyn, Mills—today a part of the Royal Bank of Scotland—has at least one other espionage connection: during World War II, its managing director, Terence Maxwell, was recruited into the Special Operations Executive (see [12:8]), for whom he served as the station head in Cairo.

Station: Bank (CE; NO; WC; DL) Take Exit 6 into Lombard Street (which Fleming compares to the Boulevard Haussmann—SPECTRE's Paris location—in Chapter 5 of *Thunderball*); the bank itself is ahead on the L.

5:15

ex Office of the Guaranty
Trust Company of New York
32 Lombard Street, EC3

Assigned to run down Mr. Big on his home ground, Bond submits to a rather humorous "Americanization" at the hands of Felix Leiter and the FBI in Chapter 3 of *Live and Let Die*. With his all new wardrobe, military haircut, and horn-rimmed glasses (!), Bond will be posing as "a New Englander from Boston" on holiday from his job in the London office of the Guaranty Trust Company. Fleming may have known of this New York-based commercial bank from his days in the city, or may simply spotted the firm on the way to or from his own bank across the street (see [5:14]). In any case, he gave Bond a short-term banking career, much as he himself had had at Cull & Co. [5:Q] during the 1930s (and as Bond would again have in *Tomorrow Never Dies*). The Guaranty Trust Company, itself merged with the J. P. Morgan and Co. in 1959 and, today, as Morgan Guaranty Trust Company, operates two London branches.

Station: Bank (CE; NO; WC; DL) Take Exit 6 into Lombard Street; No. 32 is ahead on the R, a block or so beyond the ex Glyn, Mills Bank at No. 67.

5:16

ex Rowe & Pitman Ltd
43 Bishopsgate, EC2

In June 1935, Ian Fleming joined this leading firm of stockbrokers, one whose clients included **Rolls-Royce** (*JBB*) and the **Diamond Corporation** (8:2). Ian apparently enjoyed the social aspects of the job—taking clients to lunch at **White's** (16:2) and **The Savoy** (23:8), for example—as well as writing the monthly newsletter and organizing the company darts tournament. The *real* work of researching and recommending investments, however, never seemed to engage him. Fortunately, he found a friend and mentor in Hugo Pitman, nephew of one of the firm's founders (and namesake of the Chief of Immigration in the novel *Thunderball*). Thus, the company continued to pay Fleming after he commenced his wartime service in Naval Intelligence and even offered to reinstate him at war's end. Instead, Fleming opted for an entirely different career path at *The Sunday Times* (see [3:1]). In 1985, Rowe & Pitman was acquired by SBC Warburg, which is based at 1 Finsbury Avenue. As a separate entity, Rowe & Pitman ceased to exist in 1996.

Station: Bank (CE) Take Exit 3 into Threadneedle Street and follow this to Bishopsgate, where you will turn L. The building was ahead on the R, just past the entrance to Crosby Square. For over seventy years, Crosby Square itself was the home of Robert Fleming's bank, established by Ian's millionaire grandfather in 1909. It was located at No. 8, on the western side of the square, abutting No. 34 Bishopsgate. Today, Robert Fleming Holdings Company, one of the UK's largest asset management and investment banking groups, is located at 10 Aldermanbury.

5:17

Lloyd's of London
1 Lime Street, EC3

The most famous "insurance company" in the world is more accurately described as an "insurance market" which has no shareholders and accepts no corporate liability for the risks it underwrites. Its underwriters (the so-called "Names") accept risks for personal profit or loss, being liable to the full extent of their private assets. Richard Rogers and Partners designed the company's present high-tech HQ, which opened in 1986. (Further examples of Rogers' work are Paris's famous Centre Georges Pompidou, where Bond meets Holly Goodhead in F *Moonraker*, and the **Renault** facility [*JBB*] used in *A*

View To A Kill.) Lloyd's Bondian connections are slight, but amusing. In the short story "The Property of a Lady", Bond spots the KGB Resident Director at **Sotheby's** (13:11) and notes that the man's face was nondescript, like a bank manager or member of Lloyd's. In chapter 3 of *OHMSS*, Bond reflects that Tracy's casino disgrace (a scene repeated in the film) will get her blacklisted throughout Europe, as though she had been "declared a bad risk at Lloyd's or with the City security firm of Dun and Bradstreet." Bond, of course, bails her out, just as he does in the film.

Station: Bank (CE; NO; WC; DL) Take Exit 5 into Cornhill, continue past Gracechurch Street and into Leadenhall Street. Turn R into Lime Street and look for the biggest, gaudiest thing around.

Eyes Only, 007: Lloyd's doubled as Sean Connery's HQ in the film *The Avengers* and as the target of his caper in *Entrapment.*

5:18

Tower Bridge E1, SE1

A flamboyant example of Victorian Gothic engineering, Tower Bridge, along with **St Paul's Cathedral** (5:10) and the **Houses of Parliament** (27:18), is an instantly recognizable symbol of the British capital. And yet London's most famous bridge is surprisingly new: the first stone was laid by the Prince of Wales in 1886, while construction was not completed until 1894. The venerable-*looking* bridge may be glimpsed on the monitor of the Blofeld-lookalike's wheelchair control panel in the pre-credit sequence of *For Your Eyes Only* (although the helicopter is actually some two miles upriver, approaching the **Houses of Parliament** [27:18], as the subsequent shot reveals). Tower Bridge is also briefly glimpsed during the speedboat chase down the Thames in *The World Is Not Enough*, just after the sequence at **Waterloo Pier** (23:4). The action continues across the river at **St Saviour's Dock** (30:1).

Station: Tower Hill (CI; DI) Follow the signs to the bridge, which is adjacent to the SE corner of the Tower of London. The towers, upper walkway and Bridge museum are open daily from 10am to 6:30pm (until 4:45pm Nov-Mar).

Eyes Only, 007: Adjacent to Tower Bridge is one of the most popular tourist attractions in Britain: the Tower of London. Precisely when Bond and a Scotland Yard colleague may have visited the castle is uncertain, but one of its most famous attractions was certainly on their minds in *Moonraker*. In Chapter 19, Assistant Commissioner Vallance tells Bond that he, Vallance, had better get back to the dinner at Mansion House or the assembled dignitaries will think that the Crown Jewels have been stolen. It's funny he should say that: three chapters earlier, Bond himself had reflected that the Moonraker rocket was as safe as the Crown Jewels, probably safer....

5:19

Drapers' Hall Throgmorton Street, EC2

Doubles as: The Winter Palace, St. Petersburg, Russia (interior) in *GoldenEye*

Granted its first Royal Charter in 1364, the Drapers' Company is one of the so-called "Great Companies", or craftsmen's guilds, in the City of London. Formed to regulate the wool trade, the Drapers' Company was of particular importance during the Middle Ages and thus grew to become one of the richest and most powerful of all the guilds. Like most other guilds, the Drapers' mansion boasts a gigantic banqueting hall, officially styled the Court Dining Room. It is, of course, large enough to accommodate all of the guild's 250 members, but smaller assemblies are also welcome. Thus, if you're holding an emergency meeting of the Russian Defence Council and you don't want to go all the way to St. Petersburg, the Drapers' Hall makes an ideal substitute. And so it was *here*, and not the Winter Palace, that General Ourumov offered to resign in the wake of the destruction of the Severnaya Space Weapons Control Centre. By the way, if one of the Defence Council members looks familiar, that's because it's producer Michael Wilson, who has been making regular cameo appearances since *The Spy Who Loved Me.*

Station: Bank (CE) Take Exit 2 L into Threadneedle Street, then turn L into Bartholomew Lane and R into Throgmorton Street; Drapers' Hall is ahead on the L, just past Throgmorton Avenue.

Trivia Challenge 11: Whom does Ourumov blame for the destruction of Severnaya?

Trivia Challenge 12: In which film(s) do we see an aria being performed? Three bonus points if you can name the work(s).

Quick One...

ex HQ of Cull & Company
11 Throgmorton Avenue, EC2
(behind the Stock Exchange)

Ian Fleming entered the world of banking in October 1933 with the understanding that he would be replacing one of the senior partners in two years' time and thus become a rich man at a young age. When, for complicated reasons (see Andrew Lycett's *Ian Fleming* for details), this did not occur, the future author said "goodbye" to his family's profession (see [5:16]) and joined the prestigious stockbrokers **Rowe & Pitman** (5:16). **Station: Bank (CE)**

6. COVENT GARDEN

Revitalized theatre and shopping district, centered on the site of the original Covent Garden fruit and vegetable market

6:1

Royal Opera House
Bow Street, WC2

The home of the Royal Opera Company and the Royal Ballet was opened in 1858, the third theatre to be built on this site. (The first was in 1732, the second in 1809.) Given the acoustics of its auditorium and the reputations of its two prestigious companies, the Opera House is considered one of the finest such theatres in the world. It is no surprise, then, that an attention-seeking millionaire like Hugo Drax would have a private box here, as we learn in Chapter 2 of *Moonraker*. The western side of the building was expanded in 1982; the southern side in 1998.

Station: Covent Garden (PI) Go R in James Street, L into Floral then R into Bow Street. For the **Drury Lane** (6:2), continue to Russell Street and turn L, then turn R into Catherine Street.

6:2

Theatre Royal Drury Lane
Catherine Street, WC2

Founded in 1663, the Theatre Royal Drury Lane is most famous for its elaborate musicals, at least one of which James Bond seems to have attended. In Chapter 13 of *Moonraker*, our hero stands on the cliff at Kingsdown and gazes out toward the South Goodwin Lightship. He reflects that in its permanent anchorage off the English coast, the lightship is "like a property ship on the stage at Drury Lane". The Theatre Royal also boasts one other Bond connection: it was here that Tommy "Big Tam" Connery, fresh from defeat in the 1953 "Mr. Universe" competition (see the **ex Scala Theatre** [7:2]), applied to join the chorus of the musical *South Pacific*, then due to begin an extended tour of Britain. Lacking any musical or theatrical training, the 22-year-old footballer-cum-lifeguard bluffed his way through the audition and landed the job. He also landed something else: a name-change, based, apparently, on his own fondness for the then-current film *Shane*, starring Alan Ladd. The newly-restyled *Sean* Connery (the form more directly reflecting his paternal Irish ancestry) finished out the run of the play here in Drury Lane, then embarked upon a year-long tour of Britain. By the time the company reached the King's Theatre in Edinburgh, the budding thespian had acquired a speaking part and his stage name was added to the printed program. Sean Connery had arrived.

Station: Covent Garden (PI)
See Royal Opera House, above.

6:3

The Garrick Club
15 Garrick Street, WC2

Founded in 1831 (and named after 18th-century actor David Garrick), this private gentlemen's club caters to members of the acting, writing and legal professions. In the 19th century, the Garrick's Italianate clubhouse was graced by the likes of William Thackeray, Henry Irving and Charles Dickens. Today, you might encounter anyone from publisher David Putnam and TV presenter Robin Day at one table, to actor Geoffrey Palmer (*Tomorrow Never Dies*) and **Wartski** (13:16) chairman Kenneth Snowman at another. (Snowman jokingly refers to himself as "the only 'shopkeeper' in the bunch".) Given its membership (which included Ian Fleming's brother Peter, himself a successful author, Ian's Naval Intelligence boss, John Godfrey, Bond novelist Kingsley Amis, and even Roger Moore), the Garrick has earned a reputation as the liveliest, most convivial of the Gentlemen's Clubs of London. It is perhaps for this reason that M harbors a few suspicions about one of the Garrick Club's members, the mysterious "C.C." According to Chapter 3 of *The Man with the Golden Gun*, "C.C." is the cover of the former **Oxford** (*JBB*) history professor who serves as a consultant to SIS, and a rather pampered consultant at that, at least in M's opinion. Indeed, M seems positively resentful of C.C.'s attitude, appearance, lifestyle and overly long and luxurious meals at the Garrick. Still, for all this, M appreciates the sharpness of C.C.'s mind and sincerely looks forward to reading the man's in-depth (and highly Freudian) analysis of Francisco Scaramanga.

Station: Leicester Square (NO; PI) Take the Charing Cross Road East exit L into Cranbourn Street; turn R into Garrick Street. The club is just ahead on the R. For a glimpse inside the club, check out John Wayne's 1975 thriller *Brannigan*, in which the Duke is treated to a drink and lunch at the venerable Garrick.

6:4

The Ivy
1 West Street, WC2

Located in the heart of the theatre district, this West End favorite has long been one of the most fashionably famous (and famously fashionable) restaurants in London. Ian Fleming apparently delighted in both the ambience (including stained glass and diamond lattice windows) and the traditional English cuisine, touting the Ivy as one of London's best restaurants (see the Index). What makes the restaurant even more special, though, is its role in the birth of James Bond. For it was here, on May 12, 1952, that Ian Fleming asked his friend, the author and poet William Plomer, how "you get cigarette smoke out of a woman once you have got it into her", thus tipping his hand that he had finally written "the spy story to end all spy stories". Plomer was apparently thrilled, but Fleming dismissed the book as "oafish". Plomer, a reader for the publisher Jonathan Cape, insisted that Fleming show him the manuscript, which the author eventually did, two months later. The story of Fleming's eventual literary

triumph is continued under the **ex Office of Jonathan Cape Publishers** (3:6).

Station: Leicester Square (NO; PI) Exit R into Charing Cross Road East and walk N to Lichfield Street, where you will turn R. The restaurant is ahead on the L, at the corner of West Street. **Hours:** noon-3pm; 5:30pm-midnight. Reservations are required.

7. FITZROVIA

Small, "West Bloomsbury" district named after Fitzroy Square and famous for its many restaurants

7:1

The Bamboo Spaghetti House
15 Goodge Street, W1

This is the locale where Viv and Derek Mallaby get better acquainted over spaghetti Bolognese and a bottle of "instant-Beaujolais" in Chapter 2 of *The Spy Who Loved Me*. The Bamboo opened on the ground floor of No. 15 in the 1950s and quickly expanded into the three floors above. It is now called simply the Spaghetti House.

Station: Goodge Street (NO) Go R into Tottenham Court Road then immediately R into Goodge Street. The restaurant is just ahead on the L. **Dinner:** 5:30pm-10:30pm

7:2

ex Scala Theatre
Charlotte Street, W1

If you are a Sean Connery fan then you are probably aware that at one point in the actor's career the future 007 competed for the title of "Mr. Universe". What you may not know is that he did so at the Scala Theatre here in Charlotte Street in the summer of 1953. The 22-year-old lifeguard and part-time artists' model (see **Edinburgh School of Art** [*JBB*]) had been training at the Dunedin Amateur Weightlifting Club in Edinburgh, when he heard about the competition in London and decided to give it a shot. He made his way south and, after finding a cheap bed-sit in Chelsea, spent the next three weeks rehearsing for the competition here in Charlotte Street. In the event, the shorter, bulkier entrants took most of the prizes, with Sean winning a lowly third place bronze medal in the "tall man's" category. All was not lost, however, for during his brief stay in London, Sean saw an ad recruiting extras for the chorus of *South Pacific*, then nearing the end of its long run at the **Theatre Royal Drury Lane** (6:2). It is to this location that you should turn for the rest of the story. The Scala itself was pulled down in 1970 and replaced by a ten-story apartment building called Scala House.

Station: Goodge Street (NO) Go R in Tottenham Court Road then immediately R into Goodge Street. Turn R at Charlotte Street and look for Scala House ahead on the R, between Scala and Tottenham Streets.

7:3

Bertorelli's
(now Bertorelli's Café Italian)
19-23 Charlotte Street, W1

Famous for its many charming restaurants, Charlotte Street is undoubtedly the most popular venue in London for al fresco summertime dining. Ian Fleming had several favorites in the street, including Bertorelli's (established in 1913), where he and his future wife Ann, then Lady O'Neill, frequently dined during World War II. It was also here, in 1947, that Fleming first met the beautiful Polish spy Christine Granville, née Krystyna Skarbek, who had worked for both **MI6** (27:22) and **SOE** (12:8) during World War II. Christine, with whom Fleming was to maintain a relationship for some years (whether romantic or platonic is uncertain), would later serve as the model for two different literary heroines: the tragic Vesper Lynd of *Casino Royale* and the untouchable Gala Brand of *Moonraker*. One amusing parallel, involving both Ian and Christine, occurs in the final chapter of *Moonraker*. Readers of that novel may recall that, after saving Britain from a renewed Nazi peril, Gala Brand is awarded the George Cross (which is given for acts of civilian heroism), while James Bond receives *nothing*. This reflected the real-life fact that at the end of WWII, Christine Granville was awarded the George Medal (for somewhat less heroic acts than the George *Cross*) and an OBE (Officer of the Order of the British Empire), while Naval Intelligence hero Ian Fleming received zilch, at least from his own country. Sadly, Christine Granville was killed by a jealous lover on June 15, 1952 at the Shellbourne Hotel in South Kensington. For more on Ian and Christine, see the **ex Granville Hotel** (*JBB*) in Kent.

Note: Do not confuse the Charlotte Street restaurant with the other Bertorelli's location in Floral Street, Covent Garden.

Station: Goodge Street (NO) Go R in Tottenham Court Road then immediately R into Goodge Street. Turn L into Charlotte Street and look for the restaurant, featured in the 1998 Gwyneth Paltrow fantasy *Sliding Doors*, about two blocks ahead on the R. **Hours:** *Café* Mon-Sat noon-midnight; *Restaurant* Mon-Sat noon-3pm; 6pm-11pm. Just up from Bertorelli's, at Nos. 37-39, is an Italian restaurant called Villa Carlotta. It occupies a portion of the building that once housed Schmidt's, the massive German restaurant where *Spy Who Loved Me* heroine Vivienne Michel frequently dined with her lover Kurt Rainer.

7:4

L'Étoile
30 Charlotte Street, W1

Founded in 1904, the historic L'Étoile was one of Fleming's favorite London restaurants (see the Index). During the war, he frequently lunched here with top Army and Naval brass, presumably as part of his inter-service liaison duties in Naval Intelligence. After the war, he and his future wife Ann, then Lady Rothermere, officially "graduated" to L'Étoile, after years of dining at the less expensive **Bertorelli's** (7:3). So frequent were their visits, apparently, that in a letter dated September 30, 1948, Ian told Ann that her ghost walked with him to the Étoile every night! Today, the restaurant goes by the name of Elena's L'Étoile, after the owner, Elena Salvoni. It still features the same pricey French cuisine as in Fleming's day.

Station: Goodge Street (NO) Go R in Tottenham Court Road then immediately R into Goodge Street. Turn L into Charlotte Street and look for L'Étoile ahead on the L. **Lunch:** Mon-Fri noon-2:30pm; **Dinner:** Mon-Sat 6pm-11:30pm.

8. HOLBORN

Traditional home of the legal profession, adjacent to the City

8:1

The Royal Courts of Justice (Chancery Court 3) The Strand, WC2 (near Chancery Lane)

Here, in this magnificent, late-nineteenth-century Gothic Revival complex of some 60 courtrooms (and a thousand rooms in all), the Chancery Division of the High Court heard the case of K. O. McClory and Jack Whittingham vs. I. Fleming, Jonathan Cape Limited and J. F. C. Bryce. At issue was the authorship of the novel *Thunderball*, which Fleming admitted to having adapted from a series of screen treatments co-authored by himself, Kevin McClory and Jack Whittingham in 1959-1960. Perhaps more importantly, this case would decide who owned the film rights to both the novel and the unproduced scripts. For reasons not exactly clear, in December 1963, defendants Fleming and Bryce chose to settle with McClory, ceding him the film rights and promising a credit in future editions of the novel. The following year, McClory joined forces with the hugely successful **Eon Productions** (13:31) partnership of Albert R. Broccoli and Harry Saltzman to produce the film *Thunderball*. In 1983, after years of legal wrangling, a remake of *Thunderball* appeared in the form of *Never Say Never Again*. In 1997, Mr. McClory, in conjunction with Sony Pictures, announced plans to launch a "rival" series of James Bond films, based upon the screen treatments he devised with Fleming and Whittingham. MGM/UA and Danjaq, LLC (owner of Eon Productions) promptly sued Sony, claiming sole ownership of the cinematic Bond franchise. An out-of-court settlement reached in March 1999 saw Sony concede to MGM and Danjaq, even as Mr. McClory vowed to continue his "copyright claim" against the two companies. The litigation continues as of this writing. For additional background, see Appendix two.

Station: Temple (CI; DI) Exit the station and take the stairs to Arundel Street. Walk N in Arundel Street and then turn R into the Strand. As you pass St Clement Danes Church, the Royal Courts of Justice will be directly across the Strand. **Hours:** Mon-Fri 10am-1pm and 2pm-4pm

8:2

De Beers and the Diamond Corporation Charterhouse Street, EC1

The Diamond Corporation (also known as the Diamond Syndicate, the Diamond Trading Company, and, today, officially, the Central Selling Organisation), is the marketing arm of the De Beers diamond cartel. De Beers, through its numerous African mines, produces about half of the world's uncut gem diamonds. Through its London-based Central Selling Organisation, it controls the pricing and distribution of nearly 80% of *all* uncut gem diamonds. Thus, when SPECTRE demands £100 million worth of diamonds *or else*, it's De Beers you'd better get on to, as the Home Secretary orders his assistant in the film *Thunderball*. In the novel *Diamonds Are Forever*, the Central Selling Organization, or CSO, then known as the Diamond Corporation, briefs M on the unfortunate smuggling situation, which James Bond, in turn, will have to sort out. That meeting would have taken place at nearby Morley House, the organization's temporary headquarters at 26-30 Holborn Viaduct. (German bombs destroyed the company's original **Hatton Garden** [8:3] headquarters in 1941.) In 1957, the CSO moved into an imposing structure at 2 Charterhouse, just around the corner from Morley House. It would have been here that Bond, but not M, sipped Sir Donald Munger's unusually fine solera in the film *Diamonds Are Forever* (although, of course, the actors were really on **Pinewood Studios'** [*JBB*] Stage D). Unfortunately, as with the **Bank of England** (5:12) in F *Goldfinger*, director Guy Hamilton chose not to include an establishing shot of the CSO's foreboding gray exterior. The CSO, which Fleming also refers to in his non-fictional account of *The Diamond Smugglers*, moved to its present fortress-like headquarters at 17 Charterhouse Street, directly opposite No. 2, in 1979.

Station: Chancery Lane (CE) Take Exit 2 straight into Holborn, then veer L into Charterhouse Street. A sharp L turn off Holborn takes you into Hatton Garden, where you will find the London Diamond Club (see the next entry). Continuing straight from Holborn into Holborn Viaduct will take you to Morley House.

Trivia Challenge 13: What kind of diamonds does Blofeld specify on the second tape to the British government?

8:3

Hatton Garden EC1

Jewelry craftsmen began doing business in Hatton Garden in the 1830s, but the area would become even more famous as the center of the London diamond trade. Here, dealers bought uncut gem diamonds from **De Beers** (8:2) and then sold the stones to jewelers on a commission basis. The principal venue for the trading was the London Diamond Club, whose beautiful headquarters—a white stucco house, six bays wide, with a pedimented door—was demolished in 1998. Ian Fleming visited the London Diamond Club in 1955 as part of his research for the novel *Diamonds Are Forever*; he was accompanied by his friend (and technical advisor) Philip Brownrigg of De Beers. In the novel itself, Fleming disguises Bond as "Sergeant James" of **Scotland Yard** (27:16) and sends him off to the London Diamond Club to investigate a dubious gem-merchant called Rufus B. Saye. Saye's "House of Diamonds", according to the novel, is now almost as big as **Cartier** (13:19) or Van Cleef, selling more and more diamonds each year. The problem is that they are buying fewer and fewer gems from De Beers, which costs the British Government much needed revenue. (At present, some $4.5 billion annually goes through the British banking system as a result of the gem auctions held at De Beers.) The question, then, is where are the diamonds coming from? Saye himself is a big, tough thug who doesn't seem to know a diamond from a grapefruit, so is it possible he might really be a smuggler? Hmmm, could be. Later, in the novel (chapter 7), after Bond has flown to America, Fleming describes West 46th Street as "the Hatton Garden of New York." He also mentions the street in *James Bond of the Secret Service* (see Appendix Two), when Ronnie Vallance of **Scotland Yard** (27:16) explains that it was Henrico Largo "who did the Hatton Garden job when two of my men got shot and he got away with the Goldsmith's diamonds".

Station: Chancery Lane (CE) Take Exit 2 straight into Holborn. At Holborn Circus turn L into Hatton Garden. The London Diamond Club was on the L, at No. 87.

9. KENSINGTON/HYDE PARK

Aristocratic district of west London, noted for its luxurious homes and foreign embassies

9:1

Hyde Park W2, SW1, SW7

James Bond drives through the largest of London's royal parks (presumably along Park Lane) on his way to the office, according to several novels, including *On Her Majesty's Secret Service* (see **James Bond's Route to Universal Export** [4:3]). KGB Resident Directors also enjoy a nice drive in Bayswater Road, along the northern edge of the park, according to "The Property of a Lady". However, as we learn in *Casino Royale*, something far more noteworthy than idle driving occurred here in 1948. On August 7th of that year, the SMERSH operative Goytchev, alias Garrad-Jones, shot Petchora, the medical officer attached to the Yugoslav Embassy. Goytchev, Fleming tells us, was the only such operative to ever come into the Secret Service's hands. Now, Hyde Park, as with Green Park, was certainly one of the most popular venues for the staging of duels in the 18th and 19th centuries. However, there is no record of such an assassination ever taking place here. What Fleming *may* have had in mind—and greatly embellished—was the death of PC Jack William Avery, who was fatally stabbed in Hyde Park by a suspected German spy (really a mentally-impaired tramp) on July 5, 1940. Today, Hyde Park is best known for the oratory at Speaker's Corner, boating on the Serpentine, horseback riding and even the playing of American baseball. The Serpentine Gallery, located in adjoining Kensington Gardens, hosted an exhibit of Bond production designer Ken Adam's artwork in 1999.

Station: Hyde Park Corner (PI) or **Marble Arch (CE)**, at the southeast and northeast corners of the park, respectively, will give you a Bond's eye view, but the assassination presumably happened somewhere on the western side, closer to both the Russian and Yugoslav Embassies. **Hours:** 5am-midnight daily

Eyes Only, 007: Bond uses one of the public telephones near Hyde Park's Marble Arch to ring HQ in Chapter 6 of *OHMSS*. Interestingly, he had been alerted to do so by his new "Syncraphone", an early form of the now commonplace personal pager, and one which can be seen in action in the film *From Russia With Love*.

9:2

ex Soviet Embassy (now Russian Embassy) 13 Kensington Palace Gardens, W8

A private avenue with lodge gates at either end, Kensington Palace Gardens was laid out in 1843 and subsequently filled with opulent mansions in spacious garden settings. It was quickly dubbed "Millionaire's Row" and, perhaps inevitably, went on to become "Embassy Row". As such, it has been described as the "best" street in London, which Fleming does (although note the quotation marks) in the opening of *Doctor No*. In fact, he is discoursing on Richmond Road, Kingston, which is said to be the "best" in all of Jamaica, like the Avenue d'Iéna in Paris or Kensington Palace Gardens in London. Fleming devotes even more space to this famous road in the story "The Property of a Lady", in which Bond tails a suspected Soviet spy from **Sotheby's** (13:11) to KPG. Here, the man turns into the Soviet Embassy and thereby seals his fate. Fleming actually mentions the Soviet Embassy or its staff in several Bond adventures, which is hardly surprising since 007's adventures occur largely against a Cold War backdrop. Thus, in *Moonraker*, the villain Hugo Drax is backed by the Soviets, who send a submarine to transport the former Nazi from England to Russia. When Drax's atomic bomb comes down in the North Sea (rather than London, thanks to Bond and heroine Gala Brand) and destroys the submarine, the Soviet Ambassador visits the **Foreign Office** (27:14) in a futile attempt to forestall a British salvage operation (a situation more or less reversed in the film *For Your Eyes Only*). In Chapter 5 of *From Russia, With Love*, we are told that Lieutenant-General Vozdvishensky, the head of the Intelligence Department of the Ministry of Foreign Affairs in Moscow, once "served as a 'doorman' at the Soviet Embassy in London under Litvinoff." In plain English, he was a *spy*. In Chapter 6 of *You Only Live Twice*, we learn that after the Soviets detonated a high yield warhead in northern Russia, British authorities took advantage of the public uproar to seal off the Soviet Embassy, as well as the consulates and trading offices, "for their protection". And while Fleming backed off the Soviets-as-villains theme in the Blofeld trilogy (although their threat to the western world looms large in both *YOLT* and [apparently] *OHMSS*), he never completely let them off the hook. Scaramanga, Fleming's last villain, works for the Soviets, as does SIS mole Maria Freudenstein in "The Property of a Lady". In the latter story, Bond trails Maria's boss, Piotr Malinowski, from Sotheby's directly to the Soviet Embassy. Although posing as the "Agricultural Attaché", Malinowski is, in fact, the KGB Resident Director, Moscow's top London spy. Having been spotted—and photographed—engaging in espionage activities at the famous auction house (read the story for details), Malinowsi will now be declared *persona non grata* by the Foreign Office and expelled from the country. As Bond tells M, it may take the Soviets months before they can find another Resident Director. Here, Fleming touched upon a very real concern of the day, as in the early 1960s fully 60 percent of Soviet Embassy personnel were KGB or GRU (military intelligence) agents. This was the "golden age" of Soviet espionage in London, although it would soon come to an end. Acting upon information supplied by KGB defector Oleg Lyalin in 1971, the Foreign Office declared 90 Soviet diplomats *personae non gratae* (in other words, *spies*) and promptly expelled them. A further 15 officials were refused reentry to the UK. The London Residency of the KGB never recovered. Interestingly, Fleming locates the Soviet Embassy in the first mansion on the left, as one turns down Kensington Palace Gardens from Notting Hill Gate/Bayswater Road. Today, the first mansion on the left, No. 6-7, serves as the residence of the Russian Ambassador. In Fleming's day, i.e., the 1950s and '60s, the mansion was occupied not by the Soviet Embassy, but by the *Czechoslovak* Embassy. The Soviets were safely ensconced halfway down the road at No. 13 and No. 18, which face each other across the narrow, tree-lined lane that is Kensington Palace Gardens. The Russians also leased the building at No. 5, which actually faces onto Bayswater Road, not KPG, so perhaps this is what Fleming had in mind. Then again, Fleming undoubtedly knew the first building on the left, i.e., No. 6-7, as the onetime site of the "London Cage" (where German POWs were interrogated during WWII), so it may have suited his fancy, if not his fact-checking, to locate the Soviets at this infamous address. In any case, they were all *Communists*.

Station: Notting Hill Gate (CE; CI; DI) Exit on the S side, go E in Notting Hill Gate, then turn R into Kensington Palace Gardens. No. 6-7 is at the head of the road, on the L. No. 13 is halfway down the road, also on the L. KPG also houses the Czech, Slovak, Lebanese, Philippine, Romanian and Israeli Embassies. You are free to wander past and even photograph them—but don't sit down on any of the convenient walls outside these luxury villas. A uniformed guard will immediately appear and politely ask you to hop it!

Trivia Challenge 14: During the production of which film did members of the Soviet Embassy staff visit Pinewood Studios?

Eyes Only, 007: In Chapter 1 of *The Man with the Golden Gun*, a brainwashed Bond is debriefed at 44 Kensington Cloisters, the "dull Victorian mansion" which serves as one of the Secret Service's London outposts. There never was a Victorian mansion in Kensington Cloisters, a small area adjacent to St Mary Abbotts Church in Kensington Church Street. Fleming seems to have combined elements of the "London Cage" with Latchmere House (a.k.a., Camp 020), a large, Victorian mansion near Richmond, Surrey (which **MI5** used for interrogation during the war) and transposed the setting to that of a church, nice irony there, located not far from the Cage itself.

9:3

The Roof Gardens *99 Kensington High Street, W8*

Constructed in the late 1930s, this elegant garden setting served as the venue for the premiere parties of both *For Your Eyes Only*, held on the night of June 24, 1981, and *Octopussy*, held on June 6, 1983. The former was notable because it marked the reunion of producer Cubby Broccoli and his former partner, Harry Saltzman. The two had had a less than amicable break-up in 1975, but Cubby, at the suggestion of actor Topol (Columbo), felt that this would be an appropriate occasion to bury the hatchet. As former Eon director Reg Barkshire recalled, "Cubby was a very kind, very gentle man, who would never harbor any grudges." He added that, after years of working with both men at Eon, often under very trying circumstances, "it was nice to see the two of them together again at the party." For more on the volatile partnership of Broccoli and Saltzman, see the **ex Eon Productions** entries (13:31-36).

Station: High Street Kensington (CI; DI) Exit through the arcade into Kensington High Street and go R; walk past Marks and Spencer and BHS, then turn R into Derry Street. The entrance to No. 99 is near the end, on the R.

9:4

Royal Garden Hotel *Kensington High Street, W8*

This T-shaped glass and steel hotel was all the rage when it opened in 1965. It therefore proved the ideal venue for the party held here following the dual *Thunderball* premieres on December 29, 1965. (See **ex Rialto Cinema** [19:8) and **ex London Pavilion Cinema** [19:5], for more on that memorable evening.) Unfortunately, neither Sean Connery, who was at home in Acton (see [28:1]), nor producer Cubby Broccoli could take part in the evening's festivities. Cubby was in New York, where he had been attending his beloved mother, Cristina, who died just two days before the London premieres. On a happier note, future 007 Roger Moore and his new bride Luisa enjoyed a lavish wedding reception here at the Royal Garden Hotel in April 1969. The guests included Bond girl Shirley Eaton, who appeared with Moore in several episodes of *The Saint*, as well as close friends Kenneth More, Jackie Collins, Sid James (of the *Carry On* films) and Richard Attenborough.

Station: High Street Kensington (CI; DI) Exit through the arcade into Kensington High Street and go L to the hotel.

Below:
Molly Peters and Martine Beswicke at the *Thunderball* premiere party.

9:5

Odeon Cinema *261 Kensington High Street, W8*

The cinema-going public got its first taste of Bond—James Bond here at the Odeon Kensington in August 1962. Jerry Juroe, then the head of European publicity and advertising for **United Artists** (19:13) (and later the marketing director for **Eon Productions** [13:31]), recalled the night of the *Dr. No* sneak preview:

> I was standing in the back of the cinema with Bud Ornstein [UA's European head], Harry, Cubby and Terence Young. We watched the audience's reaction and they were hysterical. When Bond said [to Professor Dent], 'That's a Smith and Wesson and you've had your six,' and then shot the guy, the audience collapsed. Terence, who was not your everyday comedy director, was a little taken aback by all the laughter. Cubby or Harry, I can't remember which one, turned to him and said 'Don't worry. It's a big plus for us.' By the time the picture was finished, Bud and I were both very excited. We got on the phone to [UA's head office in] New York and told them we had a good action movie, Sean was great, Ursula looked like a million and the audience really loved it. They weren't exactly dismissive in New York, but basically they said, 'That's great, now, go home and go to bed.' They had trouble believing that anything that wasn't made in the US could ever be that big a success.

Two months later, when *Dr. No* opened to the paying public at the **London Pavilion Cinema** (19:5), the UA execs would find out just how successful a foreign film could be.

Station: High Street Kensington (CI; DI) Exit through the arcade into Kensington High Street and go L to No. 261, just past Earl's Court Road.

9:6

ex HQ of MI6 (1919-1926)
1 Melbury Road, W14

During World War I, Sir Mansfield Cumming, a.k.a., "C", presided over his expanding Secret Service empire from the upper floor of the palatial Whitehall Court (27:8), overlooking Victoria Embankment and the **Thames** (24:1). With the resumption of peace came the inevitable budget cuts, prompting, of course, a reduction in staff and operations, as well as a move to smaller offices. Cumming found the latter in a large Victorian house at 1 Melbury Road, West Kensington, where, as was his custom, he set up both work and living quarters. He was now well away from his Whitehall masters, the **War Office** (27:6), the **Admiralty** (27:10) and the **Foreign Office** (27:14), and perhaps gladly, too, at least with regard to the War Office, which continued to press for a total absorption of Cumming's operation. (It eventually lost control to the Foreign Office, which allowed Cumming a greater degree of autonomy.) In 1921, Cumming's department, now officially styled the Secret Intelligence Service, but also known by the military cover name MI1(c) (see [27:8]), was given exclusive control of all British espionage activities abroad, as well as the responsibility for national security beyond the three-mile limit, excluding, of course, the colonies, which were the remit of MI5. (Cumming had previously shared these responsibilities with the Home Office's short-lived Directorate of Intelligence.) For the next two years, Cumming rightly focused his attention on the emerging Soviet threat, but, sadly, too, on his own declining health. Indeed, the founder of the British Secret Service suffered a fatal heart attack here in Melbury Road on June 23, 1923, having already named his successor, Admiral Sir Hugh Sinclair. Sinclair retained many of Cumming's habits and customs, including the use of green ink for handwritten messages and the cover name "C", originally, simply Cumming's initial, but now, presumably standing for "Chief" of the Secret Service. One Cumming legacy that Sinclair did not retain, however, was a life in Melbury Road, West Kensington, far from the corridors of Whitehall and the gentlemen's clubs of St James's. Thus, under its new Chief, SIS would return to Westminster, specifically to Broadway Buildings (see [27:22]), while Sinclair himself took up residence in 21 Queen Anne's Gate (see [27:23]), an adjoining building. For the early history of the Secret Intelligence Service, see **MI6 (1914-1919)** (27:8).

Station: Kensington (Olympia) (DI) Exit for Olympia, continue into Hammersmith Road and turn L. Cross into Kensington High Street and look for Addison Road to the L. Turn here then look for Melbury Road ahead on the R. The house at No. 1, which was on the S side, has been replaced by a block of flats.

10. KNIGHTSBRIDGE

Fashionable West End residential and shopping district, noted for its many high-class shops and stores, including Harrods

10:1

Scotch House
2 Brompton Road, SW1

This has been the principal and most prestigious London venue for quality kilts and knitwear, as well as traditional Scottish gifts and accessories, for well over a century.

Where else, then, would James Bond, himself a Scot, shop for a classic Scottish outfit, even if he is posing as "a kind of an inferior sort of baron"? *OHMSS* costume designer Marjory Cornelius accompanied actor George Lazenby to the Scotch House, where he was fitted for the distinctive highland outfit he would wear as Sir Hilary Bray during the Piz Gloria scenes. And given the length of the shoot and expanse of the locations (from **Pinewood Studios** [*JBB*] to Switzerland), how many different outfits did the Scotch House actually create? Director Peter Hunt recalls that "as they were the best", and therefore the most expensive, "I'm sure we could only afford one!"

Station: Knightsbridge (PI) The store is opposite the Sloane Street exit, at the junction of Knightsbridge and Brompton Road. **Hours**: Mon-Tue & Thu-Sat 9:30am-6pm; Wed 10am-7pm. Nearby, at 66 Knightsbridge, is the five-star Hyde Park Hotel, where Vivienne Michel had her "coming out" dance in *The Spy Who Loved Me* and where, thirty years earlier, her "sponsor", Ian Fleming, attended the **Eton** (*JBB*) Dance.

10:2

Harrods
87-135 Brompton Road, SW3

No trip to London would be complete without a visit to Harrods, the colossal department store (one of the largest in Europe) founded by wholesale tea merchant Henry Charles Harrod in 1849. The present terracotta palace, a true London landmark, was begun in 1901 and completed in 1905. That the store can provide *Omnia Omnibus Ubique* ("Everything for Everybody Everywhere") is Harrods' humble—and, apparently, accurate—motto. This includes, of course, the store's world-famous hampers, one of which James Bond picks up for General Koskov in the film *The Living Daylights*. Unfortunately, we aren't privy to the scene in Harrods' Wine Department, when Bond selects a more suitable champagne to replace the one on M's list. Today, that bottle of vintage Bollinger RD would cost you around £74 (or $118). As for Koskov's "peasant food", a 50g tin of Beluga Caviar ("from the largest of the sturgeons, delivering large, fragile eggs with a subtle creamy smooth flavour") will run you around £129 ($206). Throw in a little smoked salmon, pâté de foie gras and melba toast, not to mention the cost of the hamper itself, and our James could have easily spent in excess of £275 ($440). No wonder M frowned when he saw the bill.

Station: Knightsbridge (PI) Exit for Harrods. **Hours**: Mon, Tue & Sat 10am-6pm; Wed-Fri 10am-7pm

Trivia Challenge 15: How does Bond describe the brand of champagne on M's list?

11. LAMBETH

Hodgepodge commercial, cultural and educational district, as well as the London seat of the Archbishop of Canterbury

11:1

ex HQ of MI6 (1967-1994)
Century House
100 Westminster Bridge Road, SE1

Having outgrown its Broadway Buildings home of over forty years (see [27:22]), MI6 was "banished" to the *other* side of the river in 1967. (The move was actually decided in 1964 and begun in 1966.) Its tenure here, in this nondescript, 1950s-era tower (known to insiders as "Gloom Hall"), lasted nearly thirty years, during which time Britain's most secret of services officially went public. This occurred on May 6, 1992, when Prime Minister John Major, speaking in the House of Commons, acknowledged the existence of SIS, as well as its Chief, or "C", Sir Colin McColl. McColl himself had called for this new openness, believing that the very survival of his organization in a post-Cold War world depended upon soliciting the support of both politicians and the public alike. To that end, he invited news editors to lunch in his tenth floor office, with its panoramic view of London, and there cultivated favorable relations with every major British newspaper except *The Sun*, whose editor couldn't be bothered, as well as the BBC and ITV. And while most seemed to agree that Britain still needed a Secret Intelligence Service, few were happy with the cost of its flashy new, post-modern headquarters in Vauxhall Cross, whose price approached the $500,000,000 mark. See **MI6 (1994-present)** [24:2] for the rest of the Secret Service story.

Station: Lambeth North (BA) The building is next to the underground station.

11:2

Queensborough House
12-18 Albert Embankment, SE1

Hampton House
20 Albert Embankment, SE1

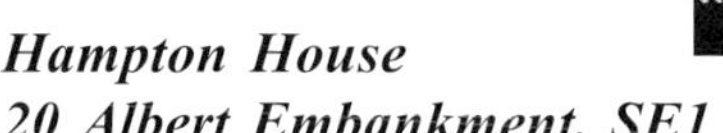

Doubles as: MI6 ("Universal Exports") in *Dr. No*

These two Thames-side buildings house, respectively, the London Fire and Civil Defence Authority and the London Fire Brigade. In 1962, they housed an altogether different agency—at least on film. Who selected these rather nondescript office buildings as the first screen incarnation of the Bondian Secret Service is not known. The Eon crew had been on the south bank at dusk to shoot the establishing shot of the **Houses of Parliament** (27:18), which would immediately precede the shot of "MI6" in the finished film. For whatever reason, they went back across to Westminster and there, near Thames House (see **MI5** [27:29]), trained their camera on Queensborough House and Hampton House (*see photo below*). It would be five more films before we got another establishing shot of MI6/Universal Exports (see **HM Treasury** [27:17]), and not until director John Glen took over in the 1980s that we would begin to see something like a consistency in the depiction of Bond's headquarters, courtesy of the **War Office** (27:6) in Whitehall. Since *GoldenEye*, of course, the real and the reel MI6 have converged in Vauxhall Cross (see [24:2]), located, ironically, just upriver from Queensborough House and Hampton House!

Station: Vauxhall (VI) Take Exit 6, cross the footbridge into Albert Embankment and carry on to the Fire Brigade buildings just up the road. Be sure to stop by the Old Father Thames Ale House for a quick one en route. To obtain the view of the buildings shown in *Dr. No*, take the Tube to **Pimlico (VI)**, exit on the Tate Gallery side, veer to the L in Drummond Gate, then turn R into Vauxhall Bridge Road/Bessborough Gardens. Turn L into Millbank and cross to the other side (along the river) as soon as you can. (You can also get some nice shots of MI6, which is directly across the river.) Continue up Millbank until you reach the enclosed area called Thames Path, opposite the southeast corner of Thames House (which is the HQ of MI5). The view of the buildings is from just inside the fence, at the southeast corner of Thames Path.

Quick Ones...

Imperial War Museum
Lambeth Road, SE1

The Imperial War Museum chronicles the history of British warfare from 1914 to the present. Tanks, planes, uniforms and artillery compete for your attention with wartime films, radio programmes, paintings, posters,

photographs and documents. Fleming fans will be pleased to note that one of the author's wartime letters—to *Daily Express* reporter Frank Goldsworthy—was donated to the museum in 1999; the exhibit *Secret War*, covers both real-life spying *and* the fictional variety, including, of course, James Bond. The museum also hosted the post-premiere party for *GoldenEye* on November 21, 1995. **Station: Lambeth North (BA)**

ex HQ of the Ministry of Works
Lambeth Bridge House
Lambeth Road, SE1

The Ministry of Works provided accommodation, furnishings, heating, cleaning and maintenance for all government departments, including (presumably) the Secret Service. Fleming refers to it on a number of occasions, including Chapter 1 of *Moonraker*, where he writes that Bond stepped out into a "drab Ministry-of-Works-green corridor" at headquarters. (Note: this is Fleming's way of describing a decorating scheme; it does not mean that Bond's office is located *in* the Ministry of Works building, as at least one fan webzine has reported.) Its former HQ was replaced by the Parliament View apartment building in 2000. **Station: Westminster (CI; DI; JU)**

12. MARYLEBONE & REGENT'S PARK

Well-kept, largely residential district that is also home to London's private medical establishment

12:1

Baker Street
W1

This broad, straight thoroughfare, running from Portman Square (near Oxford Street) to **Regent's Park**, is mentioned in a number of the novels, usually in connection with Bond's journeys to and from **Universal Export** (12:3). Its shops and offices, fast food places and souvenir shops, are, on the whole unremarkable, but then Baker Street has never been famous for its architecture or the businesses based here. What it is famous for, of course, is Sherlock Holmes, whose creator, Sir Arthur Conan Doyle, located the Master Detective at No. 221B Baker Street. (This, as Holmes scholars well know, was a fictional address; it only came into existence after the street name was extended northward and the buildings renumbered in 1930.) That Ian Fleming actually intended such a "Holmesian" evocation may seem like quite a stretch. After all, if your hero lives in Chelsea and works in Regent's Park, how else is he going to get to the office? (See [4:3] for the past and present versions of Bond's daily drive.) I certainly never gave all the Baker Street references much thought—until I re-read *From Russia, With Love*. There, in Chapter 5, the chiefs of the Soviet intelligence services (including SMERSH), discuss a plan to terrorize a Western intelligence agency. They decide on MI6 because the strength of Britain itself resides "in the myth of Scotland Yard, of Sherlock Holmes, of the Secret Service ... [and] this myth is a hindrance which it would be good to set aside." Now, all this may sound like a flimsy basis for a national myth, but there is every reason to believe that Fleming took these archetypal British institutions quite seriously. Hence the glorification of both SIS, Bond's employer, and **Scotland Yard** (27:16), which Fleming manages to work into the bulk of the 007 stories, even to the point of having Bond pose as one of their policemen. Hence, also, I believe, the ongoing references to Baker Street and the enduringly popular British myth it represents.

Station: Baker Street (BA; CI; HC; JU; ME) Take the Baker Street South exit into Marylebone Road, pay your respects to London's first and only Sherlock Holmes statue (unveiled in September 1999), then turn R and R again into Baker Street.

> **Trivia Challenge 16:** Which Bond villain played Sir Henry in the 1959 film version of *The Hound of the Baskervilles*?

12:2

Regent's Park
NW1

Regent's Park appears in nearly every one of James Bond's literary adventures because, of course, the headquarters of the Secret Service is located here (see [12:3]). In Chapter 2 of *Live and Let Die*, for example, Bond has been summoned to headquarters for an important meeting with M. Making his way up from his Chelsea flat (see **James Bond's Route to Universal Export** [4:3]), "Bond's eyes narrowed as he gazed into the murk of Regent's Park ... and drew up in the mews behind the gaunt high building". In Chapter 1 of *Moonraker*, Bond stands at his office window, "looking out at the late spring green of the trees in Regent's Park", a sight that becomes a "green panorama" in Chapter 8 of the same novel. In "For Your Eyes Only", Bond reflects on "one of the most beautiful noises of summer", that of the mowers coming up from Regent's Park through the open windows of M's office, while in Chapter 8 of *OHMSS*, Bond sits at his desk, "looking out over the triste winter twilight of Regent's Park under snow". Fleming clearly felt a great deal of affection for this elegant public park and it's easy to see why. Occupying the site of one of Henry VIII's many hunting grounds, the 500-acre estate was constructed by John Nash for the Prince Regent (later George IV) in 1817-1828. Although far less grandiose than originally envisaged, the result is still striking, with Nash's impressive cream-colored stucco terraces and villas framing the western, southern and eastern sides of the horseshoe-shaped tract. Nash's elaborate plan for an inner circle lined with a double ring of terraces was ultimately scrapped, the area eventually being filled by the gardens of the Royal Botanic Society. These, in turn, gave way to Queen Mary's Gardens, a romantic enclave containing some 40,000 rose bushes. It is to the heart of this tranquil setting that a shattered James Bond retreats in the opening of *You Only Live Twice* (and from which his office is a ten-minute walk).

Another of the park's famous attractions also has Bondian connections of its own: the London Zoo, one of the most popular educational and entertainment venues in London. Using the traditional "Universal Exports" cover, Bond claims to be in search of a great white shark for the "Regent's Park Zoo" in the film *Licence To Kill*. In the novel *Doctor No*, his literary counterpart poses as Mr. John Bryce of the Royal Zoological Society, Regent's Park. (John "Ivar" Bryce, of course, was one of Fleming's oldest and dearest friends. A further in joke is offered by way of Bond-as-Bryce's cover as an ornithologist, this being the occupation of the *real* James Bond.) Earlier in the same novel, we learn that M mistakenly believed "the Zoo" had initiated inquiries about the bird population of Crab Key, when, in fact, it was the Audubon Society of America. The Zoo is open every day except Christmas from 10:00 a.m. to 5:30 p.m. (until 4pm in winter).

Station: Baker Street (BA; CI; HC; JU; ME) Take the Baker Street North exit, go R and continue straight ahead into the park. Follow the signs to Queen Mary's Gardens. The latter is actually closer to the York Gate entrance off Marylebone Road. Enter here, cross York Bridge and the Inner Circle to see the roses Bond admired in *You Only Live Twice*. **Hours:** 5am—dusk daily. Exit at **Camden Town (NO)** for the Zoo, which is open every day except Christmas from 10am-5:30pm (until 4pm in winter).

12:3

"Universal Export" Regent's Park, NW1

Ian Fleming located the British Secret Service in a tall, gaunt, gray, building near (or, from the fourth novel on, *in*) **Regent's Park** (12:2). Its top floor was the ninth (US: tenth), according to *Moonraker*; the eighth in other novels. On its flat roof were the three squat masts of one of the most powerful transmitters in England. One of the building's tenants, and indeed, the cover for the Secret Service as a whole, was the "Universal Export Co." All this clearly represents a thinly-disguised version of the real MI6, which from 1926 to 1967 was located in a ten-story building near **St James's Park** (27:21) (cover: Minimax Fire Extinguisher Company), whose roof was surmounted by a tangle of powerful radio antennae. Fleming seems to have done little more than alter the cover and shift the building to a different park, changes he obviously felt were necessary given the fact that MI6 was then truly a *secret* service. (See **MI6 [1926-1967]** [27:22] and **ex HQ of the SOE** [12:8] for more on the real organization and its cover names.) As to whether or not the author had any other building in mind in or near Regent's Park, the answer seems to be no. From clues in *Moonraker*, *Thunderball*, *You Only Live Twice* and other novels, the building would have been located on the western side of the park, presumably on Outer Circle. Unfortunately, there is no good candidate for such a structure in this vicinity, nor was there in the 1950s. The building just north of the Baker Street tube station (which can be seen from the York Bridge Gate entrance to the park) has been suggested, but Fleming's locale was clearly at a remove from the hubbub of Baker and Marylebone Streets. In Chapter 2 of *Moonraker*, for instance, Fleming refers to "the *distant* roar of London's traffic", while in Chapter 3 of the same novel, Bond takes his "car quietly out into the park and *over* to **Baker Street** (12:1)" (emphasis added) on his way back to Chelsea. The description of Count Lippe's assault on Bond—and its lethal consequences—just outside HQ in Chapter 8 of *Thunderball* is also instructive. Note that there is ample time for a car chase in the road that runs past HQ, with Lippe's murderer then going like a bat out of hell *toward* Baker Street. Clearly, there is something of a run-up to Baker Street and, again, that suggests Outer Circle. Further, we know from Chapter 8 of *Moonraker* that, from his office window, Bond can look out across the park to the jagged horizon of London, which again suggests a western or even northwestern location, say, in the vicinity of Hanover Terrace. Interestingly, the shooting script for the film *Dr. No* also locates MI6 in Regent's Park, but apparently the filmmakers couldn't find a suitable building either.

By this point, Fleming himself was noncommittal about the location of the Secret Service, stating in a memo to the producers that it should occupy the entire upper floor of a modern office building, with shops on the ground floor. So, what the film crew came up with was the then-relatively-new London Fire Brigade buildings (11:2), located between the Lambeth and **Vauxhall Bridges** (24:3). (Coincidentally, these neighboring towers are just downriver from the current home of the real **MI6** [24:2].) On-screen, the "Universal Exports" sign (note the plural) has appeared on the **Treasury** (27:17) building in Whitehall and **Malaysia House** (27:4) in **Trafalgar Square** (27:1), not to mention the wall outside Miss Moneypenny's office in *Dr. No*, the faux company helicopter controlled by the Blofeld-lookalike in *For Your Eyes Only* and Bond's own ID card in *The World Is Not Enough*. In the latter, of course, Bond also tells Davidov that he is from "Universal Exports". It's nice to know that some things never change in the incredible world of 007.

Station: Baker Street (BA; CI; HC; JU; ME) Take the Baker Street North exit, turn R and continue into Outer Circle.

Trivia Challenge 17: In which film does Bond refer to headquarters as "UnivEx"?

12:4

The London Clinic
20 Devonshire Place, W1
(at Marylebone)

Ian Fleming suffered his first heart attack on April 12, 1961 at **Thomson House** (3:1) in Bloomsbury. He spent the following month recuperating here at the London Clinic, a prestigious private hospital founded in 1932. It was during this convalescent period that Fleming, already a successful author, wrote the first two volumes of the children's classic *Chitty-Chitty-Bang-Bang*. In the second week of May, Ian moved on to the **Dudley Hotel** (*JBB*) in Hove, near Brighton, where he completed his convalescence. On a happier note, all three of actor Roger Moore's children with third wife Luisa were born here: Deborah in 1963, Geoffrey in 1966 and Christian in 1973.

Station: Regent's Park (BA) Walk W in Marylebone Road, past **Harley Street** (12:Q), then turn L into Devonshire Place.

Eyes Only, 007: *You Only Live Twice* aerial camerman John Jordan was treated here after nearly losing his foot in a helicopter accident on location in Japan. The foot was eventually amputated, but Jordan went on film some of the spectacular action sequences in *OHMSS*. He was killed in 1969 while working on *Catch-22*.

12:5

British Broadcasting Corporation
Broadcasting House
Portland Place, W1 (at Langham Street)

Broadcasting House is the principal building of the BBC in London, as well as the base of national domestic radio services. (The television centre is located in Wood Lane, Shepherd's Bush, West London; the Foreign Service at **Bush House** [23:6].) The Art Deco building, with its rounded, almost prow-like shape, was completed in 1931, less than a decade after the BBC's inaugural broadcast from Savoy Hill (in the Institute of Electrical Engineers building behind **The Savoy** [23:8]). Although the interior suffered from blast and fire damage during World War II, the Portland stone façade remains unaltered. The lobby, too, looks much as it did in the 1930s (thanks to a careful restoration), but, unfortunately, that is about all you can see of the building's interior: "the Beeb" is not open to the public. Bondwise, a BBC correspondent—presumably from Radio 1—is on hand to provide live commentary from the Kingsdown launch site of Drax's rocket in Chapter 24 of *Moonraker*. Given the importance of this event, the Queen herself will be listening to the broadcast. In July 1958, the BBC arranged for Ian Fleming and legendary mystery writer Raymond Chandler (see also **ex Overton's** [25:4]) to record a program on thrillers. The two friends discussed everything from the difficulty in creating convincing villains to real-life "Syndicate" hit teams. Fleming gently but persistently disparaged his own works, as well as Bond himself, telling Chandler flat out, "You write better books than I do." Chandler, who was clearly a Bond fan, laconically replied, "Well, maybe or maybe not." Perhaps the most interesting revelation concerned Fleming's take on humor. "I think, basically, we're both humorists to a certain extent," he told the American. "We both rather like bringing in [humor], which possibly might not come out at first sight." Sadly, this was to be the last meeting of the Fleming-Chandler mutual admiration society. Chandler returned to his California home and died there the following March. Ian went on to acknowledge his late friend's contribution's to popular culture in Chapter 19 of *You Only Live Twice*. There, as Blofeld takes the upper hand, Bond nonchalantly sits down and lights a cigarette, reflecting that one "[m]ight as well make oneself comfortable before one went for The Big Sleep!"

Station: Oxford Circus (BA; CE; VI) Take Exit 1 R into Regent Street and continue into Portland Place. BBC Radio is the curved building directly ahead.

12:6

Langham Hilton Hotel *1 Portland Place, W1* *(at Regent Street)*

Doubles as: Grand Hotel Europe, St. Petersburg, Russia (exterior) in *GoldenEye*

Built in the style of a Florentine Palace, the 600-room hotel went on to host an astonishing number of writers, artists, statesmen and exiled royalty, including Mark Twain, Arturo, and Toscanini, Napoleon III. Severely damaged during the War, the hotel was subsequently annexed by the **BBC** (12:5). Today, under the Hilton banner, the Langham is once again regarded as one of the finest luxury accommodations in London—or, for that matter, in St. Petersburg. To convert the elegant Langham into a deluxe post-Communist venue, the film crew simply removed the Hilton Hotel flag and replaced it with the standard of the new Russian Republic. Shooting lasted throughout the night, even though in the finished film the hotel appears for all of about two seconds. The "love scene" between Bond and Xenia was shot in the studio, since the Langham did not then have a pool.

Station: Oxford Circus (BA; CE; VI) Take Exit 1 R into Regent Street and continue into Langham Place. The hotel is to the L, opposite All Souls' Church and the BBC. For the view from the film, stand opposite the hotel in front of the curved façade of the BBC.

12:7

Ian Fleming's Home *5 Montagu Place, W1*

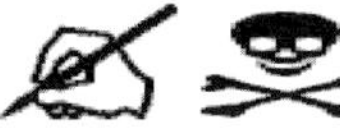

After bouncing from one temporary abode to another during the war (see, for example, the **Lansdowne Club** [13:23] and the **Athenaeum Hotel** [13:39]), Ian Fleming finally settled into No. 5 Montagu Place in the autumn of 1946. Here, he was conveniently close to his lover—and future wife—Ann, then Lady Rothermere, who resided just around the corner in Montagu Square. When the Rothermeres moved south (to Warwick House, near Green Park) the following year, Ian followed suit, relocating to a Mayfair mews cottage owned by his mother (see [13:27]).

Station: Baker Street (BA; CI; JU; ME; HC) Take the Baker Street South exit, walk S in Baker Street, turn R into Dorset Street and cross Gloucester Place to Montagu Place. Number 5—now considered Montagu *Square*—is ahead on the R.

12:8

ex HQ of SOE *64 Baker Street, W1*

The Special Operations Executive was created on July 16, 1940 to carry out subversion and sabotage operations against the German-occupied countries of Europe. SOE was actually formed from three existing organizations: section MI(R) of the **War Office** (27:6) (to which Ian Fleming's older brother Peter was attached); Section D (sabotage) of **MI6** (27:22); and the EH (Electra House) propaganda group of the **Foreign Office** (27:14). The organization was originally based in St Ermin's Hotel, Caxton Street (where Section D had been housed since the winter of 1939), but on October 31, 1940 SOE moved to a new headquarters here in Baker Street. Although conceived as a special force to "set Europe ablaze", in Churchill's words, SOE was also a de facto intelligence-gathering organization in the areas where it operated. Not surprisingly, it was quickly perceived as a rival and a threat by its "sister" (or "parent"?) agency, MI6. Attempts by MI6 to "reclaim" SOE failed and the organization survived as a separate entity until January 1946, when it was, in fact, absorbed by SIS. During the war, Commander Ian Fleming of Naval Intelligence served as a liaison with SOE, attending numerous meetings here at the Baker Street HQ. (See the **ex Admiralty** [27:10] for more on Fleming's wartime career.) Fleming undoubtedly absorbed much of what he heard at the strategy and planning sessions of SOE, whose dangerous and destructive activities clearly anticipate those of James Bond. One item in particular seems to have caught Fleming's fancy for it found its way into the heart of his fictionalized Secret Service. It is the cover name (one of several) under which SOE operated and which every die-hard Bond fan will instantly recognize: **Universal Export** (12:3).

Station: Baker Street (BA; CI; HC; JU; ME) Take the Baker Street South exit and go S in Baker Street. The building is about three blocks down on the L. During the war, a plaque outside its entrance announced the building's occupant as the "Inter-Services Research Bureau". The staff generally used a small door off Kenrick Place.

Eyes Only, 007: Among SOE's agents was none other than writer Paul Dehn, who co-scripted the film *Goldfinger*.

12:9

ex Regent Hotel (now the Landmark London) 222 Marylebone Road, NW1

On June 8, 1994, in the Drawing Room of this venerable hotel, producers Michael Wilson and Barbara Broccoli introduced 350 members of the world's press to the fifth James Bond. Having been denied the part in 1986, Pierce Brosnan finally assumed the role that nearly everyone thought should be his. Long-haired and bearded for an upcoming part as "Robinson Crusoe", Brosnan spoke quietly, almost guardedly about his vision for 007. His understated performance was perhaps a reflection of the context in which the new film would be made. In the early '90s the Bond franchise had faltered, first with the relatively disappointing box office performance of Timothy Dalton's second film, and then with a long and bitter court battle over MGM's sale of the television rights to the films. Now, five years on, the media scrutinized the new crew of filmmakers and actors to see if they could indeed revive one of the most famous and profitable series in movie history. Not unnaturally, the chief object of everyone's attention was the man who would be Bond himself. With good reason, then, Brosnan apparently felt that the responsibility for James Bond's future rested largely with him. In the event, he needn't have worried. A year and a half after the press conference, *GoldenEye* was released to favorable reviews and terrific popular acclaim. It remains the highest-grossing Bond film to date, with Brosnan's contribution to the franchise undisputed. See also the **Draycott Hotel** [4:Q] for Brosnan's retreat during his brief, but hectic stay in London.

Station: Marylebone (BA) Exit into Harewood Avenue, turn L and walk toward Marylebone Road. The original cast-iron canopy leads directly from the station to the hotel.

12:10

Madame Tussaud's Wax Museum Marylebone Road, NW1

Founded by Marie Tussaud in 1835 (and located here since 1884), this perennial favorite contains life-sized wax figures of the famous and infamous, including the Beatles, Agatha Christie, the British Royal Family, Jack the Ripper, Saddam Hussein, Telly Savalas and even Grace Jones. In December 1995, the museum rather unceremoniously but unavoidably dumped its tuxedoed figure of Timothy Dalton and replaced it with that of Pierce Brosnan, looking just a bit too casual in a three-piece suit. In 1997, with so many female patrons having tried to kiss him, Pierce's head was removed for a much-needed cleaning. It has been reinstalled and the amiable Irishman once again presides over his section, pistol in hand, as the reigning James Bond.

Station: Baker Street (BA; CI; HC; JU; ME) Exit for Madame Tussaud's, which will be just ahead. **Hours:** Mon-Fri 10am-5:30pm; Sat-Sun 9:30am-5:30pm.

Eyes Only, 007: Louis Tussaud's Waxworks, an unrelated museum in Blackpool, also boasts a Brosnan/Bond figure, this one tuxedo-clad. It is located at 87-89 Central Promenade.

Quick Ones...

Harley Street
W1

Lined with gracious Georgian houses, Harley Street is the traditional preserve of London's prestigious private medical practitioners and specialists. (These physicians are to be distinguished from their counterparts in the National Health Service, who are remunerated by the Government and provide *free* medical care to any who seek it.) According to Chapter 2 of *You Only Live Twice*, James Bond, a physical and emotional wreck after Tracy's death, tramped up and down fashionable Harley Street, as well as nearby Wimpole and Wigmore Streets, in a vain attempt to find a cure for what ailed him. **Station: Regent's Park (BA)**

John Bell & Croyden
50-54 Wigmore Street, W1

John Bell & Croyden is a large, beautifully appointed chemist's shop (pharmacy) and medical department store, specializing in aids for the physically disabled. A *mentally* disabled James Bond came here to have his new list of prescriptions made up, according to Chapter 2 of *You Only Live Twice.* **Station: Bond Street (CE; JU)**

13. MAYFAIR

Traditionally the most fashionable and elegant district of London, noted for its expensive hotels, restaurants and shops

13:0

Mayfair Walking Tour
W1

***Start*: Marble Arch Station (CE); *Finish*: Green Park (JU; PI; VI)**

This is perhaps the definitive Walking Tour in James Bond's London, with locations encompassing the life of Ian Fleming (his birthplace, later homes, and clubs), the Bond novels and films (Bond Street, Sotheby's, Wartski, Eon Productions, Les Ambassadeurs) and even real-life espionage (MI5, Naval Intelligence, OSS). From this section, you may proceed directly on to the St James's section to start the next Walking Tour.

13:1

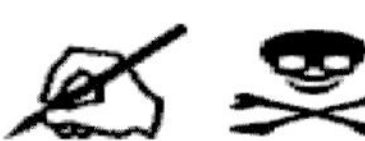

Ian Fleming's Birthplace
27 Green Street, W1

Following his marriage to Evelyn St Croix Rose in 1906 (see **St Paul's Church, Knightsbridge** [2:2]), Valentine Fleming purchased a large country place at Ipsden in Oxfordshire (see **Braziers Park** [*JBB*]) and also took a short lease on No. 27 Green Street, an attractive red brick and terracotta house constructed near the turn of the twentieth century (*see photo Page 19*). It was here, on May 28, 1908, that Eve gave birth to her second child, called Ian Lancaster Fleming, in memory of her (supposed) ancestor, John of Gaunt, Duke of Lancaster. Shortly thereafter, Valentine decided that as a rising Conservative politician he would need a proper London home and so gave up No. 27 Green Street for the far larger **Pitt House** (37:1) in Hampstead. See the next entry for another famous Green Street resident.

Station: Marble Arch (CE) Go S in Park Lane for two blocks then turn L into Green Street; No. 27 is two blocks down on the L.

13:2

ex Home of Cubby Broccoli
47 Green Street, W1

During the early days of Bondage, producer Cubby Broccoli and his wife Dana lived in an apartment at 83 Fountain House, Park Street, the back of which overlooked Park Lane. In 1964, flushed with the enormous success of *Goldfinger*, the Broccolis bought this beautiful, late Victorian home, just across the street from **Ian Fleming's Birthplace** (13:1). Unlike the majority of houses in the street, No. 47 had never been subdivided into flats and offices. The Broccolis therefore had the whole building—five floors and a basement—for themselves and their three children, Tony, Tina and young Barbara, today the co-producer of her father's famous film series. Here, Cubby and Dana could savor their magnificent art collection, which included a Picasso and a Renoir, or enjoy a simple game of backgammon in the study (where writer Tom Mankiewicz found them the day he came to resign from *The Man With The Golden Gun* production). In April 1977, as potentially enormous profits from *The Spy Who Loved Me* loomed on the horizon, the Broccolis decided it was time to escape the oppressive British tax system, which claimed so many upper bracket victims in the 1960s and '70s. Cubby therefore resigned from the Board of Eon Productions, sold his Green Street house and relocated to California. The following year, he was joined in tax-exile by both Roger Moore and director Lewis Gilbert, for which reason their next collaboration, *Moonraker*, was based in France (the troika being strictly limited on the number of days they could spend in the UK). Changes in the tax laws under Margaret Thatcher prompted a return to Britain for the production of *For Your Eyes Only*, although the Broccolis would continue to make their home in California, where Cubby died in 1996 and where Dana still lives today.

Station: Marble Arch (CE) Go S in Park Lane for two blocks then turn L into Green Street; No. 47 is two blocks down on the R.

13:3

ex Home of Robert Fleming
27 Grosvenor Square, W1

Long known as "Little America" (see the next entry), massive Grosvenor Square (the second largest in London, after Lincoln's Inn Fields) figures into the Fleming saga at several points, beginning with Ian's Scottish grandfather, Robert. The Fleming family patriarch (and founder of the bank [5:16] that still bears his name) had begun to transfer his successful operation from Dundee to London in the late 19th century, settling permanently in the capital in 1909. Three years later he hired architects Charles Mewès and Arthur Davis (designers of the London and Paris **Ritz** hotels, among many other buildings) to build a house where he and his wife Kate could entertain other members of the City's elite banking community. The renowned architects did not disappoint: their French-style creation featured an immense dining room opening on to an elegant courtyard, which was itself dominated by a two-story loggia. The Flemings moved into No. 27 Grosvenor Square in 1914 and kept the mansion as their London base until Robert's death in 1933. Unfortunately, the house was demolished in the 1950s to make way for the new American Embassy, which was completed in 1961 and looks uncomfortably like a gigantic bunker. For a hint of what the Flemings' house looked like, check out No. 88 Brook Street, a Mewès and Davis mansion located at the NE corner of Grosvenor Square. Ian Fleming, who, according to his brother Richard, spent many happy hours here in his grandparents' "family hotel", commemorates Grosvenor Square in Chapter 19 of *Moonraker*, mentioning that the villain Hugo Drax had maintained a house here until his recent move to Kent.

Station: Bond Street (CE; JU) Exit R into Davies Street and continue to Brook Street, where you will turn R; Grosvenor Square is straight ahead. The present Embassy is on the opposite (W) side of the square; No. 27 was roughly in the middle of the block.

13:4

ex American Embassy
1 Grosvenor Square, W1

During the early days of World War II, **MI5** (13:30) countersubversion chief Maxwell Knight discovered a security risk here at the American Embassy (today the site of the Canadian High Commission), but delayed informing the US Government of his find for seven months. (For more on Knight, see **ex MI5 Offices** [15:1].) The subsequent exposure and arrest of Tyler Kent, an American cipher clerk working for both the Germans *and* the Russians, ruffled many feathers in Washington, feathers which Commander Ian Fleming did his best to *un*ruffle on a May 1941 trip to the States with his Naval Intelligence Chief John Godfrey. (See the **ex London HQ of OSS** [13:6], the **ex Residence of the DNI** [13:28] and the **ex Admiralty** [27:10] for more on Ian and his wartime duties.) Fleming then had quite an affinity for America—an affinity he would go on to demonstrate in the early Bond novels. He suggested that in the interest of better relations between his department and its US counterpart, the Office of Naval Intelligence, he should have an American officer attached to him in London. As a result, Lt. Alan Schneider was transferred to US Naval Headquarters, 18 Grosvenor Square, in order to work with Fleming on a regular basis. In fact, the two became quite close and it is presumably not too much of a stretch to see in their relationship the inspiration for that between James Bond and Felix Leiter in the novels. (For more on the two real-life agents, see **Norfolk House** [16:20].) Years later, Fleming would mention the American Embassy in both *Diamonds Are Forever*, where Bond (posing as smuggler Peter Franks) is to apply for a visa to travel to the States; and *From Russia, With Love*, where we learn that Tiffany Case, Bond's live-in lover, has left him for a Marine Corps major on the Military Attaché's staff at the embassy.

Station: Bond Street (CE; JU) Exit R into Davies Street and continue to Brook Street, where you will turn R; Grosvenor Square is straight ahead. The embassy was located in the southeast corner, in the building that now houses the Canadian High Commission.

13:5

Douglas Hayward Ltd
95 Mount Street, W1

Celebrity tailor Douglas Hayward opened his famous Mount Street shop in 1967, the height of the Swinging Sixties. Prior to this, he had been in partnership with Dimitro Major (see [34:1]), whose clients included Bond editor and director Peter Hunt, as well as Hunt's James Bond, actor George Lazenby. Hayward's clients included comic superstar Peter Sellers, whom he outfitted in *Casino Royale*, as well as Sellers' friend Roger Moore. Moore had moved to the Continent in 1978 and, so, as a permanent tax-exile, could only spend a limited amount of time in Britain each year. Since most of this time was taken up at the studio, the actor needed a tailor who could come to *him*. And so, after years of collaboration with both **Cyril Castle** (13:Q) of Conduit Street and Angelo of Rome, Moore called on his old friend Doug Hayward of Mount Street. Hayward told me that he was only too happy to fly out to Moore's villa in the South of France in order to undertake the new assignment. And the result of their collaboration—a stylish, more conservative look for the character—certainly proved a welcome change from Moore's Seventies outfits. In fact, the new look is apparent in the very first frames of *For Your Eyes Only*, where the actor sports a classic three-piece suit in the graveside scene at **St Giles Church** (*JBB*). Hayward's association with the Bond films ended with Moore's departure, as Timothy Dalton preferred to choose his own wardrobe from ready-to-wear shops! James Bond's next tailor was **Brioni of Rome** (13:40), whose major London outlet is Beale & Inman, at No. 131 New Bond Street.

Station: Bond Street (CE; JU) Exit R into Davies Street and continue to Mount Street, where you will turn R. No. 90 is ahead on the L.

13:6

ex London HQ of OSS
72 Grosvenor Street, W1

The first centralized American intelligence agency, and, indeed, the forerunner of the modern CIA was founded as the Office of Strategic Services on June 13, 1942. Its remit was both intelligence-gathering and sabotage, thereby making it roughly equivalent to both **MI6** (27:22) and **SOE** (12:8). Its headquarters was in Washington, D.C., but OSS maintained a number of overseas stations, chief among which was the London Outpost, just down from the **American Embassy** (13:4) in Grosvenor Square. Ian Fleming, then working for Naval Intelligence (see [27:10]), was appointed OSS liaison officer in the summer of 1942. However, beyond sharing Intelligence with the London head of OSS, Fleming could take credit for an even greater contribution to the American "secret service": its creation. In concert with his chief, Admiral John Godfrey, Fleming attended a meeting in Washington in May 1941, theoretically for the purpose of achieving better relations with the American Office of Naval Intelligence (see [13:4]). What he actually managed to do was convince Colonel (later General) William Donovan of the pressing need for a proper American secret service, modeled upon Britain's famous SIS. Donovan, whom the British later dubbed "Q", asked for a memorandum on how such an organization should be set up and run and Fleming gladly obliged. Donovan then drafted his own recommendation and submitted it to President Roosevelt on June 10, 1941. One month later, Roosevelt appointed Donovan the Coordinator of Information, charged with collecting and analyzing intelligence that might bear on national security, disseminating it to the President and the Joint Chiefs of Staff and undertaking "supplementary activities" that might facilitate the collection of this important information. Donovan aggressively expanded his new department, taking on espionage, propaganda and subversion activities, as well as creating a Research and Analysis Division that employed assorted scholars and university types. By the summer of 1942, the organization had grown so large—and so rife with internecine strife—that Roosevelt removed the propaganda division (which became the separate Office of War Information) and retitled Donovan's creation the Office of Strategic Services. Donovan, if not most historians, acknowledged Fleming's role in the creation of OSS by presenting him with a .38 Colt Police Positive revolver bearing the inscription "For Special Services". (Ian already owned two other guns: a Browning .25 automatic, which had been issued by Godfrey, and a twelve bore shotgun which he kept at the gunmakers Holland & Holland, then at 98 Bond Street, today at 31-33 Bruton

Street.) Fleming went on to mention Donovan's organization in Chapter 2 of *Live and Let Die*, where Bond learns that Mr. Big operated as an OSS agent in France during the War; and in "Octopussy", where Major Smythe recalls how his **Combined Operations** (27:13) unit cooperated with OSS after the collapse of Germany.

Station: Bond Street (CE; JU) Exit R into Davies Street and continue to Grosvenor Street, where you will turn L. No. 72 is ahead on the R.

13:7

ex Elkin Matthews Ltd
78 Grosvenor Street, W1

In 1934, Ian Fleming began visiting this firm of rare book dealers, one of whose partners was his friend Percy Muir (see **ex Dulau's**, [13:21]). In early 1935, Ian sought Muir's assistance in starting what would ultimately become a highly-valued collection of rare and important first editions. Fleming was interested in books that had "started something"—works of social, scientific, medical and, later, literary significance. The actual job of rounding up such works fell to Percy Muir. Among his finds: a copy of Marie Curie's doctoral thesis announcing her isolation of radium, Einstein's original papers on relativity and first editions of Darwin's *Origin of Species*, Freud's *Interpretation of Dreams*, Marx's *Communist Manifesto* and Hitler's *Mein Kampf*. Of course, Fleming, who became a director of Elkin Matthews on May 20, 1936, footed the bill for the books, all of which he had preserved in black, fleece-lined buckram boxes. By the end of the decade, the "Ian Fleming Collection of 19th-20th Century Source Material Concerning Western Civilization" had grown to well over a thousand volumes. Such was its importance, in fact, that the government deemed it necessary to transfer the collection from Fleming's Ebury Street Home (2:1) to the Bodleian Library at **Oxford** (*JBB*) during the Battle of Britain. After the war, Fleming moved the collection to London, where he kept it in storage at the Pantechnicon (see [2:2]) until he could build a proper library for it. He transferred the books to **Sevenhampton Place** (*JBB*) shortly before his untimely death in 1964. In 1970, Ann Fleming sold the collection to the prestigious Lilly Library at Indiana University, Bloomington, where it now resides, along with the original manuscripts of the James Bond novels. As for Elkin Matthews, the firm moved from Grosvenor Street to 37a Duke Street, St James's in December 1938 and then, in early 1940, to Takeley, near Bishop's Stortford, Hertfordshire, where it remained until Muir's death in 1979.

Station: Bond Street (CE; JU) Exit R into Davies Street and continue to Grosvenor Street, where you will turn L. No. 78 is ahead on the R.

13:8

ex Morland & Co.
83 Grosvenor Street, W1

Gone are the days when cigarette makers like Morland's of Grosvenor Street created special blends for well-heeled customers. In the 1930s, however, young men attempting to make their way in the City did well to patronize such establishments and Ian Fleming was no exception. He apparently learned of Morland & Co. through his friend Alaric Jacob, with whom he worked at **Reuters** (5:3), although some sources credit Percy Muir of **Elkin Matthews** (13:7). In any case, James Bond's creator favored a cigarette blended from three choice Turkish tobaccos, while Bond himself would smoke a Balkan (or Macedonian) and Turkish blend. Both Fleming's (from 1939) and Bond's cigarettes sported three gold bands at the top, a reflection of their rank as naval commanders. Bond briefly gave up the distinctive Morland Specials after his stint at **Shrublands** (*JBB*) in the novel *Thunderball*. However, once he was back on the job, he reverted to the high-tar and nicotine cigarettes that he had smoked since his teens. In October 1962, Fleming wrote to Miss Julie Cohen, the head of Morlands, suggesting that the firm name these cigarettes "James Bond Special No. 1". Miss Cohen, who had earlier requested Fleming's autograph for her nephew, responded enthusiastically to this suggestion and began marketing the James Bond Specials shortly thereafter. The cigarettes featured the requisite three gold bands, in addition to the name *James Bond* printed in blue italic script. They sold for 31s. 6d. (31 shillings, 6 pence) a hundred, or a little over a pound and a half.

Station: Bond Street (CE; JU) Exit R into Davies Street and continue to Grosvenor Street, where you will turn L. No. 83 is ahead on the R.

> **Trivia Challenge 18:** Which Bond film's closing credits contain the US Surgeon General's warning about smoking?

13:9

Bond Street W1

The "Rodeo Drive" of London (it even has a Gucci's) was named after Sir Thomas Bond, Baronet of Peckham (see [46:1]), as Griffon Or explains to another Bond in Chapter 6 of *On Her Majesty's Secret Service*. The Pursuivant suggests the possibility that our Bond may be related to the Bond Street Bond—a speculator and royal favorite who went belly up building his famous street—and James, in turn, resolves to adopt Sir Thomas's family motto: "The World Is Not Enough". (Indeed, by the time of the 1999 film, James Bond clearly seems to have pinched the motto for himself.) James also seems to approve of the baronet's coat of arms, which contains three gold "balls". (Bond's reference to this as "a valuable bonus" is lost on the stuffy Pursuivant. In fact, they aren't balls at all, but bezants. For more on bezants, as well as that famous motto, see [46:1].) Griffon Or also enthuses about the number of famous people associated with the street, including Lord Nelson (Fleming's personal hero), who lived at No. 141, and his mistress, Lady Emma Hamilton, who lived at No. 145. (See **Trafalgar Square** [27:1] for more on Nelson, Fleming and Bond.) What Griffon Or fails to mention is that there are in fact *two* Bond Streets: the original lane constructed in 1686 and today called Old Bond Street; and the larger New Bond Street, which was constructed in 1720. The latter street appears in the film *Octopussy*, when Bond exits **Sotheby's** (13:11), buys a magazine at the Bond Street news kiosk (since removed) and then signals his driver to follow Kamal Khan's car. The street's cinematic Bond connection was acknowledged during a week-long celebration timed to coincide with the premiere of the film in June 1983. Actor Roger Moore himself inaugurated the festivities on Monday June 6th of that year.

Station: Bond Street (CE; JU) Exit R into Oxford Street, then turn R into Bond Street—*New* Bond Street, that is.

13:10

Church's English Shoes 133 New Bond Street, W1, et al.

One of England's premiere shoemakers (founded in

Northampton in 1873) has a prominent London outlet here in Bond Street. Fittingly enough, Church's provided the other Bond with the brown Chetwynd brogues (US: wing tips) he wore in *GoldenEye* and *Tomorrow Never Dies* and the black Presleys with the silver buckle in *The World Is Not Enough*. A pair of the former will run you £210 (about $336), and that's *without* the non-skid rubber soles with which Bond's shoes were customized (to give greater purchase during action scenes). The latter, assuming you didn't win one of two pairs autographed by Pierce Brosnan for the official Church's James Bond Sweepstakes, are a steal at £205 ($328) a pair.

Station: Bond Street (CE; JU) Exit R into Oxford Street and then turn R into New Bond Street. **Hours:** Mon-Sat 9:30am-6pm (Thu until 7pm)

13:11

Sotheby's
34-35 New Bond Street, W1
(with the second entrance at
6-7 St George Street)

Established in 1744, Sotheby's is the oldest and largest firm of fine art auctioneers in the world. Sales of furniture, jewelry, art, wine, antiquities and other valuable objects are held regularly, except in August. The firm's principal salesrooms are in New York City, on York Avenue, and here in London in New Bond Street. It was at the London location that Literary Bond, along with Fabergé expert Kenneth Snowman, tried to smoke out England's top Soviet spy in "The Property of a Lady"; and that Film Bond competed with Prince Kamal Khan for the priceless Fabergé egg (or was it the fake?) in *Octopussy*. In the short story, Mr. Snowman reminds Bond to enter via St George Street, since **Bond Street** (13:9) is now one way. He also mentions that Mr. Peter Wilson himself, for many years the chairman of Sotheby's, will be handling the important sale. Interestingly, Wilson actually worked for MI6 during World War II and claimed that his "code number" was "007", the inspiration for James Bond's! In the film, Roger Moore exits into New Bond Street, watches Kamal Khan and Magda depart with Gobinda and then signals the MI6 man to tail them in a taxi. A re-creation of the Main Auction Room (built at **Pinewood Studios** [*JBB*]) also appears in the film, the cinematic version being a bit more ornate than its real-life counterpart.

Over the years, Sotheby's has auctioned off many items of interest to Bond collectors, including rare posters, props, costumes and licensed merchandise from the '60s; Ian Fleming's suit, slippers and wartime courier's passport (the last went for a staggering $25,000 in February 2000!); first editions of the novels inscribed to various of the author's friends; a copy of the London Magazine containing the parody "Bond Strikes Camp", presented and inscribed by Fleming to his stockbroker friend Hugo Pitman (see [5:16]); and, perhaps most importantly, the James Bond File, Fleming's personal notebook of ideas for his novels. Spanning a period of some six and a half years (July 1957-January 1964), the notebook offers a fascinating insight into the evolution of James Bond and the workings of his creator's mind. Many of the ideas were subsequently incorporated into the novels (e.g., a crook cheating at gin rummy through the use of a hearing aid as a radio receiver; Bond's guard being sucked through the window of an airplane), while others, unfortunately, never saw the light of day ("a battle under Niagara Falls"; a man on a roller coaster "being shot by another man on the Big Wheel"). Amazingly, a number of the unused ideas foreshadow sequences in the later Eon films ("false fingerprints on rubber gloves"; "a masquerade ball in which the benign clown is the real killer and the crowd thinks that a real fight is part of the buffoonery"). This priceless treasure (at least to Fleming buffs) sold for £14,300 to Nicholas Fleming, Lucy Williams and Kate Grimond, Ian's nephew and nieces, on December 15, 1992.

Station: Bond Street (CE; JU) Exit R into Oxford Street, then R into New Bond Street; Sotheby's is about two and a half blocks down, on the L. The Bond Street Kiosk shown in the film was removed some years ago.

Trivia Challenge 19: Thanks to Bond bidding up the price, how much does Kamal Khan have to pay for the "priceless" Fabergé egg?

13:12

Savile Row W1

Savile Row is home to some of the finest gentlemen's tailors in London, if not the world, and has been since the early 1800s. In fact, "Savile Row" denotes not just the street itself, but a sort of upper-class tailoring district that traditionally included the neighboring streets of Conduit, Cork, Clifford and Old Burlington. In its heyday, just before World War I, Savile Row boasted 169 tailors, according to the Association of London Master Tailors. Today there are less than 50, but the street and its name still retain their traditional cachet. Fleming actually mentions three Savile Row tailors in the Bond stories, although, ironically, never in connection with 007 himself. (For details on these firms, see [13:14] and [13:15].) Of Bond, he simply tells us (in Chapter 2 of *Doctor No*) that Major Boothroyd's condescending tone (in reference to the Beretta handgun) reminded Bond of his "first expensive tailor". However, lest their be any doubt that Bond's suits were indeed Savile Row, Fleming specifically confirmed this fact in a 1964 article called "007 and Me". (For Fleming's own tailor, see **Benson, Perry & Whitley** [13:Q].) Of course, Bond mentions "my tailor, Savile Row" in F *Dr. No* (in a sarcastic response to Leiter's query as to where he was measured for his Walther pistol), but doesn't specify which one. In fact, both Sean Connery and Roger Moore were outfitted by "Savile Row" tailors (see [13:Q]), and while the current Bond, Pierce Brosnan, is outfitted by **Brioni** (13:40) of Rome, the material itself, according to costume designer Lindy Hemming, comes from—where else?—Savile Row (see the Brioni entry for details). Incidentally, at No. 3 Savile Row is the former headquarters of Apple Corps, where the Beatles performed their famous rooftop concert on January 30, 1969.

Station: Oxford Circus (BA; CE; VI) Take Exit 3 into South Regent Street, which you will follow to Conduit Street. Turn R here, then L into Savile Row.

13:13

ex Ministry of Health Fortress House 23 Savile Row, W1

Fleming mentions the Ministry of Health in several adventures, including "Risico", where the department appeals to the Secret Service for help in eliminating an Italian drug pipeline that is smuggling heroin into Britain. M, of course, had long resisted involving the Service in the illicit drug business, but, as Bond learns, the Minister of Health and the PM finally persuaded him otherwise. The ensuing adventure, involving a certain shady character called Kristatos, an amiable pirate called Colombo [*sic*] and his luscious friend Lisl, was, of course, adapted for the film *For Your Eyes Only*. (The department isn't mentioned in the film itself, although a fictional organization, "the British Narcotics Board" is.) In 1968, the Ministry became the Department of Health and Social Security; since 1988 it has been simply the Department of Health. It is now based in Richmond House, Whitehall, the **ex HQ of Combined Operations** (27:13).

Station: Oxford Circus (BA; CE; VI) Take Exit 3 into South Regent Street, which you will follow to Conduit Street. Turn R here, then L into Savile Row. No. 23—in the MOH days there was no number—is the big governmental-type building on the L.

Eyes Only, 007: The ex Ministry of Health now houses the London HQ of English Heritage, one of whose commemorative blue plaques adorns the exterior of **Ian Fleming's Home** (2:1) in Belgravia.

13:14

Anderson & Sheppard 30 Savile Row, W1

Ian Fleming claimed that James Bond patronized a **Savile Row** (13:12) tailor, although he never said which one. Cinematic Bond also claims to have a Savile Row tailor (in *Dr. No*), but, again, declines to name him. The best candidate for Bond's outfitter is probably Anderson & Sheppard, long regarded as the finest, albeit stuffiest, tailor in London. (Having never purchased a suit from them, I cannot vouch for A & S's status as the finest of Savile Row tailors. But having been accorded the most courteous of receptions and the most generous of assistance with this project, I would certainly dispute the label "stuffiest".) In fact, A & S is actually mentioned in Chapter 2 of *Thunderball*, where Bond appraises the look of the stylish Count Lippe. He reflects that the "extremely handsome ... woman-killer" was "dressed in the sort of casually well-cut beige herringbone tweed that suggests Anderson and Sheppard." Of course, the fact that Bond recognizes the firm's clothing doesn't automatically prove that he himself is a client. However, given A & S's reputation in Savile Row (and a client list that includes the Prince of Wales), one could hardly expect "the suited hero" to settle for anything less.

Station: Oxford Circus (BA; CE; VI) Take Exit 3 into South Regent Street, which you will follow to Conduit Street. Turn R here, then L into Savile Row. Anderson & Sheppard is ahead on the R. **Hours:** Mon-Fri 8:30am-5pm.

13:15

Hardy Amies Ltd
14 Savile Row, W1

Dressmaker By Appointment to Her Majesty Queen Elizabeth II, Hardy Amies is one of three **Savile Row** (13:12) tailors mentioned in a James Bond adventure. In Chapter 4 of *Thunderball*, Bond investigates the room of a suspicious **Shrublands** (*JBB*) patient called Count Lippe (a scene more or less replicated in the film). He learns that the stylish rogue wears shirts from Charvet, shoes from Peel and ties from Hardy Amies, among other places. Fleming himself actually patronized Hardy Amies, at least on one occasion, commissioning them to design a raglan dinner jacket which his own tailor, **Benson, Perry and Whitley** (13:Q), then made up. Fleming apparently hated the jacket when he saw it and, as Mr. Whitley told John Pearson, never paid for the "terrible thing"! Sci-Fi fans may also be interested to learn that Hardy Amies created the costumes for Stanley Kubrick's *2001: A Space Odyssey*.

Station: Oxford Circus (BA; CE; VI) Take Exit 3 into South Regent Street, which you will follow to Conduit Street. Turn R here, then L into Savile Row. Hardy Amies is ahead on the L. **Hours**: Mon-Fri 9:30am-5:30pm. At the end of the street, No. 1 Savile Row houses the firm of Gieves (pronounced "Geeves", not "Jeeves") and Hawkes Ltd, the prestigious military (and now civilian) tailors who made the blue and scarlet ceremonial uniform that "Octopussy" villain Major Dexter Smythe, Royal Marines (Retd), would have worn to his court martial.

13:16

ex Wartski Ltd
138 Regent Street, W1

Bond visits one of London's finest and most respected jewelers for a briefing on Fabergé orbs in "The Property of a Lady". The gentleman who conducts the briefing and attends the **Sotheby's** (13:11) auction with Bond is Mr. Kenneth Snowman (*pictured right*), the real-life owner of Wartski—then and now. Mr. Snowman (rhymes with "Roman") is one of a select group of people to appear in an Ian Fleming story *as themselves*. (Others include: Baker, the headwaiter at **Scott's** [19:6], who appears briefly in *Moonraker*; Sotheby's own Peter Wilson in "The Property of a Lady"; and, of course, Ursula Andress in *On Her Majesty's Secret Service*.) The Wartski story itself begins in Bangor, Wales in 1865, when Mr. Snowman's maternal grandfather, Morris Wartski, founded the jewelry business that still bears his name. In 1911, Morris's son-in-law, Emanuel Snowman, opened a branch in London, where the firm is now based. In 1925, Emanuel made the first pioneering trip to the Soviet Union to acquire some of the Czarist treasure that had been confiscated by the Communists. Foremost among the loot were the Imperial Easter Eggs and other objects d'art crafted by Carl Fabergé for the Russian Royal Family. Emanuel's son Kenneth, who entered the family business in 1940, went on to write a number of books on Fabergé's work, including the definitive *The Art of Carl Fabergé*, from which Fleming quotes extensively in the short story. A. (for Abraham) Kenneth Snowman became the Chairman of Wartski in March 1970, following the death of his father. Five years later, he moved the shop from Regent Street, where it had been based since 1929, to its present home in Grafton Street. His status as the "Queen's Expert" on antique jewelry (Wartski holds three royal warrants) was confirmed in June 1992 when the Grosvenor Antique Fair vetting committee, having first challenged the authenticity of a pendant displayed by Wartski, later reversed itself and gave Snowman's piece the prestigious "Artefact of the Year" award. Today in his 80s, Mr. Snowman still makes the daily commute from his Hampstead house (near the site of Fleming's childhood home, **Pitt House** [37:1]) to the small shop just off **Bond Street** (13:9), much to the delight of his loyal customers and dedicated employees. As for his "Bond connection", Mr. Snowman fondly recalls that he met Ian Fleming through the author's wife Ann and that the two men enjoyed many a pleasant lunch at The Connaught hotel and the White Tower restaurant (now defunct). In fact, Snowman faithfully recorded his contacts with Fleming in his personal diary, which he graciously showed me during my visit to the shop in July

1998. Thus, from Thursday August 1, 1963: "Wire from Ian F. Seems pleased [with the short story]". Two weeks later: "See Fleming proofs. Lunch Miss Williams (secretary to Ian Fleming)". Jumping to Friday January 10, 1964: "Bond Story published in 'Playboy'", then to June 27, 1964: "Ian F. bought a rock crystal seal from us for £18.00". The final relevant entry is dated September 15, 1964, when Kenneth attended the memorial service for Fleming at the **Church of St Bartholomew the Great** (18:1) in Smithfield. Regarding his appearance in "The Property of a Lady", this extremely modest and self-effacing man (and, remember, he knows the Queen and her family *personally*) says that he was flattered at being included in the story. However, Kenneth also points out that he has never owned a gold pencil, nor if he had, would he have ever tapped his teeth with it, as Fleming has him doing in the story (on p. 74 of the current Coronet paperback edition). As for Fleming's details concerning the Fabergé objects, well, as they came straight from the source's mouth, how can they be anything but spot on? Still, the author seems to have indulged his imagination a bit in crafting the story of a Soviet pay-off to a mole within the British Secret Service. According to Mr. Snowman, while Fabergé made at least two small, terrestrial globes out of crystal, nothing like the large, emerald globe Fleming describes has ever turned up. Yet.

Station: Piccadilly Circus (PI) Take Exit 1 into Regent Street, which you will follow N until you reach Regent Place on the R. Number 138, now home to the Cashmere Gallery, is three doors up. For the present locale, backtrack down Regent to Vigo Street, turn R and follow this (as it becomes Burlington Gardens) over to New Bond Street; turn R and follow Bond Street up to Grafton Street, where you will turn L. Wartski is just ahead on the R.

Eyes Only, 007: Just up Regent Street, at No. 170, is Mappin & Webb, one of the most fashionable and elegant of London's traditional jewelers. Look closely at the fine items on display in their magnificent showcases—you may just spot a diamond choker like the one worn by Maurice Binder's model in the title sequence of *Licence To Kill.*

13:17

ex HQ of Ladbroke & Co. Ltd
6 Old Burlington Street, W1

In Chapter 3 of *Moonraker*, we learn that, among the many amenities provided by M's Club Blades (see [16:4 and 16:6]), one is a direct wire to Ladbroke's from the Porter's Lodge. Now, today, Ladbroke's comprises a chain of over 2,000 licensed betting shops throughout the UK and Ireland. However, prior to the legalization of off-track betting in 1963, things were a little different. Then, there were only two ways to place a legal bet in Britain: at the racetracks themselves, or through Ladbroke's credit office, which was located here in Old Burlington Street. The latter had actually been established as a service to London's Gentlemen's Clubs, whose wealthy members preferred to place bets from the comfort of their St James's clubhouses, rather than at the racing venues themselves. Thus, from his lodge near the clubhouse entrance, Blades' porter would have facilitated telephone betting to a "turf commission agent" for the convenience—and potential profit—of the Club's members. Ladbroke's Old Burlington Street HQ has since been replaced by Queensbury House, at Nos. 3-9, with Ladbroke Racing Ltd now based in Imperial Drive, Harrow, Middlesex. For a glimpse of the world of off-track betting, pop into Ladbroke's shop at No. 17 Curzon Street, just down from Leconfield House (the **ex HQ of MI5** [13:30]).

Station: Piccadilly Circus (BA; PI) Take Exit 1 into Regent Street, which you will follow N. Turn L into Vigo Street, veer L into Burlington Gardens then turn R into Old Burlington Street.

13:18

Asprey & Garrard
165-169 New Bond Street, W1

One of the most luxurious jewelry and gift shops in the country, Asprey has supplied any number of expensive accessories and knick-knacks to the Bond films over the years. Among the noteworthy creations: the vanity cases issued to the Piz Gloria girls in *OHMSS* and the Fabergé eggs bandied about in *Octopussy*. Production buyer Ron Quelch, who began his association with the firm while working on *Cleopatra*, told me that Asprey's craftsmen actually made four identical eggs, of an original design, slightly larger than the real McCoys. And while all were technically "fakes", they were nevertheless crafted in exquisite detail for close-up filming. Production designer Peter Lamont, who worked with Asprey in the creation of the magnificent gem at the heart of the *Titanic* story, recalls that two additional eggs were also crafted for the scene in which Orlov smashes what he *believes* to be the fake.

Station: Green Park (JU; PI; VI) Exit on the North Side and go L (East) in Piccadilly then L into Old Bond Street. Asprey is ahead on the L. **Hours:** Mon-Fri 9am-5:30pm; Sat 9am-1pm

13:19

Cartier Ltd, et al.
175-176 New Bond Street, W1

Cartier is, of course, one of the most famous and fashionable jewelry designers in the world. Ian Fleming patronized the firm's Bond Street branch and, not surprisingly, mentions Cartier in several James Bond adventures. In *Moonraker*, for example, he tells us that millionaire Hugo Drax probably wears cuff links from Cartier, while in the original manuscript he reveals that Bond himself also shops there (presumably for the diamond chips mentioned in Chapter 8 of the book). In the short story "Octopussy", Major Dexter Smythe recalls that he had intended to spend some of his ill-gotten German loot at Cartier and in "The Property of a Lady" we are told that the interior of **Wartski**—then in Regent's Street (see [13:16])—held none of the excitement of Cartier's, Boucheron (then at No. 180) or Van Cleef, all three of which Fleming had previously plugged in Chapter 2 of *Diamonds Are Forever*. Today, Boucheron is located in nearby Dover Street, while Van Cleef & Arpels has taken up residence *within* Harrods. Only Cartier remains in the same elegant building alluded to in the short story. The firm's French headquarters also provided diamond jewelry for the party scene in *A View To A Kill* and, according to production designer Peter Lamont, some £25 million (!) worth of gems for the display cases in the Austrian hotel where Bond dazzles Kara in *The Living Daylights*. Unfortunately, as Lamont noted, the jewelry was never exploited in the finished film. Indeed, until Lamont told me, I had never even noticed the Cartier display, which is just to the right of the dress shop entrance.

Station: Green Park (JU; PI; VI) Exit on the North Side and go L (East) in Piccadilly then L into Old Bond Street. Cartier is ahead on the L, at the beginning of New Bond Street. **Hours:** Mon-Fri 10am-6pm; Sat 10am-5pm

> **Trivia Challenge 20:** In which literary adventure does Bond offer the heroine a diamond clip from Van Cleef?

13:20

David Morris International Ltd
180 New Bond Street, W1

This is the new flagship store of the renowned London jewelers, who moved here from 25 Conduit Street in December 1996. The firm's association with the James Bond films began on *Diamonds Are Forever*, for which they provided the exquisite gems on display in the title sequence, the bracelets worn by the Persian cats and a number of other items. More than a quarter of a century later, David Morris supplied the diamond and sapphire ring and the all-diamond "scalloped" necklace and matching ear studs (valued at a cool half million dollars) worn by actress Teri Hatcher in *Tomorrow Never Dies*. Two years later, the firm supplied two diamond-lined bracelets, a pair of emerald-cut diamond earrings and a diamond solitaire necklace for Denise Richards' character in *The World Is Not Enough*. Speaking of Bond heroines, you should note that next door to David Morris, at No. 25 *Old* Bond Street, is the London branch of Tiffany & Co., which was opened here in 1986. It was, of course, at their famous New York store that a certain Miss Case was born, according to the earlier film. In the novel, the heroine had received her name because that was all her father had left her mother—a case from Tiffany's.

Station: Green Park (JU; PI; VI) Exit on the North Side and go L (East) in Piccadilly then L into Old Bond

Street. David Morris is ahead on the L. **Hours**: Mon-Fri 10am-5:30pm; Sat 10:30am-5:00pm

Trivia Challenge 21: In acknowledging her untimely birth at Tiffany's, Bond tells Miss Case that he's glad for her sake she wasn't born *where*?

13:21

ex Dulau's Bookshop
32 Old Bond Street, W1

Fleming visited this small bookseller in the summer of 1929 (to buy a book of D. H. Lawrence's poems) and here began his lifelong friendship with Percy Muir, one of the shop's owners. Fleming was then living on the Continent, and asked Muir to send him regular parcels of the latest books. Later, Fleming would ask Muir's help and guidance in starting a book collection marking the "milestones of human progress". Later still, he would pinch his friend's surname for the Head of Station Z in Chapter 25 of *OHMSS*! As for Dulau's, the shop moved around the corner to Stafford Street in 1935 and around the corner again, to 29 Dover Street, the following year. The shop closed during World War II and never reopened. See **ex Elkin Matthews** (13:7) and **ex Shenval Press** (19:11) for more on Fleming's bibliophilic pursuits.

Station: Green Park (JU; PI; VI) Exit on the North Side and go L (East) in Piccadilly then turn L into Old Bond Street. The shop was ahead on the L.

13:22

Jack Barclay Ltd
Berkeley Square House
Berkeley Square, W1

According to Chapter 8 of *Moonraker*, Bond is going to speak to Bentleys about how they might relieve him of, say, £5,000 for a new Rolls-Bentley convertible. (Having only just won the money from Sir Hugo Drax, Bond can't wait to spend every penny of it. Indeed, Drax had directed Bond to "spend the money quickly", a line later appropriated for Kamal Khan in the film *Octopussy*.) At the end of the novel, Bond is, indeed, poised to take delivery of a 1953 Mark VI convertible, although the car is never mentioned in any of the subsequent books. (In *From Russia, With Love*, Bond is again behind the wheel of a Bentley, but this would appear to be the "Mark II Continental" that is more fully described in B *Thunderball*.) In any case, Bond would have had a couple of options in shopping for a new Bentley ca. 1954. One was Bentley Motors' own showroom at 14-15 Conduit Street (now defunct), a relatively small venue that also featured Rolls-Royce automobiles (Rolls having acquired the Bentley company in 1931; see **Rolls-Royce Motor Cars Ltd** [*JBB*]). In fact, Fleming wrote to the Conduit Street offices in July 1957, requesting information about a Ford Thunderbird-Bentley Continental hybrid with which he proposed to equip Bond in the novel *The Richest Man in the World* (later called *Goldfinger*), as well as an armor-plated Rolls-Royce "of rather statuesque vintage", with which he wished to equip his villain. (In the event, of course, Bond got an Aston Martin DB Mk III [see (*JBB*)].) His second option, and, indeed, the one Fleming actually mentioned at the conclusion of the original *Moonraker* manuscript, was Jack Barclay Ltd, also of Mayfair. Then, as now, the largest, most prestigious Rolls/Bentley dealership in the world, Jack Barclay had for years been located at 12-13 George Street, just off Hanover Square. In 1953, the firm made a well-publicized move to an elegant new building here in Berkeley Square, one, in fact, whose construction had begun in 1939, but was halted by the Second World War. As Berkeley Square House was an altogether larger, posher venue than the Conduit Street showrooms, it was only natural that Bond should have come here for his sales pitch.

Station: Green Park (JU; PI; VI) Exit on the North Side and go L (East) in Piccadilly, then L into Berkeley Street. Follow this to Berkeley Square, where you will see Jack Barclay on the R.

Eyes Only, 007: The woman on whose behalf James Bond has been fighting the good fight for nearly 50 years, Queen Elizabeth II, was born just around the corner at No. 17 Bruton Street, the home (since demolished) of her mother's parents, the Earl and Countess of Strathmore.

13:23

Lansdowne Club
Fitzmaurice House
9 Fitzmaurice Place
Berkeley Square, W1

Built in the 1760s by the renowned neoclassical architect Robert Adam, Fitzmaurice House was acquired in 1935 by the Lansdowne Club, the only such London establishment in which men and women had equal standing. Among its myriad amenities were a large indoor pool, squash courts, cocktail bars, fine dining facilities and a ballroom considered to be one of the most elegant in London. Commander Ian Fleming of Naval Intelligence took up temporary residence here at the Lansdowne in the autumn of 1940, after the **Carlton Hotel** (16:21) had been severely damaged by German bombs. (Fleming had moved into the Carlton after enemy bombs had hit the building adjacent to his Ebury Street Home [2:1]. See also the **ex St James's Club** [13:Q] and the **Athenæum Hotel and Apartments** [13:39] for more on his wartime accommodations.) Interestingly, Fitzmaurice House also served as the wartime HQ of the Ministry of Economic Warfare, a newly-created intelligence-gathering department which had been charged with assessing Germany's industrial capacity and output, and with which Fleming liaised as part of his Naval Intelligence duties (see [27:10]).

Station: Green Park (JU; PI; VI) Exit on the North Side and go R (West) in Piccadilly then turn R into Bolton Street. From Bolton, turn R into Curzon then L into Fitzmaurice Place. Number 9 is on the L. Try to imagine what it looked like in 1931, when the building extended out an additional 40 feet.

13:24

The Mirabelle
56 Curzon Street, W1

A favorite of the late Cubby Broccoli's, the elegant Mirabelle was also the setting for any number of lunches to which the Bond producer treated Ian Fleming in the early '60s. Broccoli, according to his autobiography, loved to spend time with Fleming, picking his brain about the world of James Bond. Fleming, too, seems to have enjoyed their time together, asking questions about the film business and about Broccoli's famous friends (Howard Hughes, for example). At times, however, the strain of transferring his hero to the screen seems to have been too much for Fleming, who had already been sued by Kevin McClory for copyright infringement over the novel *Thunderball* (see **Royal Courts of Justice** [8:1]). Thus, in an August 1961 letter to his close friend Ivar Bryce, Fleming reports on the selection of Sean Connery as star, but then rather sourly claims that he will be "dodging all those lunches and dinners at the Mirabelle and the **Ambassadeurs** (13:38) which seem to be the offices for all this huckstering." Fleming, in declining health since his April 1961 heart attack, continued to exhibit what can only be described as a mixed reaction to the emerging James Bond film series. Candid photographs from the first three productions show a smiling, engaged Fleming, frequently beaming over the world he had created on paper and to which others now gave cinematic life. On the other hand, his initial reactions to the films themselves could be downright hostile. For more on Fleming and the film world, see **ex Office of Eon Productions (1)** (13:31) and the **Travellers' Club** (16:24).

Station: Green Park (JU; PI; VI) Exit on the North Side and go R (West) in Piccadilly then turn R into Half Moon Street. The restaurant is ahead to the L, at the intersection with Curzon Street. **Hours:** Mon-Fri noon-2:30pm and 6-11:45pm; Sat-Sun 6-10:30pm.

> **Eyes Only, 007:** Fleming "salutes" Curzon Street itself in Chapter 2 of *Thunderball*. There, Bond's spotty young cab driver laments that a local Sussex prostitute recently "went mobile" in a used car, "just like the London tarts in Curzon Street"!

13:25

Geo F. Trumper
9 Curzon Street, W1

London's most fashionable barbershop was founded here in Curzon Street by George F Trumper in 1875. In addition to cutting and styling the hair of the rich and famous (including members of the Royal Family), Trumper's offers one of the world's largest ranges of "gentlemen's grooming products". Is it any wonder, then, that the shop counted among its many illustrious clients not only Ian Fleming, but a number of the **Eon Productions** (13:31) crew, who, in the 1960s, were based in nearby Audley Square? Fleming went on—in Chapter 23 of *OHMSS*—to present Bond himself with a bottle of Mr. Trumper's Eucris hairdressing, as well as a bar of Pears Soap and a

brush and comb set by Kent, each a traditional badge of fine English grooming. For more on Bondian haircuts—and a noteworthy encounter that took place during one of them—see **The Dorchester** (13:36), below.

Station: Green Park (JU; PI; VI) Exit on the North Side, go R (West) in Piccadilly then turn R into Half Moon Street. Trumper's is directly ahead in Curzon Street. A haircut from "Bond's Barbers" will run you around £17.00, a 200cc bottle of Eucris about the same.

13:26

ex Portland Club *18B Charles Street, W1*

Founded as the Stratford Club in 1816, the Portland adopted its present name (after the Duke of Portland) as a result of an 1825 reorganization, supposedly undertaken as the only way to get rid of a particularly odious member! It made the switch from whist to bridge in 1894 and is today recognized as the principal approving, or governing, body for the Laws of Contract Bridge in the United Kingdom and the Commonwealth. Here, not surprisingly, the small, highly select membership plays a more competitive game of bridge than the low-stakes fare afforded by clubs like **Boodle's** (16:4) or **White's** (16:2). Bridge fanatic Ian Fleming began playing at the Portland during World War II and finally joined the faster-paced club in 1956. It became a regular haunt for the rest of his life, *too* regular, according to his wife Ann. She complained to biographer John Pearson that Ian spent every night in London at the Portland, while, she, in turn, would have preferred him to attend the dinner parties she gave at 16 Victoria Square (see [25:1]). She was apparently mortified when, in December 1956, Ian treated their mutual friend, author Somerset Maugham, to an evening of high-stakes bridge at the club—and Maugham lost! In 1969, the Portland Club moved to its present home at 42 Half Moon Street (inside the Naval and Military Club, 94 Piccadilly). In notes to his bound copy of *Moonraker*, Fleming stated that M's club "Blades contains elements of White's, Boodle's and the Portland Club." The novel's principal Portland "element" was, of course, the high stakes bridge game that Bond plays with Sir Hugo Drax.

Station: Green Park (JU; PI; VI) Exit on the North Side and go R (West) in Piccadilly, R into Half Moon Street (past the club's current home), L into Curzon, R into Queen Street and then L into Charles Street. No. 18B is on the NW corner.

> **Trivia Challenge 22:** In the film *Moonraker*, who claims to play bridge with Hugo Drax?

13:27

Ian Fleming's Home *21 Hays Mews, W1*

In late 1947 Ian Fleming moved to 21 Hays Mews, a small cottage owned by his mother Eve and, indeed, attached to her house at 21 Charles Street. Although apparently instigated by Eve herself, the move was prompted at least in part by the fact that Ian's lover Ann and her husband, Lord Rothermere, had recently moved from Montagu Square, near which Fleming had been living (see [12:7]), to Warwick House, nestled between St James's Palace and Green Park. Ian apparently liked the mews cottage—and its proximity to Ann—but by early 1950 he was ready for a change. "It has been a wonderful home for a couple of years", he wrote to his mother on May 11, and although he was "very sorry to leave it" he simply had to have more space. Indeed, from the outside, No. 21 does appear to be quite small. However, according to the document Ian prepared for the estate agents (realtors) J. Trevor & Sons on August 17, the cottage contained no less than one large bedroom, three small bedrooms, a bathroom and lavatory, a sitting-room, a kitchen, a downstairs lavatory and a garage for a 10 h.p. car! In any case, Ian left Mayfair for Carlyle Mansions

(4:8), Chelsea, the new flat being just along from his mother's—and his—old base at **Turner's House** (4:9).

Station: Green Park (JU; PI; VI) Exit on the North Side and go R (West) in Piccadilly, R into Half Moon Street, L into Curzon Street, then almost immediately R into Queen Street. At Charles Street, turn L and either walk past No. 21 (to see Mrs. Val's one-time home) and then continue on around to the R and into Hays Mews, or turn immediately R into Chesterfield Hill then L into Hays Mews.

13:28

ex Residence of the DNI
36 Curzon Street, W1

This was the official residence of the Director of Naval Intelligence, to whom Ian Fleming served as Personal Assistant throughout World War II (see [27:10]). From September 3, 1939 until November 24, 1942, the DNI was Rear Admiral John Godfrey, with whom Fleming enjoyed a very close and warm relationship. There is probably some truth to the notion that the exacting, impatient and, at times, ruthless Godfrey was the principal model for Literary M, also known as Admiral Sir Miles Messervy. (The other model, presumably, was Sir Stewart Menzies, wartime head of **MI6** [27:22].) Fleming biographer John Pearson suggests that the stern father-naughty schoolboy dynamics between M and Bond do not adequately or accurately reflect the comradely relationship between Godfrey and his young assistant. In most of the novels, that may be true enough. But in *Moonraker*, the one novel in which M and Bond actually go on an assignment together, their relationship is extremely cordial and comradely, and one cannot help but think of Fleming and his boss on one of their many adventures together "in the field". Apart from this, there are a number of minor similarities, such as M having commanded HMS *Repulse*, which was, in fact, one of Admiral Godfrey's last ships. In any case, their wartime camaraderie came to end in November 1942, when Commodore E. G. N. Rushbrooke succeeded Godfrey as head of Naval Intelligence. Fleming remained as Rushbrooke's Personal Assistant until war's end, but nothing like a close friendship ever developed between the two men. He and Godfrey, on the other hand, maintained their friendship, enjoying, for example, the regular reunion dinners of the "36 Club" (see **ex Junior Carlton Club** [16:25]) for the remainder of Fleming's life. And clearly, Godfrey himself came to believe that he had been the model for James Bond's boss. In a letter to Ian dated April 14, 1961, just after the author's heart attack, the admiral told his former Personal Assistant that he "enjoyed visiting Old Mitre Court [Fleming's office (5:2)] and felt quite 'M'ish [*sic*]."

Station: Green Park (JU; PI; VI) Exit on the North Side and go R (West) in Piccadilly, R into Half Moon Street then L into Curzon Street. No. 36 is ahead on the L. Just past this, at No. 30, is the current home of **Crockford's** (16:23), the exclusive club which, according to B *Moonraker*, counted James Bond among its members.

13:29

ex White Elephant
28 Curzon Street, W1

The White Elephant was a stylish restaurant and gaming club frequented by both the Beatles and assorted members of the **Eon Productions** (13:31-36) team, including the producers, directors and actors. It was, as former Eon director Reg Barkshire recalls, "our local café". Indeed, it was here, shortly before the filming of *Live and Let Die*, that Roger Moore had a memorable lunch with his six-year-old son Geoffrey. According to Moore's *James Bond Diary*, their exchange was as follows:

Geoffrey: "Can you beat anybody here?"
Roger: "Oh, yes."
Geoffrey: "Supposing James Bond came in."
Roger: "Daddy is going to play James Bond."
Geoffrey: "I know that. I mean the *real* James Bond. Sean Connery."

It was also here that director Guy Hamilton first spoke to Christopher Lee about playing the title role in *The Man With The Golden Gun*. Lee had read the novel, Fleming's last, and felt that he didn't remotely resemble the literary Scaramanga, who, in the actor's words, "was just a very unattractive, unpleasant thug." Yet, Hamilton reassured him that the whole thing would be "a breeze", especially since Lee would be working with a host of old friends, including Roger Moore, whom he had known for 25 years, Lois Maxwell, Desmond Llewelyn and even Cubby Broccoli, for whom the actor had appeared in *The Cockleshell Heroes* in 1955. Hamilton gave him a copy of the script, which depicted a much more amusing and attractive villain than that of the Fleming opus, much to Lee's relief. The actor also noted that the cinematic Scaramanga earned a million dollars a hit, prompting him to ask if that was going to be his salary as well. "Unfortunately," Lee recalled, "I never did get an answer on that one."

Station: Green Park (JU; PI; VI) Exit on the North Side and go R (West) in Piccadilly, then R into Half Moon Street and L into Curzon. The ex White Elephant is ahead on the L.

13:30

ex HQ of MI5 (1945-1975)
Leconfield House
Curzon Street, W1

MI5, or, to use its official name, the Security Service, is the United Kingdom's internal counterespionage agency, a partial equivalent to the FBI in the United States. According to the Security Service Act of 1989, "[t]he function of the Service shall be the protection of national security and, in particular, its protection against threats from espionage, terrorism and sabotage, from the activities of agents of foreign powers and from actions intended to overthrow or undermine parliamentary democracy by political, industrial or violent means." MI5 began as the "home section" of the **War Office**'s (27:6) new Secret Service Bureau in October 1909. It was tasked with combating espionage *within* the United Kingdom, while the responsibility for gathering secret intelligence *outside* the country was given to the department that would eventually become **MI6** (27:8). It's first Chief, Captain (later Major-General Sir) Vernon Kell, used "K", the initial letter of his surname, as cover, just as his counterpart in the foreign section, Commander (later Captain Sir) Mansfield Cumming, used "C" as his. (The code name "K" did not survive Kell, who was sacked by Churchill in 1940, while "C" survives to this day in MI6 parlance.) In 1916, the counter-espionage department was absorbed into the War Office's newly-formed Directorate of Military Intelligence, where it was given the cover name MI5, i.e., Military Intelligence, Section Five. It was reorganized as the civilian Security Service in October 1931, although the military title MI5 would remain in popular—and semi-official—usage. (For more on the military cover names MI5 and MI6, see [27:6] and [27:8].) The Security Service was originally based in modest Victoria Street premises with Cumming's nascent intelligence section (see [27:8]); it would later move to the War Office; 124-126 Cromwell Road; Thames House; Wormwood Scrubs Prison (at the start of World War II) and, finally, to joint bases at Blenheim Palace (*JBB*) and 58 St James's Street for the duration of the war. Its greatest triumph was probably the "Double Cross System" of World War II, in which some 120 enemy agents were "turned" (into double agents) in order to pass false intelligence to Germany (notably that the D-Day landings would occur at the Pas de Calais, not Normandy). Its greatest shame was undoubtedly the failure to identify the legion of Soviet "moles", or penetration agents, operating within its own organization, MI6 and other government departments during and after the war. (For more on the exposure of these spies—Burgess, Maclean, Philby, et al.—and the resulting scandals, see the **University of Cambridge** [*JBB*]). Fleming, who liaised with MI5 as part of his Naval Intelligence duties during WWII (see [27:10]), refers to these scandals, as well as to the bitter rivalry between "Five" and her sister Service, MI6, in several novels. In Chapter 5 of *From Russia, With Love*, one of the Soviet Intelligence chiefs praises MI5, but then adds that the "Secret Service is still better [i.e., better still]." In Chapter 4 of *Live and Let Die*, Bond tells Felix Leiter that the Secret Service is "always rubbing MI5 up the wrong way" and that MI5, in turn, is always stepping on the corns of **Scotland Yard**'s (27:16) Special Branch. In *Moonraker* and "The Property of a Lady", M tries to avoid stepping on MI5's corns even as he conspires to send Bond on missions *within* Britain. In the latter, Bond actually liaises with MI5 agents and apparently visits Leconfield House itself as part of his investigation of the **Soviet Embassy** (9:2). Strictly speaking, of course, only MI5 can operate *within* the UK, while MI6 can only operate *outside* the UK (an exception, ironically, being foreign embassies, which are technically not on British soil). Fleming acknowledges the famous "parallel system" in Chapter 9 of *Moonraker*, but seems to have overlooked (or simply ignored) the fact that British colonies are also considered part of the United Kingdom. Thus, Fleming, or, if you prefer, M, sends Bond off to British possessions such as Jamaica, the Bahamas, and the Seychelles whenever it suited his purpose. The filmmakers, too, have violated the parallel system (as if accuracy mattered!), sending Bond off to the Bahamas (in *Thunderball*) and Hong Kong (in *You Only Live Twice*, *The Man With The Golden Gun*) while both were still British colonies and, thus, technically, outside the jurisdiction of MI6. Another possible error occurs in *The Living Daylights*. Gibraltar was and is a British possession and responsibility for its security rests with MI5 (although, as author Nigel West reminded me, both services did maintain operatives there during WWII). For more on the Security Service and its operations, see (13:4), (15:1) and (27:29).

Station: Green Hyde Park Corner (PI) Exit for Park Lane, walk N (away from Hyde Park Corner) and then turn R into Curzon Street. Leconfield House, once known to its MI5 occupants as the "Pink Elephant" (a joking allusion to the **ex White Elephant** [13:29] across the street), is just ahead on the L. For the current home of the Security Service, see (27:29).

13:31

ex Office of Eon Productions Ltd (1)
3 Audley Square, W1

One of the most important partnerships in motion picture history began here in June 1961, when American producer Albert R. "Cubby" Broccoli joined with Canadian producer Harry Saltzman to secure financing for a series of films based upon Ian Fleming's James Bond novels. The previous December, Saltzman had met with Fleming at **Les Ambassadeurs Club** (13:38) and there secured a six-month option on all the existing Bond novels except *Casino Royale*, the rights to which were owned by producer Charles K. Feldman. Broccoli himself had been interested in Fleming's books for some time and, rather than wait for Saltzman's option to expire—at which point someone else might beat him to the punch—he decided to team up with the Canadian producer. From Saltzman's solicitors, Harbottle and Lewis, the pair acquired Eon Productions Ltd, a shelf company whose name did *not* stand for "Everything or Nothing", as some writers would later claim. (Shelf companies are ready-made corporations, kept "on the shelf" of an accounting or law firm for immediate transfer to clients in a hurry.) They incorporated themselves in Lausanne, Switzerland (where both capital-gains taxes and US corporate income taxes could be avoided) under the name Danjaq, S.A., an amalgam of their wives first names, Dana (Broccoli) and Jacqueline (Saltzman). (S.A. itself stands for *Société Anonyme*, i.e., a limited liability corporation established under French law in Francophone countries. Danjaq was later registered as a Limited Liability Company in the United States, hence the current name Danjaq, LLC.) Eon would then operate as a subsidiary of the Swiss corporation, producing UK-based films with money provided by **United Artists** (19:13). The producers took separate offices in 3 Audley Square, while Eon itself was officially registered at 38 Soho Square, both outposts of Broccoli's former company, Warwick Film Productions (see [19:10]). Indeed, many of Broccoli's former Warwick crew, including director Terence Young, screenwriter Richard Maibaum, cameraman Ted Moore and art director Ken Adam, would be hired for the new production. Among the newcomers to the fold was a relatively unknown Scottish actor named Sean Connery, who came here to audition for the part of James Bond in August 1961. Striding confidently into Broccoli's first floor (US: second floor) office wearing an open-necked shirt and brown suede shoes, Connery impressed the two producers with his "take me as I am" attitude. As Cubby would recall in his autobiography, "[e]verything about Connery that day was convincingly James Bond.... [His] looks and explicit body language cast him irresistibly as 007." United Artists executives were not so sure, but the producers went ahead with their plans, officially announcing their selection in November of that year. And the rest, as they say, is history. During the '60s, Eon also maintained

The former Eon Productions Office at 2 South Audley Street.

offices at 27 Hill Street (13:34) and 1 Tilney Street (13:32), which is directly across from Audley Square. In 1972, Eon relocated to the ground floor of 2 South Audley Street, a striking Victorian townhouse adjacent to Audley Square. See the next three entries for more of the Eon story, as well as (9:5) and (13:38) for the birth of the Cinematic Bond.

Station: Hyde Park Corner (PI) Exit for Park Lane, walk N (away from Hyde Park Corner) and turn R into Curzon Street, then L into South Audley. No. 2 is ahead on the R and just past this is Audley Square. Opposite is No. 1 Tilney Street.

13:32

ex Office of Eon Productions Ltd (4)
1 Tilney Street, W1

For *Dr. No* they had been based in Cubby Broccoli's old Warwick Productions headquarters at 3 Audley Square (13:31); for *From Russia With Love* they had largely switched to 38 Soho Square (19:10); for *Goldfinger* and *Thunderball* to 27 Hill Street (13:34); and now, in January of 1966, with a gigantic Japanese production looming on the horizon, Eon relocated its administrative offices to No. 1 Tilney Street. The new headquarters, located directly across from 3 Audley Square, was by far the largest of any Eon office before or since. According to former company director Reg Barkshire, Eon occupied the entire four-story building, over 30 rooms in all. In fact, there was more space than Eon actually needed, so the remainder was subsequently allotted to one of producer Harry Saltzman's many side ventures, Lowndes Productions. Of course, it was these very side ventures that eventually led to the break-up of the Broccoli-Saltzman partnership. As former Eon marketing director Jerry Juroe explained: "Cubby was content to make Bond pictures. Harry, on the other hand, was always trying to be the next Irving Thalberg [the legendary MGM mogul of the 1930s]." Indeed, while Cubby concentrated exclusively on Fleming properties (including *Chitty Chitty Bang Bang*), Saltzman spent more and more time on outside projects like *The Ipcress File*, with Michael Caine, and *The Battle of Britain*, directed by Guy Hamilton. In fact, Lowndes Productions actually grew so large that, at Barkshire's suggestion, Eon surrendered its lease on the building to Saltzman's company, becoming the *tenant* of No. 1 Tilney Street, instead of its owner. Cubby, of course, continued to operate from his traditional base in 3 Audley Square, where he would remain until Eon's next official move, to 2 South Audley Street, in 1972. By this time, of course, the two producers communicated largely through intermediaries and actually took turns producing the Bond films themselves. (Harry supervised *Live and Let Die*, for example, while Cubby would take charge on *The Man With The Golden Gun*.) The partnership was most assuredly doomed, as you will see in the next entry.

Station: Hyde Park Corner (PI) Exit for Park Lane, walk N (away from Hyde Park Corner) and turn R into Curzon Street, then L into South Audley. No. 2 is ahead on the R and just past this is Audley Square. Opposite is No. 1 Tilney Street.

13:33

ex Office of Eon Productions Ltd (5)
2 South Audley Street, W1

Eon Productions officially relocated from 1 Tilney Street (see the previous entry) to 2 South Audley Street in February 1972. The move was initiated by producer Cubby Broccoli, who had finally decided to sell his long-time base at 3 Audley Square (see [13:31]). Eon accountant (and future company director) Reg Barkshire was the first to recce this stylish Victorian house, which is located just two doors down from 3 Audley Square. Reg recalled that when he first showed the building to Broccoli, the producer said simply: "Look no more. This is it." And so it would be, at least for Broccoli, who quickly settled into his new ground floor (US: first floor) office. Contrarily, his estranged partner, Harry Saltzman, remained across the road in his massive Lowndes Productions offices. The two men now spoke primarily through "intermediaries", one of whom, marketing manager Jerry Juroe, recalled that he once stopped to marvel at how many times he had nearly been run over darting back and forth between Harry's office on one side of the street and Cubby's on the other! Reg Barkshire, another intermediary, echoed the sentiment, recalling that he himself often felt like a "Ping-Pong ball in a vise"! Things finally came to a head in late 1975, when the woefully overextended Saltzman decided to sell his share of Danjaq, S.A., Eon's Swiss holding company. However, instead of approaching Broccoli for a buyout, the mercurial producer turned to **United Artists** (19:13), the company that financed and distributed the Bond films. (For the lengthy legal battle that preceded this sale, see Cubby's autobiography, *When the Snow Melts*.) UA was only too happy to oblige and thus, in December of that year, became the official co-producer of the James Bond film series. Barkshire attended the sale of Saltzman's shares, which was held in Lausanne, Switzerland. He explained that the sale was actually "an open, public auction, where anybody could have attended. But it was not publicized, so no one else showed up. The United Artists lawyer simply stood up and said, '*I'll* buy the shares.' It lasted all of ten minutes, but it was quite a formal little auction." The new arrangement was something of a mixed blessing for Cubby because while UA agreed to leave the actual creative producing to him, the company still insisted upon having its own director, Bernard Coote, on the Eon board. In fact, as Barkshire recalled, "UA actually had one of their production executives, Danton Rissner, sitting at the desk across from Cubby all during the production of *The Spy Who Loved Me*." One good thing that came out of all this was that Cubby's stepson, attorney Michael G. Wilson, was able to assist in both the legal proceedings *and* the film production itself. Their successful partnership, with Michael eventually becoming co-producer of the films, would continue through 1989's *Licence To Kill*. In the '90s, sadly, both Harry Saltzman and Cubby Broccoli were sidelined by illness. Harry died in Paris on September 28, 1994, while Cubby succumbed to heart disease in California on June 27, 1996. In the meantime, Cubby's daughter Barbara had joined Michael as co-producer of the Bond films, ensuring that the most successful series in cinema history would continue as a vital franchise into the 21st Century. The company currently operates out of a stylish Georgian building in Piccadilly, not far from its historic Mayfair premises.

Station: Hyde Park Corner (PI) Exit for Park Lane, walk N (away from Hyde Park Corner) and turn R into Curzon Street, then L into South Audley. No. 2 is ahead on the R and just past this is Audley Square. Opposite is No. 1 Tilney Street.

13:34

ex Office of Eon Productions Ltd (3)
27 Hill Street, W1

As pre-production began on *Goldfinger* in the summer of 1963, Eon Productions switched from their Soho Square premises (19:10) to this attractive stucco house, just around the corner from Cubby Broccoli's Audley Square office (13:31). The company occupied some half a dozen rooms on the third floor (US: fourth floor), remaining here through the production of *Thunderball* in 1965. By that time, Bond had become a certifiable global phenomenon, and the Eon directors decided to find an even larger facility in Mayfair. Thanks to company director (and associate producer) Stanley Sopel, their search ended at 1 Tilney Street, directly across from Audley Square (see the three previous entries for more on the Eon locations).

Station: Hyde Park Corner (PI) Exit for Park Lane, walk N (away from Hyde Park Corner) and turn R into Curzon Street, then L into South Audley. Continue past Audley Square and turn R into Hill Street. No. 27 is on the R.

13:35

ex London Playboy Club
45 Park Lane, W1

James Bond's connection with Hugh Hefner's *Playboy* magazine began in 1960, with the publication of Ian Fleming's short story "The Hildebrand Rarity". Over the next few years, two more stories and three full-length novels would appear in the pages of *Playboy*. In November of 1965, the first of twelve Bond pictorials appeared, this one called "James Bond's Girls" and featuring revealing glimpses of all the Bond women up to that point, including Miss Moneypenny! The text of the article was penned by Richard Maibaum, who had co-written all the Bond screenplays then extant. As if to return the favor, cinematic Bond ogled a copy of *Playboy* magazine in *On Her Majesty's Secret Service* and even pinched the centerfold! In the next film, *Diamonds Are Forever*, the Playboy-Bond connection was deepened with the revelation that 007 actually belonged to the Playboy Club in London (card number UK 40401). Membership in these clubs, the first of which opened in Chicago in 1960, entitled you to high-class entertainment, good food and drink, and, of course, service with a smile from the famous Playboy bunnies. In all this, the clubs, indeed, the entire Hugh Hefner empire, provided a perfect complement to the world of Ian Fleming and James Bond. No wonder **Eon Productions** (13:33) and **United Artists** (19:13) chose the London Club as the site of the grandiose premiere party for *The Spy Who Loved Me*, the biggest and most expensive Bond production to that time. And producer Cubby Broccoli, himself a member of the club, certainly had a lot to celebrate the night of July 7, 1977: the completion of a spectacular new Bond film after years of legal and financial battles with his erstwhile partner Harry Saltzman; an almost certain box-office smash in the offing; a new partnership with his beloved stepson, Michael Wilson, with whom Broccoli would later co-produce the series; and even a commitment from his star, 49-year-old Roger Moore, that the actor, having completed the three pictures for which he was originally contracted, would indeed be signing on for one more. At least! And in spite of the rather "constricted setting", as former Eon director Reg Barkshire remembers it, the Playboy Club went on to host the post-premiere party for

Moonraker, on June 26, 1979. Two years later, this vestige of the chauvinistically Swinging Sixties was forced to close its doors when the British Gaming Board revoked Playboy's gambling license. The building itself, a precast concrete affair built in the mid-1960s, was subsequently acquired by the Sultan of Brunei (the richest man in the world, prior to the advent of Bill Gates), whose controversial brother continues to cavort here behind the smoked glass windows of his own private "playboy club". In the spring of 2000, Ladbroke (see [13:17]), a division of the Hilton Group, signed a deal with Playboy Enterprises to open a new Playboy Casino Club here in Mayfair. Perhaps, bunnies, like diamonds, are also forever.

Station: Hyde Park Corner (PI) Exit for Park Lane, walk N (away from Hyde Park Corner); the ominous-looking gray building is ahead on the R, just before the Dorchester, which is also owned by the Sultan.

Trivia Challenge 23: Which issue of *Playboy* magazine does Bond peruse in *OHMSS*?

13:36

The Dorchester
53 Park Lane, W1

One of the Leading Hotels of the World and certainly one of London's most luxurious, the Dorchester opened its doors with great fanfare on April 18, 1931. Since then, the concrete-reinforced hotel has accommodated everyone from General Dwight Eisenhower, who used the "bomb-proof" building as a headquarters during World War II, to the Duke of Edinburgh, who held his stag party here in November of 1947. During the war, the Dorchester also saw a great deal of a young naval officer named Ian Fleming, who happened to be in love with one of the hotel's residents, a certain Anne O'Neill (she hadn't yet dropped the *e* in her first name), the future Lady Rothermere *and* the future Mrs. Ian Fleming. Ian also played bridge here with Lord Kemsley, owner of the vast newspaper empire then headquartered in Grays Inn Road. Fleming would go on to work for Lord Kemsley at **Kemsley House** (3:1) shortly after the war. Years later, author Fleming would enshrine the hotel in *Goldfinger*,

August 1972: Producers Cubby Broccoli and Harry Saltzman (center and right) announce the new James Bond, Roger Moore, at The Dorchester.

or at least in the original manuscript of the novel. There, on page 3, we learn that a Mexican smuggler leaves a package at the **Victoria Station** (25:3) left-luggage office and then mails the ticket to a man called Schwab at the Dorchester hotel. For some reason, perhaps to avoid libeling a favorite hotel, Fleming ultimately changed this to "Boox-an-Pix, Ltd, WC1". The Dorchester also has a number of cinematic Bond associations, as well. It was here that director Terence Young and his assistant, Johanna Harwood, spent ten days in late 1961, rewriting the script for *Dr. No*. According to Young, it was Harwood's idea to include the recently-stolen portrait of the Duke of Wellington in Dr. No's quarters (see the **National Gallery** [27:2]). On October 7, 1968, Producers Harry Saltzman and Albert R. Broccoli introduced the world to their new James Bond—George Lazenby—here at the Dorchester. Interestingly, Broccoli had first spotted George Lazenby in Kurt's barbershop, which was then located in the basement of this very hotel. According to legend, young George—then a model—actually "set up" the veteran producer. Hoping to be discovered by Broccoli, Lazenby, then appearing in a series of television commercials for Fry's Chocolate Creams, supposedly researched the producer's lifestyle and habits, learning of the renowned—and high-priced—Kurt's. Thus, when Broccoli came in for a haircut, Mr. Lazenby just happened to be sitting in the next chair. Lazenby himself, in a 1994 interview with *007 Magazine*, described the encounter with Broccoli as a coincidence, but did admit to having selected Kurt's because they did Sean Connery's hair! And speaking of Connery, the Dorchester also served as the venue for an important meeting in February 1971 between associate producer Stanley Sopel and the ex-Bond star, who was about to be lured back into the Eon fold for *Diamonds Are Forever*. It was also in a penthouse suite here at the Dorchester, on August 1, 1972, that Roger Moore was announced as the third James Bond. Future Bonds would be introduced in Vienna (Timothy Dalton) and Marylebone (Pierce Brosnan). For the latter, see the **ex Regent Hotel** (12:9).

Station: Hyde Park Corner (PI) The hotel is just up Park Lane, on the R. Afternoon tea is served on the Promenade each day from 3pm-5pm.

> **Eyes Only, 007:** Fleming mentions Park Lane itself in the opening of *Thunderball*, where we learn that James Bond parties here at an undisclosed address.

13:37

London Hilton on Park Lane
22 Park Lane, W1

A 30-story "Manhattanism" which towers above **Hyde Park** (9:1), the London Hilton opened in 1963 and is today considered the flagship property of Hilton International. The hotel's Windows Restaurant (then the Rooftop), with its striking panoramic view of London, was chosen as the venue for the introduction of the *OHMSS* cast to the world press on October 13, 1968. Adjacent to the restaurant was the "007 Night Spot", which opened at the height of '60s Bondmania. Here, you could sip 007 Vodka or a "Live and Let Die" champagne cocktail, all the while ogling assorted film props (both real and recreated) and listening to selections from the superspy's hit parade. The bar itself closed in 1978, while many of the props ended up in the hands of private collectors. Some of these props—for instance the "Disco Volante" life preservers—were sold at auction by **Christie's South Kensington** (21:1) in September 1998. That they were created for a bar, not an actual movie, seems not to have mattered in the least to the avid aficionados who snapped them up.

Station: Hyde Park Corner (PI) The hotel is just up Park Lane, on the R. The Windows Restaurant serves lunch and dinner Mon-Fri; dinner Sat; and brunch Sun. Jacket and tie are required for dinner.

> **Eyes Only, 007:** Fans of *The Man from U.N.C.L.E.* should recognize the Hilton as U.N.C.L.E.'s London headquarters in the fourth season episode "The Deep Six Affair".

13:38

Les Ambassadeurs Club
5 Hamilton Place, W1
(just off Park Lane)

In the summer of 1958, Ian Fleming and American film producer Irving Allen met here at the fashionable Les Ambassadeurs Club to discuss bringing James Bond's adventures to the big screen. The meeting did not go well, primarily because Allen didn't really like Fleming's books. But Allen's New York partner did. His name was Albert R. Broccoli and he was not about to give up on James

Bond. (It has been reported that Broccoli himself attended the "Les A" luncheon, but Cubby flatly contradicted this assertion in his autobiography, *When the Snow Melts*.) In December 1960, Canadian producer Harry Saltzman met with Fleming here at Les A, coming away with a six-month option on all the Bond novels, except *Casino Royale*, which the author had sold to actor-director Gregory Ratoff in 1955 and which Ratoff's widow, in turn, had sold to producer Charles K. Feldman in 1960*. Fleming was to receive $100,000 for each novel, plus 2° % of the net profits on each film. In the event that the filmmaker exhausted all of Fleming's novels, he was granted the movie rights to the character of James Bond and thus could create original Bond adventures. Unfortunately, Saltzman could not secure financing and it was not until he teamed up with Broccoli in June 1961 that the cinematic Bond was off and running (see all the **ex Offices of Eon Productions Ltd** [13:31-34] and **ex Office of United Artists** [19:13]). And what better place to introduce their version of "Bond, James Bond" than the elegant Les Ambassadeurs Club. Specifically, the filmmakers set the scene in Les Ambassadeurs' Le Cercle casino, a chemin de fer salon that had caused something of a sensation when it opened in May of 1961. At the time, no other London club possessed such an exclusive, French-styled gaming room (casino gambling had only recently been legalized), a fact that did not go unnoticed by the makers of *Dr. No*. (Nor, apparently, did it go unnoticed by writer Fleming, who mentions that Bond has "been losing a lot of money at one of these new gambling clubs" in Chapter 2 of *You Only Live Twice*.) Unfortunately, the film's modest budget could not be stretched to include location filming in Hamilton Place. So, the "Le Cercle Les Ambassadeurs" sign was mocked up in the studio, and the scene itself, with Sean Connery and Eunice Gayson, was shot on a Ken Adam set at **Pinewood Studios** (*JBB*). Adam assigned production buyer Ron Quelch the task of obtaining props for the casino set, which proved to be something of a challenge given the dearth of French-style gaming clubs in London. "We were restricted in the amount of equipment we could rent," Ron explained, "so, in the end, we borrowed a lot of props from old film productions. The result wasn't particularly brilliant." However, for verisimilitude, Ron *did* commission replicas of actual Les Ambassadeurs plaques, which can be seen in the film itself and in publicity shots of Connery and Eunice Gayson taken on the casino set. Les A continued its Bondian association through the opening of *Dr. No*, on October 5, 1962, when the club hosted the film's post-premiere party. In fact, producer Cubby Broccoli frequently treated Ian Fleming to lunch here at Les A, as well as the nearby **Mirabelle** (13:24), where the two would discuss the ongoing development of the cinematic Bond. As Cubby told Fleming biographer John Pearson (and as he presumably tried to reassure Fleming himself), the intention wasn't to "send up" the material, but rather to include "an occasional joke, an occasional 'sick' line to make the sadism acceptable...to let the audience know that this violence really was fantasy." (See the entry on The Mirabelle for Fleming's reaction to all of this.) Interestingly, both Sean Connery and Roger Moore were members of the club, posing here for a famous 1969 photo, three years before Moore himself would become James Bond. Eleven years later, in July 1980, Moore again visited Les A, this time confiding to writer Paul Donovan that as Eon had been screen-testing potential replacements, he, Moore, had no intention of returning as Bond. "Two weeks later," as Donovan notes in his biography of the actor, "Roger Moore signed to play Bond in *For Your Eyes Only*."

Station: Hyde Park Corner (PI) Walk N in Park Lane and take the first R into Hamilton Place. For a glimpse of Les A as it actually appeared in the 1960s, look no further than your personal copy of *A Hard Day's Night*. The Beatles shot two brief scenes here on March 17 and April 17, 1964. The "Le Cercle" scene even featured Margaret Nolan, the amply-endowed actress who played "Dink" in *Goldfinger*.

*Feldman produced the big-budget comedy *Casino Royale* in 1967 for Columbia Pictures, after which he sold his rights in the novel to United Artists. UA and Columbia jointly owned these rights until 1998, when Columbia sold its interest to MGM/UA and Eon Productions.

Trivia Challenge 24: Name the *other* performer who appears in both *Goldfinger* and *A Hard Day's Night*.

13:39

Athenæum Hotel & Apartments 116 Piccadilly, W1

Considering his home at 22B Ebury Street (2:1) a tempting target for German bombers (No. 20 had already been hit), Commander Ian Fleming took up residence in a number of hotels and clubs (including the **Carlton** [16:21], the **Lansdowne** [13:23] and the **St James's** [13:Q]), finally settling here in the Athenæum Court Apartments, as they were then called, toward the end of 1941. Fleming complained about the lack of space in this "concrete monstrosity", claiming to have tested—and verified—the old adage about there not being room enough to swing a cat, or, at any rate, a bottle on the end of a tie. Still, the Athenæum flat was handy for the Curzon Street home of his Naval Intelligence superior Admiral John Godfrey (see [13:28]), as well as for **The Dorchester** (13:36) in Park Lane, where Ann O'Neill, the future Mrs. Ian Fleming, was staying at the time. Fleming would remain here until the fall of 1946, when he moved into a house in Montagu Place (12:7). Today, the refurbished hotel and apartments are considered one of the more luxurious accommodations in Mayfair. Celebrity guests have included Val Kilmer, late of *The Saint*, and Charles Dance, who appeared in *For Your Eyes Only* and later starred as Ian Fleming himself in the British biopic *Goldeneye*.

Station: Green Park (JU; PI; VI) Exit on the North Side and go R (West) in Piccadilly, past the **ex American Club** (13:Q) and the former St James's Club. Turn R into Down Street to see the apartment complex itself, which is attached to the back of the hotel. The flat that Fleming occupied is not known.

13:40

Brioni Roman Style (UK) Ltd 1 Old Bond Street, W1

Founded in 1945 by Nazareno Fonticoli and Gaetano Savini, Brioni of Rome is today esteemed as one of the finest men's tailors in the world. In addition to foreign and domestic royalty, their celebrity clients have included Hollywood he-men Clark Gable, John Wayne, Gary Cooper, Kirk Douglas, Rock Hudson and, since 1995, Pierce Brosnan. Costume designer Lindy Hemming explained the "switch" from Bond's traditional **Savile Row** (13:12) tailors to Brioni:

> I wanted the look of a *modern* Savile Row suit, but Savile Row only produces a suit a *month* and we need everything in bulk. For every suit Bond wears, the tailor has to provide up to 20 identical suits, for the stuntmen and stand-ins and to replace any damaged clothes. I knew that I simply wouldn't be able to get the numbers I needed in Savile Row. So, I did a lot of research and finally discovered Brioni of Rome. Their suits were something a modern man could wear. They had ease and grace and sophistication—everything I thought a modern Bond should have. I flew out to their factory in Penne, on the Adriatic, and saw that they had enough tailors [some 900, in fact] to do the job in the time we had. I also saw that they were very flexible and, most importantly, that I could work with them to get my own designs produced.

So, in addition to driving German cars, James Bond would now sport Italian-made suits. However, as Lindy pointed out, the material itself actually comes from Savile Row. "I design the suits and then I buy the material from Holland & Sherry or Wain Shiell of Savile Row or Dormeuil of Sackville Street. Then I send it to Brioni in Rome, tell them what I want and they make it. We've done three films together without a 'hiccup'—even in a crisis." One such "crisis" occurred on *The World Is Not Enough* and it involved the suit Bond wears during the pre-credit boat chase. As originally scripted, the MI6 explosion/boat chase sequence would take place the same day as the initial scene in the Swiss bank—originally set in Switzerland itself, but ultimately lensed in Bilbao, Spain. Thus, the lightweight charcoal gray suit Bond wears in Spain would also be the one in which he survives the explosion, pursues Cigar Girl downriver, crashes through assorted buildings and tumbles down the **Millennium Dome** (35:1). For some reason, however, the filmmakers de-

cided that "some time had passed" between the opening scene and the scene at headquarters, which meant, of course, that Bond would now be wearing two different suits in the pre-credit sequence. So Hemming had to scrap the order for thirty identical copies of the "Spain suit" and come up with thirty versions of a new dark grey, three-piece suit for Bond to wear at MI6 *and* during his cruise down the **Thames** (24:1). "Only Brioni could cope with that kind of madness!" she enthused. And just how many suits did the master tailors provide for our hero (and his stand-ins) on this particular assignment? Well, not counting the boiler suit Bond wears in the "Kazakhstan" sequence, there were seven different outfits and approximately 100 suits in all. James Bond truly is "the suited hero". And if you can't quite swing the price of one of Bond's outfits (£2,500-£3,000), Brioni offers a range of off the peg suits for around £1,900 ($3,040)! For more on Bond's clothes, see Appendix One. Brioni's other London outlet is Beale & Inman of 131 New Bond Street.

Station: Green Park (JU; PI; VI) Exit on the North Side and go L (East) in Piccadilly. Turn L into Old Bond Street and look for Brioni on the corner. The shop is open by appointment only.

> **Trivia Challenge 26:** Who said of the Cinematic Bond, "On you everything looks good"?

Quick Ones...

ex Shop of Anthony Sinclair
29 Conduit Street, W1

Anthony Sinclair was one of the finest "Savile Row" tailors in London. Among his clients was Terence Young, the elegant director of *Dr. No*, who naturally thought of Sinclair when it came time to dress the new James Bond, Sean Connery (*see phot overleaf*). Sinclair decided that Bond's suits should be simple and sensible, with just a touch of the military about them (longer jacket, fitted waist, narrower trousers) in keeping with the character's naval background. The lightweight Sinclair suits were classic, not "trendy", which is why the Connery Bond of the '60s still looks so good today. Sinclair ultimately relocated to No. 43 Conduit Street, right next door to his friend (and rival) Cyril Castle, at No. 42 (see below). **Station: Oxford Circus (BA; CE; VI)**

ex Shop of Cyril Castle
42 Conduit Street, W1

In the film *Moonraker*, Dr. Goodhead asks Bond, slightly ruffled from the fall the two of them have just taken, if he has broken something. "Only my tailor's heart," he laments. At that time, actor Roger Moore, and therefore Bond himself, wore outfits designed by "celebrity tailor" Cyril Castle of Mayfair. Castle actually collaborated with Moore on the actor's wardrobe for both *The Persuaders* television series and the Seventies Bond films. Ironically, *Moonraker* would be the final collaboration between the tailor and actor. For the neo-conservative '80s, Moore—and Bond—would turn to a more traditional tailor, **Douglas Hayward** (13:5) of Mount Street. **Station: Oxford Circus (BA; CE; VI)**

ex Shop of Benson, Perry and Whitley
9 Cork Street, W1

Ian Fleming had his three-piece, light-weight worsted suits tailored here in Cork Street, just two streets over from the famous **Savile Row** (13:12). Why Cork Street and not the more fashionable Savile Row? Because, as the author wrote in "007 and Me": "It's slightly cheaper." Cheaper indeed, especially given the fact that, according to his tailor, Fleming wore his suits until they were in threads. Mr. Whitley also revealed to Fleming biographer John Pearson that Ian dressed for comfort, not for show, that he usually had three suits at a time and that these suits cost 58 guineas (around £61 or $170). **Station: Piccadilly Circus (BA; PI)**

ex St James's Club
106 Piccadilly, W1

The St James's membership was originally drawn from the Diplomatic Service, which explains why Ian Fleming joined the rather stuffy club, essentially an outpost of the **Foreign Office** (27:14), in 1931. He was then working as a journalist for **Reuters** (5:3), but dreamed of a diplomatic job in the Foreign Office. His dreams were dashed, however, when he failed to obtain a high enough score on the rigorous FO exam that July. Still, he remained a member of the St James's for years, even taking up temporary residence here during World War II, prior to finding a more permanent home in the Athenaeum Court Apartments off Piccadilly (see [13:39]). In 1975, the club was absorbed by **Brooks's** (16:5), which, ironically, is located just a few doors down from the St James's original home at 54 St James's Street. **Station: Green Park (JU; PI; VI)**

Tailor Anthony Sinclair ensures that Sean Connery is "dressed to kill."

ex Showrooms of Aston Martin Lagonda Ltd 96-97 Piccadilly, W1

The manufacturers of some of the finest luxury sports cars in the world have long maintained showrooms in Mayfair. Today, they are located in nearby Berkeley Street (No. 40, if you care to drop by), but in the 1960s they were located in Piccadilly, opposite Green Park. And it was here, on September 14, 1964, that the company unveiled a rather special automobile to an elite cadre of reporters and photographers: a customized Aston Martin DB5 (registration number: BMT 216A), which, in three days' time, would make its cinematic debut in the film *Goldfinger*. Company employees demonstrated the car's many exotic gadgets (some of which had been slightly modified since filming) and the assembled media representatives lapped it up. Clearly, there was going to be a promotional bonanza unlike any the carmaker or the filmmakers had ever seen. **Station: Green Park (JU; PI; VI)**

> **Trivia Challenge 25:** What is the first gadget Bond uses on the DB5?

ex American Club 95 Piccadilly, W1

Rufus B. Saye, alias Jack Spang, eats lunch here each day, according to Chapter 2 of *Diamonds Are Forever*. He is the head of the London office of the "House of Diamonds" (see **Hatton Garden** [8:3]), but in reality is the boss of the American Spangled Mob. His Club, now defunct, was founded by a group of American businessmen at **The Savoy** (23:8) on October 21, 1918. Shortly thereafter, the Club relocated to No. 95 Piccadilly, where it would remain until its closure in the 1980s. **Station: Green Park (JU; PI; VI)**

ex Turf Club 85 Piccadilly, W1

Considered the finest sporting club in London, the terribly exclusive Turf counted among its roster of dukes and similarly-landed members of the upper class a thriller writer named Ian Fleming. Ian presumably took great delight in the afternoons he spent here: the Turf, along with **Boodle's** (16:4), is one of only two clubs the author name-dropped in his famous *Playboy* interview in 1963. (Note: the interview was published in December 1964, but was actually conducted sometime in the spring of 1963, just prior to Fleming's 55th birthday on May 28th.) The club moved from its rather gloomy Piccadilly clubhouse (where it was founded in 1864) to 5 Carlton House Terrace, SW1 in 1965. Incidentally, the Turf offers reciprocal temporary membership in the aristocratic Jockey Club of Paris, which hires the pompous detective Achille Aubergine to investigate Max Zorin in the film *A View To A Kill*. **Station: Green Park (JU; PI; VI)**

Max Meyer's Flat Albany Albany Court Yard Piccadilly, W1

According to Chapter 6 of *Moonraker*, Sir Hugo Drax's metal broker friend and bridge partner, Max Meyer, lives in a "quiet flat in Albany", where he keeps his "soothing collection of Battersea snuffboxes." The Albany was—and is—an exclusive apartment complex centered around an 18th-century Palladian-style house built for the 1st Viscount Melbourne. Distinguished residents have included Lord Byron, William Gladstone, Aldous Huxley, Dame Edith Evans, Graham Greene, Edward Heath, and even "proto-Bond" Sidney Reilly (see [27:8])! **Station: Green Park (JU; PI; VI)**

14. PADDINGTON

Mostly residential area centered around the enormous Paddington Train Station, noted for its many budget bed and breakfasts

14:1

St Mary's Hospital Praed Street, W2

Sir James Molony, one of the most famous neurologists in the world—and a consultant to the British Secret Service—practices here, according to Chapter 2 of *Doctor No*. M calls on the good doctor (whose name Fleming pinched from that of his own **Harley Street** [12:Q] dentist) for an evaluation of Agent 007, whom Sir James had just released from the hospital the day before. (Fleming fans may recall that Bond had *nearly* succumbed to the poison-tipped shoe-knife of a certain Rosa Klebb at the end of the previous novel, *From Russia, With Love*. This incident is alluded to in the film *Dr. No*—as is the hospital stay—but without specific reference to Rosa Klebb, since her story had yet to be filmed!) Sir James Molony also advises M on the state of Bond's health in the novels *You Only Live Twice* and *The Man with the Golden Gun.* St Mary's, which opened in 1851 and was named after a nearby church, also boasts another "Fleming connection", although it has nothing to do with Ian. It was here, in 1928, that Sir Alexander Fleming discovered penicillin.

Station: Paddington (CI; DI) The hospital is just E of the tube station. The Paddington Railway Station, one of the most impressive train stations in London, is mentioned in the novel *The Spy Who Loved Me*—it is the terminus from which heroine Vivienne Michel departs for her weekly trip to Windsor and the waiting arms of young Derek Mallaby.

Trivia Challenge 27: What special event in the life of Ian Fleming occurred here on August 12, 1952?

15. PIMLICO

Once-fashionable riverside residential district, sandwiched between Chelsea and Westminster

15:1

ex MI5 Office
308 Hood House,
10 Collingwood House
Dolphin Square, SW1

Here, in the once-elegant Dolphin Square, **MI5**'s (13:30) legendary Maxwell Knight presided over the countersubversion department known as B5(b) during World War II. Hood House contained his office and a safe house—actually a flat—while Collingwood House contained the rest of the staff, including Knight's beautiful agent (and companion), Joan Miller. Among Knight's more famous operations was that in which he unmasked Soviet spy Tyler Kent, a cipher clerk stationed at the **American Embassy** (13:4) in Grosvenor Square at the start of the war. It has been claimed that Ian Fleming based the fictional M, at least in part, on Knight, who, for obvious reasons, was known to his colleagues as "M". However, Fleming's own Naval Intelligence superior, John Godfrey, is a more obvious model (see [23:10]), as is Sir Stewart Menzies of **MI6** (27:22). Fleming and Knight were certainly friends, though, and, in fact, it was to the unorthodox chief of B5(b) that Ian turned for help on one of the most controversial, indeed, bizarre schemes, of wartime intelligence. Here, in Knight's Hood House office, Fleming developed a plan to lure a top Nazi to Britain, someone gullible enough to believe that a pro-German organization known as The Link was preparing to overthrow Churchill—by this time the Prime Minister—and sue for peace with Germany. Knight was apparently quite enthusiastic about the plan, even as Fleming's own chief was anything but, and the two conspired to use their mutual friend, the occultist Aleister Crowley, to lure Deputy Führer Rudolf Hess from Germany. And so they did...For the rest of this incredible story, see the **ex Cavendish Hotel** (16:16). As for Knight, he and his section remained here in Dolphin Square until 1946, when the new MI5 Chief, Sir Percy Sillitoe (another Fleming friend), closed the offices and transferred all personnel to the new HQ (13:30) in Curzon Street, Mayfair. Knight left the service in the 1950s, going on to host a series of highly popular nature programs for the **BBC** (12:5). He died of complications from pneumonia in 1968.

Station: Pimlico (VI) Go R out of the station and into Lupus Street, then L into St George's Square. Pass the school and then turn R into Chichester Street. The Dolphin Square flats are ahead to the L.

16. ST JAMES'S

Exclusive clubbing and shopping preserve of upper class English gentlemen

16:0

St James's Walking Tour
SW1

***Start*: Green Park Station (JU; PI; VI); *Finish*: Buckingham Palace**

Although there are several film-related locations on this walk, the majority derive from the Bond novels, particularly *Moonraker*. Along with a Mayfair visit, the walking tour of St James's will give you great insight into the life and habits of Ian Fleming and the character of the Literary James Bond.

16:1

The Ritz, London
150 Piccadilly, W1

How much—or how little—can one say about this magnificent hotel? It bears the most famous name in the business—that of Swiss hotelier César Ritz, who, unfortunately, suffered a nervous breakdown and went into seclusion shortly before construction began. The building itself has the distinction of being the first major steel-framed structure in London, built in the manner of American skyscrapers of the late 19th century. Its exterior draws upon a number of French sources, including its sister hotel in Paris, the first to bear the name of Ritz. (Charles Mewès and Arthur Davis, the architects of both hotels, went on to design a number of homes and public buildings in London, including the **Royal Automobile Club** [16:26] and **Robert Fleming's House** [13:3] in Grosvenor Square.) The Ritz officially opened on May 24, 1906 and immediately established itself as one of the most fashionable social settings in London. It was quite simply, *the* place to be seen, and remains so to this day. Ann Fleming obviously knew this, for she frequently dined here with one or more of her many name-droppable friends (author Evelyn Waugh, for example). Her less socially-conscious husband also knew the Ritz, for he listed its Grill as one of his 12 favorite restaurants and mentioned the hotel itself in no less than three James Bond adventures. In *Moonraker*, the Ritz serves as Hugo Drax's London base, while Bond himself takes up temporary residence here in *Diamonds Are Forever* and *The Man with the Golden Gun*. In the former, Bond poses as diamond smuggler Peter Franks, and, as part of his cover, stays in one of the suites overlooking Green Park. In the latter, he is on the Russians' expense account and makes a rather conspicuous exit from the Arlington Street side of the hotel. (Read the novel to find out what happens when he does.) Fleming defended this name-dropping technique in a 1962 article for *Show* magazine called "How to Write a Thriller". He claimed that he was "interested in things and in their exact description" and therefore saw "no point in changing the name of the Ritz to the Grand Hotel Majestic, or the Dorchester to the Porchester" (although see the **Trafalgar Palace Hotel** [27:3] and the **Royal St George's Golf Club** [*JBB*] for two instances in which he *did* change the names). Today, Claridge's, the Lanesborough or **The Dorchester** (13:36) itself is apt to cost you more than the Ritz. But at £300 (nearly $500) for a double room, the legendary hotel has few worries about keeping out the riffraff. In fact, a two-room "James Bond Suite", overlooking Green Park à la *Diamonds Are Forever*, will run you no less than £900 ($1440) a night. Just remember, no price is too great when you are following in the footsteps of a legend...

Station: Green Park (JU; PI; VI) Exit on the South Side for the Ritz, which is just E of the station. Afternoon tea is served each day from 2pm-5pm. The park itself—which Bond views from the window of his bedroom in *Diamonds Are Forever* (Chapter 6)—is open daily from 5 am to midnight.

Trivia Challenge 28: In which novel does Bond stay—and nearly die—at the Paris Ritz?

16:2

White's
37-38 St James's Street, SW1

With a waiting list of nearly eight years and a membership that includes the Prince of Wales, White's is by far the most prestigious and exclusive of the London Clubland establishments. It is also the oldest, having been founded as White's Chocolate House in 1693, on the site of what is now **Boodle's** (16:4). The club moved into its present, vaguely French-styled home, in 1788. During the 18th and 19th centuries, White's was renowned for its high stakes gambling, and for a membership that would bet on literally anything. (The most infamous example of White's betting mania involved a man who had collapsed on the club's doorstep in 1750 and was then carried inside; members wagered on whether the stricken man was already dead or merely unconscious.) During the constitutional crisis of 1788 (involving the appointment of a regent for the mentally ill George III), White's fell in line squarely behind William Pitt and the Tories, leaving those members who supported the Whigs to resign from the club and head for **Brooks's** (16:5). During World War II, White's became a virtual annex of **MI6** (27:22), as Secret Intelligence Chief Sir Stewart Menzies not only dined at the club, but also conducted business here, including the recruitment of new officers. (Indeed, Menzies's indiscretion is said to have outraged his No. 2 at the Service, Claude Dansey, the veteran spymaster who formed the ultra-secret "Z Organisation" in 1936 [see **Bush House** (23:6)].) Young man about town Ian Fleming joined White's in July 1936 and regularly dined here for the next several years. By 1944, however, he had apparently tired of the relentless Tory politicking (although he himself was hardly a leftist), as well as the hectic social scene here, and so switched to the more relaxed **Boodle's** (16:4) down the street. (Note the comment in the novel *You Only Live Twice* that White's was "noisy and 'smart'".) Nevertheless, Fleming could still be counted on to turn up at White's whenever he was invited to do so. During one memorable evening in October 1951, he dined here with Sir Stewart Menzies himself, who revealed that he would soon be stepping down as the head of MI6. (His successors, including the hapless Sir John Sinclair, are discussed under **ex Home of the Secret Service Chief** [27:23].) Three years later, in the novel *Moonraker*, Fleming would endow the head of his fictional Secret Service with a membership at the exclusive "Blades", an amalgam of **Boodle's** (16:4), **Pratt's** (16:6), the **Portland Club** (13:26) and White's.

Station: Green Park (PI; VI; JU) Exit on the South Side and walk E in Piccadilly, then turn R into St James's Street. No. 37 is on the E side of the street, unmarked, of course.

16:3

Davidoff of London
35 St James's Street, SW1

The famous Swiss-based cigar manufacturer and retailer was founded by Russian-born Zino Davidoff in 1946. The branch here in St James's, with its walk-in humidor and incomparable collection of smoking requisites, is considered one of the finest such shops in London. Given its reputation, as well as the Russian connection, it's no wonder that Davidoff attracts customers like Xenia Onatopp, who smoked Romeo y Julieta Shakespeares in the film *GoldenEye*, Roger Moore, who regularly pops in to replenish his stock of Davidoff 2000s, and current Bond Pierce Brosnan, who favors the Davidoff No. 2's. For *The World Is Not Enough*, the firm also supplied a box of the famous Romeo y Julieta Churchills, one of which Miss Moneypenny unceremoniously consigns to the bin.

Station: Green Park (JU; PI; VI) Exit on the South Side and walk E in Piccadilly, then turn R into St James's Street. Look for Davidoff across the street from **Swaine Adeney** (16:14). **Hours:** Mon-Fri 9am-6pm; Sat 9:30am-6pm

> **Eyes Only, 007:** Bond also makes use of a Romeo y Julieta aluminum cigar tube in *Thunderball*—it's the container for his miniature breathing device!

16:4

Boodle's
28 St James's Street, SW1

Doubles as: "Blades" in the novels *Moonraker*, et al. (see also **Pratt's Club** [16:6])

Boodle's is one of the oldest and most exclusive gentlemen's clubs in London. It was founded in 1862 by Edward Boodle, the former headwaiter and manager of Almack's Club. (Fleming refers to the fashionable Almack's, which was located at 49-50 Pall Mall, in Chapter 3 of *Moonraker*.) Boodle's club settled into this Adam Style building in 1783 and has been based here ever since. It is directly across from **Brooks's** (16:5) and just down the street from **White's** (16:2), which together represent the top three such establishments in London. Ian Fleming actually gave up the politically conservative White's for Boodle's in 1944, preferring the more relaxed (and apolitical) atmosphere here at No. 28. According to his SIS counterpart and frequent lunch companion, Philip Johns, Fleming also esteemed the wartime cuisine at Boodle's to be the best in London. In this, he was apparently seconded by Sir Claude Dansey, the No. 2 man at **MI6** (27:22) and the former head of the ultra-secret "Z Organisation" (see [23:6]). Years later, Fleming mentioned the club by name in both *Moonraker* (Chapter 19) and *You Only Live Twice* (Chapter 2), using the latter novel as an excuse to poke gentle fun at Boodle's membership of "superannuated country squires talking of nothing but the opening of partridge season". More importantly, Boodle's was the principal inspiration for the fictional club "Blades", which counts among its members none other that the head of the British Secret Service. At Blades, for exam-

ple, only freshly minted money is used; at Boodle's, the coins were boiled before being given in change so as not to dirty the hands of its members. Blades occupies the site of the former Sçavoir Vivre Club, as does the real-life Boodles (although Fleming locates the older club in Park Street [*sic*], when, of course, it was in St James's Street). At Blades, newspapers are ironed before they are sent to the reading room, a practice which Boodle's phased out after the advent of non-smudge ink. And, of course, the description of Blades' bow window and Adam style front accord perfectly with those of Boodle's. Thus, in *Moonraker*, although Bond and M are ostensibly dining at "Blades", it is chiefly the ambience, amenities and trappings of Boodle's that Fleming lovingly, almost nostalgically describes over the course of several chapters. For the actual location of the fictional club, see **Pratt's Club** (16:6).

Station: Green Park (PI; VI; JU) Exit on the South Side and walk E in Piccadilly, then turn R into St James's Street. The club is just down from **Davidoff** (16:3).

Trivia Challenge 29: Which of Fleming's villains owes his or her surname to a member of Boodle's?

16:5

Brooks's
St James's Street, SW1
(across from ***Boodle's****)*

Founded in Pall Mall in 1764, William Brooks's club moved to this elegant, purpose-built structure in 1778. With **Boodle's** (16:4) and **White's** (16:2), it is one of the three most prestigious private clubs in London. (Interestingly, the club "flaunts" its exclusivity by refusing to use, or even acknowledge that it has, a street number. In fact, Brooks's *does* have a number—60—but don't tell them you heard it here.) The club's illustrious membership has included thirteen prime ministers, as well as notables from a variety of different fields, including historian Edward Gibbon, philosopher David Hume, painter Joshua Reynolds and actor David Garrick, after whom the **Garrick Club** (6:3) is named. During the Revolutionary War, Brooks's was the haunt of anti-Royalist Whig politicians who ardently supported their American cousins in the struggle to form the United States. The lead water tanks to the left of the clubhouse entrance, now used as planters, bear witness to this support through the simple legend "1776". James Bond, whose own moderate politics are tinged with an occasionally disconcerting leftist streak (cf. his remarks in support of Castro's rebels in "Quantum of Solace"), parks outside the august club in Chapter 4 of *Moonraker*. Brooks's is also mentioned in the preceding chapter of the same novel, in which Fleming expounds upon the history of London's prestigious gentlemen's clubs. Interestingly, in the original *Moonraker* manuscript, Fleming wrote that Bond generally had lunch at Brooks's, but, for some reason, changed this to the Secret Service canteen in the final draft.

Station: Green Park (PI; VI; JU) Exit on the South Side and walk E in Piccadilly, then turn R into St James's Street. The club is ahead on the R, just before Park Place.

16:6

Pratt's Club
14 Park Place, SW1

Doubles as: "Blades" in the novels *Moonraker*, et al. (see also **Boodle's** [16:4])

Literary M belongs to the prestigious private gentlemen's club Blades, an amalgam of Fleming's clubs **Boodle's** (16:4) and **White's** (16:2), which were located just around the corner from Blades, in St James's Street, as well as the **Portland Club** (13:26), then located in Charles Street, Mayfair. In terms of amenities and appearance, Blades seems more like Boodle's (see the entry). However, as Blades is the "most exclusive club in London", according to Chapter 3 of *Moonraker*, it also evokes comparisons with White's, which is considered the father of all such establishments and boasts the most aristocratic and conservative membership roster of them all. In its high-stakes bridge games, Blades recalls the Portland Club, to which Fleming switched shortly after the publication of *Moonraker*. Finally, in terms of actual location, Blades occupies the site of Pratt's, whose clubhouse, unique in Clubland, is a relatively small town house, in contrast to the country house-style buildings of, say, Boodle's and **Brooks's** (16:5). In fact, Pratt's is more of a private dining club than a traditional gentlemen's club. It dates from 1841, when William Nathaniel Pratt, steward to the Duke of Beaufort (and former croupier at **Crockford's** [16:23]), began hosting informal dinners here for the Duke and his aristocratic friends. Indeed, Pratt's was actually considered a hotel until 1857, when it was officially rated a club. Winston Churchill was a regular visitor during the 1920s and '30s and Tory MPs still constitute a large percentage of the club's 600 members. One reason for this may be the club's relatively low profile—in a group whose profiles are extremely low to begin with! (None of the St James's area clubs advertise themselves on the outside for the obvious reason that they simply aren't open to the public. However, one, the **Travellers' Club** [16:24], actually admits visitors for guided tours.) Whether any of this influenced Fleming's decision to locate the fictional Blades on the site of Pratt's is unknown. In any case, Bond dines with M at Blades in *Moonraker*, and also out-cheats Blades member Sir Hugo Drax, later revealed to be a *Nazi* (no true *English* gentleman would have cheated at bridge). Auric Goldfinger, another foreign cad, is also a member—and also a cheat! Who on earth was screening potential members in the fifties? The club is also mentioned on several other occasions, including Chapter 1 of *Thunderball*, where we learn that "some friend of [M's] at Blades…told him about [**Shrublands** (*JBB*)]"; in Chapter 20 of *OHMSS*, where Bond dreams that he and Tracy, now his wife, are attending some uncomfortably lavish do at an embassy and he wishes "he was playing a tough game of bridge for high stakes at Blades"; Chapter 2 of *You Only Live Twice*, where the building seems to have moved from Park Place (or Park *Street*, as Fleming calls it in *Moonraker*) out into St James's Street itself; and Chapter 17 of *The Man with the Golden Gun*, where we learn that the fraternity of ex-Secret Service men known as the Twin Snakes Club holds its annual dinner here. See the **ex Junior Carlton Club** (16:25) for the real-life version of the Twin Snakes Club.

Station: Green Park (PI; VI; JU) Exit on the South Side and walk E in Piccadilly, then turn R into St James's Street. Park Place—Fleming calls it Park *Street*—is ahead on the R, just past **Brooks's** (16:5) and opposite **Boodle's** (16:4).

16:7

John Lobb
9 St James's Street, SW1

Ian Fleming mentions James Bond's shoes on a number of occasions, telling us, for example, that Bond wears well-polished black moccasins (*Moonraker*), that he abhors shoelaces (*OHMSS*), that his toe-caps are lined with steel (*Live and Let Die*), that he has a concealed knife in the sole of each shoe (*Goldfinger*) and that he (presumably) prefers English shoes to Italian ones ("Risico"). In *Diamonds Are Forever*, he even tells us that Bond wears golf shoes from Saxone, a famous, but now defunct, Scottish firm whose name has since been acquired by Stylo plc of Bradford. On no occasion, however, does Fleming actually identify Bond's regular bootmaker. Nor do the Eon films, merely confirming—in the case of *Live and Let Die*—that Bond does have a bootmaker and that he shared him with a late, lamented colleague called Baines. However, in his posthumous autobiography, producer Cubby Broccoli describes the trappings associated with the fictional character, mentioning Bond's penchant for **Savile Row** (13:12) suits, honey from **Fortnum's** (16:13) and his patronage of the "royal bootmaker". And *that* reference brings us straight to No. 9 St James's Street. Bootmaker to the Crown since Queen Victoria's day, John Lobb is generally considered to craft the finest bespoke shoes in the world. (And at £1500 a pair, they can afford to.) Fleming may well have mentioned the firm during one of his many discussions with Broccoli, or else in the lengthy background memorandum he provided the producer. Either way, the filmmakers certainly came to Lobb, as actor Sean Connery recalled in the 1999 British television documentary *The James Bond Story*. Connery's first successor as Bond also came to Lobb—for a pair of riding boots—and apparently created quite a stir to boot (sorry about that). According to *OHMSS* costume designer Marjory Cornelius, George Lazenby shocked Lobb's conservative staff by asking for zips (i.e., zippers) on his boots, an addition that he felt would be both stylish and practical. Mrs. Cornelius recalled the incident as if it were yesterday: "They simply told him, 'If you want zips, you can go and have [the boots] made elsewhere.'" And that was that. Lazenby acquiesced and Bond got his traditional Lobb boots—without the zips! Today, of course, Bond buys his shoes from **Church's** (13:10), whose principal London outlet is at 133 New Bond Street.

Station: Green Park (PI; VI; JU) Exit on the South Side and walk E in Piccadilly, then turn R into St James's Street. Lobb's is near the end of the street, on the L. **Hours:** Mon-Fri 9am-5:30pm; Sat 9am-4pm

16:8

James Lock & Co., Ltd
6 St James's Street, SW1

The most famous name in English headgear dates back to 1759 when James Lock inherited his father-in-law's hatmaker's shop, which, in turn, had been founded in

1676. In 1764, Lock moved the shop to No. 6 St James's Street, where it has been based ever since. Among the firm's many famous customers: Lord Nelson (see **Trafalgar Square** [27:1]), the Duke of Wellington, Beau Brummel, Winston Churchill, Prince Charles, Sir Paul McCartney and even Pierce Brosnan himself. In the early 1960s, Lock's supplied a number of hats for the James Bond films, including the black Homburg that Bond tosses onto the hat rack in *Dr. No*; the dark gray felt trilby, called a Sandown (after the race course near London), that Bond wears in *Dr. No*, *From Russia With Love* and *Goldfinger*; and the square crowned bowler (which Lock's calls a square crowned coke) with which Oddjob dispatches his victims in *Goldfinger*. In fact, Harold Sakata wore several hats in the film, so to speak. One was simply an ordinary square crowned bowler, for which the actor was measured right here in the shop; two others were specially crafted by special effects supervisor John Stears and technicians Bert Luxford and Jimmy Ackland-Snow. One of these bowlers, which John called the "spinning hat", was fitted with a spring steel brim and was used for the scene in which Oddjob decapitates the statue. That sequence is interesting for a couple of reasons. First, while the throw itself was filmed at **Stoke Poges Golf Course** (*JBB*), the actual decapitation was shot at **Pinewood Studios** (*JBB*). Second, as Bert Luxford laughingly explained: the hat was already spinning before it was even thrown! How is that possible? Alimentary, Dr. Leiter. The hat was motorized. What's more, it had a small eyelet inserted through the top (also made of steel), through which a very thin wire was run. The prop man simply switched on the electric motor (mounted to the inside of the top) and then sent the spinning bowler sailing along the wire. (If you watch the golf course throw *very closely*, you can just spot the silver eyelet atop the hat.) The other customized bowler, called the "throwing hat", was made with a softer, more pliable steel so that it could be wedged into the bars of the grill in the gold vault scene. This hat was sold at auction in 1998 and fetched an amazing £61,750. The seller: Graham Rye, President of the James Bond International Fan Club; the buyer: Eon Productions. (See **Christie's South Kensington** [21:1] for more on the auction.) Lock's still carries all the classic Bondian hats, including the black Homburg, which will run you £130 ($208); the Sandown, priced at £105 ($168); and the square crowned coke à la Oddjob, a "steel" at £175 ($280).

Station: Green Park (PI; VI; JU) Exit on the South Side and walk E in Piccadilly, then turn R into St James's Street. Lock's is near the end of the street, on the L. **Hours:** Mon-Fri 9am-5:30pm; Sat 9:30am-4:30pm

16:9

Spink & Son Ltd
5-7 King Street, SW1

London's most prestigious dealers in rare coins, medals, militaria and other antique treasures, was founded by goldsmith John Spink in 1666. Nearly three centuries later, Spink & Son assisted Ian Fleming in gathering research material for the novel *Live and Let Die*. The author acknowledged this help in the book itself by having M tell Bond that both Spink's and the **British Museum** (3:5) have confirmed that Mr. Big's coins came from the pirate Bloody Morgan's treasure. See **Sir Henry Morgan's Birthplace** [*JBB*] for more on the colorful buccaneer.

Station: Green Park (PI; VI; JU) Exit on the South Side and walk E in Piccadilly, then turn R into St James's Street, then L into King. Spink's is ahead on the L. **Hours:** Mon-Fri 9:30am-5:30pm

Note: Next door, at No. 8, is Christie's auction house, whose South Kensington branch (21:1) hosted important sales of James Bond collectibles in 1998 and 2001.

16:10

Turnbull & Asser
71-72 Jermyn Street, SW1

A Jermyn Street fixture since 1885, this celebrated shirtmaker has preserved every bit of its 19th-century elegance, from the original fireplace with mother-of-pearl inlay to the horseshoe store sign hanging above the door. T & A has also maintained a dazzling and diverse Who's Who of celebrity clients, including Winston Churchill, David Niven, the Prince of Wales, Michael Caine, the Duke of Windsor, Ian Fleming (who favored the firm's Sea Island cotton shirts) and, of course, James Bond. Bond's connection—apart from Fleming—derives from the fact that T & A supplied custom-made shirts to director Terence Young, a sophisticated gentleman who imbued the screen version of James Bond with much of his own style and taste. For Connery-Bond, T & A created a signature shirt with distinctive turnback cuffs, fastened not with cuff links but with two pearl buttons. Bond wears the trademark T & A shirts in every film from *Dr. No* through *The Man With The Golden Gun* and then again, after a twenty-three-year respite, in 1997's *Tomorrow Never Dies*. The firm also supplied the white, blue and cream shirts that Brosnan wears in *The World Is*

T&A's Michael Fish selects material with actor Sean Connery.

Not Enough. His new ties—and Turnbull & Asser does refer to these as "James Bond Ties"—were designed by Lindy Hemming and made by T & A subsidiary Charles Hill Silk of Union Street, SE1. All are available at T & A for around £45-£50 ($72-$80). Oh, yes, in case you ever wondered, James Bond also gets his white boxers here at T & A. How's that for an "undercover job"?

Station: Green Park (JU; PI; VI) Exit on the South Side and walk E in Piccadilly, then turn R into St James's Street and then L into Jermyn Street. **Hours:** Mon-Sat 9:30am-5pm

16:11

Wilton's
55 Jermyn Street, W1

In Ian Fleming's day, this aristocratic West End favorite was located in Bury Street, just across the way. In 1984, Wilton's moved out into Jermyn Street, bringing much of the original Edwardian décor and accoutrements to its new premises. It is still considered one of the finest—and most formal—restaurants in London, renowned for its seafood, fish and game dishes, as well as traditional desserts. When you stop by, be sure to have a chat with Head Oysterman Patrick Flaherty—he used to hand-deliver special parcels of smoked salmon, lobster and oysters to Ian Fleming at the author's Victoria Square home (25:1)! See the Index for the rest of Ian Fleming's Favorite Restaurants.

Station: Green Park (JU; PI; VI) Exit on the South Side and walk E in Piccadilly, then turn R into St James's Street and L into Jermyn Street. **Hours:** Sun-Fri 12:30pm-2:30pm; 6:30pm-10:30pm (Sun until 10pm); reservations required; jacket and tie required

16:12

Alfred Dunhill
50 Jermyn Street, SW1

Founded by the eponymous saddler in 1893, Alfred Dunhill is famous for its quality cigars and smoking requisites, as well as an expensive range of men's fashions and accessories. (The two divisions are now separately-owned companies.) Ian Fleming smoked his famous Morland Specials in an ebonite Dunhill cigarette holder and was apparently only too happy to plug the firm whenever he could. Thus, in *From Russia, With Love* we learn that SMERSH executioner Donovan Grant possesses a number of "membership badges of the rich man's club", including a well-used gold Dunhill lighter, while in *Thunderball*, we are told that a local Bahamian tobacconist is "the Dunhills of Nassau". Other references occur in "The Living Daylights" and *You Only Live Twice*. Dunhill also has a long and distinguished association with the cinematic Bond, dating back to the very first film, *Dr. No*, in 1962. Production buyer Ron Quelch recalled that the filmmakers wanted a gunmetal cigarette lighter and case, just as Fleming had described, for the scene in which Bond is introduced in **Les Ambassadeurs Club** (13:38) (see **Pinewood Studios** [*JBB*] for the background to this story). He contacted a number of London firms in a vain attempt to find just such a set, at a price the producers could afford, before finally ringing Dunhill's here in St James's. Yes, the sales manager told him, Dunhill carried just the items, made of silver, with a gunmetal finish. In fact, the lighter and case were duplicates of a set that had been specially made for a woman whose husband was a fan of Fleming's novels! That set was acquired by Eon Productions and went on to appear throughout the series, "whenever we needed to show Bond smoking", Quelch explained. Between films, the lighter and case would be sent back to Dunhill for refinishing "because it was a pewter finish, or gunmetal finish, on silver and it marked." Watch for these historic props in *From Russia With Love*, *OHMSS* and *The Spy Who Loved Me*, and for the gold Dunhill that Roger Moore uses to light his cigar in *Live and Let Die*. On a more contemporary note, *GoldenEye* sees James Bond traveling to Russia (actually to **Epsom Racetrack** [*JBB*]!) with a stylish Dunhill attaché case, while in *Tomorrow Never Dies*, 007 sports a pair of Dunhill ADvantage cuff links at Elliot Carver's Hamburg party. In the pre-credit sequence of the same film, a gold-plated Alfred Dunhill Unique Sports Lighter (appropriately modified by Q Branch) comes in handy as a mini-grenade. In *The World Is Not Enough*, Bond again wears a pair of ADvantage steel and gold cuff links, as well as a pair of Millennium mother of pearl cuff links. (Look for the latter in the "tuxedo scenes", i.e., the casino, the test facility and the finale, and the former everywhere else.) He also sports three different Dunhill leather belts: a brown one with silver buckle during the boat chase; a brown one with gold buckle during the torture and submarine scenes (when he wears the cream linen suit); and a black one with silver buckle in all other non-tuxedo scenes. All these items—save the attaché case—are available at any Dunhill shop, as is the ordinary "civilian" version of the *TND* lighter. And if you can't quite justify £200 for a pair of Bondian cuff links, you can always plump for the cheaper AD2000 blue cuff links worn by the late Sir Robert King. Hey, if they're good enough for a billionaire oil baron…

Station: Green Park (PI; VI; JU) Exit on the South Side and walk E in Piccadilly, then turn R into St James's Street and L into Jermyn Street. **Hours:** Mon-Fri 9:30am-6pm

16:13

Fortnum & Mason Ltd
181 Piccadilly, W1

Founded as a grocer's shop in the 1770s, Fortnum & Mason is today one of the poshest department stores in London. (Although it looks old, the present building is in fact *neo*-Georgian and dates from the 1920s.) Fortnum's caters to a very high-class clientele, indeed, including several members of the Royal Family and—surprise, surprise!—a secret agent named James Bond. As we learn in Chapter 11 of *From Russia, With Love*, Bond garnishes his breakfast toast with "Tiptree 'Little Scarlet' strawberry jam; Cooper's Vintage Oxford marmalade and Norwegian Heather Honey from Fortnum's." (In the original manuscript, Bond savored Kielers Oxford marmalade and Mount Hymetus honey from Fortnum's.) Another Fortnum customer pops up in B *The Spy Who Loved Me*. This is Oxford-bound Derek Mallaby, the young cad who callously broke it off with heroine Vivienne Michel, then attempted to make amends by sending her a dozen bottles of Fortnum's best pink champagne. Viv responded by sending the champagne right back where it came from!

Station: Piccadilly Circus (PI; BA) Exit for Piccadilly (South side), go L in Piccadilly and look for Fortnum's ahead on the L. The eastern portion of the building, at 185, is the former site of **Swaine Adeney** (see the next entry). **Hours:** Mon-Sat 9:30am-6pm

16:14

ex Swaine Adeney Brigg
185 Piccadilly, SW1

Originally located at 185 Piccadilly (which is now part of **Fortnum & Mason** [16:13]), Swaine Adeney has been manufacturing high-quality leather riding and travel goods since 1750. In 1943 the company merged with the Royal umbrella makers Brigg and Sons and today, from its new shop at 54 St James's Street, provides whips and gloves by appointment to Her Majesty the Queen and leather goods by appointment to HRH the Prince of Wales. Fleming mentions the firm in Chapter 10 of *You Only Live Twice*, where Bond watches Tiger Tanaka's commandos fight with six-foot staves and then tours "the museum of *ninja* armament". Unimpressed by all the low-tech weaponry, Bond deflates his beaming host by sarcastically remarking that he "must get Swaine Adeney to make me a two-yard-long walking stick." Tiger is not amused. A few years earlier, according to Chapter 13 of *From Russia, With Love*, James Bond had carried a Swaine Adeney attaché case—specially modified by Q Branch, of course—on his assignment in Istanbul. For a Jamaican assignment in 1962, the Cinematic Bond opted for a lid-over-body model with handstitched black leather, red skiver (sheepskin) lining and solid brass key locks. The following year, Q Branch adapted that very case for another mission to Istanbul, although Bond himself didn't think he would need it. This time the lethal accessories included everything from an exploding tear-gas canister to an AR-7 folding sniper's rifle. In fact, the filmmakers used *three* cases in *From Russia With Love*: the original Swaine Adeney lid-over-body model from *Dr. No*, which production buyer Ron Quelch actually purchased from the location here in Piccadilly; and two others designed by Syd Cain and built from scratch by John Stears' special effects team. The Swaine Adeney case is an inch smaller in depth than the special effects cases and, of course, has the distinctive lid-over-body design; the gadget versions, based on a simple box case design, do not. Today, Swaine Adeney will sell you the 3 °" lid-over "James Bond Attaché Case", with red skiver lining, for £860 (nearly $1400). A black, 4 ∫" bridle hide box case, more like the film's purpose built version, will run you £820 (around $1300). As for the special effects cases, one was loaned out in 1994 (for possible reproduction) and unfortunately never returned; the other, which actor Desmond Llewelyn once used for promotional purposes, is now in the Eon archives.

Station: Green Park (JU; PI; VI) For the original location, exit the station on the south side and walk E in Piccadilly until you come to Fortnum's; Swaine Adeney was in the easternmost portion of the building. For the current location, again, exit on the south side, walk E in Piccadilly, then turn R into St James's Street. The shop is just ahead on the R, at No. 54. Don't be surprised if you run into Roger Moore here, or across the street at the **Davidoff** (16:3) cigar shop. **Hours**: Mon-Sat 9:30am-6pm (Thu until 7pm)

16:15

Hatchard's Booksellers
187 Piccadilly, W1

London's oldest and most prestigious bookseller was founded by publisher John Hatchard in 1797. Four years later, Hatchard moved his shop from 173 Piccadilly to Nos. 189-190 (now No. 187), where it has remained ever since. (It used to adjoin **Swaine Adeney** [16:14], at No. 185, but now borders the expanded **Fortnum & Mason** [16:13].) In addition to serving the Royal Family with distinction, Hatchard's has enjoyed the custom of numerous prime ministers, the Duke of Wellington, Lord Byron, George Bernard Shaw, Oscar Wilde, Rudyard Kipling and Virginia Woolf. Another big name associated with the bookseller, at least indirectly, is James Bond. According to Chapter 8 of *On Her Majesty's Secret Service*, the firm provided the **College of Arms** (5:11) with a copy of G. W. Marshall's famous *Genealogist's Guide*. The College, in turn, passed the book along to James Bond, who, in the guise of Sir Hilary Bray, hoped that it wouldn't take more than a few props to turn 007 into a Herald. Sadly, Marshall's book (1903 edition) has not been reprinted since 1980 and, as the staff of Hatchard's concedes, no single genealogical reference work has come along to take its place. In the film version, Bond consults a copy of C. W. Scott-Giles' 1958 edition of *Boutell's Heraldry* (which he takes to Ruby's room and inadvertently [?] leaves behind). Production buyer Ron Quelch recalled that while he did call on Hatchard's, all the prop books, including copies of Marshall's famous guide and *Burke's General Armoury* (see the **London Library** [16:19]), actually came from Heraldry Today, a specialist shop then located at 10 Beauchamp Place, SW3, and today based in Ramsbury, Wiltshire.

Station: Piccadilly Circus (PI; BA) Exit for Piccadilly (South side), go L in Piccadilly and look for Hatchard's ahead on the L. **Hours:** Mon-Sat 9am-6pm; Sun noon-6pm

16:16

The Cavendish Hotel
81 Jermyn Street, SW1

The present luxury hotel opened in 1966 on the site of what is now known as the "old Cavendish Hotel". It was at the old Cavendish that Commander Ian Fleming took part in one of the most bizarre schemes in the annals of wartime espionage. Naval Intelligence (see the **ex Admiralty** [27:10]) had come to believe that Adolf Hitler relied heavily upon astrological advice in planning military and political strategy (this claim has since been challenged). His deputy, Rudolf Hess, was believed to be even more entranced by both astrology and the occult. Somehow (there is still a great deal of mystery about all this), the British Intelligence community learned that Hess wanted to fly to England in pursuit of his own peace accord between the two warring nations. Therefore, Fleming wondered, why not find out what kind of advice Hess was receiving, and try to supplement it with a little bogus astrological propaganda? His Naval Intelligence chief, Admiral Godfrey, was skeptical, but Fleming pursued the plan with zeal. In this he was aided and abetted by MI5 countersubversion chief Maxwell Knight, who was then headquartered in Dolphin Square, well outside the realm (and reach?) of Whitehall (see **ex MI5 Offices** [15:1]). Their goals were to convince Germany that a negotiated peace with England was indeed possible (it wasn't, of course, but such a stalling tactic might delay the German invasion until Britain was better able to cope with the enemy) and to encourage the gullible Hess to make the trip in pursuit of this settlement. To this end, Fleming, with Knight's blessing, held a series of meetings at the Cavendish Hotel with their mutual friend Aleister Crowley, who was then staying there. A highly controversial figure variously known as "the Great Magician" and "the Great Beast", Crowley was an expert on astrology, mysticism and all things occult, particularly the German variants thereof. With his help, not only would the Department of Psychological Warfare, with whom Fleming was working, concoct false horoscopes to be planted on Hess, but also undertake occult rites to further influence Hess's actions. And thus, according to Fleming biographer Donald McCormick (quoting Crowley's son, Amado), a "high ritual" was performed to this end in Ashdown Forest, East Sussex, in September 1940. Fleming was apparently fascinated by the complex ceremony, which involved a "fireworks display" and an effigy of Hess dressed in a Nazi uniform and sitting on a "throne". To what extent Bond's creator may have believed in the efficacy of such a ceremony is, of course, another question. In any case, as history records, Deputy Party Leader Rudolf Hess did, indeed, fly to Scotland on May 10, 1941, and attempt to undertake a negotiated peace between Britain and Germany. His efforts were dismissed on all sides (in fact, Hitler ordered that Hess was to be shot on sight if he ever set foot in Germany again) and, after the Nuremberg trials, the former Nazi leader would spend the rest of his life in Spandau Prison. That British Intelligence was involved in the scheme to lure Hess was suspected at the time, but vigorously denied. Why? Because Joseph Stalin was convinced that Britain and Germany were plotting to join forces against the Soviet Union and Hess's flight was the prelude to such a double-cross. Churchill couldn't have his Russian ally believing such a thing, nor could he lend any credence whatever to the notion that a pro-German faction existed within the UK. Therefore, Hess was simply "insane", precisely the assessment leveled by the Germans. Ian was apparently bitterly disappointed that the Government refused to exploit the Hess Affair, or to allow Crowley to interrogate the man. Still, he was thankful for the Great Magician's help and, at the conclusion of the affair, sent Aleister a small token of his appreciation: a bottle of toilet water from **Trumper's** (13:25) of Curzon Street.

Station: Green Park (PI; VI; JU) Exit on the South Side, go E in Piccadilly, then R into St James's Street and L into Jermyn Street.

16:17

J. Floris Perfumes
89 Jermyn Street, SW1

Ian Fleming was a frequent patron of this small but prestigious perfume shop, established in this very locale by Spanish merchant Juan Famenias Floris in 1739. Not surprisingly, the author plugged the firm in several of James Bond's adventures, beginning with *Moonraker*. There, in Chapter 3, we learn that Floris provides the soaps and lotions in the bathrooms and bedrooms at the "most exclusive club in London" (see [16:6], although you should know what it is). In Chapter 21 of *Diamonds Are Forever*, Bond plans to cable May, his elderly Scottish housekeeper, with instructions to "get things fixed" for the arrival of Tiffany Case. In addition to airing the sheets and stocking up on flowers, May will have to purchase bath essence from Floris. Finally, we are told in Chapter 13 that the firm even provides the lime bath essence for the mink-lined prison run by *Doctor No*.

Station: Green Park (JU; PI; VI) Exit on the South Side, go E in Piccadilly, then R into St James's Street and L into Jermyn Street. **Hours:** Mon-Fri 9:30am-5:30pm; Sat 10am-5pm

16:18

ex À l'Écu de France Restaurant
111 Jermyn Street, SW1

German Interrogation, Take Two: After the failure of his "Scott's plan" to elicit secrets from captured German U-boat officers (see **ex Scott's Restaurant** [19:6]), Commander Ian Fleming gamely decided to give it another go. This time, the German prisoner would be taken to see his old flat in Eaton Square, wined and dined here, at his favorite restaurant (also one of Fleming's favorites), then escorted to a beautiful house near **Sloane Square** (4:1), one which Ian had wired for sound. Unfortunately, by the time his escorts got him to the house, "Captain-lieutenant" von Ostheim was too drunk to talk, and all Fleming got for his trouble was a worthless recording of an inebriated Nazi. Interestingly, the former restaurant is now home to a Church's English Shoes store, so while you can no longer dine here à la Fleming you can at least shod your feet here à la Bond.

Station: Piccadilly Circus (BA; PI) Take the Piccadilly (South side) exit R into Lower Regent Street, then turn R into Jermyn Street. The ex restaurant, current shoe store, is ahead on the L.

16:19

London Library
14 St James's Square, SW1

The London Library was founded as a sort of "scholars' library" in 1841; today it contains over a million volumes, which makes it one of the largest independent lending institutions in the world. Its subject range runs to the "high-brow" (literature, history, philosophy, theology, fine art and so on), with lighter fair being admitted to the shelves only after the exercise of "much discrimination". The library charges £130 ($208) for an annual membership, around £3,000 for a life membership (depending on the applicant's age), and this only after the would-be subscriber has passed a credit examination and furnished proper references (I am serious). James Bond appropriates a copy of *Burke's General Armoury*, stamped 'Property of the London Library', as part of his Hilary Bray disguise in the novel *On Her Majesty's Secret Service*. Fleming does not say whether Bond himself was a member of the Library, or whether **Universal Export** (12:3) maintained an account there. Still, one can just imagine the scene in the Library Membership Administrator's office: "It says here that the applicant is a sort of 'licensed troubleshooter' and that he's been recommended by an Admiral Sir M____ M_______. Hmm. Works for a Regent's Park firm called 'Universal Export'. Better have them checked out, Miss Philpott. No degree but he does have a CMG. Annual income seems a bit on the low side *and* he isn't married. Still, the banking references are legitimate and the cheque itself is good. Issue a provisional membership for a probationary period of, say, two months. Full twelve-month membership pending return of the borrowed item...." Unfortunately, as readers of the novel may recall, James Bond left Piz Gloria in such a hurry that he forgot to stuff that copy of *Burke's General Armoury* into his ski pants. One can only hope that Universal Export promptly purchased a replacement volume, thereby saving Bond's face—and borrowing privileges—at the prestigious London Library.

Station: Piccadilly Circus (BA; PI) Take the Piccadilly (South side) exit R into Lower Regent Street; turn R into Jermyn Street, then L into Duke of York Street, which leads into St James's Square. The library is in the NW corner, to your R as you enter the square. **Hours:** Mon-Sat 9:30am-5:30pm (Thu until 7:30pm).

16:20

Norfolk House
31 St James's Square, SW1

Built on the site of the square's first house (erected in the late 1660s), the present office building was completed in 1939, on the eve of the Second World War. Fittingly, Norfolk House became the HQ of General Dwight Eisenhower's 1st Allied Army, as well as that of the joint Anglo-American intelligence operations. Regularly attending conferences here, where both the Normandy invasion and the parallel deception operation were discussed, were Commander Ian Fleming of British Naval Intelligence and his American counterpart and friend, Lt. Alan Schneider. The American officer was presumably the inspiration for Felix Leiter, whom Fleming assigns to NATO's Joint Intelligence Staff in both *Casino Royale* (Chapter 7) and *Live and Let Die* (Chapter 1). For more on Lt. Schneider, see the **ex American Embassy** (13:4) and the **Royal Seven Stars Hotel** (*JBB*).

Station: Piccadilly Circus (BA; PI) Take the Piccadilly (South side) exit R into Lower Regent Street; turn R into Jermyn Street, then L into Duke of York Street, which leads into St James's Square. No. 31 is in the SE corner of the square.

Eyes Only, 007: St James's Square was also the venue for the *TWINE* premiere party, held here under a lavishly-appointed marquee on the night of Monday, November 22, 1999.

16:21

ex Carlton Hotel & Grill
Corner of Pall Mall and Haymarket, SW1

On May 24, 1939, Ian Fleming lunched with Admiral John Godfrey, the Director of Naval Intelligence, at the Carlton Grill, conveniently located just across the Mall from the Navy's administrative headquarters at the **Admiralty** (27:10). Fleming had been recommended to Godfrey as a Personal Assistant by no less an eminence than Montagu Norman, Governor of the **Bank of England** (5:12). Then, as now, who you know can matter more than what you know: Norman was acquainted with Ian through his Chief of Staff, Bernard Rickatson-Hatt, Fleming's old boss at **Reuters** (5:3) and a close friend of Eve Fleming, Ian's mother. (According to Donald McCormick's sources, Norman actually knew Fleming himself, as the governor could have hardly recommended someone whom he had never met for such an important position.) Fleming impressed Godfrey, got the job, and remained PA to the DNI until the close of the war. The Carlton was not so fortunate: German bombs effectively ended its life in the autumn of 1940, even as Fleming himself was a resident here. The magnificent building, whose interior was modeled after the Paris Ritz, lay dormant until 1957, when it was demolished to make way for New Zealand House. The latter building, home to the New Zealand High Commission (i.e., embassy), was opened by Queen Elizabeth in 1963. The drab, nineteen-story office tower, located in the traditional heart of London, is, to quote a local tour director, "not to everyone's taste".

Station: Charing Cross (BA; JU; NO) Take the Cockspur Street exit, turn L into Cockspur Street and continue to the corner of Pall Mall and Haymarket; the Carlton was in the NW corner. For an idea of what the hotel actually looked like, walk up Haymarket to the building just N of New Zealand House. This is Her Majesty's Theatre, which was built by the same architect (C. J. Phipps) at the same time (1896-97) in the same style (French Renaissance). Apart from the different signage, Her Majesty's is literally the twin of the grand hotel, right down—or, rather, up—to its impressive dome.

16:22

ex United Service Club,
a.k.a., "The Senior"
116-119 Pall Mall, SW1

The Senior began as a "General Military Club" for higher ranking army officers who had fought in the Napoleonic Wars. Then the membership of the Royal Navy Club expressed an interest in merging with their army brethren, hence the new name: United Service Club. When junior army and navy officers formed a similar club the following year, they called it, appropriately enough, the Junior United Service Club. The older club, in turn, was dubbed "the Senior". The Senior's expanding membership quickly outgrew the original clubhouse at the northeast corner of Charles II Street and Regent Street, so in May 1826, they hired architect John Nash to construct a lavish new headquarters here in Pall Mall, the first building especially commissioned by such a club. One of the Senior's more important members, at least from a Bondian perspective, was Admiral John Godfrey, the Head of Naval Intelligence from 1939-1942 (see the **ex Admiralty** [27:10]). The admiral frequently dined here with Commander Ian Fleming, who served as Personal Assistant to both Godfrey and his successor, Captain (later Rear Admiral) Edmund Rushbrooke, during World War II. Although it was never really Fleming's club, the creator of James Bond would later write that the Senior was "the greatest of all Services' clubs in the world." In fact, according to Chapter 2 of *You Only Live Twice*, M would have stuck to the Senior but too many people knew him here and there was too much shop talked. By the time Fleming wrote those words, the United Service Club had already merged with the Junior and had even begun admitting civilians to make ends meet! The club's fortunes continued to decline, however, and the Senior finally closed its doors in 1976. Some of its members transferred to the other military clubs (the Army and Navy Club, at 36 Pall Mall, and the Naval and Military Club, at 94 Piccadilly), while others opted for the prestigious **Brooks's** (16:5) in St James's Street. Still others took advantage of a generous invitation to join the Institute of Directors, an organization of British business leaders that took up residence here in 1978. To the extent that ex-Senior members continue to enjoy the Institute of Directors club facilities, the Senior can be said to live on in its traditional Pall Mall home.

Station: Piccadilly Circus (BA; PI) Take Exit 3 for Lower Regent Street and follow this into Waterloo Place. The building is to the L, on the southeast corner of Pall Mall and Waterloo Place. It is open by appointment only.

16:23

ex Crockford's
16 Carlton House Terrace, SW1

According to Chapter 1 of *Moonraker*, James Bond spends his evenings at this exclusive gambling establishment, away from the more traditional "Clubland" world of St James's Street, the site of M's club "Blades" (see [16:6]), as well as the real-life clubs **Boodle's** (16:4) and **White's** (16:2). Interestingly, the original club, founded by William Crockford in 1828, was located right in the heart of Clubland, at 50 St James's Street. Popularly known as the "Temple of Chance", Crockford's was esteemed as the most luxurious of the 18 gaming houses in the vicinity of St James's Street, thanks largely to the talents of its celebrity chef, Eustache Ude. Thanks to celebrity members like the Duke of Wellington (and to the influence of Crockford himself), it was also the only St James's gaming house to escape periodic raids by **Scotland Yard** (27:16). Crockford, who lived at 11 Carlton House Terrace, died in 1844, and with him, the club itself. In 1934, a new Crockford's was founded at 16 Carlton House Terrace, a private home with no less than 23 bedrooms. The fashionable gambling den, which was not unknown to Ian Fleming, remained here for over half a century, finally transferring its gaming license to 30 Curzon Street (near the former Mayfair HQ of **MI5** [13:30]) in 1986. No. 16 Carlton Terrace Home is now the HQ of the Crown Estate, which manages the properties owned by Queen Elizabeth.

Station: Piccadilly Circus (BA; PI) Take Exit 3 for Lower Regent Street, continue through Waterloo Place and then turn L into Carlton House Terrace. No. 16 is ahead on the R.

16:24

Travellers' Club
106 Pall Mall, SW1

Founded in nearby Waterloo Place in 1819, the Travellers' was intended as a reunion point for English gentlemen who had journeyed abroad. In fact, the original members were required to have traveled at least 500 miles from London, a relatively rare feat at the time. Today, the qualification is simply one trip abroad, with special consideration given to those who have actually lived abroad. The present clubhouse, a small, but attractive Italianate palace built around a central court, was completed in 1832. Cinematic Bond's first director, Terence Young, certainly a well-traveled man by any standard, was a member and occasionally dined here with his friend Ian Fleming. (The two had met several years before the Bond films, through Ian's wife, Ann.) "He knew everybody in the **Foreign Office** (27:14)," Young told Richard Schenkman in a 1981 interview, "and the Travellers' Club is a great Foreign Office Club." Young also selected the Travellers' as the venue for a celebratory dinner party following the first, private screening of *Dr. No*, on July 25, 1962. (According to editor Peter Hunt, this screening took place in the basement cinema of **Eon Productions**' Audley Square offices [13:31], and not at the Travellers' itself, as some writers have claimed.) Among the assorted dignitaries were Ian and Ann Fleming, who, in a letter to her friend Evelyn Waugh, claimed that "it was an abominable occasion." Apparently, no one really liked the film, including Ian, although his reaction to the "Eon Bond" certainly softened in time. Interestingly, the Travellers' is the only one of the traditional Clubland establishments to admit visitors for guided tours.

Station: Piccadilly Circus (BA; PI) Take the Piccadilly (South side) exit R into Lower Regent Street and continue through Waterloo Place. Turn R into Pall Mall and look for No. 106 across the street. Tours are Mon-Fri by appointment. Across the street, at No. 15 Pall Mall, stood the London office of the American Automobile Association, which Vivienne Michel visited in Chapter 6 of *The Spy Who Loved Me*. Next door, at No. 16, was the showroom of Wilkinson Sword Ltd., the firm which manufactured the concealable throwing knives for Bond's attaché case in the novel *From Russia, With Love*.

16:25

ex Junior Carlton Club
29 Pall Mall, SW1

This famous Clubland establishment was founded in 1864 as an offshoot of the Carlton Club, which, in turn, had been set up in 1832 to promote the interests of the Conservative Party. The first of its purpose-built headquarters was opened on this site in 1869; major expansion and renovation followed in the 1880s and 1920s. After World War II, the Junior Carlton became the venue for the regular dinners of the "36 Club", a semi-formal association of some 70 former members of the Naval Intelligence Division. The club was organized by Admiral John Godfrey, the former Director of Naval Intelligence, whose official residence had been 36 Curzon Street, whence the club's name (see **ex Residence of the Director of Naval Intelligence** [13:28]). Godfrey, in concert with other former Intelligence chiefs, felt that such reunions would be a good way to keep the old gang together—and functioning—in the event of another war. (His former **SOE** [12:8] counterpart, Colin Gubbins, had undertaken something similar with his Special Forces Club in Kensington.) Sitting around Disraeli's Cabinet table, an artifact of the Conservative statesman's now preserved in the Carlton Club itself, the former spooks were free to drink, dine and discourse on the ins and outs of intelligence-gathering. According to Admiral Sir Norman Denning, it was at one of the club's dinners in 1948 that his one-time subordinate, Commander Ian Fleming, "held forth on his own ideas of the ideal agent he would employ." Fleming, of course, had been Personal Assistant to both Godfrey and his successor as DNI, Edmund Rushbrooke, during the Second World War (see the **ex Admiralty** [27:10]). As Denning related the story to John Pearson in 1965, Fleming claimed that an agent "must be tough, ruthless, promiscuous, so as to avoid long-term emotional entanglements, patriotic, reasonably affluent." Sound familiar? It certainly did to Denning—at least after he began reading Fleming's novels some years later. "I realised that [Fleming] had been presenting us with an early mock-up of Bond himself." The 36 Club continued to meet here in the Junior Carlton until 1963, when the building was demolished to make way for a more modern clubhouse. At that time, the members of the Junior Carlton were invited to enjoy the hospitality of the Army and Navy Club, located just across the entrance to St James's Square at No. 36 Pall Mall. Godfrey's dinners were duly transferred to the new venue, long known as "the Rag" (from a disgruntled member's remark about the meager late-night meal being a "Rag and Famish affair", with this, in turn, alluding to a low-class brothel then operating off Cranbourn Street). That Fleming may have eventually grown tired of these "Old Boys" dinners—or simply saw them for what they really were—is suggested by Bond's comments in Chapter 17 of *The Man with the Golden Gun*. There, having been offered a knighthood (which he respectfully declines), 007 reflects that he only wears his CMG (Companion of the Order of St Michael and St George) and other decorations at the annual dinners of "The Twin Snakes Club", the fraternity of ex-Secret Service men who hold their "grisly reunion[s]" at Blades (see [16:6]). These men—and women, apparently—were brave and resourceful in their day, but now (like Fleming, himself) had old people's diseases and repeated stories of dusty triumphs and tragedies that could never be told in the history books. But Bond, the young man of action, concerned only with tomorrow, continued to show up at these functions, bedecked in his "lettuce", because it gave "pleasure and reassurance to the 'Old Children' at their annual party." That Bond gave pleasure and reassurance to Ian Fleming is certainly true, but the words are also tinged with irony, even bitterness. For as Bond remained young and vital, concerned only with "what was going to happen tomorrow", Fleming himself was growing older, weaker, sicker. Indeed, the author would succumb to heart disease less than six months after these words were typed.

Station: Piccadilly Circus (BA; PI) Take the Piccadilly (South side) exit R into Lower Regent Street and continue through Waterloo Place. Turn R into Pall Mall. The final incarnation of the Junior Carlton, completed in 1967, occupies the space between the two entrances to St James's Square. In 1977, the financially-troubled club abandoned its purpose-built headquarters to merge with the Carlton Club at No. 69 St James's Street.

16:26

Royal Automobile Club
89 Pall Mall, SW1

The newest, largest and least class-conscious of the Clubland establishments was founded in 1897 "for the Protection, Encouragement and Development of Automobilism". It occupied four rooms in the massive Whitehall Court complex until 1902, when it moved to larger premises at 119 Piccadilly. (For another temporary tenant of Whitehall Court, see **MI6 [1914-19]**[27:8].) Nine years later, the club moved to its present Edwardian headquarters, which was designed by Mewès and Davis, architects of **The Ritz** (16:1). The RAC is mentioned, along with the AA (the Automobile Association, then in Fanum House, Leicester Square), in connection with Bond's enquiry in Chapter 19 of *Moonraker* as to whether the missing Gala Brand could have been involved in an auto accident on the road from Dover to London. The reports from both organizations are "negative". In Chapter 25 of *From Russia, With Love*, SMERSH killer Donovan grant poses as "Captain Norman Nash" of the Royal Automobile Club, according to the visiting card he presents to James Bond. (The Cinematic Grant also gives Bond a card, but we never see what it says.) Finally, in the summer of 1969, the club had the chance to exhibit the Aston Martin DB5 "road car" (registration number: FMP 7B), which was used for many of the driving and "non-gadget" scenes in the films *Goldfinger* and *Thunderball*. The chosen venue for the display was the club's first floor (US: second floor) reception area. This meant that the DB5 had to be hauled to the RAC on a transporter truck and backed down ramps *through* the first floor French windows! The sight would have been enough to stop traffic in Pall Mall—which is just what it did....

Station: Piccadilly Circus (BA; PI) Take the Piccadilly (South side) exit R into Lower Regent Street and continue through Waterloo Place. Turn R into Pall Mall. The club is located ahead, on the S side of the street. At the end of Pall Mall, to the left, is St James's Palace, the Tudor landmark mentioned by Fleming (ever the tour guide) in Chapter 19 of *Moonraker*.

Eyes Only, 007: MI6 founder Mansfield Cumming was an ardent motor enthusiast and, not surprisingly, an early member of the RAC. He often retreated to the RAC—in all three of its homes—for staff meetings, lunches, etc., thus establishing the tradition of using gentlemen's clubs as virtual annexes of the Secret Service. For another famous "annex", see **White's** (16:2).

16:27

Buckingham Palace
The Mall, SW1

The Official London Residence of the British Sovereign was actually built for John Sheffield, the 1st Duke of Buckingham and Normanby, in 1702-1705. In 1762, King George III purchased "Buckingham House" for £28,000 (about £2.7 million in today's money) and eventually bestowed it upon his wife, after whom it was called "The Queen's House". When the king died in 1820, his son and successor, George IV, decided that, with a little work and a lot of money, a refurbished "King's House" (as it had been called since the Queen's death) would make the perfect permanent residence for the British monarch. Therefore, with Parliament's grudging approval (and an initial budget of £200,000), a rather elaborate rebuilding project was begun in 1826. By 1837, some £700,000 had been expended, both George IV and his successor William IV were dead and the place was still scarcely habitable. Nevertheless, the new Queen, Victoria, decided to make the rechristened Buckingham Palace her official London residence. Since Victoria's day, each of her successors has lived in "Buck House" (as the inner circle calls it), which, along with **Windsor Castle** (*JBB*) and the Palace of Holyrood House in Edinburgh, is one of the three Official Residences of the Sovereign. The present queen, Elizabeth II, ascended the throne in 1952 and it is in her name that the British government conducts all official business, hence the phrase "On Her Majesty's Service" (or, in MI6 parlance, "On Her Majesty's *Secret* Service", an amalgam of the traditional "OHMS" and the phrase "on secret service", applied to someone officially engaged in clandestine activity). Interestingly, Queen Elizabeth came to the throne just as James Bond himself first emerged from the typewriter of Ian Fleming (who would later name her as one of his personal heroes*). Half a century on, she remains the only sovereign the superspy has ever served. In Chapter 25 of *On Her Majesty's Secret Service*, Bond shudders to think how she would feel about the string of crimes he had just committed in her name. In Chapter 17 of *The Man with the Golden Gun*, he passes up a trip to Buckingham Palace to be knighted by the Queen, explaining to M that he is content to remain a "Scottish peasant". (A few years earlier, at the conclusion of the *Moonraker* affair, M himself had precluded Bond's trip to the Palace, reminding the PM that the Secret Service does not go in for such honors.) In the film *OHMSS*, Bond actually apologizes to the Queen's portrait prior to taking a drink on duty, even though he is about to resign from her Secret Service. Bond's enemies, on the other hand, have taken a far less respectful approach to the Queen. In the novel *Moonraker* (written in 1954), the vengeful Nazi Sir Hugo Drax aims his atomic weapon at London, specifically, at a small house within a hundred yards of Buckingham Palace (see **Hugo Drax's House** [25:2]). The idea of targeting the young Queen herself—who will be listening to **BBC** (12:5) coverage of the historic launch—makes him seem particularly abhorrent. Forty years later, with the Queen now a living institution, the plot was resurrected by the writers of *GoldenEye*. There, the traitorous Trevelyan intends to destroy London à la Drax in order to avenge an ancient wrong perpetrated against his family by the British government. His ironic comment as he contemplates the destruction: "God save the Queen". A lighter, but even more direct reference occurs in the finale of the film *Moonraker*, when the Mission Control Director tells the Minister of Defence that he will have the audio-visual feed from Bond and Holly's shuttle patched directly through to the White House and Buckingham Palace. "I'm sure Her Majesty will be fascinated," the Minister confidently replies. Indeed.

Station: Green Park (VI; PI; JU) Exit on the South Side, go R in Piccadilly, then R through the iron gates into Queen's Walk, which you will follow all the way to the Mall. Turn right into the Mall and look for the Palace straight ahead. The Changing of the Guard takes place at 11:30am daily from April 1 to August 7 (on alternate days from August 8 to March 31) when the Sovereign is in residence. (Be sure to stand outside the palace like one of the "middle-aged Americans with cameras" that Fleming describes in Chapter 2 of *Goldfinger*.) The State Rooms (including the Throne Room and the State Dining Room), Queen's Gallery and Royal Mews are open in August and September Mon-Fri 9:30am-5:30pm daily.

The royal standard, with the Queen's Coat of Arms, flies from the palace mast whenever the sovereign is in residence. In front of the palace is the impressive Queen Victoria Memorial, the "culmination" of Sir Aston Webb's triumphal processional route, otherwise known as the Mall (rhymes with *shall*). The white marble sculpture includes a 13-foot-high seated figure of Victoria herself, facing eastward down the Mall. It is this "great architectural and scenic change" (as Webb's project was dubbed) that Fleming evokes at the beginning of the climactic car chase in Chapter 19 of *Moonraker*. There, having just passed St James's Palace, Bond does "a racing change round the island in the Mall with Drax already passing the statue in front of the Palace." For more on the chase—and its dramatic outcome—see ***Moonraker* Car Chase Route** (*JBB*).

*In the Foreword to H. Montgomery Hyde's *Room 3603*, Fleming names the Queen, the Duke of Edinburgh, Winston Churchill and William Stephenson—wartime head of MI6's New York station—as among his "miscellaneous cohort of heroes".

Trivia Challenge 30: Who disparages the Cinematic Bond's reward of "a hearty 'Well done!' from Her Majesty the Queen and a pittance of a pension"?

17. ST PANCRAS

Rail transportation hub centered on St Pancras Station and the massive new British Library

17:1

St Pancras Station
Euston Road, NW1

Doubles as: Moskovsky Vokzal (Moscow Railway Station), St. Petersburg, Russia (interior) in *GoldenEye*

Constructed in the 1860s as the terminus of the Midland Railway, St Pancras Station is fronted by the former Midland Grand Hotel, a Victorian Gothic marvel designed by Sir George Gilbert Scott and now used for offices. The train shed itself is also considered a masterpiece of Victorian engineering: 689 feet in length, 245 feet in width (the widest span in the world until it was eclipsed by Jersey City's Pennsylvania Station in 1888) and standing 100 feet above the rails at its apex. The 25 main ribs comprising its massive vault weigh 55 tons each! Remember that the next time you watch *GoldenEye*, for it is here, on Platform 5 of the briefly-glimpsed St Pancras Station that Natalya Simonova emerges from the train and proceeds to the IBM computer store (itself a shop front built at the **ex Eon Studios** [*JBB*] in Leavesden, Hertfordshire).

Station: King's Cross St Pancras (CI; HC; ME; NO; PI; VI) Follow the signs from the Underground to the St Pancras railway station and look for Platform 5.

18. SMITHFIELD

Historic district on the fringe of the City, famous for its wholesale food market, churches and remnants of the Roman wall

18:1

The Priory Church of St Bartholomew the Great
West Smithfield, EC1

Founded as an Augustinian priory in 1123, St Bartholomew the Great was restored and rebuilt to its present form in the 1880s and '90s. It remains the only surviving large-scale Norman building in London, as well as the sole extant monastic church from the twelfth century. By virtue of its age, size and splendor, it serves as the senior parish church in the City. In September 1964, St Bartholomew also served as the venue for the memorial service to Ian Fleming, who had died the previous month in Canterbury and was buried in the cemetery of **St James's Church** (*JBB*), Sevenhampton, Wiltshire. Present were his widow, Ann, their 12-year-old son Caspar, Ian's brother Peter, who read the lesson, and their half-sister Amaryllis, who played a Bach saraband for cello. (The life of Amaryllis herself was commemorated here in November 1999.) Also present were Ian's former Naval Intelligence boss, John Godfrey, several distinguished writers and members of the nobility and, of course, William Plomer, Fleming's "gentle reader", who would remember his dear friend "on top of the world, with his foot on the accelerator". Film buffs may also recall St Bartholomew as the setting for the wedding that *didn't* take place in the Hugh Grant comedy *Four Weddings and a Funeral* and for a brief bit in *Robin Hood: Prince of Thieves*.

Station: Barbican (HC; CI; ME) Turn R (S) into Aldersgate, then immediately R into Long Lane. At West Smithfield turn L and look for the church on the L. Nearby, in Charterhouse Street, is the famous Smithfield Market, which Fleming mentions in the story "007 in New York".

19. SOHO

Multi-cultural entertainment hub renowned for its many theatres, cinemas, clubs and international restaurants

19:1

Piccadilly Circus
W1

The most famous intersection in England, Piccadilly Circus, i.e., Circle, is also the London equivalent of New York's Times Square. It is a garish explosion of neon signs, shops, restaurants, cars, crowds and tourist traps, one that apparently delighted both Fleming and Bond from their corner window table at **Scott's** (19:6). Thus, in Chapter 19 of *Moonraker*, Bond sits at his favorite restaurant table and watches "the people and the traffic in Piccadilly and down the Haymarket." As one of London's most famous landmarks, the circus is invoked by several non-British characters in the Bond saga, beginning with the obnoxious American millionaire Milton Krest in "The Hildebrand Rarity". Having introduced his English wife, Liz, to James Bond, the intellectually-challenged Krest is sure that the two Britons will want to swap stories about Piccadilly Circus and the "Dooks" they both know. Another American, Felix Leiter, invokes the circus in Chapter 12 of *Thunderball*, noting that Count Lippe's assault on Bond near **Regent's Park** (12:2) "[s]ounds more like The Loop around Chicago than a mile or so from Piccadilly." In the film *From Russia With Love*, starry-eyed Tatiana Romanova slips into a new negligée and proudly proclaims that she will wear "this one in Piccadilly". Bond informs her that she won't because they've just passed some new laws there. Still, with everything else going on in the circus, I wonder if anyone would even notice the sultry cipher clerk. And speaking of not noticing things, Bond himself evokes the bustling intersection in *The Man With The Golden Gun*, when he apologizes to Andrea Anders for being late. "Bangkok traffic is worse than Piccadilly," he continues, still not noticing that his newfound friend is just dead!

Station: Piccadilly Circus (BA; PI)

Trivia Challenge 31: According to Bond, in Chapter 8 of *OHMSS*, whose Coat of Arms "looks like a mixture between a jigsaw puzzle and Piccadilly Circus at night"?

19:2

Café Royal
68 Regent Street, W1

Founded at 15-17 Glasshouse Street in 1865, this fashionable French café-restaurant had expanded southward to Regent Street by 1870. It was the favorite haunt of a number of famous writers and artists, including Oscar Wilde, T.S. Eliot, James McNeill Whistler and Augustus John, as well as the future kings Edward VIII and George VI. It was also a favorite rendezvous of Ian Fleming, who entertained lady friends here during his pre-war bachelor days. Fleming's friend Aleister Crowley, the notorious "warlock" (see **Cavendish Hotel** [16:16]), is reputed to have once patronized the place in nothing but a cape. Years later, actor George Lazenby patronized the Café Royal wearing long hair and a beard, much to the chagrin of producers Cubby Broccoli and Harry Saltzman. The occasion was the London premiere of *OHMSS*, which took place at the **Odeon Cinema** (19:9) in Leicester Square on the evening of December 18, 1969. After the film, the cast and crew made the short trip to Regent Street, where the festivities were somewhat marred by the strain between Lazenby and the producers and the knowledge that this would be the actor's first and last Bond picture. Still, the setting itself proved popular among UA and Eon execs, and the post-premiere party for *Live and Let Die* (July 5, 1973) would be held here as well. The restaurant has since undergone major renovation and reconstruction, but the present incarnation still preserves something of the atmosphere of the old Café Royal.

Station: Piccadilly Circus (BA; PI) Take Exit 1 into Regent Street (East side) and look for the restaurant ahead—and around—on the R. Lunch and dinner are served Mon-Sat, with reservations recommended.

> **Trivia Challenge 32:** What are the connections between painter Augustus John and the Fleming family? (two possible points)

19:3

Lillywhite's Ltd
24-36 Regent Street, SW1

Britain's largest, most comprehensive sports department store was founded by cricketer James Lillywhite in 1863; it has been based in **Piccadilly Circus** (19:1) since 1925. Its six floors are crammed with over 70,000 different products, covering some 35 different sports, including snow skiing. It should come as no surprise, then, that Lillywhite's supplied the sensible, old-fashioned ski trousers that Bond wears during his visit to Piz Gloria in Chapter 11 of *On Her Majesty's Secret Service*. Nor should it come as any surprise that the firm also supplied the sensible cold weather outfits (coats, trousers and boots) worn by the *OHMSS* film crew on location in Switzerland. Lillywhite's did not, however, provide the stylish skiing outfits worn by the actors themselves. These, according to costume designer Marjory Cornelius, came from Ski Bogner of Munich, the firm founded by the father of Bond ski sequence cameraman Willy Bogner (and today run by Willy himself). The Bogner firm also provided the skiing outfits for *The Spy Who Loved Me* and *For Your Eyes Only* (note the "B" logo on Roger Moore's zipper).

Station: Piccadilly Circus (BA; PI) Take Exit 3 for Lower Regent Street; the store is adjacent to the tube station, on the E side of Lower Regent Street. **Hours:** Mon-Fri 9:30am-7pm; Sat 9:30pm-6pm; Sun 11am-5pm

19:4

Burberrys Ltd
18-22 Haymarket, SW1

Inspired by a conversation with a medical doctor, Surrey draper Thomas Burberry invented a new type of waterproof fabric in 1856. He called it "gabardine" (from an old name for a type of long outer garment) and began selling it in his Basingstoke shop. During World War I, Burberry, by now based in London, modified his popular raincoat for the use of officers in the trenches of France, thus giving rise to the enduring "trench coat". Today, with its trademark plaid lining of beige, cream and red, the practical, yet fashionable "Burberry" (as Edward VII dubbed the coat) remains a true status symbol. This fact was not lost on Ian Fleming, who favored the firm's dark blue belted raincoats for himself and, apparently, also for James Bond. The first reference (implied) to a Burberry occurs in Chapter 10 of *The Spy Who Loved Me*, when Vivienne Michel describes Bond's "uniform" as comprising just such a dark blue raincoat, as well as a "a soft black hat pulled rather far down." The second reference, in *The Man with the Golden Gun*, is explicit: at the direction of his (temporary) KGB superiors, a brainwashed Bond purchases a new raincoat from Burberry's in order to look the part of a high-living secret agent.

Station: Picadilly Circus (BA; PI) Take Exit 4 for the Haymarket and turn R. The shop is just down the Haymarket on the L. **Hours:** Mon-Sat 10am-6pm (thu until 7pm); Sun noon-6pm

> **Trivia Challenge 33:** In which film(s) does Bond carry a traditional Burberry into Miss Moneypenny's office?

19:5

ex London Pavilion Cinema
3 Piccadilly
Piccadilly Circus, W1

James Bond made his *official* big screen debut here at this prominent West End cinema, on Friday October 5, 1962. (The press showing had occurred the day before, with the first reviews appearing in the next morning's papers. A sneak preview was also held at the **Odeon Cinema** [9:5] in Kensington two months earlier.) Ian Fleming attended the World Premiere, as did the filmmakers, members of the cast and a number of international celebrities including J. Paul Getty and Anita Ekberg. The film was a critical—and, more importantly, financial—success, stunning **United Artists** (19:13) executives in America, who thought that *Dr. No* might well die a quiet death upon its release in the States. The next two films premiered at the nearby Leicester Square **Odeon** (19:9), but Bond was back at the Pavilion for the premiere of *Thunderball* on December 29, 1965. Attendees that night included Claudine Auger and Luciana Paluzzi, as well as Honor Blackman and Tania Mallet. Sean Connery, already weary of the Bond phenomenon, stayed home with the wife and kids (see [28:1]; for the premiere party, see **Royal Garden Hotel** [9:4]). Indeed, Bond was now so big that he required *two* simultaneous premieres, the other being held at the neighboring **Rialto Cinema** (19:8). This was to be the last Bond premiere for both cinemas, as all future films would open at the Leicester Square Odeon. Sadly, after 44 years in operation, the Pavilion's cinema closed its doors in 1978. Today, the upper floors of the London Pavilion are occupied by Madame Tussaud's Rock Museum.

Station: Piccadilly Circus (BA; PI) Exit for Shaftesbury Avenue to come up in front of the Pavilion.

19:6

ex Scott's Restaurant
18-20 Coventry Street, W1

Scott's was—and is—a rather elegant seafood restaurant, which, until 1966, was located in the very heart of the English capital, in what is today the Trocadero Centre. According to Chapter 19 of *Moonraker*, Bond's favorite restaurant table in London is the right-hand corner table for two on the first floor (US: second floor), where he could look out of the window and watch all the people that come and go in **Piccadilly** (19:1) and the Haymarket. In the original manuscript, Fleming actually mentions Scott's by name; in the novel itself, he does not. He *does*, however, mention Baker, the headwaiter, by name, in spite of—or perhaps because of—a rather amusing incident during the war. It seems that Commander Fleming of Naval Intelligence (see [27:10]) and another officer had taken two German POWs to Scott's in the hope of getting them drunk enough to reveal some very important secrets about German U-boats. In the end, the German officers revealed nothing. The headwaiter, however, did—to **Scotland Yard** (27:16). Having overheard Fleming's group speaking in German, in London, in the middle of the war, the patriotic Baker reasoned that something fishy was afoot. Eventually, a group of detectives, or "narks", as Ian called them, infiltrated the restaurant to observe the suspicious foursome for themselves. No arrests were made, but Admiral Godfrey, Fleming's NID superior, was informed of the incident and later gave his subordinate a good tongue-lashing. Nevertheless, Fleming continued to try to pump German POWs for information (see [16:18]), and also continued as a regular at Scott's for the rest of his life. He first mentions the restaurant by name in Chapter 3 of *Diamonds Are Forever*, wherein Bond invites his friend Bill Tanner, M's chief of staff, to a lunch of dressed crab and black velvet (stout and champagne) at Scott's. Another reference occurs in Chapter 3 of *You Only Live Twice*, when Bond makes plans to take Mary Goodnight to Scott's in order to celebrate his promotion and new assignment. Today, the closest a Bond fan can come to dining in Fleming and Bond's former hangout, at least geographically, is the **Planet Hollywood** (19:7) restaurant in the Trocadero Centre, just down the block. The current incarnation of Scott's itself may be found at 20 Mount Street, just down from The Connaught hotel, and it, too, has a Bondian connection: According to his *James Bond Diary*, newly-cast Roger Moore discussed the 007 role at Scott's Mount Street restaurant with director Guy Hamilton in August 1972.

Station: Piccadilly Circus (BA; PI) Exit on the Shaftesbury Avenue side and go E in Coventry Street toward the Haymarket. Look for the massive Trocadero Centre just ahead on the L; Scott's was in the western corner. If you want to check out the location of the famous table, take the escalator up to the first floor (US: second floor) and turn L into "Funland". Walk straight ahead, all the way to the end of the arcade, and then turn to the L. You are now facing the corner immortalized by Bond and his creator.

19:7

Planet Hollywood
13 Coventry Street
Piccadilly Circus, W1

The restaurant chain founded by Hollywood action stars Stallone, Schwarzenegger and Willis is not shy about acknowledging the legacy of the *original* action-adventure hero. The London incarnation boasts an extensive collection of Bond props and models, including a full scale replica of "Little Nellie", built by Wing Commander Ken

Wallis himself, a model of a SPECTRE helicopter, also from *You Only Live Twice*, the Snooper from *A View To A Kill*, the ATAC from *For Your Eyes Only*, assorted smaller props and outfits from various films, and a decidedly odd-looking gun also said to have been used in *You Only Live Twice*.

Station: Piccadilly Circus (BA; PI) Exit on the Shaftesbury Avenue side and look for the big building ahead on the L. **Meals served:** Mon-Sun 11:30am-1am.

Planet Hollywood's Little Nellie.

19:8

ex Rialto Cinema
3-4 Coventry Street, W1

Bond mania reached its height with the "dual premiere" of *Thunderball* on December 29, 1965. That night, thousands of fans packed **Piccadilly Circus** (19:1) and Coventry Street hoping for a glimpse of the stars in attendance at the **Pavilion** (19:5) and Rialto, respectively. Guests at the latter included villains Adolfo Celi and Guy Doleman (Count Lippe), and "Bond Girls" Molly Peters and Martine Beswick. This was the only brush with Bondage for the Rialto, as every subsequent premiere would be held at the nearby **Odeon Cinema** (19:9) in Leicester Square. Today, the former cinema is occupied by the tony Fashion Café.

Station: Piccadilly Circus (BA; PI) Exit on the Shaftesbury Avenue side and go E in Coventry, past the Trocadero. The ex Rialto is just ahead on the L.

19:9

Odeon Cinema
22-24 Leicester Square, WC2

The London premieres of every Bond film save *Dr. No* and *Thunderball* have been held at the prestigious Leicester Square Odeon, the largest cinema in town. Indeed, Bond mania really began in earnest here, at the World Premiere of *Goldfinger*, on September 17, 1964. That night, barely a month after the death of Ian Fleming, 5,000 fans crowded into Leicester Square, hoping for a chance to see the living incarnation of the author's creation. Unfortunately, Sean Connery, already uneasy about his bondage to the role, was in North Africa shooting *The Hill*. Still, the crowd got to ogle Pussy Galore herself, as well as other members of the cast and production company. Since the Connery days, Messrs. Lazenby, Moore, Dalton and Brosnan have attended their respective premieres here, often in the presence of royalty. (Indeed, all five '80s premieres were attended by the Prince and Princess of Wales.) The Art Deco style cinema celebrated its 60th anniversary in 1997 and underwent extensive renovation in 1998. Fortunately, the distinctive exterior, with its *moderne* black tower, still looks much as it did in the sensational '60s.

Station: Leicester Square (NO; PI) Take the Charing Cross Road (West) exit for Leicester Square. Turn L into the Square and look for the cinema on the L.

Trivia Challenge 34: What important Bond-related event took place here on November 17, 1996?

19:10

ex Office of Eon Productions Ltd (2)
38 Soho Square, W1

Prior to the formation of **Eon Productions** (13:31) in 1961, producer Cubby Broccoli had been partnered with Irving Allen in a company called Warwick Film Productions Ltd. The Warwick offices were located at 3 Audley Square, with a dubbing theatre and other production facilities here in Soho Square. When Broccoli teamed up with Harry Saltzman to produce the Bond films, his new company, Eon Productions, rented space in both Warwick facilities. The producers themselves were based in the Mayfair building, while the company's "registered office", or official address, was here in Soho Square. Thus, the very first screenplay commissioned by Eon, Richard Maibaum's August 1961 draft of *Thunderball*, bears the Warwick address of 38 Soho Square. The company retained its third-floor (US: fourth-floor) offices here through the production of the second Bond film, *From Russia With Love*, in 1963. At that time, Eon moved to 27 Hill Street in Mayfair, just around the corner from Audley Square. For more of the Eon story, see the Mayfair entries (13:31-36).

Station: Tottenham Court Road (CE; NO Take Exit 1 L into Oxford Street. At Soho Street turn L and continue into Soho Square. No. 38 is around to the R, on the W side of the square.

19:11

ex Shenval Press Ltd
58 Frith Street, W1

Shenval Press was for some years the printer and distributor of the *Book Collector*, a highbrow journal catering to the serious bibliophile. From 1955 to 1964, the owner of the *Book Collector* was none other than Ian Fleming, ably supported by his friends and fellow enthusiasts Percy Muir and John Hayward (see **ex Dulau's** [13:21] and **ex Elkin Matthews** [13:7] for more on Fleming and Muir). The venture actually began in 1952, when, at Ian's urging, his *Sunday Times*' boss, Lord Kemsley, resurrected a prestigious but moribund publication called the *Book Handbook*, which he had acquired some years before. Kemsley eventually tired of the magazine, which cost £1,000 an issue to produce and seemed unlikely to ever turn a profit. He first sought to unload the publication, then, having failed in this, to shut it down completely. Fleming, already serving on the editorial board of the rechristened *Book Collector*, offered the publisher £50 to take it off his hands. Kemsley agreed and thus Ian, to his great delight, became both an author *and* a publisher. Muir and Hayward, the other two members of the board, drummed up financial support from their wealthy friends, and the *Book Collector* entered perhaps the most interesting phase of its existence, coming under the personal direction of James Bond's creator. For budgetary reasons, the trio never opened a permanent office: John Hayward did most of the editorial work from his home at 19 Carlyle Mansions (in Fleming's old building [4:8]), while business matters were handled here at the printer itself. Nevertheless, as biographer Andrew Lycett notes, the *Book Collector*, under Fleming, "developed into the most authoritative publication in its field in the world." Under the stewardship of Mr. Nicholas Barker and Mrs. Pat Cooper, it remains so to this day. See also **ex Queen Anne Press Ltd** (3:2) for more of Fleming's life as a publisher.

Station: Tottenham Court Road (CE; NO) Take Exit 1 L into Oxford Street. At Soho Street turn L, continue into Soho Square, veer around to the R, and then at the bottom of the square, continue into Frith Street.

19:12

Quo Vadis
26-29 Dean Street, W1

Established by P. G. Leoni in 1926, this Gallic brasserie was one of Ian Fleming's favorite restaurants (see the Index for the complete list). Famous for its fine French cuisine, Quo Vadis, or at least the building it occupies, can also boast another famous literary connection. For it was here, in two small rooms at No. 28, that Karl Marx lived with his wife and young children from 1851 to 1856.

Station: Tottenham Court Road (CE; NO) Take Exit 1 L into Oxford Street. Dean Street is ahead to the L, just past Soho Street. The restaurant will be on the L. **Hours:** Mon-Fri noon-2:30pm and 6-11:15pm; Sat 6-11:15pm; Sun 6-10:15pm

19:13

ex Office of United Artists Corporation Ltd
Film House
142-150 Wardour Street, W1

Founded by legendary Hollywood film artists Charles Chaplin, D. W. Griffith, Mary Pickford and her husband Douglas Fairbanks in 1919, United Artists successfully distributed quality independent films for nearly thirty years. Its fortunes declined rapidly after World War II, however, and the company found itself on the verge of bankruptcy by 1951. To the rescue came New York lawyers Arthur B. Krim and Robert S. Benjamin, who began to *finance* independent productions, in addition to distributing them. With no permanent studio (and therefore none of the overhead that plagued the big film companies), the new UA could devote the bulk of its resources to the films themselves, films over which the producers, not the UA backers, exercised creative control. As a result, United Artists' pictures not only tended to give the audience, as well as the company, the most bang for the buck, but also to rack up an impressive number of critical hosannas and Academy Awards. (Its pictures won in 12 out of 19 categories in 1959 alone.) Indeed, during the first decade under Krim and Benjamin, UA released dozens of films now regarded as classics, including *The African Queen, High Noon, Marty, Around the World in 80 Days, Twelve Angry Men, The Defiant Ones, Paths of Glory, Some Like It Hot, The Apartment, Inherit the Wind, Judgment at Nuremberg* and *West Side Story*. By this time, 1961, UA had opened its European production headquarters here in Wardour Street, the center of the British film industry since the 1930s. Heading the office was George H. "Bud" Ornstein, who would later be joined by David Picker, nephew of one of UA's New York bosses. In June 1961, Ornstein met with British-based American producer Albert R. Broccoli, who, in partnership with Harry Saltzman, had taken an option on Ian Fleming's James Bond novels (see **ex Eon Productions Ltd [1]** [13:31]). The producers needed to secure financing for their first film and Broccoli believed that he would at least get a polite hearing from his old friend Arthur Krim. Obtaining Ornstein's blessing here in London, the producers immediately flew to New York for a meeting with Krim, Benjamin and Picker at UA's Seventh Avenue headquarters. On June 21, 1961, Broccoli and Saltzman struck the now-legendary deal for the production of the first James Bond film: UA would put up 100% of the financing, pegged at just under $1 million, of which $100,000 would go to Ian Fleming, $80,000 for the producers' fee, $40,000 for the director, $40,000 for the screenplay and $140,000 for the cast, including the yet-to-be-chosen star. Fleming would also receive 2° % of the profits off the top, after which the producers and UA would split the remainder on a 50-50 basis.* (UA subsequently increased the producers' take to 75% of the profits.) Neither UA nor, one suspects, the canny producers really had any idea that they were about to launch one of the most important cinematic phenomena of all time. Indeed, Saltzman later recalled that upon first screening *Dr. No*, one of the UA execs groused, "Well, all we can lose is $950,000, Harry." Of course, *Dr. No* not only recouped its costs (in London alone!), but went on to become a certified blockbuster all over the world. And so it goes, after nearly 40 years.... In April 1967, UA was purchased by San Francisco-based insurance giant Transamerica Corporation, a match-up that seemed sensible at the time but which later proved a serious mistake. In December 1975, UA paid $36 million for producer Harry Saltzman's half of Danjaq, S.A, the Swiss-based company which owned Eon Productions (see [13:33]). UA was now technically the co-producer of the Bond films, although Cubby Broccoli would, in fact, go on to function as the sole *creative* producer. During the Transamerica years, UA scored a number of non-Bond successes, including the *Pink Panther* and *Rocky* series, as well as such box-office and critical triumphs as *One Flew Over the Cuckoo's Nest* and *Annie Hall*. However, after chafing inside the TA conglomerate for more than a decade, the visionary management team of Krim and Benjamin decided they had had enough. On January 13, 1978, the pair left United Artists to form their own production company, Orion Pictures, taking several other top UA execs with them. TA shrugged the whole thing off, replaced the irreplaceable Krim and Benjamin and then immediately embarked upon the *Heaven's Gate* project, one of the costliest fiascos in Hollywood history. In May 1981, Transamerica sold its former corporate jewel to Metro-Goldwyn-Mayer, perhaps the most famous film production company in the world. In 1983, MGM reconstituted itself as a new corporate entity, MGM/UA Entertainment Company, under whose banner the film *Octopussy* was released. Years of disintegration and reintegration followed, as first one tycoon, then another bought and sold portions of the legendary company. By the late 1990s, United Artists was again operating as a subsidiary of MGM, financing the Bond pictures (through *The World Is Not Enough*) and distributing them in the United States and Canada. In the rest of the world, the films were released through United International Pictures, a company formed through the merger of UA's old London arm with Cinema International Corporation, a Paramount-Universal overseas distribution partnership. In June 1999, MGM announced that United Artists would no longer finance and distribute the Bond films. Rather, MGM itself would now take on those jobs, which is why *its* famous logo, and not UA's, appears at the start of *The World Is Not Enough*. In November 2000, Fox Filmed Entertainment replaced UIP as MGM's international distributor.

Station: Piccadilly Circus (BA; PI) Exit for Shaftesbury Avenue, turn L at the top of the stairs then R into Shaftesbury Avenue and follow this to Wardour Street, where you will turn L. No. 142 is ahead on the right.

*Fleming biographers Pearson and Lycett state that Fleming received 5% of the *producers' profits*. However, author Tino Balio, who examined United Artists' records, claims that Fleming's percentage came off the top, meaning that both UA and Eon absorbed the cost. Since UA and Eon split the profits on a 50-50 basis, Fleming's cut would have been the same in either case.

Quick One...

ex 400 Club
28 Leicester Square, WC2

Derek Mallaby genuinely impresses young Vivienne Michel when he takes her to London's top nightclub in Chapter 2 of *The Spy Who Loved Me*. Prior to this, the best Viv had managed was the cellar clubs in Chelsea. As

Fleming suggests, the 400 was indeed the "in" place to be and be seen: no less a personage than HRH Princess Margaret frequented the club in the late 1940s and early 1950s. Today, the site is occupied by the Moon Under Water pub. **Station: Leicester Square (NO; PI)**

20. SOUTH BANK

Thames-side commercial and cultural area distinguished by its up-market museums and theatres

20:1

James Bond "Big Ben" Photo Site Westminster Bridge, SE1

George Lazenby posed here, pistol in hand, for a famous series of publicity shots from *On Her Majesty's Secret Service*. The best time to take photographs here, assuming it's a sunny day, is morning, since the view is almost directly due west.

Station: Westminster (CI; DI; JU) Exit for Westminster Bridge, cross the bridge, and just as you reach the other side of the river, look for steps off to the right side, leading down to the Albert Embankment river walk. Lazenby posed on the L side of the lamppost at the base of the steps. Climb up on, nonchalantly lean against the lamppost and revel in the fact that you are literally standing in the footsteps of James Bond. Well, near enough...

21. SOUTH KENSINGTON

Southwest residential area also noted for its many museums

21:1

Christie's South Kensington 85 Old Brompton Road, SW7

Founded by James Christie in 1766, this celebrated firm of fine art auctioneers is actually based at No. 8 King Street, St James's (next to **Spink and Son** [16:9]). Those premises are famous for such record-breaking sales as Van Gogh's *Sunflowers* for £24.75 million in 1987 and the same artist's *Portrait of Dr Gachet* for £49.1 million three years later. The South Kensington branch, in contrast, handles a less pricey range of paintings, ceramics, books, jewelry, toys, collectibles and pop memorabilia. It was thus considered the perfect venue for one of the largest sales of James Bond-related items in history. On September 17, 1998, nearly 300 lots of Bond memorabilia were sold for a half million pounds (approximately $835,000), some two and a half times more than had been predicted. Among the items for sale: Roger Moore's customized Rolex watch from *Live and Let Die*; a prop tarantula from *Dr. No*; a Lotus Esprit "shell" from *The Spy Who Loved Me*; and, most memorably—if CNN's coverage is any clue—Oddjob's steel-rimmed bowler from *Goldfinger*. It fetched the seller, Graham Rye, President of the James Bond International Fan Club, a whopping £61,750—over $100,000! The hat, actually one of three used in the film (see **James Lock & Co.** [16:8]), was purchased by none other than Bond producer Michael Wilson for the Eon Archives. On February 14, 2001, Christie's followed up with another high-profile Bond auction, this one featuring one of the DB5s from *GoldenEye*, a Walther P99 from *Tomorrow Never Dies* and Ursula Andress's bikini from *Dr. No*. The latter sold for £35,000 ($52,000) to Planet Hollywood co-founder Robert Earl, who described it as "the most important piece of memorabilia ever sold at auction." Indeed....

Station: South Kensington (CI; DI: PI) Exit into Old

Brompton Road and go W; Christie's is just ahead on the L.

21:2

Natural History Museum Cromwell Road, SW7

Opened in 1881, this magnificent twin-towered, terracotta-and-slate-blue "Romanesque cathedral" was created by architect Alfred Waterhouse to house the **British Museum**'s (3:5) burgeoning Natural History Collection. The museum also functions as a library and research institute, a fact that James Bond exploits in Chapter 16 of *Live and Let Die*. There, in preparation for his assault on Mr Big's Caribbean lair, 007 asks Lieutenant-Commander Strangways to have London obtain diving equipment from the **Admiralty** (27:10) and "[a]ll the dope they can get from the Natural History Museum on barracuda and shark."

Station: South Kensington (CI; DI: PI) Follow the signs to the Museum. **Hours:** Mon-Sat 10am-5:50pm; Sun 11am-5:50pm

21:3

Victoria and Albert Museum Cromwell Road, SW7

Founded on this site in 1857, the South Kensington Museum quickly became the repository for a hodgepodge collection of masterpieces from all countries, styles and periods. Queen Victoria laid the cornerstone of the present building in 1899, directing that it be renamed after herself and her late husband Albert (see also **Royal Albert Hall** [21:5]). Today, with its grand Cromwell Road façade by Sir Aston Webb, the Victoria and Albert Museum houses the largest and finest collection of decorative art in the world. Fleming mentions the V & A, as it is popularly abbreviated, in the short story "The Property of a Lady", telling us that the museum will probably bid against Kenneth Snowman of **Wartski** (13:16) for the valuable Fabergé globe at the **Sotheby's** (13:11) auction.

Station: South Kensington (CI; DI; PI) Follow the signs to the Victoria and Albert Museum. **Hours:** Mon noon-5:50pm; Tue-Sun 10am-5:50pm

21:4

Royal Geographical Society 1 Kensington Gore, SW7

Stockbroker Ian Fleming began attending lectures here in 1939, his brother Peter, already a successful travel writer and explorer, having become a Fellow some years earlier. Ian's attendance was presumably motivated by a belief that the better informed he was about the world the better chance he stood of obtaining some kind of Intelligence job during the war that was sure to come. After the war, during which he served with distinction in the Naval Intelligence Division of the **Admiralty** (27:10), Fleming actually applied to become a Fellow of the Society and did so on May 27, 1946, the day before his 38th birthday.

Station: South Kensington (CI; DI; PI) Exit into Exhibition Road and follow this to Kensington Gore; the building is on the L.

21:5

Royal Albert Hall Kensington Gore, SW7

The largest concert hall in London—with some 8,000 seats—was completed in 1871 and named for Queen Victoria's late and much lamented Consort, Prince Albert. According to *Moonraker*, Sir Hugo Drax staged a Coronation Ball for Nurses here at the Albert Hall in 1953, just one more way to feign patriotism and get his name in the newspapers. According to the shooting script for *The Living Daylights*, Kara Milovy's triumphant westbloc début takes place in the Royal Albert Hall, with Prince Charles and Princess Diana in attendance. Thus, for such an important occasion, M, General Gogol and Felix Leiter are all on hand to explain that Bond is away "on an important case". In the film itself, however, the scene has been shifted to a much smaller Viennese venue (note the German signs on the doors), which makes you wonder why the hell M was schmoozing with a Czech cellist in Austria, and one whom he had chastised Bond for not killing, at that!

Station: South Kensington (CI; DI; PI) Follow the signs to the Royal Albert Hall, which will lead you into Exhibition Road. Follow this to Prince Consort Road, where you will turn L then R into the curved Albert Court.

21:6

Royal College of Art
Kensington Gore, SW7

Founded in 1837, the RCA moved to its present location in 1962. The only wholly postgraduate university of art design in the world, it is also the only art college, Royal or otherwise, to have had Ian Fleming as one of its governors. Fleming had actually attended **Eton** (*JBB*) with Robin Darwin, the Principal (or Head) of the college. In September of 1955, Darwin arranged for his old friend to be elected to the school's governing council, a flattering gesture which Fleming happily embraced. Six years later, the author sought to return the favor, inviting Darwin to publish "The Living Daylights", a short Bond adventure that Fleming had just completed. Originally intended for the debut issue of *The Sunday Times* color magazine, "Daylights" or, rather, artist Graham Sutherland's painting of an arrow-pierced heart that was to accompany it, was proving a bit too technically daunting for the printers. (Or, as Andrew Lycett reports, the paper simply didn't like the artist's work.) Fleming, in a letter dated November 21, 1961, therefore suggested that Darwin, through his new Lion and Unicorn Press, might be better able to render both the story and the cover painting, which would be donated free of charge to the College. (Fleming promised that Sutherland would agree to this—and he did.) Now according to its 1955 Prospectus, one of the RCA's stated "Objects" (Number 7, ironically) was that "[i]t may publish and sell books, pamphlets, magazines or other literature whose sole or main purpose is to further the educational or research work of the College." Precisely how a James Bond story would accomplish either of those goals is unclear, but, in any case, Fleming offered 007 to Darwin. He further suggested that the two of them should meet for lunch in the school's common room, where Darwin could appraise both the painting and the story for himself. Darwin, an acknowledged Bond fan, was only too happy to see Fleming, and the materials. Unfortunately, he concluded that the 8,000-word story was simply too short to justify its printing as a book, not to mention the expense of reproducing the cover painting. As a result, "The Living Daylights" debuted, as originally planned, in the inaugural issue of *The Sunday Times* magazine, in February 1962. This, of course, infuriated the management of the *Daily Express*, which held what it assumed were the exclusive serialization rights to James Bond's adventures. For more on *that* story, see the **ex *Daily Express*** (5:4).

Station: South Kensington (CI; DI; PI) Follow the signs to the Royal Albert Hall, which will lead you into Exhibition Road. Follow this to Prince Consort Road, where you will turn L then R into the curved Albert Court. The College is to the left (west) of Albert Hall, in Kensington Gore. For the location in the 1950s, follow the signs to the V & A. From the corner of Cromwell Road and Exhibition Road, walk N in the latter and look for the archway on the R, at the end of the museum's Henry Cole Wing. This leads straight back to the former RCA building.

22. SOUTH LAMBETH

Downmarket residential area, somewhat rehabilitated in recent years

22:1

Roger Moore's Childhood Homes
4 Aldebert Terrace; 16 Albert Square, SW8

Roger George Moore was born at the Annie McCall maternity hospital in Jeffreys Road on 14 October 1927. His parents George and Lily lived one half mile away in the three rented rooms which formed the first floor (US: second floor) of 4 Aldebert Terrace. Young Roger spent a fairly happy childhood here until the threat of German bombs forced his evacuation to Northern England in 1939. In 1943, the family moved to a larger flat around the corner, at 16 Albert Square. For more on Roger's early life, see **RADA** (3:8).

Station: Stockwell (NO, VI) Walk N in Lambeth Road and then turn R into Aldelbert Terrace. No. 4 is ahead on the L. Albert Square is just past this, to the L.

> **Trivia Challenge 35:** Which Bond Girl appeared in three episodes of Moore's *The Saint* television series?

23. STRAND

Thames-side commercial and theatre district linking the western areas to the City

23:1

Hungerford Bridge
WC2, SE1

Completed in 1864 (and subsequently described as "the

ugliest thing seen on the Thames"), this wrought-iron lattice girder structure is the only central London bridge to combine train and pedestrian crossings. The Hungerford, also known as the Charing Cross Railway Bridge, marks the turning point of the **Thames** (24:1) (see **Charing Cross Station** [23:10]), and may be spotted as the top-most of the three bridges in the magnificent aerial shot near the beginning of the *TWINE* boat chase. It also marks the spot where Cigar Girl swerves to cut off Bond, splashes him and ends up crashing into **Waterloo Pier** (23:4), which is in fact located next to **Waterloo Bridge** (23:3), not Hungerford Bridge. This sequence occurs immediately after the pair pass beneath **Westminster Bridge** (27:19), which is, in fact, more than a quarter of a mile upriver. Those boats really do travel fast! See the next entry for the "missing" *Queen Mary* footage, which would have "linked" the bits at Hungerford and Waterloo Bridges.

Station: Embankment (BA; CI; DI; NO) Follow the signs to the South Bank Arts Centre, which is reached via the bridge. Walk out to the middle of the bridge for spectacular views up and down the Thames.

23:2

TS Queen Mary
Waterloo Pier
Victoria Embankment, WC2

Commissioned as a Scottish pleasure steamer in 1933, TS *Queen Mary* was converted to a restaurant and conference center in the 1980s. The ship, along with a number of other Thames-side landmarks, was to have been featured in the pre-credit sequence of *The World Is Not Enough*. Specifically, after being cut off by Cigar Girl at **Hungerford Bridge** (23:1), Bond was to have maneuvered the tiny Q Boat past Cleopatra's Needle and then through the narrow gap between the *Queen Mary* and Victoria Embankment, emerging unscathed on the other side of **Waterloo Bridge** (23:3). Though actually staged and filmed, this sequence was ultimately cut for time. Thus, in the finished film, the action skips immediately from the Hungerford to the **Waterloo Pier** (23:4) bit. However, if you look closely, you can spot the *Queen Mary* in the background, under Waterloo Bridge, as Cigar Girl smashes into the pier.

Station: Embankment (BA; CI; DI; NO) Exit to the Embankment and follow the signs to the Needle, which is just downriver from the station, and look for the restaurant just ahead.

Below (main photo): The Q boat races towards the gap between the Embankment and Queen Mary, in a sequence cut from the finished film. *Inset:* The false section built on to Waterloo Pier awaits destruction!

23:3

Waterloo Bridge
WC2, SE1

Waterloo Bridge is a great place from which to view the heart of London, with the **Houses of Parliament** (27:18) just upriver, and the City just downriver. It is also a good place from which to survey both the **TS *Queen Mary*** (23:2) and **Waterloo Pier** (23:4), two locales featured in the *TWINE* pre-credit boat chase. Waterloo Bridge itself provides a nice punctuation mark for the scene, as Cigar Girl smashes through the nearby floating shelter (see the next entry) with one of the bridge's massive piers in the background. The high angle shot of the boats continuing downriver was taken from the bridge itself.

Station: Embankment (BA; CI; DI; NO) Exit to the Embankment and follow the signs to the Needle, which is just upriver from the bridge and Waterloo Pier.

23:4

Waterloo Pier
Victoria Embankment, WC2

Until November 1998, this was one of only two floating police stations in the world, the other being in Hong Kong. Waterloo Pier now serves as a mooring point and rest stop for the patrol craft of the Thames Division of the **Metropolitan Police Service** (27:16), whose headquarters is in Wapping High Street (see [52:1]). In April 1999, the Met kindly obliged when the makers of *The World Is Not Enough* wanted to destroy the pier for the film's pre-credit boat chase. In fact, what Cigar Girl's Sunseeker smashed through was a small, breakaway "shelter" that the filmmakers added just for the occasion. To ensure that the wood, glass and polystyrene building disintegrated on cue, small explosive charges were placed beneath the windows and detonated at the moment of the boat's impact. Supervising art director Neil Lamont explained that the original choice for this stunt was Charing Cross Pier, just upriver. However, when he and location manager Richard Sharkey went there on a recce, they happened to spot the ***Queen Mary*** (23:2) and Waterloo Pier just downriver, and decided that the juxtaposition of the ship, bridge and pier might make for a more interesting set-up. Second-unit director Vic Armstrong agreed and the stunt was subsequently staged at the new location. Unfortunately, as noted in previous entries, much of this sequence ended up on the cutting room floor. Also shot here at the Waterloo Pier location was *The Golden Salamander* tourist boat, which pulled away just as Cigar Girl smashed into the pier. This bit, too, was deleted. However, for your reference, the boat is a private charter operated by Livett's Launches Ltd, HMS *Belfast*. It is based at Charing Cross Pier, beneath **Hungerford Bridge** (23:1), and operates every day, year-round, cruising from Putney in the west to the **Millennium Dome** (35:1) in the east. A three-hour cruise during the week will run you £585 ($936); a four-hour cruise on the weekend £840 ($1,344).

Station: Embankment (BA; CI; DI; NO) Exit to the Embankment and follow the signs to the Needle, which is just upriver from the bridge and Waterloo Pier. From Waterloo Pier, the boat chase action switches to **Tower Bridge** (5:18), thereby skipping the entire King's Reach stretch of the **Thames** (24:1).

23:5

Somerset House
Strand, WC2

Doubles as: Unnamed square, St. Petersburg, Russia (exterior) in *GoldenEye*; the Ministry of Defence, London (exterior) in *Tomorrow Never Dies*

A neoclassical structure intended to rival the great public buildings of other European capitals, Somerset House was the first large-scale structure in London specifically designed to house government offices. The Board of Inland Revenue (equivalent to the American IRS) moved into the complex in 1789 and has remained there, more or less continuously, ever since. *GoldenEye*'s view of the complex comes during the scene in which Jack Wade works on the engine of his vintage Moskvich, with Bond's able assistance, of course. In *TND*, we first see Bond turning into Somerset House from the Strand and then driving the DB5 back into the courtyard. Production designer Allan Cameron explained that the filmmakers were not allowed inside the actual MOD and that Somerset House gave the director exactly what he was looking for. "Roger [Spottiswoode] wanted the sweep of the Strand and the DB5 coming into this grand building and that's what we got," Cameron recalled. Indeed, part of that very scenic sweep includes the elegant little Italianate church St Mary-le-Strand, which was completed in 1718 and which, with the widening of the Strand in 1910, became "St Mary-le-Stranded"! (*see photo overleaf*).

Station: Temple (CI; DI) Go L in Temple Place, R into Surrey Street, then L into the Strand. The complex is ahead on the L. If you continue on to the intersection you can turn around and look back toward the nondescript entrance through which Bond drives the DB5 in the film. Follow his route inside the complex for the impressive view of the Inland Revenue Offices, er, the Ministry of Defence. Two years earlier, "Jimbo" handed Jack Wade the hammer ("No, the bigger one. The sledge.") in the NW corner of the courtyard, to the R of the entrance.

Eyes Only, 007: From 1836 to 1973, Somerset House also contained the offices of the General Register of Births, Deaths, and Marriages, for which reason both Griffon Or and Sable Basilisk mention searching it for family records in Chapters 6 and 7, respectively, of *On Her Majesty's Secret Service*.

Somerset House.

23:6

Bush House
Aldwych, WC2

Developed by American businessman Irving T. Bush as a vast trade center, Bush House is today famous as the HQ of the BBC's External Radio Services. (For more on the "Beeb", see [12:5].) During WWII, the government's new Political Warfare Executive, a spin-off of **SOE** (12:8), ran its propaganda operation from here. PWE worked in conjunction with the BBC to influence opinion against the Germans in occupied countries, as well as to influence German opinion against the Nazis themselves. In 1941, PWE tapped Commander Ian Fleming of Naval Intelligence, a fluent German speaker, to broadcast "white propaganda" from Bush House as part of the BBC's German Service. (So-called "white propaganda" is fact-based information, distorted to favor those reporting it; "black propaganda", usually done clandestinely so that governments can disavow it, relies upon deception and outright lies. The latter operation was run out of Woburn Abbey, Bedfordshire, by Fleming's friend Sefton Delmer of the ***Daily Express*** [5:4].) Fleming was apparently fascinated by propaganda and deception and so delighted in reporting of the German Navy "that all their U-boats leak". (Rather more "gray", than "white", eh?) Also based here, from 1936 to 1939, was the "Z Organisation", a semiautonomous, ultra-secret branch of **MI6** (27:22), run by the legendary—and controversial—Colonel Claude E. M. Dansey, then the No. 2 man in the Secret Service. Z's headquarters was on the eighth floor of the north-west wing; its cover was the export branch of an actual diamond company owned by Dansey's millionaire friends (and financial backers), Solomon and Jack Joel, on the floor below. Fleming apparently had no official involvement with Z, although he certainly knew Dansey from **Boodle's** (16:4) and through at least one friend, Conrad O'Brien-ffrench, who was one of Dansey's agents. In that Z used a commercial cover, in contrast to the vaguely diplomatic Passport Control Offices employed by MI6 (see [27:14]), the organization more closely resembled the fictional Secret Service Fleming would later create. (The Joel Brothers themselves, who, apart from diamonds, were famous for their successful racehorses, bear at least a passing resemblance to the Spang brothers of *Diamonds Are Forever*). Fleming would also commemorate the founder of Z himself in Chapter 15 of *From Russia, With Love*, where we learn that "Major Dansey" preceded Darko Kerim as Head of Station T. (Ironically, one of the real Heads of T during the early post-war period was Soviet spy Kim Philby, who is discussed under the **University of Cambridge** [*JBB*].) Finally, in the film *Thunderball*, Bond and his Nassau crew listen to BBC Radio's foreign service to learn that Big Ben did indeed strike seven times at six o'clock, just as SPECTRE had directed. That broadcast would have emanated from Bush House.

Station: Temple (CI; DI) Exit the station and take the steps up to Arundel Street. Walk N in Arundel Street and then cross the Strand. On the other side of the street, veer to the L into the Aldwych and look for the large building complex to the L.

23:7

ex HQ of the Air Ministry
Adastral House
Kingsway, WC2

The Air Ministry was created in January 1918 to administer the Royal Air Force, a brand new military service formed from the merger of the Army's Royal Flying Corps and the Navy's Royal Naval Air Service. A counterpart to the **Admiralty** (27:10) and **War Office** (27:6) departments in Whitehall, the Air Ministry took up residence here in Kingsway in 1919, where it would remain until 1955. Fleming mentions the Air Ministry a number of times in the novel *Moonraker*, which was written and set in 1954. He tells us that the department supplied both weather reports to Hugo Drax and Intelligence to Special Branch Agent Gala Brand (see **Scotland Yard** [27:16]). The Air Ministry also provided the RAF service personnel who guard the exterior of Drax's Kingsdown base (see **Drax's Plant** [*JBB*]), as well as the men who supervise the fueling of the rocket and take charge of the firing point on the day of the historic launch. In 1955, the year of the novel's publication, the Air Ministry moved from Kingsway to a new Adastral House in Theobald's Road, WC1. Meanwhile, the Secretary of State for Air himself had relocated to the Board of Trade building in Whitehall. Thus, when Fleming sets part of the action of *James Bond of the Secret Service* (see Appendix Two) in the Operations Room of "the Air Ministry in Whitehall", the reference is to the Board of Trade building. Fleming also mentions the ministry in Chapter 9 of *Thunderball*, when Petacchi wonders how long it will take for them to learn of the missing bomber he has just hijacked. In 1964, three years after the publication of *Thunderball*, the Air Ministry, the Admiralty and the War Office were absorbed by the new **Ministry of Defence** (27:7), which would be headquartered in the Board of Trade building.

Station: Temple (CI; DI) Exit the station and take the steps up to Arundel Street. Walk N in Arundel Street and then cross the Strand. On the other side of the street, veer to the L into the Aldwych and look for the large building at the corner of Kingsway, opposite the BBC.

23:8

The Savoy
Strand, WC2 (at Savoy Court)

The luxurious Savoy hotel was built as an annex to the Savoy Theatre in 1889. Renowned for both its American Bar (where the world's first martini is said to have been mixed in 1910) and the Grill Room restaurant (long a favorite of parliament members), the Savoy remains one of the grandest and most expensive hotels in London. Indeed, it's just the kind of place you'd expect to find Ian Fleming, who listed the Grill Room as one of his 12 favorite restaurants (see the Index). In fact, during the pre-production phase of *Dr. No*, Fleming invited Sean Connery to lunch here at the Savoy, where Janet, Marchioness of Milford Haven (a cousin of Fleming's friend Ivar Bryce), gave the actor her personal stamp of approval. Not surprisingly, Fleming mentioned the Savoy in a number of novels, starting with *Diamonds Are Forever*, where he tells us that the hotel is home to gem-smuggler-*cum*-mob boss Rufus B. Saye, alias, Jack Spang. Later in the same novel, Saye operative Shady Tree pays Bond $1,000 for smuggling diamonds into America, the cover story being that Tree owed him the money from a bridge game they had played at the Savoy. Ironically, the Savoy is *not* the kind of place you will actually find James Bond, at least according to the story "Quantum of Solace". Here, at a dinner party given by the Governor of the Bahamas, Bond is forced to make small talk with the pretty, but dull, English wife of a Canadian millionaire. She insists that the Savoy Grill is the nicest place for supper, pressing Bond to agree. Bond, unfortunately, cannot, since all he has is "dusty memories" of London nightlife. Poor fellow. His memory really is slipping: only two years earlier he had compared the menus in *Doctor No*'s elegant, mink-lined prison to those of the Savoy Grill!

Station: Charing Cross (BA; JU; NO) Exit on the Strand (South) side and go R (East) in the Strand; look for the entrance to the Savoy on the R, just past Shell-Mex House and nearly opposite the Strand Palace Hotel. Afternoon tea is served each day in the Thames Foyer from 3pm-5:30pm. The Grill Room is open for lunch from 12:30-2:30 Monday through Saturday.

Trivia Challenge 36: With what legendary playwright, actor, director and raconteur did Ian Fleming frequently dine at the Savoy?

23:9

ex HQ of the Ministry of Supply
Shell-Mex House
Strand, WC2 (at Ivybridge Lane)

A successor to the nineteenth-century Board of Ordnance and the WWI-era Ministry of Munitions, the Ministry of Supply was formed in August 1939 to provide the Army (and later the Air Force) with materiel and stores. It was headquartered here in Shell-Mex House, a colossal Art Deco-style office block completed in 1931. In addition, the MOS also maintained a "war department" in Westminster, where the real-life "Q", Charles

Fraser-Smith, created his gadgets (see [27:24]). In Chapter 10 of *Moonraker*, Bond visits the MOS to learn about Hugo Drax's atomic rocket, and why it is so important for Britain's defense. In fact, the MOS was responsible for security at **Drax's Plant** (*JBB*) and it is the murder of one of their agents, Major Tallon, that prompts the Minister of Supply to request SIS's help in securing the area. (SIS was already involved in the affair to the extent that it had originally screened—and cleared—the man who murdered Major Tallon: a German, as were all of Drax's other employees.) Normally, of course, **MI5** (13:30), not SIS, would have been called in on a domestic case such as this one, but at the Minister's urging the PM gave permission for Bond to work *inside* the UK, just this once. Also, Britain's nuclear weapons were formerly identified by Ministry of Supply numbers, hence the "MOS" in the serial numbers of the bombs stolen by SPECTRE in both the novel and the film *Thunderball*. The latter actually errs in suggesting that "MOS" is a "type" of weapon, not to mention the fact that by 1965 such weapons were designated with Ministry of Defence numbers in place of the old MOS numbers. In fact, the Ministry of Supply had been dissolved in 1959, with some of its functions going to the **Air Ministry** (23:7), some to the Ministry of Aviation and still others to the **War Office** (27:6), all of which were ultimately subsumed in the new **Ministry of Defence** (27:7) in 1964. Many of the MOS's functions are today performed by the Ministry of Defence Procurement Executive in Filton, near **Bristol** (*JBB*).

Station: Charing Cross (BA; JU; NO) Exit on the Strand (South) side and go R (East) in the Strand; look for Ivybridge Lane ahead on the S side of the street. The riverside façade, famous for its large, Deco-style clock, is best appreciated from the Embankment or the other side of the river.

23:10

Charing Cross Station WC2

The major railway terminus nearest to the heart of London, Charing Cross Station was opened in 1864, along with the Charing Cross Hotel above it. The station enters the Bond saga in Chapter 5 of *Diamonds Are Forever*. There, we accompany the beautiful smuggler Tiffany Case as she exits the **Trafalgar Palace Hotel** (27:3), crosses **Trafalgar Square** (27:1) and enters Charing Cross Station. Here she uses a pay phone to get instructions from a mysterious voice known only as "ABC". (We later learn that ABC is none other than Rufus B. Saye, alias Jack Spang of the Spangled Mob, the shadowy villain of the tale.) In crafting this incident, Fleming presumably recalled the famous bust that took place near the Strand entrance to Charing Cross Station on the night of January 18, 1938. Operating at the behest of **MI5** (13:30), **Scotland Yard** (27:16) arrested Soviet spy Percy Glading and his contact, Albert Williams, as the latter handed over a parcel of classified military documents that he had surreptitiously removed from Woolwich Arsenal, his place of employment. Credited for the arrest were MI5 agent Olga Gray, who had penetrated Glading's spy ring several years earlier, and Gray's case officer, Maxwell Knight, with whom Fleming himself would work during World War II (see [15:1]). Incidentally, if the new Charing Cross Station (completed in 1990) looks familiar, it's because the architect, Terry Farrell, also designed the current headquarters of **MI6** (24:2)!

Station: Charing Cross (BA; JU; NO) Just across from Charing Cross Station, at 440 Strand, is Coutts & Co., bankers to the Royal Family since the reign of George III. Fleming namedrops this venerable British institution in the midst of the short story "The Property of a Lady".

Eyes Only, 007: Fleming invokes this area at the conclusion of *Casino Royale*, telling us that heroine-cum-double agent Vesper Lynd received her instructions from an "accommodation address" at 450 Charing Cross Place. According to Fleming (or Vesper), this was the site of a newsagent. In fact, there was no such street as "Charing Cross Place", and the only newsagent in the vicinity of the station in 1951 was "P. Bond" at 9 Adelaide Street. Do you suppose Fleming knew...?

24. VAUXHALL

Densely-populated riverside district, noted for the tangled road junction known as Vauxhall Cross

24:1

River Thames and TWINE Boat Chase Route

Although generally thought of as "London's river", Britain's longest and most famous waterway actually rises in the Cotswalds, Gloucestershire, and meanders eastward through six southern counties (and several Bond locations in Berkshire, Buckinghamshire and Oxfordshire) before it finally reaches the North Sea some 210 miles later. Fleming mentions the historic river on a number of occasions, but his most poetic evocation occurs in the opening of *The Spy Who Loved Me*, where narrator Vivienne Michel recalls the romantic boat trips she and young Derek Mallaby used to take down the Thames at Windsor. (For more on those trips, see **Vivienne Michel's Boat Trip** [*JBB*].) The Thames is also shown in the films *Dr. No* (see [11:2]), *From Russia With Love*, *Goldfinger*, *For Your Eyes Only* (see [52:1]) and, most dramatically, in *The World Is Not Enough*. In the latter, the river provides the setting for the spectacular pre-credit boat chase, which begins at **MI6** (24:2) and **Vauxhall Bridge** (24:3), after Cigar Girl's assassination of Sir Robert King and attempted assassination of Bond himself. Bond launches the new, but unfinished, Q Boat from the bomb-damaged Secret Service HQ, while Cigar Girl speeds off in the sleek Sunseeker Hawk 34, customized with a one-of-a-kind machine gun and mortar-launchers. The two boats pass a number of riparian landmarks at a relatively leisurely pace, including: the Tate Gallery, **MI5** (27:29), the **Houses of Parliament** (27:18), **Westminster Bridge** (27:19) and Victoria Embankment. Then, in rapid sequence, the chase encompasses **Hungerford Bridge** (23:1), **TS *Queen Mary*** (23:2), **Waterloo Bridge** (23:3), **Waterloo Pier** (23:4), **Tower Bridge** (5:18) and **St Saviour's Dock** (30:1). From here the action continues *out* of the river itself, first in Docklands, East London (**Millwall Docks** [41:2], **Royal Victoria Dock** [31:1], **West India Docks** [41:1] and **Tobacco Dock** [52:1]), then at the **Historic Dockyard** (*JBB*) in Chatham, Kent. Bond finally returns to the Thames at **Trinity Buoy Wharf** (44:1), then follows Cigar Girl to the **Millennium Dome** (35:1) in Greenwich for the explosive climax of the sequence.

Station: Vauxhall (VI) Exit to Vauxhall Bridge and the river. The best place to begin a *TWINE*-esque boat trip is at Westminster Pier, near the Westminster Bridge end of Victoria Embankment.

24:2

MI6 (1994-present)
Vauxhall Cross
85 Albert Embankment, SE1

On May 6, 1992, John Major became the first British Prime Minister to officially acknowledge the existence of the Secret Intelligence Service, or MI6 (see **MI6 [1967-1994]** [11:1]). Two years later, Parliament passed the Intelligence Services Act, which put MI6 on a statutory basis for the first time in its 85-year history. That same year, MI6 made a highly-publicized move from Century House, near Lambeth Station, to an elaborate structure called Vauxhall Cross. (The location is actually mentioned in the British Government publication *Central Intelligence Machinery*, published by Her Majesty's Stationery Office.) This "theatrically ominous" post-modern marvel, designed by Terry Farrell and said to have cost nearly $500,000,000, has been described as everything from an "architectural landmark" to a gaudy "Aztec or Mayan temple". Either way, Vauxhall Cross is hard to miss. The building contains a sports hall, library, computer rooms, restaurant and covered parking garage for the convenience and use of its employees, as well as bomb-resistant walls and enough foliage to suggest a small park. (Note the plane trees, gazebo and fountain on the ground level, facing the river, and the 14 yew trees, grown in Italy and acclimatized in Scotland, along the fifth level.) Built into its nine-story concrete framework is a Faraday cage, a grounded metal screen that prevents electromagnetic signals from passing in or out of the building. Its state-of-the-art internal security system includes an array of sci-fi-like entry tubes that form a barrier between the lobby and the interior of the building proper. To gain entry, an employee swipes his identification card through the electronic reader on the lobby side of the tube; the outer door slides around permitting him access, then shuts, locking him inside the tube. He must then enter a PIN number to open the inner door and pass inside. Some things never change though: the World War II cover name, Government Communications Centre, remains the same; SIS employees still call it "the Firm" while the Foreign Office still refers to them as "the Friends"; the head of the Service, Richard Dearlove, is still called "C" and handwrites internal memos in green ink (as *The Sun* reported on page 2 of its February 26, 1999 issue); and, most importantly, the agency continues to earn its keep in a post-Cold War world. Case in point: the 1996 operation against the French Navy (that's right, the *French* Navy), in which a real-life James Bond managed to obtain the plans for a revolutionary *submarine tracking system* from a French civilian engineer. Four years later, life again imitated art when terrorists fired a rocket from a Russian-built anti-tank weapon at the (relatively) impregnable fortress! (Damage was confined to a window and two wall panels on the eighth floor; the most sensitive areas, including the command centre, are underground.) For the history of SIS/MI6, including the proper usage of its various names, see **MI6 (1914-1919)** (27:8) and **MI6 (1926-1967)** (27:22).

The striking green and beige-colored exterior of Vauxhall Cross appears briefly in the film *GoldenEye* (the first time that the location of James Bond's Secret Service coincided with that of the actual Secret Service), as well as in the pre-credit sequence of *The World Is Not Enough*. In the former, the shot is from Vauxhall Bridge, in the latter from Millbank, on the other side of the river. A red double-decker bus—the sine qua non of London establishing shots—crosses the bridge on both occasions. Later *TWINE* shots—of the explosion and Q Boat launch—utilized John Richardson's magnificent quarter-scale replica, which at over 80 feet in length can scarcely be called a "miniature"! The dozen or so interiors, including M's and Moneypenny's offices, "Q Division" [*sic*], the security area and several corridors, were, of course, designed by Peter Lamont and built at **Pinewood Studios** (*JBB*). Lamont did not model his interiors on those of the real McCoy, which he had the chance to visit only *after* the start of production and which he found to be "rather disappointing". Instead, he delivered a series of brilliant, high-tech originals (not all of which appear in the film*) that accord with both the exterior of the real building and with our own sense of how Vauxhall Cross *should* look on the inside.

Station: Vauxhall (VI) Take Exit 6 and cross the footbridge into Albert Embankment. The best views of the building are obtained form the bridge itself or the west bank of the river. MI6 also maintains a Training Centre at 296-302 Borough High Street, The Borough, South London; and a school for sabotage and demolition at Fort Monkton, Gosport, near **Portsmouth** (*JBB*), in Hampshire.

Note: You may photograph the exterior of MI6, preferably from the bridge or the other side of the river, but do not try to enter the building itself. *YOU ARE NOT WELCOME*.

*For example, Lamont built a corridor leading from the **Thames** (24:1), where Bond arrives by seaplane, to a security checkpoint featuring an optical scanner. Bond was to pass through this "entrance corridor" en route to the vault and thence to M's office. The scene was filmed but ultimately cut, either for time or because the seaplane arrival itself had been dropped.

Eyes Only, 007: In the "gap" between MI6 and the neighboring building, the Eon crew erected a small section of the damaged wall through which Bond (and the audience) views Cigar Girl. The crew also built the ramp from which the Q Boat was actually launched into the river. The "splashdown shot" shows the Q Boat landing in the river, with the stucco terraces and office blocks adjacent to Riverside Gardens, Millbank in the background, as well as the corner of the real MI6 building on the extreme left.

Left: Ian Fleming's home, 16 Victoria Square, London.

25. VICTORIA

Largely commercial "travelers' quarter" centered on Victoria Station

25:1

Ian Fleming's Home
16 Victoria Square, SW1

Given its location between majestic **Buckingham Palace** (16:27) to the north and bustling **Victoria Station** (25:3) to the south, tiny Victoria Square is an incongruously simple, even tranquil residential setting. Its most famous house, No. 16, is a yardless Regency structure—built in 1838-39—with a cream-colored stucco exterior and a handsome domed turret. It was to be Ian Fleming's last London home: the author moved into No. 16 in March 1953, just before the publication of *Casino Royale*, and lived here until his untimely death in August 1964. During this time, the ground floor (US: first floor) contained the dining room and kitchen; the first floor the drawing room; the second floor his wife, Ann's, bedroom; and the third floor Ian's bedroom and study. Here, on the top floor, the author retreated from the incessant, and frequently annoying, parties given by his wife for their many rich friends. After Ian's death, Ann divided her time between Victoria Square and their home in Wiltshire (see [*JBB*]). In March 1973, after precisely 20 years of residence at No. 16, Ann sold the house for £50,000 and retreated to Wiltshire. She died there, at Sevenhampton Place, on July 12, 1981. In 1996, the English Heritage organization sought permission to commemorate the Flemings' Victoria Square home with the prestigious Blue Plaque award, but could not obtain permission from the owners. The plaque was installed at **Ian Fleming's Home** (2:1) in Ebury Street, Belgravia, instead.

Station: Victoria (VI; CI; DI) Go L out of the station and turn R into Buckingham Palace Road. Pass Eaton Lane and then look for the entrance to Victoria Square just ahead on the left. No. 16 is in the NW corner of the tiny square.

25:2

Hugo Drax's House
Ebury Street (now Beeston Place), SW1

According to Chapter 19 of *Moonraker*, Sir Hugo Drax lives at **The Ritz** (16:1) but also keeps a small place in Ebury Street. Bond tails Drax from Blades (see [16:6]) to the Ebury Street house, which, following Fleming's description of the route, would be located just off Lower Grosvenor Place, in what is today Beeston Place. (Fleming provided the number, 14, in the original manuscript, but omitted it from the final draft.) Bond watches Drax remove the captive heroine, Gala Brand, from this house, and then follows the villain's car to the Moonraker Plant in Kent. What Bond does not yet know is that Drax has installed a radar homing device on the top floor of the building, equipment designed to bring the *Moonraker* atomic weapon crashing down in the heart of London. Bond was apparently also unaware that just round the corner from Drax's house was 16 Victoria Square, the London home of a certain writer of popular spy novels. See also ***Moonraker* Car Chase Route** (*JBB*) in Kent.

Station: Victoria (VI; CI; DI) Go L out of the station, turn R into Buckingham Palace Road and look for Victoria Square on the left, just before Lower Grosvenor Place. Proceed through the square (noting, of course, No. 16) and then on to Beeston Place. The building that Fleming presumably had in mind is to the right, at the corner of Beeston Place and Victoria Square (just across from the Goring Hotel at No. 15).

25:3

Victoria Station
Victoria Street, SW1

According to Chapter 1 of *Goldfinger*, this august railway station, just a few minutes walk from **Ian Fleming's Home** (25:1), once served as a drop site for Mexican heroine smugglers. Each month, a diplomatic courier named Santos would deposit a suitcase full of dope in the left-luggage office and then mail the claim ticket to a man called Schwab. Schwab, in turn, would claim the suitcase, distribute its contents (valued at £20,000) to the junkies of London and grow very wealthy in the process. **Scotland Yard** (27:16) eventually twigged all this and, given the Mexican connection, promptly turned the case over to the Secret Service. James Bond himself was then dispatched to Mexico to find the courier's source and destroy it. As we see in the film *Goldfinger*, Bond blows up the Mexican heroine refinery and kills one of the big man's *capungos*, just as in the novel, but now you know ... *the rest of the story*.

Station: Victoria (VI; CI; DI) In Fleming's day the Left Luggage Office was located approximately where the W. H. Smith shop now stands. Across the street is the Victoria Bus Station, where Hugo Drax claimed to have dropped off Gala Brand in Chapter 19 of *Moonraker*.

25:4

ex Overton's
Terminus Place, SW1
(opposite Victoria Station)

Following his move to nearby Victoria Square (see [25:1]), Ian Fleming dined regularly at this famous seafood establishment, going on to list it as one of his favorite restaurants (see the Index for the complete list). Indeed, he recommended Overton's to all his friends, including the celebrated crime novelist Raymond Chandler, who briefly lived in nearby Eaton Square in the spring of 1955. When Chandler offered to pen a plug for the next Bond novel, Fleming did two things. First, he sent Chandler a copy of *Live and Let Die*. Then he treated the American master to lunch here at Overton's, whose *pâté maison* Fleming rated as the best in London. Chandler must have really enjoyed the lunch, or Fleming's company, or the book or perhaps all three: his letter of June 4, 1955 praised Ian as "probably the most forceful and driving writer of what I suppose must still be called thrillers in England." Ian thanked him effusively for the encomium, forwarded copies of the letter to both **Jonathan Cape** (3:6) and Macmillan, his British and American publishers, respectively, and, perhaps most importantly, found his confidence in his own writing abilities restored by the generous praise of a fabled author. Chandler returned to the States shortly thereafter, but continued to visit London—and Fleming—until some months before his death in 1959. See the **BBC** (12:5) for more on the two legendary writers.

Station: Victoria (VI; CI; DI) The site, occupied until recently by Maxine's Café Brasserie, is opposite the station entrance, at the junction of Victoria Street and Wilton Road.

26. WEST BROMPTON

Southwest district on the fringe of Central London, centered upon the vast Brompton Cemetery

26:1

The Chapel, Brompton Cemetery
Old Brompton Road, SW10

Doubles as: Church of Our Lady of Smolensk, St. Petersburg, Russia (exterior) in *GoldenEye*

One of several large cemeteries ringing central London, Brompton is distinguished by its domed, octagonal chapel, which was built for the Church of England in the 1840s. (The original plans called for additional, smaller chapels for Catholics and Dissenters, but the architect, Benjamin Baud, ran out of funds.). It was here that Natalya Simonova came for her fateful rendezvous with Boris Grishenko. At least for the exterior shot. The interior scenes were filmed at the **Cathedral of St Sophia** (1:1)

Station: West Brompton (DI) The cemetery is opposite the station; the chapel is at the other end of the cemetery, near Fulham Road.

27. WHITEHALL WESTMINSTER

Central London district containing most of the government buildings, including the Houses of Parliament and the residence of the PM

27:0

Whitehall Walking Tour
SW1

***Start*: Charing Cross Station (BA; JU; NO) *Finish*: St James's Park Station (CI; DI)**

Connecting **Trafalgar Square** (27:1) to the **Houses of Parliament** (27:18), Whitehall—formerly King Street—contains many, if not most, of the principal offices of the British Government. Indeed, its name (which derives from Henry VIII's Palace of Whitehall) has become a synonym for the government itself, as when Q comments to Bond in F *For Your Eyes Only* that "your signal sent Whitehall into shock." The street itself is actually shown in the films *Octopussy, A View To A Kill, Licence To Kill* and, stretching a point, *For Your Eyes Only*. It is also referred to in Chapter 10 of *Moonraker*, where Bond, visiting **Scotland Yard** (27:16), reflects that "the noise of the traffic on Whitehall and on the Embankment had sounded far away"; in Chapter 14 of *Thunderball*, where the Bahamian Police Commissioner tells Bond that he is "not used to the crash treatment from Whitehall" (see **Prime Minister's Residence** [27:12] for the lead-up to this remark); and in "The Property of a Lady", where Bond leaves **Wartski**'s (13:16) enchanting shop at 138 Regent Street "to spend the rest of the day in drab offices around Whitehall", making arrangements to expose the top Soviet spy in London (see **ex Soviet Embassy** [9:2] for more on this story). There are many important landmarks along this street, Bondian and otherwise, so no trip to London would be complete without a Whitehall Walk.

27:1

Trafalgar Square
WC2, SW1

Located in the traditional heart of London (between the City to the east and Whitehall to the south), Trafalgar Square commemorates one of the most famous battles in British history. On October 21, 1805, off the coast of Cape Trafalgar, Spain, British naval forces under the command of Admiral Horatio Nelson defeated the combined French and Spanish fleets, thereby making Britain safe from almost certain invasion. Nelson himself, mortally wounded during the fighting, emerged as the hero of the Battle of Trafalgar and, indeed, as the greatest naval hero in British history. His monument, located on the south side of the square, comprises a fluted Corinthian column surmounted by a 17-foot statue of the admiral himself (overall height: 185 feet), which, with the four bronze lions at its base, has become one of the most famous landmarks in London. The Hero of Trafalgar is also commemorated in the British English phrase "the Nelson touch", which the OED defines as a "masterly or sympathetic approach to a problem" (Nelson being famous for both the compassion with which he treated his men and his ability to triumph against overwhelming odds). Now, what does all this have to do with James Bond? Well, for a start, Trafalgar Square (and Nelson's Column) appear as a backdrop for establishing shots of MI6 in the films *Octopussy*, *Licence To Kill* and, most obviously, *The Living Daylights*, where "Universal Exports" has taken up temporary residence in the square itself. (Director John Glen told me that he wanted something "immediately recognizable" as London—and you can't get much more recognizable than Trafalgar Square. It has appeared in more films than you can count [or at least than I am inclined to count], including the ill-fated *Avengers* movie.) Literary Bond conjures up images of the square in two novels, and, interestingly, both of the images are bird-related. In Chapter 13 of *Live and Let Die*, Bond reflects that the "oldsters" seated in rows of davenports along the sidewalks of St. Petersburg, Florida remind him of the starlings in Trafalgar Square. Four years later, recovering from his wounds at the end of *Doctor No*, Bond daydreams of a romanticized London, where "people [are] being photographed with pigeons on their head in Trafalgar Square." And, of course, Commander Bond himself possessed what almost amounted to "the Nelson touch", or so M wrote in the "Obituary" that constitutes the penultimate chapter of *You Only Live Twice*. (For more on the obituary, see the **ex *Times*** [5:7].) Of course, it's no surprise that one of Britain's greatest fictional heroes should inspire comparisons with one of the nation's greatest real-life heroes. Bond's creator not only idolized Lord Nelson (keeping a miniature of the admiral in his bedroom), but also endorsed hero worship in general. As Fleming wrote in the Foreword to *Room 3603* (H. Montgomery Hyde's 1962 account of Sir William Stephenson and the wartime MI6 station in New York [see (27:22)]): "In this era of the anti-hero, when anyone on a pedestal is assaulted (how has Nelson survived?), unfashionably and obstinately I have my heroes.... I am convinced they are necessary companions through life."

Station: Charing Cross (BA; JU; NO)
Exit for Trafalgar Square.

27:2

The National Gallery Trafalgar Square, WC2

Constructed in the 1830s as the "climax" to **Trafalgar Square** (27:1), London's most famous art gallery houses one of the finest collections of Western European paintings in the world. One of these paintings, as well as the gallery itself, is referred to in the story "The Property of a Lady". During a discussion with art expert Dr Fanshawe (who becomes "Jim Fanning, our art expert" in the film *Octopussy*), the "philistine" M refers to one of the famous Fabergé globes as an "[e]xpensive hunk of jewellery." The fussy Dr Fanshawe takes umbrage at the remark and indignantly asks M if he considers the Goya that was sold at **Sotheby's** (13:11) for £140,000 and subsequently stolen from the National Gallery just "an expensive hunk ... of canvas and paint". The reference is to Francisco de Goya's famous painting of *The Duke of Wellington*, which was stolen from the gallery in August 1961. During its four-year absence, *The Duke* took up temporary residence in Crab Key, at least according to the film *Dr. No*. The idea for this clever visual joke (note Sean Connery's double take as he spots the painting on the way up to Dr. No's dining room) is generally credited to director Terence Young's assistant, Johanna Harwood. However, production buyer Ron Quelch recalls that it was mercurial producer Harry Saltzman who first got a bee in his bonnet about including the painting. Either way, the instructions to Ron and production designer Ken Adam were clear: have a copy of the painting on the set, ready for filming, the following morning. As Ron recalled, "I went straight to the National Gallery, bought a transparency and a postcard of the painting, copied down its exact dimensions [64.3 x 52.4 cm] and took these to the Carltograph [a specialist printer] in South London. I told them I needed a photo enlargement of a certain size, that it had to be 'washed out' for later 'overpainting' and that I need it this afternoon!" After insuring that the enlargement would indeed be ready that afternoon, Ron set off to rent an ornate frame for the finished product. At precisely 4:30 p.m. he slipped the rolled-up enlargement and photos through the letterbox of Ken Adam's Kensington home and the following morning, the man who would later design the Fort Knox vault brought in his own expert "forgery" of the Goya painting. I asked Ron why the photo needed to be overpainted. "To give it depth," he explained. "A simple enlargement would have lacked the depth of the actual painting. It would have been a dead giveaway." In May 1965, the real painting was finally restored to its rightful spot in Room 39 of the National Gallery's East Wing, where it remains to this day. The domed exterior of the gallery itself may be glimpsed in the background of the Universal Exports establishing shot near the beginning of *The Living Daylights*. And just to round out the gallery's Bondian connections, you should be aware that during WWII, Commander Ian Fleming often lunched here with his friend Pamela Tiarks, for whom he had obtained a job in the Citadel of the **Admiralty** (27:10).

Station: Charing Cross (BA; JU; NO) Exit on the Strand (North) side and veer R into Duncannon Street, which leads directly to the gallery. **Hours**: Mon-Sat 10am-6pm (Wed until 8pm); Sun noon-6pm

27:3

"Trafalgar Palace Hotel" Near Trafalgar Square, WC2

Bond, posing as Peter Franks, meets the beautiful blonde smuggler Tiffany Case in Room 350 of this hotel in Chapter 5 of *Diamonds Are Forever*. She always stays here when she is in London, in spite of—or because of (?)—the fact that it has one of the highest crime rates of any large hotel in the city. At the time (ca. 1955), there was no such hotel in the vicinity of **Trafalgar Square** (27:1). So which, if any, hotel did Fleming actually have in mind? An inspection of the original manuscript provides the answer. There, Tiffany exits the Trafalgar Palace, looks at her watch and then "walk[s] *along the Strand* to Charing Cross Station (emphasis added)." The logical starting point for *that* journey would have been the famous Strand Palace Hotel, at No. 372 Strand. Apparently, renaming the hotel wasn't enough, so Fleming also relocated it to the western side of Trafalgar Square (which Tiffany must cross in order to reach the station). In this way, he was free to describe the large amount of crime in the hotel and avoid a libel suit at the same time. The film version ignores the problem by staging Bond's initial meeting with Tiffany in her Amsterdam apartment. Here, the wary female smuggler verifies Bond's bona fides by comparing a photo of his right thumbprint to one of the real Peter Franks' thumbprint. Thanks to Q, Bond's print matches Franks'. Uncredited for his role in providing *both* fingerprints was production buyer Ron Quelch, whose right thumb bears the faint scar seen in the film. "I said to [art director] Peter Lamont, 'One print looks like another, so you should use something distinctive—mine!" Quelch told me that he got the scar as the result of a childhood injury, never dreaming, of course, that it might one day lead to cinematic "immortality"! Years later, Ron secured an additional "role" for himself, and one for his wife Jean, as well, in *The World Is Not Enough*. If you look closely at Elektra King's desk, you will see a photo of her mother—that's Jean—and one of her parents' wedding. That's actually Jean and Ron's 1950 wedding photo. Mind you, Ron's head was replaced by that of Elektra's father, but, hey, that's show biz!

Station: Charing Cross (BA; JU; NO) Exit on the Strand (North) side and go L (East) in the Strand; the Strand Palace is ahead on the N side of the street, opposite **The Savoy** (23:8).

27:4

Malaysia House
57 Trafalgar Square, WC2

Doubles as: Universal Exports (MI6), London (exterior) in *The Living Daylights*

In *The Living Daylights*, Universal Exports, i.e., MI6, relocated from the **War Office** (27:6) building in **Whitehall** (27:0) to the **Trafalgar Square** (27:1) offices of the Malaysia Tourism Promotion Board! One might wonder if this was an attempt to strengthen ties with a former British Colony or if they were simply renovating the Old War Office Building. In fact, director John Glen told me that he selected Trafalgar Square because he "wanted something recognizable, with tourists, to establish a London locale." Moreover, he "didn't intend to show the actual building, just the [Universal Exports] sign." Production designer Peter Lamont added that since no one really knew (or felt free to disclose) the actual location of MI6 (this was before the highly-publicized move to Vauxhall Cross [24:2] in 1994), it was up to whoever shot the film to select his own Secret Service headquarters. The criterion was purely visual, not historical, although in the case of the Old War Office Building, the filmmakers got both. Indeed, after the brief sojourn to Trafalgar Square, Eon's MI6 moved back to the venerable Whitehall building for *Licence To Kill*.

Station: Charing Cross (BA; JU; NO) Take the Cockspur Street/Mall exit (which appears in the film) to come up near the spot where the establishing shot was photographed. For the precise view from the film, go to the narrow, wedge-shaped island in the Mall, where that street intersects with Whitehall, and look back toward Canada House (the gold-colored building west of the square). The latter, incidentally, doubled as John Gielgud's headquarters in Peter Hunt's *Gold*, which, of course, starred Roger Moore.

27:5

Ministry of Agriculture, Fisheries and Food
3-8 Whitehall Place, SW1

The top pest-control man from "Ag. And Fish.", Mr. Franklin, briefs Bond and M on the ins and outs of Biological Warfare in Chapters 21-22 of *On Her Majesty's Secret Service*. According to Franklin, the subject is very much alive in his Ministry because Britain is the most highly agriculturalized nation in the world and thus ripe for such an attack. Were this to happen, all poultry and animals would have to be destroyed and all crops burned; Britain would be bankrupt within months. This, of course, is precisely what Ernst Stavro Blofeld has in mind, not for purposes of extortion, as in the film, but for revenge. Incidentally, as a blue plaque outside the entrance indicates, the Ministry of Ag. and Fish. stands on the site of the original HQ of the (London) Metropolitan Police Service, a.k.a., Scotland Yard. For more on the famous police force, see (27:16).

Station: Charing Cross (BA; JU; NO) Exit on the Strand (South) side and go L, past **Trafalgar Square** (27:1), then L into Whitehall. The building is on the E side, before Whitehall Place.

27:6

ex HQ of the War Office
Old War Office Building
Whitehall, SW1

Doubles as: MI6 in *Octopussy*, *A View To A Kill* and *Licence To Kill*

The War Office was the government department responsible for the administration and supervision of the British Army. Its counterparts were the **Admiralty** (27:10), which oversaw the Royal Navy, and, from 1918, the **Air Ministry** (23:7), which oversaw the RAF. In 1873, the government established the first Army, or Military, Intelligence Branch under the aegis of the War Office, a successor to both the Depot of Military Knowledge (1803-15) and the Topographical and Statistical Department (1855-57; 1871-73). The Intelligence Branch, then headquartered at 4 New Street, Spring Gardens (on the site of the present Admiralty complex), was tasked with gathering strategic military intelligence during peacetime, i.e., spying, an important complement to the tactical or field intelligence operations that were generally set up on an ad hoc basis during wartime. It's brief, still largely in force today, was to "... collect and classify all possible information relating to the strength, organization and equipment of foreign armies, to keep themselves acquainted with the progress made by foreign countries in military art and science and to preserve the information in such a form that it can readily be consulted and made available for any purpose for which it may be required."* The Intelligence Branch relocated to Adair House, St James's Square, in 1874 (the War Office itself was then located in nearby Pall Mall), moving on to 16 and 18 Queen Anne's Gate in 1884 and to Winchester House, back in St James's Square, in 1901. During this time, the Branch underwent a number of reorganizations and name changes, becoming the Intelligence Division in 1888, the Department of Mobilization and Military Intelligence in 1901 and the Directorate of Military Operations (MO) in 1904. In 1906, the MO Directorate, along with the rest of the War Office department, moved into an impressive new Whitehall headquarters, the Victorian baroque complex now known as the Old War Office Building. It was here, in October 1909, that the government created the new Secret Service Bureau under MO5, the "Special Duties" section of Military Operations. Formed in response to the growing threat from Germany, the Bureau was divided into two sections—one to handle counterespionage at home and another to conduct espionage abroad. Both the home and foreign sections were eventually removed from Military Intelligence (as the MO Directorate was renamed in 1914) and reorganized as civilian agencies under the aegis of the **Home Office** (27:15) and the **Foreign Office** (27:14), respectively. Notwithstanding this change of status, the two secret services are still best known, both popularly and semi-officially, by their former Military Intelligence cover names: MI5 and MI6. (For more on their history, see **MI5 [1945-1975]** [13:30], **MI6 [1914-1919]** [27:8] and **MI6 [1926-1967]** [27:22].) Indeed, Eon Productions continues to locate MI6 within the Military Intelligence hierarchy, as the crest in *The World Is Not Enough* makes clear. Director John Glen actually went a step further in three of his five films, locating the Secret Service in the Old War Office Building itself (see photo inset, page 125). He explained that he simply admired the look of this elegant complex and was unaware of its MI6 connection. As to why he—or the Secret Service—opted for a temporary relocation to **Trafalgar Square** (27:1) in *The Living Daylights*, see **Malaysia House** (27:4). Today, of course, the cinematic Secret Service coexists with the real Secret Intelligence Service in Vauxhall Cross (see [24:2]).

During World War II, the Directorate of Military Intelligence employed Ian Fleming's older brother, Peter, in its sabotage section, MI(R), while Ian himself liaised with that very section as part of his Naval Intelligence duties at the Admiralty. (MI[R] was subsequently absorbed into the **Special Operations Executive** [12:8] in **Baker Street** [12:1].) Years later, Author Fleming would refer to both the War Office and its Military Intelligence Directorate on several occasions, including Chapter 2 of *Moonraker*, where he tells us that the former helped the "amnesiac" Hugo Drax to establish his "true" identity. In the same novel, he also tells us that Major Tallon, the **Ministry of Supply** (23:9) officer who was murdered by a Drax henchman, had worked for Army (i.e., Military) Intelligence. In Chapter 1 of his last novel, *The Man with the Golden Gun*, Fleming describes Captain Walker of the Secret Service's Liaison Section as "an extremely bright ex-prisoner-of-war interrogator from Military Intelligence". It is Captain Walker who, after consultation with his superior, directs a brainwashed Bond to the "Soft Man" at the Secret Service Interrogation Centre (see [9:2]) in Kensington. Later, after Bond has attempted to kill his Chief with a Soviet cyanide pistol, the War Office sends a Chemical Warfare squad to disinfect M's office. Ironically, this may well have been the department's last official act, for even as Fleming typed those words in

1964, the War Office was being dissolved. Its place was taken by a powerful new **Ministry of Defence** (27:7), which amalgamated the former Admiralty, Air Ministry and War Office departments under a single roof in Horse Guards Avenue. Military Intelligence itself, along with the Naval and Air Intelligence departments, was absorbed into the new Defence Intelligence Staff, which is based in the MOD's main building. It is headed by the Chief of Defence Intelligence, who answers to the Minister of Defence.

Station: Charing Cross (BA; JU; NO) Exit on the Strand (South) side and go L, past **Trafalgar Square** (27:1), then L into Whitehall. The building is on the E side, just past Whitehall Place; for the view of the War Office Building in *A View To A Kill*, see **Horse Guards** (27:9).

* Quoted in Gudgin, *Military Intelligence: The British Story*, p 27.

Trivia Challenge 37: During WWII, the War Office adopted the American designation "Top Secret" for highly classified documents. What older security classification, shown in the film *Moonraker*, did "Top Secret" replace?

27:7

Ministry of Defence Main Building Horse Guards Avenue, SW1

As is discussed below under **ex Ministry of Defence** (27:20), the original MOD was created in 1946 to coordinate the activities of the three independent defense ministries, viz., the **Admiralty** (27:10), the **War Office** (27:6) and the **Air Ministry** (23:7). By 1964, when it moved to its present home, the new, more powerful Ministry of Defence—which Fleming refers to in the opening chapters of his final novel, *The Man with the Golden Gun*—had absorbed all three departments under a single Secretary of State for Defence, or Minister of Defence. This is the British Cabinet member portrayed by Geoffrey Keen in six consecutive films (starting with *The Spy Who Loved Me*) and by Julian Fellowes in *Tomorrow Never Dies*. The exterior of the actual Ministry of Defence, a massive, rather austere fortress completed in 1959, was shown for the first and only time in *For Your Eyes Only*. Thanks

to a thorough cleaning in the 1980s, the dark façade that appears in the film is now significantly lighter. You are free to take as many pictures as you like of the exterior of the building, including the MOD plaque shown in the film, but no unauthorized personnel may enter the Ministry of Defence. Ironically, this prohibition extends to James Bond himself, for which reason he is shown entering **Somerset House** (23:5) and not the real MOD in *Tomorrow Never Dies*. Incidentally, while both the Fleming and Eon versions of the Secret Service operate under the MOD, the real SIS/MI6 is supervised by the **Foreign Office** (27:14).

Station: Charing Cross (BA; JU; NO) Exit on the Strand (South) side and go L, past **Trafalgar Square** (27:1), then L into Whitehall. Look for Horse Guards Avenue on the E side, just past the Old War office Building.

Eyes Only, 007: Prior to its occupation by the MOD, this complex housed the Board of Trade, the powerful regulatory department whose Permanent Secretary briefed M on the diamond smuggling situation one week before the events described in Chapter 2 of *Diamonds Are Forever*. In 1970, the Board of Trade merged with the Board of Technology to become the Department of Trade and Industry, located at 1 Victoria Street.

27:8

ex HQ of MI6 (1914-1919)
2 Whitehall Court, SW1

Yes, Virginia, there *is* an MI6. It is, in the words of one of its officers, "the Secret Intelligence Service of popular fiction, with the task of gathering information from all over the world about the intention, plans, etc., of any country which may be at war with Great Britain or may be a potential enemy."* Along with **MI5** (13:30; 27:29), it is the oldest and most important of Britain's so-called "secret services", government departments that were, until quite recently, officially unmentionable in Parliament, in the press, in open correspondence or on unscrambled telephones. The checkered history of both organizations begins in October 1909, with the creation of the Secret Service Bureau of the Directorate of Military Operations (MO). Administratively, the new bureau was placed under MO5, the "Special Duties" section of the MO Directorate, which was headquartered in the **War Office** (27:6) (to which you should turn for the pre-1909 history of Military Intelligence). It consisted of two sub-sections: one concerned with counterespionage, i.e., spy-catching, at home; the other with secret intelligence-gathering, i.e., spying, abroad. Both were initially housed in a small office in Victoria Street (on the site of the present Lord Chancellor's Department at 54-60), the idea apparently being to literally distance the new bureau from its masters in Whitehall. The Home Section was headed by Captain (later Major General Sir) Vernon Kell (known as "K"), who would continue in the post until 1940; the Foreign Section was headed by Commander (later Captain Sir) Mansfield (Smith) Cumming (known as "C"). The following year, Cumming opened his own office in nearby Vauxhall Bridge Road, where he also maintained a flat for himself. As cover, he acquired a post office box under the name of Rasen Falcon & Co., a shipping and exporting firm (cf. Fleming's "Universal Export"). 1910 was also the year that responsibility for Cumming's section shifted, at least in part, from the War Office—where it was known as MO5(j)—to the **Admiralty** (27:10), the Navy being considered the chief customer for overseas intelligence. Since the **Foreign Office** (27:14) actually financed the Secret Service Bureau (from the so-called "Secret Vote"), Cumming, in effect, had three masters, a frequently unhappy situation that would obtain for over a decade. In the autumn of 1914, just after the start of World War I, Cumming transferred the bulk of his expanding operation to the top floor (and roof) of 2 Whitehall Court, a huge, French Renaissance-style block of mansion flats completed in 1892. His new headquarters comprised an odd assortment of strangely-shaped rooms and passages that included his own overcrowded office, with its massive table, file cabinets and impressive collection of leather-bound books; a two-story workshop (a kind of an early "Q Branch"); a staff canteen; and an apartment for himself and his wife, May. Although someone apparently forgot to inform the London Post Office of the cover name, "Captain Spencer's Flat" (its directory matter-of-factly listed the tenant of 2 Whitehall Court as "Commander Mansfield G. Smith-Cumming, C.B."!), the overall set-up at Whitehall Court seems to have delighted the eccentric spymaster. (In addition to his monocle, assorted disguises and wooden leg—the result of an automobile accident in which his son was killed—Cumming also used a small scooter to navigate the corridors of Whitehall.) What *didn't* delight Cumming was the War Office's attempt to reassert its control over his section. In January 1916, as part of its wartime reorganization, the War Office had replaced the DMO with a new and more powerful department called the Directorate of Military Intelligence. Each of the directorate's sections was given a cover name beginning with the prefix "MI", including Kell's MO5(g), henceforth to be known as MI5. The Secret Service, although now largely responsible to the Navy, was rechristened MI1(c), i.e., Military Intelligence, Section 1(c), a cover it would retain until the 1930s. (Its far more famous byname originated during the Second World War, when MI6, i.e., Section Six of Military Intelligence, both liaised with and provided cover for the Secret Service.) As the war progressed, Cumming managed to steer a course away from both his military and naval masters and into the arms of the Foreign Office, under whose jurisdiction the department was reorganized as the Secret Intelligence Service (still its official name). Apart from Cumming himself, the WWI-era Secret Service is perhaps most famously associated with Russian-born Sidney Reilly (né Sigmund Rosenblum), an agent whose story was glowingly recounted in the book and television series *Reilly—Ace of Spies*. Reilly, who conducted a number of successful operations against the Bolsheviks in Russia, had a penchant for expensive clothes, elegant digs (see **Albany** [13:Q]), fashionable restaurants and high-stakes gambling. Not unnaturally, he has been described as the "model" for James Bond. Fleming himself modestly demurred, averring that Bond was "not a Sidney Reilly". Indeed, for Bond was no more and no less than an idealized version of Fleming himself (see **ex Admiralty** [27:10]). Still, as Rosenberg and Stewart note in *Ian Fleming*, it must have reassured Bond's creator to know that such flamboyant spies as Sidney Reilly, Sir Paul Dukes (another of Cumming's agents) and Du√ko Popov actually existed. Unfortunately for Reilly, life did not imitate art, where the hero (generally) triumphs in the end. The "Ace of Spies" traveled to the Soviet Union in September 1925, walked into an obvious trap and was subsequently executed for his trouble. In the meantime, of course, the

War had ended, Cumming's budget had been slashed, and SIS/MI1(c) had relocated to more modest premises in Melbury Road, West Kensington (see [9:6]). Cumming's former HQ (which is depicted in the *Reilly* series) is now occupied by the Royal Horse Guards Thistle Hotel. For the later history of SIS, including Fleming's version of the organization, see **MI6 [1926-1967]** (27:22) and **ex Home of the Secret Service Chief** (27:23).

Station: Embankment (BA; CI; DI; NO) Exit for the Embankment, into which you will turn R and continue to Victoria Embankment Gardens; Whitehall Court will be the massive building to the R. Cumming's rooms were in the upper right-hand corner, overlooking the gardens and the river.

*Quoted in *The Faber Book of Espionage*, p 436.

27:9

Horse Guards
Whitehall, SW1

Constructed in the 1750s, this Palladian barracks—known simply as Horse Guards—serves as the headquarters of the Household Division of the British Army. The Household Division includes the two regiments of the Household Cavalry, whose soldiers provide mounted escorts for the Royal Family and carry out various ceremonial duties, including the Trooping the Colour on the Queen's official birthday in June. Members of the Household Cavalry mount the Queen's Life Guard here at Horse Guards Arch, which is the official entrance to **Buckingham Palace** (16:27). The Guard provides two mounted sentries, or "boxmen" (so called from their stations inside boxes outside the Arch), who are posted from 10:00 a.m. to 4:00 p.m. each day. It is one of these colorful, helmeted boxmen who rides across the screen immediately after the credits in the film *A View To A Kill.*

Station: Charing Cross (BA; JU; NO) Exit on the Strand (South) side and go L, past **Trafalgar Square** (27:1), then L into Whitehall. The building is on the W side, opposite Horse Guards Avenue. The Changing of the Guard takes place daily at 11am and Sundays at 10am. Stand near the Guard to the left of the Arch, face **Trafalgar Square** (27:1) and then "pan" across Whitehall to the corner of the **ex War Office** (27:6) building. Could that be Miss Moneypenny in the window?

Below (main photo): Horse Guards, Whitehall. *Insert:* the Old War Office as shown in *A View To A Kill*

27:10

ex HQ of the Admiralty
Old Admiralty Building
Whitehall, SW1

The Admiralty was the government department responsible for the administration of the Royal Navy. Its headquarters was the purpose-built Admiralty Building, constructed in the 1720s and today known as the Old Admiralty. Fleming refers to the Admiralty department—which actually co-directed MI6 during its early years (see [27:8])—on a number of occasions, starting with *Live and Let Die*, where Bond asks them to supply the underwater equipment he will need for an assault on Mr. Big's Jamaican lair. In *Moonraker*, the BBC commentator speculates that having a submarine on hand for the launching of Drax's rocket must have been "an idea of the Admiralty's", while in the short story "For Your Eyes Only", M alludes to the Admiralty in a lecture on decision-making. In "The Hildebrand Rarity", Bond conducts a security check of the Seychelles Islands on behalf of the Admiralty, which may have to transfer its fleet base there from the Communist-infiltrated Maldives. In *James Bond of the Secret Service*, the screen treatment that led to the novel and film *Thunderball* (see Appendix Two), Fleming actually set a short scene in the Operations Room of the Admiralty. Finally, in the novel itself, Bond simply cables them a report from the Bahamas. The Admiralty was abolished in 1964, when administration of the Navy, as well as the Royal Army and Royal Air Force, was transferred to the new **Ministry of Defence** (27:7), located just off Whitehall in Horse Guards Avenue. Some of its functions were taken over by an MOD committee known as the Admiralty Board or, more properly, the Navy Board. This is presumably the referent in the film *Thunderball*, when the Air Vice Marshal tells Dawson to "notify the Admiralty at once" regarding the missing Vulcan bomber; in *For Your Eyes Only* when the captain of the *St George's* orders his junior officer to "verify and advise Admiralty" about the decode of Russian satellite data; and in *Tomorrow Never Dies*, when both the commander of the *Devonshire* and Admiral Kelly of the *Bedford* order that signals be sent to the Admiralty advising that their respective ships are under attack. The head of the Navy Board is the Chief of the Naval Staff, also known by the traditional title, First Sea Lord. The First Sea Lord is responsible for the efficiency and fighting effectiveness of the Royal Navy and answers to the country's top military leader, the Chief of the Defence Staff (CDS), who, in turn answers to the Minister of Defence. The Bond films omit the CDS, showing the First Sea Lord reporting directly to the Minister of Defence in both *For Your Eyes Only* and *Tomorrow Never Dies*. (Look fast in the latter. The First Sea Lord, whose role was originally larger, may be spotted over Admiral Roebuck's right shoulder in the MOD scene near the conclusion of the film.) Today, the Admiralty's former headquarters serves as an annex of the **Foreign Office** (27:14), which is located farther down Whitehall.

It was also here, in the Admiralty's famous Room 39, that Ian Fleming spent the war years as Personal Assistant to the Director of Naval Intelligence, thoroughly enmeshed in the real-life world of espionage. Fleming had been appointed a lieutenant in the Special Branch of the Royal Naval Volunteer Reserve on July 26, 1939, with a promotion to commander following on September 8. His duties in Section 17—the "co-ordinating section" or "bridge"—of the Naval Intelligence Division, included analysis of secret signals and reports, formulation of strategy and tactics, and overall responsibility for 30 Assault Unit, a group of intelligence-gathering commandos that he created in 1942 (and which inspired the MOB "A" Force in which Major Dexter Smythe served in the short story "Octopussy"; see **ex HQ of Combined Operations** [27:13] for more details). Fleming, whose code name was "17F", also liaised with both political leaders and senior members of the other intelligence services, including the heads of the Special Operations Executive, the Political Warfare Executive, the Ministry of Economic Warfare and the Secret Intelligence Service (James Bond's future employer). (See **ex HQ of SOE** [12:8], **Bush House** [23:6], **Lansdowne Club** [13:23] and **MI6 [1926-1967]** [27:22], respectively, for more on these organizations.) His desk remained in the same place throughout the war, on the far side of the room, by one of the three windows overlooking Horse Guards Parade (behind **Horse Guards** [27:9]). From here he would pass through a green baize door into the office of the Director of Naval Intelligence, Rear Admiral John Godfrey (and later in the war, Commodore E. G. N. Rushbrooke), much as the Chief of Staff and Bond himself would pass through the green baize door that led to the offices of M and his staff in *Moonraker* and other novels. (See the **ex Residence of the DNI** [13:28] and **ex Carlton Hotel** [16:21] for more on Godfrey.) Indeed, a great deal of Fleming's Naval Intelligence experience found its way into the James Bond novels, from the admiral at the head of the Service to the "Eyes Only" stamped on secret documents; from Bond's rank as a Commander in the Royal Naval Volunteer Reserve, to 007's self-effacing description of himself as "strictly a chocolate sailor" in Chapter 20 of *Thunderball.* (One of Ann's supercilious friends had so dubbed Fleming during the war.) Given all this, it is difficult to see how the character of James Bond could have been "based" on one or more British or foreign spies, as is often claimed. Plainly

Bond was Fleming, or, at any rate, a romanticized version of Fleming: the author as he would like to have been. True, Fleming frequently denied there was anything more than a superficial similarity between Bond and himself. For example, during his 1958 BBC radio chat with Raymond Chandler (see [12:5]), Ian said of Bond: "I suppose he's got some foibles I've got, but I wouldn't have said he's got any relation to the person I think I am. But there it is." In the same program, however, Fleming also admitted that "one writes about what one knows" and what he knew was Intelligence. Of course his exploits *outside* the office were not always rousing successes (see **ex Scott's** [19:6], **Cavendish Hotel** [16:16] and **Port of Dover** [*JBB*] for examples), but occasionally Fleming was given the chance to prove that, like Bond, he had something of the "Nelson touch". (See **Trafalgar Square** [27:1] for more on Nelson, Fleming and Bond.) In June 1940, for instance, Ian was sent to France on an important liaison and intelligence-gathering mission. While abroad, he was called upon to take charge of the evacuation of British refugees from Bordeaux, a task that he handled with great skill and courage. Among those whom he had to shepherd aboard a boat to England were ex-King Zog of Albania and his extended family, who left behind a fleet of luxury cars as spoils for the advancing German Army! One scheme that Fleming did *not* take part in was the abduction of Nazi leader Martin Bormann at the end of the war. This was alleged of Bond's creator in a recent book, but biographer Andrew Lycett categorically denies that the incident ever occurred. (Bormann was nowhere to be found when Germany collapsed in May 1945, prompting later speculation that he had somehow escaped—possibly with Allied help [!]—to South America. His body was unearthed near Hitler's Berlin bunker in 1972 and positively identified as such by forensic experts.) With six years of *real* espionage adventures behind him, Commander Ian Fleming left Naval Intelligence at the end of 1945. It would be another six years before he would begin the first James Bond novel at *Goldeneye*, the Jamaican home he had named after one of his wartime operations. Yet, in a very real sense, Agent 007 began here, in a large ground-floor room of the Admiralty building, overlooking Horse Guards Parade. Naval Intelligence itself, which Fleming mentions in Chapter 1 of *Casino Royale* and Chapter 4 of *The Man with the Golden Gun*, would survive as a separate organization until 1964, when it was merged with the two other service intelligence agencies (the Army's and the Air Force's) to form the Defence Intelligence Staff (see **ex War Office** [27:6]).

Station: Charing Cross (BA; JU; NO) Exit on the Strand (South) side and go L, past **Trafalgar Square** (27:1), then L into Whitehall. Pass through the Horse Guards entrance and look for the Admiralty across the parade ground, to the R. Now look for the Green dome on the L side of the Admiralty. Rooms 39 (with three windows) and 38 (with two) are directly below this on the ground floor (the level *beneath* the columns). Fleming's desk was adjacent to the middle window of the group of five. Just below and to the R of the rooms is the so-called "private exit", from which the First Sea Lord (the head of the Admiralty) would depart for meetings with the PM at 10 Downing Street, just across the Parade. The Directors of Naval Intelligence were also privileged to possess a key to this door. The entrance that Fleming himself used faces onto the Mall. It is known as Cook's Entrance, from the statue of Captain James Cook located just outside it.

Trivia Challenge 38: Name the other film(s) in which the First Sea Lord is mentioned.

27:11

ex Whitehall Radio Communications Centre Whitehall, SW1 *(Beneath Horse Guards Parade and St James's Park)*

Whitehall Radio, also known as the Admiralty Radio Station, Whitehall Wireless or Whitehall W/T, was a vast underground communications complex located beneath Horse Guards Parade and **St James's Park** (27:21). As the Royal Navy's principal radio station, Whitehall W/T maintained communication links with all naval radio stations in the British Colonies and the Commonwealth, as well as links with the country's main port communication centres, e.g., **Portishead Radio** (*JBB*), and with Her Majesty's ships at sea. Personnel, all bound by the Official Secrets Act, entered through the **Admiralty** (27:10) itself, then proceeded down a long corridor, through a single door and down a stepladder into the "dungeons". Ian Fleming obviously knew of the set-up, given his Naval Intelligence work right here in the Admiralty. He mentions the station in several Bond adventures, including *Goldfinger* (chapter 23), where Bond radios Weathership Charlie from Goldfinger's disabled plane, proposes to ditch the aircraft in the ocean near the ship and asks them to contact Whitehall Radio to verify that he is British Secret Service agent Number 007. In *James Bond of the Secret Service*, the Chief of Staff has Moneypenny cipher a signal to all stations by Whitehall Radio, a scene repeated with even more routing instructions (to the Heads of the CIA, the Deuxième Bureau, NATO Intelligence,

MI5, et al.) in Chapter 7 of *Thunderball*. Although it is not specifically mentioned in the film *Dr. No*, the MI6 Communications Room shown near the beginning of the film is also located *underground*, a fact revealed to me by production buyer Ron Quelch. (Note the absence of any windows.) Production designer Ken Adam was quite specific in his description of the set as underground, Ron recalled, which suggests the possibility that Fleming himself may have conveyed this bit of arcana to the producers. (The author is known to have provided Cubby Broccoli with a lengthy memorandum on the world of James Bond and the fictional Secret Service.) Ron's job was to come up with the necessary radio equipment. Fortunately, he knew a chap called Mike Lustig of the Racal Aerotronics firm in London. Racal had just completed an order for several radio transmitter/receiver units, six of which Mike happily loaned to Eon. After returning the sets to Racal, Eon paid for a retest and the now slightly-used transmitters were sent on to their *original* destination: the New Delhi airport! (For more of Ron's early adventures in "buying for Bond", see **Les Ambassadeurs Club** [13:38].) A remnant of the real Whitehall radio station is still here beneath the old Admiralty building, although the Navy's principal communication centre is now based at HMS Warrior, Sandy Lane, Northwood, Greater London.

Station: Charing Cross (BA; JU; NO) (see above). The entrance was off the Mall, near the back of the Whitehall Theatre.

27:12

Prime Minister's Residence
10 Downing Street, SW1

The head of the British Government is referred to in several novels, notably *Moonraker*, where he gives permission for Bond to operate *inside* England for one assignment, then later orders Bond out of the country until the disastrous Drax affair blows over. In Chapter 14 of *Thunderball*, Bond threatens to go above the Bahamian Police Commissioner's head to the Prime Minister himself in order to get permission to conduct an underwater recce of Largo's yacht. M telephones the PM about Blofeld in Chapter 8 of *OHMSS*, withholds information from him in Chapter 22 of the same novel, takes orders from the PM in "Risico" and notes that he is a Privy Councillor [*sic*] in Chapter 7 of *Thunderball*. The Prime Minister even "proposes to recommend to Her Majesty Queen Elizabeth the immediate grant of a knighthood" to Bond at the end of *The Man with the Golden Gun*. (Bond politely refuses the honor.) In the films, both the Prime Minister and Number 10 itself are referred to on several occasions, e.g., *Thunderball*, where the SPECTRE ransom demand was "received at No 10 this morning"; *On Her Majesty's Secret Service*, where "Number 10's been making ugly noises about Operation Bedlam"; *GoldenEye*, where M relays to Bond that "the Prime Minister's talked to Moscow" about the destruction of the Space Weapons Control Centre at Severnaya; and *Tomorrow Never Dies*, where we learn that Elliot Carver "has spoken to the Prime Minister in London" regarding the crisis in the South China Sea. The PM, in the form of Margaret Thatcher, actually appears—along with the ever-faithful Denis—in *For Your Eyes Only*. The relatively modest Georgian residence—home to British Prime Ministers since Robert Walpole accepted the key from George II in 1735—is also shown briefly in the same film. The famous entrance, which dates from 1760, was faithfully recreated by Peter Lamont's art department, right down to the atmospheric fog and helmeted London bobby standing guard outside the door. Since 1990, the entrance to Downing Street itself has been gated and guarded for security reasons, although you can easily see the dark brick building, located at the end of the street, on the right.

Station: Charing Cross (BA; JU; NO) Exit on the Strand (South) side and go L, past **Trafalgar Square** (27:1), then L into Whitehall. Downing Street is on the W side, just before the massive **Foreign Office** (27:14) complex.

Trivia Challenge 39: In which film does M worry that "If the PM gets to hear of this, he'll hang me from the yardarm"?

27:13

ex HQ of Combined Operations
Richmond Terrace
Whitehall, SW1

Fleming tells us that during World War II, Major Dexter Smythe, the protagonist-villain of the story "Octopussy", was "seconded from the Royal Marines to Combined Operations Headquarters under Mountbatten". Speaking excellent German, he was assigned "the unenviable job of being advanced [*sic*] interrogator on Commando operations across the Channel". Fleming, of course, knew whereof he spoke. Combined Operations was formed by Winston Churchill in June 1940 as a successor to the Inter-Services Training and Development Centre of 1938.

Initially based at the **Admiralty** (27:10), where Fleming himself worked for Naval Intelligence, the new organization was tasked with training commando units for cross-Channel assaults, building and testing landing craft and advising the Chiefs of Staff (COS) on the inter-services problems posed by amphibious warfare. It was subsequently relocated to Richmond Terrace and placed under the command of Churchill's own protégé, Louis Mountbatten, who became the "mounting authority" for all amphibious raids. The organization grew even larger and more important under Mountbatten, who was subsequently promoted to the rank of vice-admiral and given the title Chief of Combined Operations (CCO). Indeed, the success of the Normandy invasion in June 1944 can, in no small measure, be attributed to the work of Mountbatten and his Combined Operations staff, a fact which Churchill himself duly acknowledged. As for Major Smythe, to return to "Octopussy", he spent two years as a translator-commando before being asked to form an intelligence-gathering commando unit for the "Miscellaneous Objectives Bureau". The MOB, Fleming relates, was formed by the Secret Service and Combined Operations and it was tasked with cleaning up Abwehr and Gestapo units after the collapse of Germany. This, as we now know, was pure autobiography. Fleming himself had conceived of the unit, which would be tasked with obtaining sensitive or intelligence-related enemy equipment, including cipher machines and codebooks. The Special Engineering Unit, as it came to be called, was approved by the Joint Intelligence Committee (overseer of MI6) in 1942, but with the provision that it be run by Mountbatten's Combined Operations. This, of course, irked Fleming's Naval Intelligence boss, John Godfrey, although administration of the naval unit, called 30 Assault, was eventually turned over to none other than Commander Ian Fleming. As for Smythe, he later killed an Austrian ski instructor who had led him to a cache of hidden Nazi gold, a crime for which James Bond ultimately threatens to arrest him. I'm sure we can safely assume that this part of the story was fictitious!

Station: Charing Cross (BA; JU; NO) Exit on the Strand (South) side and go L, past **Trafalgar Square** (27:1), then L into Whitehall. The building is on the E side, opposite Downing Street.

27:14

Foreign (& Commonwealth) Office
King Charles Street, SW1

References to the Foreign Office, the government department responsible for overseas relations and foreign affairs (roughly equivalent to the US State Department), occur in the majority of Fleming's novels, starting with the very first, *Casino Royale*. Here, the Chief of Staff learns that M had won a bit of a victory at the FO earlier in the day; what the victory was we are not told. At the end of *Moonraker*, the Soviet Ambassador visits the FO in order to discuss the fate of the Russian submarine destroyed by Hugo Drax's nuclear missile. In *From Russia, With Love*, SMERSH killer Donovan Grant is to be briefed by a former Foreign Office employee who is now in Moscow. (This is a veiled reference to British traitor Donald Maclean, who, along with Guy Burgess, another FO mole, had defected to Moscow in 1951—a fact not officially confirmed until 1956, the year in which Fleming wrote the novel.* Fleming actually mentions Burgess and Maclean by name in Chapter 11, as Bond has been assigned to a Committee of Inquiry to investigate their treachery. For more on these real-life spies, see the **University of Cambridge** [*JBB*].) In *Goldfinger*, Bond cynically describes his work for Universal Export as selling small arms to "anyone the Foreign Office decides doesn't want the stuff to shoot at us with", while in *The Spy Who Loved Me*, Vivienne Michel tells us that her flatmate, Susan, has a job at the Foreign Office ("in something called 'Communications', about which she was very secretive"). The FO is also mentioned in *Doctor No*, *On Her Majesty's Secret Service*, *The Man with the Golden Gun*, and "The Property of a Lady". The Foreign Office and the Commonwealth Office were merged in 1968 and are thus now, technically, the Foreign and Commonwealth Office. The real MI6 has been under the control of the FO/FCO since ca. 1919, in contrast to the Fleming/Eon version of the Secret Service, which answers to the **Ministry of Defence** (27:7) and still seems to be a part of the former Military Intelligence Directorate (see **ex War Office** [27:6] and **MI6 [1994-present]** [24:2]).

Also based here in the Foreign Office was the Passport Control Office, the cover organization under which SIS operated its overseas stations. The FO set up PCO in 1919 with the aim of giving its new charges a more suitable cover than the MI5 Military Control offices through which they had been operating. As PCO was technically separate from the Foreign Office (and actually run by an organization, SIS, that did not officially exist) the FO could deny knowledge of or responsibility for any compromising activities on the part of the local offices. The new system even afforded the local station heads, or passport control officers, a chance to earn additional income through the visa fees they charged foreigners wishing to enter Britain. Unfortunately, many host countries quickly saw through the cover and complained about British spies in their midst. By 1936, on the eve of war, the PCO system had been so thoroughly compromised in Europe that Sir Hugh asked his deputy, Claude

Dansey, to form a parallel network of foreign outposts, one that later became famous as the Z Organisation (see [23:6]). When this, too, was blown, by the disastrous Venlo Affair (in which the Gestapo captured the heads of the two Dutch SIS stations), Sir Stewart, the new C, essentially started from scratch, building up a wartime operation that relied upon a number of different covers, including the "Inter-Service Liaison Department" and, in the US, "British Security Co-ordination". Thus, by the time Ian Fleming wrote his novels in the 1950s and '60s, he could safely speak of the Secret Service station heads operating under the (now-defunct) cover of Passport Control Officers, as he does, for example, of John Strangways in Chapter 3 of *Doctor No*. He could even have them fix up a good (fake) passport in the name of a Scottish baronet, as they apparently do for James Bond in Chapter 8 of *OHMSS*. Today, the London Passport Office is located in Clive House, 20 Petty France, just west of the St James's Park Underground station. Its duly authorized function of Passport Control is subsumed under HM Immigration department and you enact one of its minor rituals every time you enter the United Kingdom and show your passport to the poker-faced folks behind the little counters. Incidentally, if anyone ever says there's a message for you at Passport Control, think twice before you check it out. The last fellow who did was Peter Franks, in the film *Diamonds Are Forever*, and look what happened to him!

Station: Charing Cross (BA; JU; NO) Exit on the Strand (South) side and go L, past **Trafalgar Square** (27:1), then L into Whitehall. The building is on the W side, just past Downing Street. The FCO's palace-sized, Italianate HQ, constructed between 1861 and 1875, actually comprises four buildings, each with its own courtyard. The original arrangement was as follows: Foreign Office, northwest corner, India Office southwest corner (both overlooking **St James's Park** [27:21]); Colonial Office, northeast corner, **Home Office** (27:15) southeast corner (both overlooking Whitehall).

*Interestingly, the two men were unearthed in Moscow by one of Fleming's own foreign correspondents at *The Sunday Times*—Richard Hughes, the model for Dikko Henderson in the novel *You Only Live Twice*. Indeed, Hughes had been directed to secure an interview with the two men by none other than Fleming himself.

27:15

ex Home Office
Foreign & Commonwealth Building (Southeast Wing)
Whitehall, SW1

The Home Office is the government ministry responsible for the administration of law and order, immigration,

The Foreign Office as seen from St James's Park

community relations and other matters of public order. To a certain extent, its functions coincide with those of the American Department of Justice, as well as the State Department and the Department of the Interior. Its minister, the Secretary of State for Home Affairs, or Home Secretary, oversees the internal Security Service, or **MI5** (27:29), an approximate counterpart to the American FBI. In the short story "Risico", the Home Secretary persuades a reluctant M to take on an Italian gang that is smuggling heroin into Britain. In the film *Thunderball*, the Home Secretary serves as the liaison between the Secret Service and the Prime Minister (although the character is actually called "*Foreign* Secretary" in the closing credits, which, ironically, would be correct in the real-life intelligence bureaucracy). In fact, the screenplay indicates that the conference room (where M has gathered all the Double-0 agents) is actually located in the Home Office itself. Contrarily, the film suggests that the grand room is just down the hall from M's office at Universal Exports (see **Residence of the Argentine Ambassador** [2:4]). In any case, there is no connection between the real British Secret Intelligence Service, which operates *outside* the United Kingdom, and the Home Office, which is concerned with matters of *internal* security. The real MI6 answers to the **Foreign Office** (27:14), while Fleming's version—and Eon's version apart from *Thunderball*—is affiliated with the **Ministry of Defence** (27:7). The Home Office moved out of the southeast wing of the Foreign Office Building, facing Whitehall, in 1978. It is presently located at 50 Queen Anne's Gate, very near the former Broadway Buildings home of MI6 (see [27:22]).

Station: Charing Cross (BA; JU; NO) See the **Foreign Office** (27:14).

27:16

ex HQ of the Metropolitan Police Service (informally Scotland Yard)
Norman Shaw Building (formerly New Scotland Yard)
Victoria Embankment, SW1

The Metropolitan Police Service was originally headquartered at 4 Whitehall Place, on the site of the present **Ministry of Ag. And Fish.** (27:5). The building backed on to a street called (Great) Scotland Yard, whose name was subsequently extended to the Met itself. In 1890, "Scotland Yard" relocated to a new building here, on the Victoria Embankment, which, appropriately enough, was named *New* Scotland Yard. Within a decade, expansion and specialization had prompted the demand for an even larger facility, hence the second building just to the south, linked to its predecessor by a bridge. It is this Baroque stronghold, designed by Richard Norman Shaw, that James Bond visits in the novels *Moonraker, Diamonds Are Forever* and *OHMSS*, as well as the screen treatment *James Bond of the Secret Service*. In the first, Bond is briefed by Assistant Commissioner of Police Ronald Vallance and reflects that the courtyards and cul-de-sacs of the Yard remind him of a prison without roofs. (Later in the same novel, Bond liaises with Gala Brand, a member of the Special Branch of the Yard's famous Criminal Investigation Department, or CID.) In *Diamonds*, Bond is again briefed by Assistant Commissioner Vallance here at the Yard before himself posing as "Sergeant James" of the CID! (Bond again poses as a CID man in "The Property of a Lady", tells Tilly Masterton [*sic*] that he works for the Yard in *Goldfinger* and repeats the same cover story to Judy Havelock in "For Your Eyes Only".) In *OHMSS*, Bond delivers the list of the Piz Gloria girls to Scotland Yard and confers with Vallance on the final stages of the operation to get Blofeld. In *JBSS*, Bond again liaises with the Assistant Commissioner here at the Yard and Vallance himself plays his biggest role in any Bond adventure (see Appendix Two). He briefs Bond several times throughout the story, essentially usurping M's role, and organizes much of the action both before and after the theft of the atomic warhead. Scotland Yard itself, for which Fleming seems to have had limitless admiration, enters the fray in *Diamonds Are Forever, Goldfinger*, "Risico", *The Spy Who Loved Me, On Her Majesty's Secret Service* and "Octopussy". In *From Russia, With Love*, the author evokes a romantic, even nationalistic image of the venerable police department as the Soviet intelligence chiefs assess the "English myth" of Sherlock Holmes, Scotland Yard and the Secret Service. In 1967, the mythical Met moved to 10 Broadway, off Victoria Street, this building also being named New Scotland Yard. Appropriately—albeit rather awkwardly—the Victoria Embankment site is sometimes called *Old* New Scotland Yard, although its proper name is the Norman Shaw Building, after its renowned designer. It is currently used as an office building for members of Parliament, and is therefore not open to the public. Watch for its bright orange-red façade just north of the **Houses Parliament** (27:18) in the opening boat chase of *The World Is Not Enough*.

Station: Westminster (CI; DI; JU) Exit for Victoria Embankment and turn L; the complex is just ahead on the L.

27:17

HM Treasury Treasury Chambers Great George Street, SW1

Doubles as: Universal Exports, London (exterior) in *On Her Majesty's Secret Service*

HM Treasury is the government department responsible for the management of Britain's finances and economy. It enters the Bond market in several novels, often playing an unexpected, behind-the-scenes role in 007's adventures. In *Casino Royale*, for example, it supplies the funds for Bond's gambling assault on Le Chiffre, while in *Live and Let Die*, we learn that M constantly battles with the department over the Secret Service budget. In *Moonraker*, the Treasury asks **Scotland Yard** (27:16) to investigate some of Hugo Drax's business practices; in *Diamonds Are Forever*, a Treasury official visits M to discuss a suspected smuggling operation; in *Goldfinger*, the department informs M that the Double-0 Section is redundant (!); and in *OHMSS*, the Treasury (read overburdened British taxpayer) has to cough up "a great chunk of foreign currency" to replace the three million or so birds that died after exposure to the "fowl pest" Blofeld unleashed at the National Poultry Show at **Olympia** (36:1). The Treasury's magnificent early Victorian headquarters, designed by Sir Charles Barry and incorporating much of William Kent's 18th-century original, also plays an unexpected role in the cinematic version of *OHMSS*: it is the site of "Universal Exports", a.k.a., the British Secret Service. Director Peter Hunt actually discovered the building on a recce of Whitehall and personally supervised the shot of the "Universal" plaque (which immediately follows the opening gun-barrel sequence) one quiet Sunday morning. "I wanted to show 'London'," Peter recalled, "so that was the perfect location because you could get Big Ben [reflected] in there, which is very recognizable." I asked Peter why he specifically wanted a "Universal Exports" establishing shot when none of the previous directors had bothered. He replied quite simply: "Because it was in the book." Peter also decided to "pull a Hitchcock" and make a cameo appearance in the film. That's him, reflected in the plaque, walking toward the camera. (Since then, director Lewis Gilbert has appeared in *Moonraker* [in the St. Mark's Square crowd scene] and producer Michael Wilson has appeared in every film since *The Spy Who Loved Me*.). **Pinewood** (*JBB*) matte artist Cliff Culley actually made the one-of-a-kind brass nameplate, which, sadly, has long since vanished. (A near-replica was sold at **Christie's South Kensington** [21:1] in 1998.)

Station: Westminster (CI; DI; JU) Take the Whitehall (West) exit into Parliament Street, turn L at the top of the stairs, then immediately R into Great George Street. The "Universal" plaque was placed near the base of the second tower, just past the three archways. Your view of **Parliament** (27:18) will be obscured by a red telephone booth (placed there since the film), the fourth one along from Parliament Street.

27:18

Houses of Parliament (formally the Palace of Westminster) Parliament Square, SW1

Undoubtedly the most recognizable building in London, the Palace of Westminster, seat of the Houses of Parliament, dates largely from the mid-19th century, a devastating fire having destroyed nearly all of the older structure. Upon its completion in 1860, the neo-Gothic masterpiece boasted over 1,000 rooms, 100 staircases, 11 courtyards, two miles of corridors and a 316-foot clock tower that would become the most famous landmark in London. (Note: While both St Stephen's Clock Tower and its massive timepiece are popularly known as "Big Ben", that nickname properly belongs to the 13-ton bell inside the tower. Fleming seems to have it right when he notes that Big Ben sounded three in Chapter 5 of *Goldfinger*. I have lost count of the number of times the famous chime—a symbol of the nation itself to generations of Britons at home and abroad—is heard in the films.) Establishing shots of this majestic building, by *all* accounts a true architectural triumph, serve to identify London and/or the British government in both *Dr. No* and *Goldfinger*. The Palace also appears in the reflection of the Universal Exports plaque in *On Her Majesty's Secret Service* (suggesting that MI6 is located in the **Treasury** (27:17) in Great George Street); in *For Your Eyes Only*, as Bond travels by helicopter to **Beckton Gas Works** (29:1); and as a striking backdrop to the Westminster section of the pre-credit boat chase in *The World Is Not Enough*. Parliament in general, or the House of Commons in particular, is referred to in several novels, e.g., *Moonraker*, where we are told that Parliament considers the rocket "sound"; and *You Only Live Twice*, where we learn that a Secret Service scandal known as the Prenderghast case had led to Questions in the House and a trial at the **Old Bailey** (5:8).

Station: Westminster (CI; DI; JU) Exit for the Houses of Parliament. The Houses are generally in session from mid-October to late-July, with a three-week recess for the Christmas holiday. For access, queue at the St Stephen's Gate entrance (clearly marked) in St Margaret's Street. The lines are shortest after 6pm (while Parliamentary business may go on till 10pm). **Hours:** Mon-Thu 2:30pm-indefinite (Wed also 10am-2pm); Fri 9:30am-3pm. Tickets for a guided tour or a seat at Prime Minister's Question Time must be obtained in advance from your embassy or MP.

27:19

Westminster Bridge SW1, SE1

This extra-wide cast-iron structure (its 84-ft width was considered exceptional at the time) may be seen in the establishing shot of the **Houses of Parliament** (27:18) in *Goldfinger*; when Bond's helicopter passes the Houses of Parliament in the *For Your Eyes Only* pre-credit sequence; and as Bond overtakes Cigar Girl at—where else?—the Houses of Parliament in the *TWINE* boat chase. (Look for several shots of the bridge's light green arches in the latter.) It is, without a doubt, the best place in London from which to view the Palace of Westminster.

Station: Westminster (CI; DI; JU) Exit for Westminster Bridge. For a noteworthy spot on the South Bank side of the bridge, see **James Bond's "Big Ben" Photo Site** (20:1).

Above: The TWINE boat chase beneath Westminster Bridge.
Below: Parliament as seen from Westminster Bridge.

27:20

ex Ministry of Defence Storey's Gate, SW1

During World War II, the British Government set up the so-called War Cabinet to oversee and coordinate the activities of the country's three separate defence ministries, the **Admiralty** (28:12), which administered the Navy, the **War Office** (27:6), which governed the Army and the **Air Ministry** (23:7), which oversaw the Air Force. After the war, the Government decided to expand the War Cabinet into a permanent department called the Ministry of Defence, which would formulate and coordinate Britain's overall defense policy and allocate defense expenditures. In purely internal matters, i.e., those having to do exclusively with the Navy, Army and Air Force, the Admiralty, War Office and Air Ministry, respectively, would remain supreme. It is this early, relatively modest incarnation of the MOD that Fleming refers to in Chapter 4 of *Moonraker*, where both Bond and M pose as Ministry employees; Chapter 15 of *The Spy Who Loved Me*, where Bond gives the actual Storey's Gate address as his business address (in a letter to Vivienne Michel); and Chapter 8 of *OHMSS*, where Bond plans to use a Ministry of Defence cutout as a liaison between himself and Sable Basilisk of the **College of Arms** (5:11). And it is to the three traditionally separate departments that Fleming alludes in *Casino Royale* when he describes the Secret Service as an "adjunct to the British Defence Ministries" (note the plural). Over the years, indeed, even as Fleming was evolving James Bond's world, the original Ministry of Defence dramatically increased both its power and scope, prompting the government's 1963 decision to simply scrap the old defense ministries in favor of one super ministry. For the rest of the story, see the **Ministry of Defence** (27:7).

Station: Westminster (CI; DI; JU) Take the Whitehall (West) exit into Parliament Street, turn L at the top of the stairs, then immediately R into Great George Street. Storey's Gate will be ahead on the L; the Ministry headquarters was on the W side of the street, at the corner.

27:21

St James's Park SW1

In the last chapter of *Moonraker*, a battered James Bond is dropped off at the corner of Birdcage Walk and Queen Anne's Gate, opposite London's oldest and most ornamental royal park. He had been test-driving a 1953 Mark VI Bentley, battleship gray in color (like its predecessor), with dark blue leather upholstery. Bond tells the test-driver from Bentley's (actually **Jack Barclay Ltd** [13:22]) that he will buy the car, providing they have it at the ferry terminal at Calais by the next evening. He then limps into the park, sits down opposite the island in the lake and anxiously awaits the arrival of Gala Brand, the new love of his life. Unfortunately, Gala batters Bond even further, explaining that she cannot run off to France with him because she is to be married the following day. Bond puts on a brave face, of course, pretending that he is only mildly disappointed. Ironically, the rebuff couldn't have happened in a more romantic spot, as Fleming doubtless knew and as you will, too, when you visit St James's Park.

Station: St James's Park (CI; DI) From the station walk straight up Queen Anne's Gate (past the new Home Office to the L and the former home of MI6 [see (27:22)] to the R), across Birdcage Walk and into the park. Duck Island is off to the R. **Hours:** 10am-9:30pm daily in summer; 10am-4pm daily in winter

27:22

ex HQ of MI6 (1926-1967) Broadway Buildings 54 Broadway, SW1

The Secret Intelligence Service has occupied a number of buildings since its inception, including the palatial Whitehall Court (27:8), where it was based during World War I, and the far more modest house at 1 Melbury Road (9:6), which, under its founder, Captain Mansfield Cumming, it occupied in the years immediately afterward. Cumming's successor as Chief of the Secret Service, or "C" (see below), was Rear Admiral (later Sir) Hugh Sinclair, a former Director of Naval Intelligence (see [27:10]) and something of an empire builder. Sinclair's vision for SIS included not only a return to Westminster but also an absorption of two other secret services, **MI5** (13:30) and the Government Code & Cypher School (GC&CS). In the end, he scored two out of three: the government placed GC&CS under his control in 1923 and authorized new Westminster offices for both organizations in 1926.* (MI5 remained under **War Office** [27:6] control until 1931, when it was made a civilian agency answerable to the **Home Office** [27:16].) Sinclair chose to base his new empire in Broadway Buildings, a nine-story, mansard-roofed office block located near **St James's Park** (27:21) and, more importantly, just around the corner from his own flat in Queen Anne's Gate (see next entry). One of Broadway Buildings' covers—since SIS did not officially exist until the 1990s—was the Minimax Fire Extinguisher Company; another, the Government Communications Centre, is still in use (see **MI6 [1994-present]** [24:2]). SIS—also known, since 1940, as MI6 (see [27:8])—would remain here until 1967, a period encompassing the Second World War, the height of the Cold War, and, of course, Ian Fleming's entire literary career. Sadly, the early Broadway years were not among the most stellar for SIS, which, in the absence of any overseas crisis (and in consequence of the 1930s Depression), was largely starved of funds by its **Foreign Office** (27:14) masters. The result, of course, was that the organization often produced unreliable intelligence for its clients in Whitehall. Government confidence in the Secret Service was further eroded by the fact that Sinclair had focused most of his limited resources on the Soviets, instead of the Germans, who, as it happened, posed a slightly more serious threat to Britain come 1939. That very year, Sinclair died and a new Chief took over his "amateur organisation with a limited budget" (as historian—and former SIS officer—Hugh Trevor-Roper dubbed it). He was Colonel (later Major General Sir) Stewart Menzies (pronounced "Mingis") and he slowly but surely began to rebuild and restore the Secret Intelligence Service. Indeed, by the end of the war, Menzies's SIS had achieved a number of important successes, perhaps none more crucial than the "Ultra" intelligence produced by GC&CS at **Bletchley Park** (*JBB*), Buckinghamshire. Unfortunately, being a *secret* organization, SIS's failures and scandals have tended to attract enormous publicity (see, for example, the **University of Cambridge** [*JBB*], recruiting ground for Soviet Spy Kim Philby, later of MI6; and **HM Naval Base Portsmouth** [*JBB*], scene of a botched MI6 operation involving a visiting Soviet ship), while its successes have gone virtually, and of necessity, unrecognized. Still, the organization retains its hold on the public imagination, something it has done since the 1920s, when its successes in the First World War inspired the American belief that SIS was one the six institutions that ruled the world. (The others were: **Buckingham Palace** [16:27]; the White House; the **Bank of England** [5:12]; the Federal Reserve Bank; and the Vatican.) Thus, when Ian Fleming crafted "the spy story to end all spy stories" in 1952, he installed his hero *not* in the Naval Intelligence Division of the **Admiralty** (27:10), where he himself had served, but in the legendary Secret Intelligence Service. (In fact, during World War II, Fleming actually served as a liaison between his department and SIS's Naval Section here at No. 54.) His fictional version of SIS, which was also located near a park (see **Regent's Park** [12:2]), in a nine-story building, with the cover "Universal Export" ("Universal Exports" in the films), clearly evokes Broadway Buildings. (In *Moonraker* alone Fleming writes that the top floor is the *ninth*, elsewhere, he specifies that it is the eight, which means that the building itself has nine stories, counting the ground floor. Entrance to Menzies's fourth floor (US: fifth floor) office, at least during the war, was through a padded, double door, over which was positioned a red lamp ("do not enter") and a green lamp ("enter"), just as Fleming described for the fictional Secret Service Chief. (See, for example, Chapter 12 of *From Russia, With Love*; in earlier novels, the privacy light was either blue or green.) Further, Menzies's secretary—and the guardian of his inner sanctum—was the formidable Miss Pettigrew, whom Fleming converted into the more glamorous Miss Moneypenny. (Note that in the original *Casino Royale* manuscript, M's secretary is "Miss Pettavel".) Of course, Menzies himself was known as "C", which Fleming converted to "M" for his fictional Service Chief. The title "C" had originated with the Service's founder, Sir Mansfield Cumming, who simply followed Whitehall custom and used the initial letter of his surname as an abbreviation/cover. (Similarly, his counterpart at MI5, Sir Vernon Kell, used "K".) When Cumming died in 1923, his successor, Sir Hugh Sinclair, retained "C" as *his* cover, but apparently with the understanding that the initial also stood for "Chief". Precisely why Fleming chose the initial "M" is still debated (although plainly he could not have used "C" itself). Some sources suggest that he pinched it from Maxwell Knight, the wartime head of MI5's counter-subversion section (see [15:1]), others from Colin McVean Gubbins, one of the wartime heads of **SOE** (12:8). Both were known as "M" within their respective organizations and both were friends of Fleming's. Freudians, of course, like to point out that Ian called his mother, Eve, "M". I prefer to think that he borrowed the initial from Sir Stewart Menzies, with whom he worked during the war and with whom he maintained a cordial friendship afterward. In any case, like Cumming, Fleming's Sir Miles Messervy used the initial letter of his surname as his cover. That "M" may have stood for anything else is never explicitly stated in the novels. Still, it must now be accorded an additional significance, since, as with the real-life "C", the title "M" has been transferred to Sir Miles Messervy's cinematic successor.† So, if "C" is the "Chief", perhaps "M" is the "Manager" of the Secret Service, a title suggested by his cover as "Managing Director" of Universal Exports (see, for example, Chapter 22 of *Diamonds Are Forever* and Chapter 24 of *From Russia, With Love*), as well as by Mansfield Cumming, who referred to himself and Kell as "managers" of their respective services. In writing of the organization itself, Fleming generally stuck to the traditional name "Secret Service", although in the later novels he also used "SIS". (The change may have been prompted by the fact that Fleming had sought and received Foreign Office clearance to depict the Secret Service in the aborted screenplay he devised with Jack Whittingham and Kevin McClory in 1959 [see Appendix Two].) The Eon films have employed both "British Secret Service" (e.g., *From Russia With Love*, *Diamonds Are Forever* and *Tomorrow Never Dies*) and "MI6" (*Dr. No*, *GoldenEye* and *The World Is Not Enough*, with the last clearly suggesting that the Service remains part of the Military Intelligence organization; see **MI6 [1994-present]** [24:2] and the **ex War Office** [27:6]). All are in some sense correct: Secret Intelligence Service (SIS) is the actual name of the organization; MI6 (Military Intelligence, Section Six) is its World War II-era cover, still in popular use (see [27:8]); and Secret Service is its original name, which officially survived in the title of the "Chief of the Secret Service" until 1994. (Since then, the title has been "Chief of the Intelligence Service".) Finally, regarding Bond's famous "licence to kill", one must acknowledge that Fleming—or his American editor—invented the phrase, if not the concept. (The first appearance comes in Chapter 14 of *Diamonds Are Forever*: In the British edition, Leiter asks if Bond still has "that double 0 number that means you're allowed to kill"; in the American edition, Leiter asks about "that double-0 number that licenses you to kill". Fleming, if he didn't actually suggest the rephrasing, certainly ran with the punchier version in subsequent stories, starting with *Doctor No*.) But were there—*are* there—MI6 agents who are permitted—or "licensed"—to kill? There certainly were during the Second World War (although they weren't code-named "00"-something, "00" being the prefix used on classified government documents). One such assassination—of a German spy working in New York in 1941—was apparently authorized by MI6's American bureau head William Stephenson, whom Fleming met there that very May. (Indeed, it was from Stephenson that Ian learned of the Japanese cipher expert operating in Rockefeller Center, one floor below British Security Coordination, i.e., MI6, which, in turn, Fleming adapted for Bond's back story—his first assassination—in *Casino Royale*. Whether he also knew of the elimination of the German spy is unclear.) Following the war, MI6 certainly undertook, or at least backed, "wet ops", including the elimination of General Mahmud Afshartus, Chief of the Iranian National Police, as part of the U.S.-British operation to overthrow the country's prime minister. (Dr. Mohammad Mossadeq had nationalized the Anglo-Iranian Oil Company [afterward British Petroleum] in 1953 and Britain wanted it back; the U.S. joined in the belief that Mossadeq's populist movement would turn communist and the Middle East would topple in an early variant of the "domino theory".) As a result of its success in Iran, MI6 formed a Special Political Action section to undertake propaganda, sabotage, assassination and other "disruptive actions". Its most notable early target was Egyptian leader Gamal Abdel Nasser, whose life was spared in October 1956 when the three-man SPA hit team apparently got cold feet. After nearly two decades of toppling (or attempting to topple) any number of unfriendly dictators and regimes (actions cynically alluded to by Alec Trevelyan in *GoldenEye*), SPA was shut down in 1973 by the new "C", Maurice Oldfield. (Following the Soviet invasion of Afghanistan in 1979, Margaret Thatcher re-instituted the famous "disruptive actions", also known among certain insiders as "James Bond operations". These included, fittingly enough, the dispatch of MI6 agents and materiel to aid mujahedin units fighting the Soviets in Afghanistan.) That SIS has since been involved in assassinations remains a hotly debated topic, with allegations of plots against Libya's Qaddafi and Yugoslavia's Milosevic at the top of critics' most recent "hit lists". One thing that is not debated, however, is that, per Section 7 of the *Intelligence Services Act 1994*, the Foreign Secretary may authorize MI6 agents to perform acts abroad for which they might be liable to criminal prosecution at home. Does that sound like a "licence to kill"...?

Station: St. James's Park (CI; DI) The building with the longest SIS association—now used as offices by London Regional Transport—is opposite the Broadway exit of the tube station. Next to it is The Old Star pub, the one-time after-hours haunt of the Broadway Buildings "cowboys". For the later history of the organization, see **ex MI6 (1967-1994)** (11:1), **MI6 (1994-present)** (24:2) and, especially, **ex HQ of the SOE** (12:8) for more about those covers. For a photo, see page 169.

*Writers have traditionally listed the year of the move to Broadway Buildings as 1925, or even 1924. However, recently released Foreign Office documents (specifically, the Secret Service Committee Report of 1925) make it clear that as of December 1925 SIS was still based in Melbury Road and the move to Westminster, while recommended, had not yet been approved.

†I say "successor", singular, because I do not subscribe to the theory that Robert Brown's M was actually Admiral Hargreaves from *The Spy Who Loved Me*. Were any such switch to have been intended, the filmmakers would have clearly indicated this in *Octopussy*. In fact, if anything, they would have wanted to stress the continuity of their series, in contrast to the "rival" Bond, *Never Say Never Again*, which was released a few months after *Octopussy*. Moreover, there is certainly ample precedent in the Bond films for recasting the same part with different actors. However, just to confirm that Robert Brown was indeed Sir Miles Messervy, I put the question to the film's director, John Glen. Here is his response: "No, Bob Brown was not Admiral Hargreaves. He was playing the same character as Bernard [Lee]. Quite frankly, I wouldn't have thought that apart from Bob himself and some of us [the filmmakers] that anybody would have

even remembered his part in *The Spy Who Loved Me*." Case closed.

Trivia Challenge 40: In British Intelligence circles, MI6 is known as "the Firm". In which film does Bond refer to his organization as such?

27:23

ex Home of the Secret Service Chief (?)
21 Queen Anne's Gate, SW1

Ian Fleming never gave us the address of M's London home, merely implying that the Secret Service Chief maintained such a residence, in addition to his country house in Windsor. (See Chapter 2 of *Diamonds Are Forever* and Chapter 20 of *On Her Majesty's Secret Service*, as well as **Quarterdeck** [*JBB*].) What the author undoubtedly knew, but chose not to exploit in any way, was that the real head of MI6 lived here, on the first floor (US: second floor) of 21 Queen Anne's Gate, a beautifully preserved brick house dating from 1704. The first Chief of the Secret Service (CSS, or simply "C") to live here was Admiral Sir Hugh Sinclair (known to his Whitehall cronies as "Quex"), who succeeded Sir Mansfield Cumming in 1923. At that time, the Service itself was based in rather modest premises in West Kensington (see [9:6]) and Sinclair determined to change this. In 1926, with the financial support of the new Conservative government, he engineered the transfer of SIS to Broadway Buildings (27:22), a large office block that conveniently backed on to 21 Queen Anne's Gate. A concealed door in his new fourth floor (US: fifth floor) office led to a hidden passage connecting the two buildings. This meant, of course, that Sinclair never had to venture outside the secure world of home and office, unless it was to **White's** (16:2), the St James's club to which the Secret Service Chiefs traditionally belonged. In 1940, Sir Hugh was succeeded by Sir Stewart Menzies (pronounced "Mingis"), who successfully presided over MI6 during World War II and, somewhat less successfully, during the early years of the Cold War. Menzies is probably the most famous "C" (after Cumming) and an obvious model for the character of M. Fleming knew Menzies personally and even pinched his surname for a minor character—Corporal Menzies—in "The Living Daylights". Major-General (later Sir) John Sinclair, the former Director of Naval Intelligence, took over from Menzies for a brief but disastrous period known as "the horrors" (when MI6 was publicly humiliated for a number of botched espionage and assassination plots), to be followed by MI5 Director-General (!) Sir Dick White in 1956. Sir Dick, the only person to head both MI5 *and* MI6, was the last Secret Service Chief to live at Number 21. (See also **ex MI6 (1967-1994)** [11:1].)

Station: St. James's Park (CI; DI) Take the Broadway exit, walk straight up Queen Anne's Gate and follow it around to the R. The building is just ahead on the R. The War Office Intelligence Branch, the forerunner of Britain's present-day intelligence machinery, including MI6, was housed just across the street at Nos. 16 and 18 from 1884 to 1901

27:24

ex Ministry of Supply Office (1939-1945)
Portland House
Tothill Street, SW1

Although based in Shell-Mex House (see [23:9]), the MOS also operated a special "war department" here in Westminster, just down the street from **MI6** (27:22). The real-life "Q", gadget-maker Charles Fraser-Smith, worked here in CT6 (Clothing and Textile, Section Six, a cover identity linked to that of MI6), crafting ingenious devices and concealed weapons for use by British spies, Resistance fighters and escaping POWs in Europe. One day, during the war, Commander Ian Fleming of Naval Intelligence paid a call on Fraser-Smith, hoping to secure some hollowed-out golf balls for a scheme he had in mind. Whether Fleming ever got the balls is unclear, although 007 certainly did, in Chapter 6 of *Diamonds Are Forever*. Bond himself replicates Fleming's trip to the Ministry in Chapter 10 of *Moonraker*, although that meeting would have taken place at the Shell-Mex House headquarters.

Station: St James's Park (CI; DI) The site is just down from Broadway Buildings, on the NE corner of Dartmouth and Tothill.

Trivia Challenge 41: The MOS procured the supplies that the Army's "Q" Staff then distributed. This is the source of Fleming's—and Eon's—"Q Branch". What does "Q" stand for?

27:25

ex Head Office of Vickers Ltd
Vickers House
Broadway, SW1

Naylor, Hutchinson, Vickers & Company began as a Sheffield steel manufacturing firm in 1829. Through expansion, merger and acquisition, Vickers (Naylor and Hutchinson were quickly dropped) went on to become one of the largest and most famous armament companies in the world—a true British icon. At one time or another, the firm manufactured planes, trains and automobiles, as well as ships, tanks, subs, guns, ammunition and airships—all of them quite large and quite effective. Vickers not only contributed mightily to the British effort in both World Wars, it also produced the first of the famous "V-Bombers", the Vickers Valiant, which were to provide the nation's nuclear deterrent during the early decades of the Cold War (see **RAF Waddington** [*JBB*] for more on the V-Bombers). Between the wars, Vickers, or, rather, its subsidiary Vickers-Armstrongs, marketed its vast range of armaments both at home and abroad. (The policy was abandoned when it was realized that these weapons could theoretically be used against Britain. See the **Foreign Office** [27:14] for Fleming's cheeky reference to this problem.) One of Vickers' foreign representatives, according to the Obituary in *You Only Live Twice*, was Andrew Bond of Glencoe, Scotland (see [*JBB*]). In fact, Andrew's son James obtained most of his early education in Europe as a consequence of his father's travels on behalf of the company. Later, during the war, an old Vickers colleague of his father's helped young James join "a branch of what was subsequently to become the Ministry of Defence [i.e., the Secret Service]." Another Vickers subsidiary, the Metropolitan-Vickers Electrical Company (known as "Metrovick"), is also connected to the Bond saga, in this case through Ian Fleming. Metrovick, which Vickers formed in 1919 and sold in 1928 (the name was kept by the new owners, Associated Electrical Industries, Ltd), had cozied up to the Soviet Union in the early 1920s and, as a result, won a number of sizeable contracts to build and install heavy electrical machinery in the newly-formed Communist nation. In March 1933, six Metrovick engineers were arrested in Moscow and charged with sabotage and espionage. The incident shocked and outraged the British public, which assumed the whole thing to have been a frame-up. (The Soviets were apparently seeking a scapegoat to blame for the failure of their myriad "reforms".) As a result, all the major British news organizations sent reporters to cover the show trial in Moscow the following month. Journeying to Russia on behalf of Reuters was none other than novice reporter Ian Fleming, who had joined the famous news agency in 1931. His coverage of the trial, in which five of the men were found guilty (and subsequently deported), is described under **ex Reuters** (5:3). Throughout the Fleming/Bond period—indeed from 1911 until 1962—Vickers was based in Vickers House, Broadway, on part of the site now occupied by New Scotland Yard (see [27:16]). In 1962, the firm took over the top half of gleaming Millbank Tower (which may be glimpsed during the *TWINE* boat chase), naming it, what else, Vickers House. It was during this period, specifically in 1980, that Vickers bought **Rolls-Royce Motor Cars Ltd** (*JBB*), then, as now, based in Crewe, Cheshire. The match was never a good one, though, and Vickers sold the famous automaker to Volkswagen in July 1998. Four months later, the firm completed its move to yet another Vickers House, this one in Bessborough Gardens, just around the corner from Millbank Tower.

Station: St James's Park (CI; DI) Take the Broadway exit R into Broadway; the site is ahead on the L.

27:26

ex Colonial Office
Church House
Great Smith Street, SW1

The Colonial Office was one of three government departments concerned with Britain's external relations. (The others were the Foreign Office and the Commonwealth Relations Office [mentioned in B *The Man with the Golden Gun*], which are today combined in a single ministry, the **Foreign & Commonwealth Office** [27:14].) This particular department was responsible for the administration of Britain's many dependent territories (some 50 colonies, protectorates and other dependencies in 1957), including the appointment and supervision of colonial governors. Its presence is felt more or less strongly in a number of Bond's literary adventures. In Chapter 16 of *Live and Let Die*, for example, we learn that the Colonial Office had tried to help the Secret Service gain access to Mr. Big's Jamaican stronghold, but to no avail. In *Doctor No*, the Colonial Office works with the Secret Service and the **Ministry of Defence** (27:7) in the investigation of the mysterious island of Crab Key, while in "The Hildebrand Rarity" the department pronounces the Seychelles Islands "safe as houses", though M dispatches Bond to do a security check in any case. In "Quantum of Solace", Bond liases with the Bahamian Governor and listens to the man's extended anecdote about Philip Masters of the Colonial Office; in "Octopussy" the department will facilitate an exchange of cables between Government House in Jamaica and the Secret Service and **Scotland Yard** (27:16) in London regarding the prosecution of Major Smythe. Of course, in the real world, Bond would seldom if ever have liaised with the Colonial Office or its overseas officials since British colonies come under the jurisdiction of **MI5** (13:30), not SIS. But then, M never did have any compunction about stepping on MI5's toes, did he? In 1966, the Colonial Office and the Commonwealth Relations Office were merged into a single Commonwealth Office, which was housed in the Foreign Office building in Whitehall. The Commonwealth and Foreign Offices were, in turn, merged into a single ministry in 1968.

Station: St James's Park (CI; DI) Exit the station into Petty France/Broadway (opposite the new Home Office), turn R and follow this straight into Tothill Street. At Victoria Street (near Westminster Abbey), look for Great Smith Street across the way to the R. Cross Victoria Street to Great Smith Street, walk toward the Westminster Abbey Choir School on the L and look for the entrance to Dean's Yard. Enter through the archway into Dean's Yard and look for Church House on the R.

27:27

Marquis of Granby Pub
Dean Bradley Street, SW1

Ian Fleming always claimed to have pinched the name of his fictional hero from that of American ornithologist James Bond, author of the seminal reference work *Birds of the West Indies* (one of Fleming's "bibles" in Jamaica). Yet, according to biographer Donald McCormick, Fleming may well have settled upon Bond's name and number here in the venerable Marquis of Granby—nine years before he put the paper in the typewriter at *Goldeneye*. McCormick's source is a gentleman named G.H. Forster, who, in a 1991 letter to *The Daily Telegraph*, claimed to have spent an hour with Fleming in this pub in 1943. During their chat, Forster convinced Fleming of the significance—and utility—of the lucky number 7, and gave him the names of two school mates, James Aitken and Harry Bond, which, through simple transposition, would yield the character names Harry Aitken and...well, you get the idea. In fact, McCormick does not name the pub at which Forster claimed to have met Fleming, but others have. Rightly or wrongly, the pub has now become a part of Bond's London. In addition to references by writers such as York Membery (author of *Pierce Brosnan: the Biography*), the Marquis of Granby is now described by local tour guides as the "birthplace" of James Bond!

Station: St James's Park (CI; DI) Follow Broadway S as it becomes Horseferry Road; continue past Marsham Street, and look for Dean Bradley Street ahead to the L. The pub is on the L side of the street.

27:28

ICI Group Headquarters
Imperial Chemical House
9 Millbank, SW1

Amalgamated from four major British chemical manufacturers in 1926, Imperial Chemical Industries is the largest such concern in the United Kingdom. In fact, ICI operates 200 facilities in over 50 countries, manufacturing some *50,000 products*, including industrial chemicals, paints, explosives, drugs, pesticides, plastics and synthetic fibers. As the epitome of a British, indeed, an international corporate giant, ICI is briefly mentioned in Chapter 4 of *You Only Live Twice*. There, Dikko Henderson explains the seemingly mysterious Japanese social hierarchy to James Bond, noting that the buck stops with the Emperor, who must make peace with his ancestors and the gods. In fact, it's all rather similar to the operation of a big corporation, like ICI or Shell, except that the ladder stops with a Board of Directors, and not with the Almighty or your great-grandfather. Somewhat astonishingly, the company is still headquartered in the same purpose-built office block into which it moved in 1928.

Station: Westminster (CI; DI; JU) Exit for the Houses of Parliament, turn L into St Margaret's Street and continue past Parliament into Millbank. Just before Lambeth Bridge, look for the first of the three large, Edwardian-era blocks. This is ICI; the second and third belong to **MI5** (27:29).

Trivia Challenge 42: In the film adaptation, Bond poses as the new managing director of what thinly-disguised version of ICI?

27:29

MI5 (1995-present)
Thames House
***Millbank, SW1** (near Lambeth Bridge)*

The current home of MI5 is in fact an old home: the Security Service was briefly located on two floors of the impressive Thames House in 1937. In the 1990s, the Edwardian complex was refurbished to the tune of £245,000,000, presumably providing all the mod cons a busy counter-espionage agent might require. (Sharp-eyed viewers may spot the gleaming white corner of the building just beyond Millbank Tower in the aerial shot near the beginning of the *TWINE* boat chase.) As with **MI6** (24:2), the new MI5 now officially acknowledges its own existence and even openly advertises for recruits with an informative promotional brochure. At the time of its move from 140 Gower Street (which it had occupied for twenty years), the head of MI5 was Stella Rimington, the first woman to hold such a position in the history of the British Intelligence Services. She is said to have inspired, at least in part, the decision to make M a woman in the film *GoldenEye*. That said, it must be remembered that Mrs. Rimington was (until 1996) the head of *MI5*, while Bond's boss, of course, is the head of *MI6*. For the history of the organization, see **MI5 (1945-1975)** (13:30).

Station: Westminster (CI; DI; JU) Exit for the Houses of Parliament, turn L into St Margaret's Street and continue past Parliament into Millbank. Look for the building ahead on the R, just past Lambeth Bridge. Opposite the SE corner of the building is the spot where the *Dr. No* crew filmed the establishing shot of Universal Exports (see [11:2]).

GREATER LONDON

28. ACTON/EAST ACTON

28:1

ex Home of Sean Connery
Acacia House
Centre Avenue, W3

During the mid- and late-1950s, struggling actor Sean Connery lived in a number of small London flats, including No. 12 Shalcomb Street (off the King's Road, in Chelsea), a shared accommodation in Brondesbury Villas, Kilburn, and, finally, his own "bachelor pad" in Wavel Mews, Acol Road, South Hampstead, which he bought in 1957 (see photo on page 1). Following the successful premiere of *Dr. No* in October 1962 (see [19:5]), Connery acquired this solid, but unspectacular 12-room house, formerly occupied by 25 nuns of the Order of Adoratrices. It was here that the actor, his wife Diane Cilento, her daughter Gigi and the Connerys' newborn son Jason would spend the early years of "Bondage". Indeed, by the time of *Goldfinger*, obsessed fans were camping outside the walls of Acacia House, desperately hoping to catch a glimpse of the man himself. (Ironically, one occasion on which fans might have spotted the globe-hopping star here in Acacia House was during the "double premiere" of *Thunderball*, on December 29, 1965, when all eyes were focused on the **Rialto** [19:8] and Pavilion Cinemas. Connery forewent the Leicester Square frenzy in order to spend a quiet evening at home with the family.) A series of burglaries, which began during the production of *Thunderball*, prompted the actor to put the house up for sale in April 1966. The property was quickly sold and the family moved to a Victorian mansion in Putney (see [47:2]). The only dwelling in this tiny cul de sac, Acacia House is still privately owned, and underwent extensive renovation in 1998.

Station: Ealing Common (DI; PI) or **Shepherd's Bush (CE)** It is quite a hike from either station in the Uxbridge Road, so you may want to grab a cab or take the bus (get off at Acton Park). The house is at the end of the very short Centre Avenue, on the R.

28:2

Farley and H. J. Spiller Hire Ltd 1-17 Brunel Road, W3

Ever wonder where James Bond gets his art? Or where M acquires his naval prints? Or how about where Moneypenny gets those decorative flower prints for her office? The answer to all these questions is H. J. Spiller, now a part of the prestigious Farley group of antique prop and furniture hire firms. Spiller provided the vintage automobile prints for Bond's flat in *Dr. No*, as well as the assorted prints and portraits on view in his later *Live and Let Die* digs. Coming right up to the present, Spiller supplied the paintings for both MI6's Scottish HQ and Elektra King's bedroom in *The World Is Not Enough*. Farley itself has supplied a number of furnishings, fixtures and paintings to the Bond productions, including the 17th-century Italian bed where we first meet Anya in *The Spy Who Loved Me* (look for the distinctive silver eagle atop the headboard) and the assorted paintings that grace the walls of Dr. No's Crab Key lair, all of them original. (The exception—Goya's portrait of the Duke of Wellington—was a "forgery", although Spiller itself provided the ornate frame. For more details, see the **National Gallery** [27:2].) Some years ago, Farley acquired the inventory of another film and television hire firm, Louis Koch and Son, of Cleveland Street, W1, which production buyer Ron Quelch also used on the Bond films. Koch items included Miss Taro's suite of Chinese furniture (managing director Mark Farley today relaxes in the very chair from which Bond shot Professor Dent) and M's griffin motif ink stand, a prop used on the majority of the Bernard Lee films. (Farley sold the latter at **Sotheby's** [13:11] in 1998—a rare event since the firm generally retains all of its props. Mark Farley told me that he was curious to see how much one of Bond-related items would fetch and was quite pleased with the result.)

In most cases, of course, it's the hire firms that supply Eon with furnishings. However, on one memorable occasion, Eon turned the tables—literally. Leon Pettitt, a former Koch employee who now works for Farley, laughingly recalled the day Ron Quelch came into the Cleveland Street shop and said, "We've just bought a *tree*." And indeed they had—for £1,000! In fact, Eon went on to spend another £5,500 having that tree made into the 34-foot-long table from which Karl Stromberg would shoot his last bolt in *The Spy Who Loved Me*. Ron Quelch elaborated: "Ken Adam wanted a long refectory table under which the villain would fire that nasty piece of weaponry [at Bond]. We looked and looked, but couldn't find the right table anywhere. Finally, someone discovered a man down in Hawkhurst, Kent who specialized in top-quality reproduction furniture. He then made the table and chairs to our design." Oh, yes, he also supplied the enormous lime tree from which the furniture was actually crafted. After production wrapped, Eon sold the deadly dining table (minus the lethal accessory) to Koch, who removed a six-foot section from the middle and crafted two 14-foot pieces for use in the store itself. But don't look for the remains of Eon's $10,000 table here at Farley. The tops eventually warped so badly ("the timber was very green," Quelch recalled) that the firm had no choice but to scrap them.

Station: East Acton (CE) Exit into Fitzneal Street, turn R into Old Oak Common Lane, then L into Brunel Road.
Hours: Mon-Fri 8am-5:30pm

> **Trivia Challenge 43:** Talking of art, which of Fleming's characters painted orchids?

29. BECKTON

29:1

Beckton Gas Works Royal Docks Road, E6

In November and December 1980, the *For Your Eyes Only* crew shot Bond's hair-raising encounter with the Blofeld lookalike at Beckton's 300-acre gas works, which was built in 1876 and remained operational for nearly a century. The principal locales showcased in the film include the Benzole Plant Building, from which "Blofeld" (temporarily) controls the action, and the chimney down which Bond drops the wheelchair-bound baddie. Doubling for Roger Moore in the latter scene was American pilot Marc Wolff, who made three separate runs at the chimney for the climactic shot. According to special effects supervisor Derek Meddings' (interviewed in *American Cinematographer*), the pilot successfully hit the target on every take! For the sequence in which the helicopter enters (or *appears* to enter) the Purification Shed, Meddings scaled down a section of the building for use as a foreground miniature. Wolff then flew the helicopter *between* the real building, in the background of the shot, and the miniature shed section in the foreground of the shot. The impressive result literally defies detection. (For another spectacular use of the foreground miniature technique, see **RAF Northolt** [49:1].) To achieve the effect of Moore himself actually flying the Jet Ranger inside the shed, Meddings constructed a hydraulically-controlled mock helicopter which could be maneuvered up and down the length of the building along some 1,000 feet of rails. Again, the results were superb. Interestingly, before settling on the Beckton facility, which had also appeared in *The Avengers* television series and the John Wayne thriller *Brannigan*, the filmmakers considered a derelict gas works on the other side of the river, in North Greenwich. *That* spot would actually become a Bond location nearly twenty years later in *The World Is Not Enough*: it is the site of the **Millennium Dome** (35:1)!

Station: Bank (CE) From here transfer to the Docklands Light Railway line and take this to the Beckton station, exit and go R into Winsor [*sic*] Terrace, which ends at the gas works. Note that while the gas works is located miles from the heart of London, the scenic journey through the renovated Docklands area is a worthwhile treat in itself, and one with the added benefit of taking you fairly close to the *TWINE* locations described under Isle of Dogs and Canning Town, below.

Trivia Challenge 44: How is the Blofeld look-alike billed in the closing credits?

30. BERMONDSEY

30:1

St Saviour's Dock
SE1

This narrow inlet on the south bank of the **Thames** (24:1) provides a convenient means of segueing from the river itself to the enclosed—and more manageable—docks of East London during *The World Is Not Enough* boat chase. Here, on the eastern side of **Tower Bridge** (5:18), Cigar Girl passes Butler's Wharf and the striking new Design Museum, then abruptly swerves into the tiny inlet. Bond shoots past St Saviour's Dock, does an about face, then follows the Sunseeker Hawk 34 down what is, in fact, a dead-end. Where the two boats emerge is actually **Millwall Docks** (41:2)—some two miles down the Thames! The buildings along this "muddy creek", as *Time Out London* calls it, are in fact renovated warehouses that now serve as blocks of luxury flats.

Station: London Bridge (NO) Exit into Tooley Street and head E past Tower Bridge. Look for signs to Butler's Wharf and the Design Museum, which are located along the river itself; St Saviour's Dock is just beyond this. The Design Museum showcases classic designs of the recent past, present and future, including such everyday items as typewriters, televisions, household appliances, office equipment, cars and bicycles. **Museum hours:** Daily 11:30am-5:30pm (last admission)

31. CANNING TOWN

31:1

Royal Victoria Dock
E16

After his "barrel roll" over Cigar Girl's Sunseeker Hawk and before the "low bridge" bit, both filmed at **Millwall**

Docks (41:2), Bond has a near miss with a stationary boat and watches his antagonist incinerate an old sailing barge called the *Wyvenhoe*. These bits and more were staged here at Royal Victora Dock for the opening boat chase of *The World Is Not Enough*. Prior to filming, rehearsals and special effects testing were conducted in the small Pontoon Dock, near the North Woolwich Road. Later, in addition to the near miss and explosion, second unit director Vic Armstrong filmed Cigar Girl firing at Bond in the Q Boat, as well as the latter itself darting between the plumes of water, all along the southern edge of the dock. Then, on May 14, 1999, director Michael Apted brought the first unit here to film close-ups of Pierce Brosnan getting splashed by the explosions and briefly submerging the Q Boat, also along the southern edge of the dock. This footage was then edited into the Glengall Bridge sequence, which Vic Armstrong shot in Millwall Docks. Of his memorable stint in the water, Brosnan noted on *The Tonight Show* (November 4, 1999) that he had "a wetsuit on underneath and then I had the James Bond suit and the tie, but I had these big kind of galoshes underneath, which is kind of half Bond, half duck!"

Station: Bank (CE) to **DLR**, exit at Royal Victoria.

32. CHISWICK

32:1

Hogarth Roundabout W4

Having infiltrated the smuggling pipeline as Peter Franks, James Bond is taken for a fateful ride in Chapter 6 of *Diamonds Are Forever*. The Brooklyn-accented chauffeur presses his passenger to "sit up front" ("it was not an invitation," Fleming tells us), a scene that actually survives in the Eon adaptation of the novel. After the roundabout at the end of the Great West Road, the driver pulls over (presumably in Hogarth Lane), gets out of the car, and adds six new Dunlop golf balls to the ones already in Bond's bag. The new balls contain the merchandise that Bond will be smuggling to America, a rather more straightforward method of clandestine transport than the corpse-insertion one employed in the film. From here the pair travel on to **London Airport** (43:1), or, as it is known today, Heathrow. And while we're in the neighborhood, we may as well note that it was in the Great West Road that some rich idiot married a Mark II Continental Bentley to an apparently unforeseen telegraph pole. Bond bought the bits, according to Chapter 7 of *Thunderball*, and had **Rolls** (*JBB*) straighten the chassis and replace the engine with that of the more powerful Mark IV.

Station: Turnham Green (DI) Go L into Turnham Green Terrace, R in Chiswick High Road and immediately L into Devonshire Road, which ends at Hogarth Roundabout.

33. FELTHAM

33:1

IBM UK Ltd 1 New Square Bedfont Lakes, TW14

Doubles as: Carver Media Group Complex, Hamburg, Germany (exterior and interior) in *Tomorrow Never Dies*

Building 2 of IBM's UK headquarters provided its exterior and a good deal of its interior for mad media mogul Elliot Carver's Hamburg complex. IBM footage includes the exterior establishing shot and the interior party scenes where Bond not only meets Carver and Wai Lin but also renews his friendship with Paris. The scenes of Carver's bloated speech in the CMG newsroom (on which a battered Bond thankfully pulls the plug) were shot not at IBM, but rather at the **ex Eon Studios** (*JBB*) in St Albans, Hertfordshire. Bond's subsequent assault on the complex was filmed partially at IBM, partially on a Hamburg rooftop and partially on an Eon soundstage. The latter contained Gupta's lab and office, as well as a replica of the "strange hatch" which production designer Allan Cameron had spotted on the real IBM rooftop. The footage of Bond dodging the bad guys' bullets and Wai Lin making her vertical escape was shot here in the IBM atrium, apart from the bit where she fires her piton into one of the columns. "We obviously couldn't do that to the IBM building," Cameron laughingly recalled, "so we just repeated a bit of a column on the stage." From Feltham, the "Hamburg" action shifts to **Harmsworth Quays Printing** (48:1) and **West Ferry Printers** (41:3) for the press room sequences.

Note: The IBM complex is not open to the public.

Trivia Challenge 45: By what sobriquet does Paris refer to her husband?

34. FULHAM

34:1

Major's Ltd
11A Royal Parade
Dawes Road, SW6

Just as director Terence Young sent neophyte Bond Sean Connery to his tailor, **Anthony Sinclair** (13:Q) of Conduit Street, Mayfair, director Peter Hunt sent neophyte Bond George Lazenby to *his* tailor, Dimitro Major of Fulham. In collaboration with *OHMSS* costume designer Marjory Cornelius, Mr. Major successfully bridged the gap between old styles and new, outfitting Lazenby with conservative, three-piece suits that evoked the Connery years, as well as modish two-piece suits (with bolder colors, wider pocket flaps and lapels) that foreshadowed the Moore years. In fact, Major outfitted all the principal actors in the film, including Telly Savalas, Gabriele Ferzetti and Bernard Lee. Interestingly, Mr. Major had been in partnership with **Douglas Hayward** (13:5), who, in 1967, opened his own shop in Mount Street, Mayfair and would later outfit Roger Moore's Bond.

Station: Fulham Broadway (DI) Exit into Fulham Broadway and continue straight into Dawes Road. Royal Parade is at the end of Dawes Road, on the L.

35. GREENWICH

35:1

The Millennium Dome
Drawdock Road, SE10

The origins of this controversial white elephant (which cost the over-burdened British taxpayers over one billion dollars!) lie in the fact that the world's day—and hence the millennium—may be said to "begin" here in Greenwich, home of the zero degrees, or prime, meridian, the point from which other longitudes—and time zones—are reckoned. (The old astronomical observatory is still here in Greenwich, although the official royal facility for the calibration of world clocks is now located at **Cambridge University** [*JBB*].) To capitalize on the traditional association between London and the measurement of world time, the government hired a private contractor to construct the world's largest dome (duly noted by the *Guinness Book*) here in Greenwich. The glass and steel structure was designed to usher in the year 2000 with all due hype and media fanfare (although, technically, the fanfare should have been reserved for the year 200*1*), as well as to celebrate the best of British ingenuity and technology through a series of themed exhibits and attractions. Given all the media attention surrounding its cost and construction, the content of its exhibits, the

strains it would place on the public transport system, etc., not to mention its place in the record book, it's no wonder the Bond filmmakers chose to incorporate the admittedly impressive-looking locale in *The World Is Not Enough*. Here, after the dramatic chase down the **River Thames** (24:1), Bond has his final showdown with the deadly Cigar Girl. The action picks up from **Trinity Buoy Wharf** (44:1), directly across the river, where Bond reenters the water following his cruise through the London Canoe Club and Viktor's Restaurant (see **Tobacco Dock** [52:1] and the **Historic Dockyard** [*JBB*] in Chatham). Cigar Girl heads for shore, ditches her boat, which Bond's torpedoes promptly incinerate, then commandeers a convenient hot-air balloon, poised for ascent. Bond pilots the Q Boat up out of the water (using the wrecked Sunseeker as a ramp), dives for one of the balloon's ropes, watches helplessly as Cigar Girl destroys the balloon and then crash-lands, more or less safely, on the dome itself. The sequence was filmed here on location, as well as at **Pinewood Studios** (*JBB*). The studio footage combines full-sized mock-ups with John Richardson's exquisite miniatures.

Station: North Greenwich (JU) London's newest Underground station, one of the largest in Europe, takes you right to the Dome, which is being redeveloped as a high-tech business park.

Below: The balloon's basket is suspended over The Dome from a crane. *Right:* The miniature version!

36. HAMMERSMITH

36:1

Olympia
Hammersmith Road, W14

Founded as the National Agriculture Hall in 1884, this large exhibition center went on to host some of Britain's most popular car, horse, dog and home shows. Today, many of the larger shows and exhibits are held at the nearby Earl's Court Exhibition Hall, at the NEC in Birmingham or, in the case of the National Poultry Show, at the National Agriculture Centre, in Stoneleigh, Warwickshire. In the 1960s, however, the Poultry Show was held at Olympia and, as we learn in Chapter 21 of *OHMSS*, something truly frightening happened at the most recent December exhibit*. This, at any rate, was the conclusion reached by Franklin, "the Man from Ag. and Fish" (see [27:5]), in his Christmas Day briefing of Bond and M at the latter's country home. It seems that turkey flocks all over East Anglia, as well as Suffolk and Hampshire, were recently ravaged by a virus called Fowl Pest—and all the birds that died first were exhibited at the National Poultry Show at Olympia. (Three million birds were killed in all, with the result that Britain had to import its Christmas turkeys from the US.) Unfortunately, the exhibition hall had been cleared and cleaned for the next show before anyone from the Ministry of Agriculture could inspect it. But it all points to one thing: Biological Warfare against Britain, waged by Blofeld through the Piz Gloria girls!

Station: Kensington (Olympia) (DI) Follow the signs to Olympia.

**OHMSS* was written in January-February 1962 and published in the spring of 1963. That the story is set in the autumn and winter of 1962 has been inferred from the fact that in Chapter 7, Sable Basilisk tells Bond that Ernst Stavro Blofeld was born on May 28, 1908 (as was Fleming himself), and then adds that the would-be count "is now 54, as I reckon it." However, an argument can also be made for a setting of 1960. In the same chapter, Bond refers to "the Thunderball affair about a year ago", and the earlier novel explicitly dates the SPECTRE ransom demand to June 3, 1959. Further, in Chapter 8, Sir Hilary receives a letter from Blofeld on December 16, which would have fallen on Sunday in 1962, but on Friday in 1960. (The context suggests that this was an ordinary workday, not the weekend.) Perhaps in his autobiographical haste, Fleming forgot that it was supposed to be 1960 (there are two other references to events of that year in the novel) and simply imposed his own age on Blofeld. Either that, or Sable Basilisk cannot subtract. And to confuse the issue even more, M writes in the Obituary at the end of *You Only Live Twice* that "James Bond was briefly married in 1962", which would therefore mean that the bulk of *OHMSS* takes place from September to December 1961!

> **Trivia Challenge 46:** What is the name of M's country home?

37. HAMPSTEAD

37:1

ex Pitt House
North End Avenue, NW3
(near Hampstead Heath)

Aspiring Tory politician Valentine Fleming acquired this ivy-clad Georgian mansion, originally known as North End House, and later Wildwoods and North End Place, in 1909. He renamed it Pitt House, in honor of its one-time occupant, the Conservative statesman William Pitt the Elder. An immense, forbidding place, more Victorian in appearance than Georgian, Pitt House contained 12 bedrooms and dressing rooms, three bathrooms, four reception rooms, a large lounge, a magnificent billiard room, a palm house and six extra rooms to be used as the owner might see fit. Val's children, including young Ian, would divide their time between Pitt House, on the edge of Hampstead Heath, and the family home at **Braziers Park** (*JBB*), Oxfordshire. Valentine was killed in battle during the First World War and Ian's widowed mother Eve sold the property in 1923. During the next World War, Pitt House suffered severe bomb damage and was finally pulled down in 1952. Today, all that's left are the gates and a plaque commemorating the fact that Pitt lived here in 1767. The so-called "Pitt House" occupying a portion of the original estate has no connection apart from the name.

Station: Golders Green (NO) Walk—or take a bus two stops—down North End Road; turn L into North End then R into North End Avenue. Pitt House was on the R. Note: Pitt House is just down the Northern Line from **Brent Cross Shopping Centre** (39:1), so the two locations can be visited on the same trip.

Trivia Challenge 47: Which Hampstead resident—and controversial architect—inspired the name of one of Fleming's villains.

38. HAREFIELD

38:1

ex Harefield Quarry
Summerhouse Lane
Harefield
Uxbridge

Doubles as: Swiss forest in *Goldfinger*; Fort Knox (vicinity) in *Goldfinger*

In addition to locations at **Black Park Country Park** (*JBB*), **Burnham Beeches** (*JBB*) and **Pinewood Studios** (*JBB*), all in Buckinghamshire, the *Goldfinger* car chase also features one important stunt filmed just outside of Harefield: the bad guys' Mercedes bursting into flames as it bounces down the side of a hill. This immediately follows a shot of the car driving through the oil slick and careening off the road (filmed in Burnham Beeches); and precedes one of the car, engulfed in flames, crashing into the wall of Goldfinger's factory (filmed at Pinewood). The brilliant pyrotechnics were, of course, courtesy of the late special effects genius, John Stears. That same cliff face appears later in the film, when Goldfinger's truck convoy prepares to move in on the Fort Knox Bullion Depository. (Look for Oddjob tossing a gas mask to Bond in the back of one of the trucks.) The convoy pulls away from the cliff and the action then dissolves to a duplicate convoy in the real Fort Knox, before switching back to England, in the form of Black Park Country Park, Buckinghamshire.

Station: Uxbridge (ME; PI); exit on the right to the bus station and take a U9 bus to the Harefield West stop (Belfry Avenue). Exit the bus, continue in Park Lane and then turn R into Summerhouse Lane; the cliff is at the end of the road, just beyond the new housing development.

38:2

Denham Quarry Lakes
Harvil Road
South Harefield
Uxbridge

Doubles as: Abandoned quarry en route from Shrublands, Southern England to London in *Thunderball*

According to *Thunderball* art director Peter Murton, SPECTRE assassin Fiona Volpe ditched the rocket-firing BSA 650cc Lightning motorcycle at the water-filled quarry here in South Harefield. Of course, it wasn't really Luciana Paluzzi (or at least it wasn't *only* Luciana Paluzzi) and it wasn't one of the two customized BSA 650s. Special effects technician Bert Luxford actually rode the bike, a four-year-old BSA 10, modified to look like the Lightnings, while the actress was on hand for the close-up of the biker removing "his" helmet. Bert recalled that Ms. Paluzzi actually pushed the bike into the lake, although "with great difficulty as she was so small." In the finished film, you can't tell that it's actually her because the biker is still wearing a helmet. Bert and John Stears customized all three bikes, only one of which was rigged to fire Stears' specially-prepared missiles. That particular 650 is on display at the **Cars of the Stars Motor Museum** (*JBB*) in Cumbria. The other 650 was returned to BSA, while the stand-in, which was purchased solely for the drop in the lake, is now in private hands. Bert himself owned the stand-in during the years immediately following *Thunderball*, but sold the bike when he grew too old to ride it!

Station: Uxbridge (ME: PI); exit on the right to the bus station and take a U9 bus toward Harefield. Exit in Harvil Road at the Hillingdon Outdoor Activities Centre and walk down the path to the lake.

Left:
Director Terence Young supervises the 'dumping' of the BSA motorcycle at Denham Quarry Lakes.

39. HENDON

39:1

North Car Park,
Brent Cross Shopping Centre
Hendon Way, NW4

Doubles as: Kempinski Hotel Atlantic Parkhaus, Hamburg, Germany (interior) in *Tomorrow Never Dies.*

Here, at Greater London's faithful recreation of the All-American Mall, James Bond field-tested his beautiful new BMW 750iL. Filming took place throughout the North Car Park, but principally on Level Four. Bond parked the BMW in Row 4D, then exited the garage through a convenient door. That door—and its wall—were actually built by production designer Allan Cameron. "The garage is quite large, as you know," Cameron recalled, "so I built about 120 feet of wall to divide it off because Brent Cross still wanted to use part of the car park while we were shooting!" Also added were the large steel shutters that Bond blasts with one of the BMW's rockets (to no avail, as you will recall). The sequence concludes on the roof of the real hotel Parkhaus, with the BMW smashing through a wall (built at the studio) and landing in the Avis rental shop across the street. "I built the whole of the Avis shop there in Hamburg", Cameron recalled with justifiable pride. "We found a store set back about 20 feet from the street, so we could use the space in front to build the shop and crash the car." And, as luck would have it, the building across the street proved a perfect substitute for the back of the Atlantic Hotel!

Station: Brent Cross (NO) Exit the station and take a No. 210 bus to Brent Cross Shopping Centre. The car park is behind the mall, on its northern side. To find the exact spot where Bond parked, go to the back, i.e., northern side, of Level Four and look for the last pillar marked 4D. As you face the pillar (and the back of the garage), look down at the two rows of parking spaces, one on the L, one on the R. The BMW was parked in the fourth space on the R. **Hours:** Mon-Fri 10am-8pm; Sat 9am-6pm; Sun 11am-5pm

Eyes Only, 007: Also located in Hendon is the Metropolitan Police Training College where, according to Chapter 14 of *Moonraker*, Gala Brand received her training.

40. HOUNSLOW

40:1

London (Heathrow) Airport
Hounslow, TW6

Europe's busiest airport (and the fifth largest in the world) boarded its first passenger in 1946. Then, it was called simply London Airport. Heathrow, from the name of the ancient Iron Age settlement where the airport was constructed, came into use in the 1960s, after the opening of a second major London airport at Gatwick. Literary Bond departs from London Airport in several adventures, including *Diamonds Are Forever*, where he has time before his BOAC flight to America to size up his fellow passengers in the Departure Lounge; *James Bond of the Secret Service*, where he receives an extended airport briefing from Ronnie Vallance of **Scotland Yard** (27:16) prior to his flight to Nassau; and *On Her Majesty's Secret Service*, where, disguised as the baronet Sir Hilary Bray, he sips brandy and ginger ale in the VIP Lounge and has to keep reminding himself to stop acting like a stage nobleman. Bond presumably also departs from here in the films, although the only explicit reference occurs in *Octopussy*, when he hastens to the airport after telling M that "our tail followed [Kamal Khan] to Heathrow". The shooting script for *Tomorrow Never Dies* includes a scene where M drops Bond off at Heathrow, but apparently, this was never filmed. Other Bondian airports include **London Southend Airport** (*JBB*), London Stansted Airport (see [*JBB*]) and **London Gatwick Airport** (*JBB*).

Station: Heathrow Terminal 1 (PI)

Below: North Car Park, Brent Cross.

40:2

ex Ariel Hotel (now Forte Posthouse Heathrow) 118 Bath Road Hayes, Middlesex, UB3

Vivienne Michel checks into this new circular hotel after her return from Switzerland in Chapter 6 of *The Spy Who Loved Me*. Her stay is a short one, however, as she has already decided that she has had enough of London. She plans to buy a Vespa motor scooter and go off and tour America (see [42:42]). The distinctively-shaped Ariel became a Posthouse hotel in the early 1970s and is now part of the Forte chain.

Station: Heathrow 1,2, 3 (PI) A shuttle service runs from the airport to the hotel.

41. ISLE OF DOGS

41:1

West India Docks, Canary Wharf and Blackwall Basin E14

Recent editions of the *Time Out London Guide* describe the West India Docks area as having a "toytown look from the Docklands Light Railway", while "at ground level it looks more like the set of a James Bond film." Indeed. But the "epic buildings" of Canary Wharf represent a relatively recent transformation of an area once dominated by London's commercial shipping industry. After the closure of the the docks themselves in 1980, the area was developed as a sort of mini city, centered on the massive Canary Wharf Tower (a.k.a., One Canada Square), which at 774 feet is the tallest building in Britain and the fourth-tallest in Europe. (The tallest, at 981 feet, is the Commerzbank Tower in Frankfurt.) The result is visually impressive, if somewhat jarringly "American". (Cesar Pelli, architect of the Canary Wharf Tower, also designed New York's World Trade Center.) Of course, the Cinematic Bond is himself something of an Anglo-American hybrid, so it seems only fitting that he should make an appearance beneath this symbol of the new, high-rise London. Thus, for *The World Is Not Enough*, Vic Armstrong's second unit crew came here to shoot the sequence in which Cigar Girl crashes through a police boat (a balsa wood "stunt double" covered with the fiberglass shell of an actual police craft), detonates a yachting fuel station (see photo overleaf), and then speeds off beneath the Trafalgar Way bridge and out into Blackwall Basin. (This occurs immediately after the Glengall Bridge sequence at **Millwall Docks**, which is described in the next entry.) Blocked by the fiery wreckage, Bond consults his onboard map of the Isle of Dogs (which indicates that he is in the river itself, near Canary Wharf Pier), figures out a way to head her off at the pass (so to speak), then performs an about-face and speeds back past Billingsgate Fish Market (the red building on the right). The next leg of his journey actually takes place several miles *upriver* at **Tobacco Dock** (52:1), Wapping, although according to the map, Bond will be passing through the very West India Docks he has just left!

Station: Canary Wharf (JU); or, for a more scenic route: **Bank (CE)**; transfer to Docklands Light Railway (Island Gardens) and exit at **Canary Wharf (JU)**. Filming took place at the eastern end of the North Section, opposite Billingsgate Market, near the southern end of the bridge and in Blackwall Basin.

41:2

Millwall Docks E14

The two large docks in the Millwall area of the Isle of Dogs were completed in 1868, their name recalling the windmills that once stood on the adjacent bank. As with their larger counterparts to the north (see above), the docks provided a safer, more controlled environment for several of the more hair-raising stunts in the pre-credit boat chase of *The World Is Not Enough*. Our first glimpse of the Docks—actually the southeast corner of Millwall Outer Dock—occurs immediately after the footage of Bond and Cigar Girl speeding down the narrow **St Saviour's Dock** (30:1), near **Tower Bridge** (5:18). One by one, they emerge from beneath the footbridge here, with Cigar Girl then stopping to fire her big gun at Bond. Bond—actually stuntman Gary Powell—proceeds to undertake a stunning barrel roll over the back of the Sunseeker, taking out the lovely's lethal accessory. Close-ups of a wet Pierce Brosnan barrelling down on Cigar Girl were actually filmed in **Royal Victoria Dock** (31:1), to which the action then switches for shots of the pair weaving among stationary boats and the explosion of the *Wyvenhoe*. Then it's back to Millwall Inner Dock for the sequence where Cigar Girl and Bond approach the very low Glengall Bridge. Cigar Girl makes it just as the lifting bridge is closing; Bond—Powell again—manages to squeeze through *after* the bridge has closed. The footage of Brosnan actually submerging the Q Boat was also shot at the Royal Victoria Dock. From here the action jumps—almost logically, in fact—to **West India Dock** (41:1).

Station: Canary Wharf (JU); transfer to Docklands Light Railway and exit at **Crossharbour & London Arena** station. Follow the signs to the Millwall Inner and Outer Docks. Pepper Street, above Glengall Bridge, is just ahead. The barrel roll was filmed along the southern edge of Millwall Outer Dock, more or less opposite the SE corner of **West Ferry Printers** (see the next entry). Continue past the printers and around the footpath to the Outer Dock.

41:3

West Ferry Printers Ltd 235 Westferry Road, E14

Doubles as: Lower press room, Carver Media Group Complex, Hamburg, Germany (interior) in *Tomorrow Never Dies*

The interiors of Carver's press room (as in "Stop the presses!") were filmed here at West Ferry Printers, as well as **Harmsworth Quays Printing** (48:1) in Rotherhithe. The West Ferry print hall is, in fact, the largest in Europe, responsible for seven national periodicals, including the *Daily Telegraph*, the ***Daily Express*** (5:4), the *Guardian* and the *Financial Times* (for whom Bond claimed to work in *A View To A Kill*). (Prior to 1995, the venerable financial journal was printed at 240 East India Dock, a location originally earmarked for—but subsequently dropped from—the *Tomorrow* shoot.) In fact, the makers of *TND* had originally planned a more extensive shoot here in Westferry Road. In addition to the fight and chase scenes with Bond and Carver's thugs, party scenes involving the principals and numerous extras were to be filmed in the Viewing Gallery above the press room. According to West Ferry Technical Services Manager David Moore, who coordinated the shoot with Eon Productions, the set was dressed, the lights were up, the actors assembled and the cameras in place, when it was discovered that Miss Hatcher had actually left the country and returned to America! Production designer Allan Cameron concurs that additional filming had been planned for West Ferry, but denies that Teri Hatcher's availability had anything to do with its cancellation. "Roger [Spottiswoode, the director] liked the idea of a more direct link between Carver and the presses and considered staging Jonathan Pryce's big speech at West Ferry. But for practical reasons, we ended up shooting those scenes at **IBM** (33:1) and the studio (see **ex Eon Studios** [*JBB*])." The fight scene originally earmarked for the West Ferry press room was ultimately staged at Harmsworth Quays because the Isle of Dogs facility literally couldn't stop the presses for the two days required by the filmmakers. In the end, what we see of West Ferry is Bond passing the Carroge office (the control room for the ro-

Cigar Girl's explosive exit from West India Docks (*see page 149*)

botic Automated Guided Vehicles that roam the press room), dodging bullets, diving onto the dolly and rolling into the reel store room. He is then nearly crushed by a clamp truck and its 1.25-ton reel of newsprint—a sequence actually staged at the studio, according to Cameron. The action then switches back to West Ferry, where Bond launches himself off the loading dock into a *mock* Hamburg street, after which we cut to a shot of Pierce Brosnan—on location in a *real* Hamburg Street!

Station: Canary Wharf (JU); transfer to Docklands Light Railway and exit at **Crossharbour** station. The print works is on the other side of Millwall Inner Dock, along the northern edge of Millwall Outer Dock, both of which are featured in the *TWINE* boat chase (see [41:2]).

42. KENSAL GREEN

42:1

Bapty & Company Ltd *703 Harrow Road, NW10*

This North London firm, the largest supplier of prop weaponry in the world, has armed both the hero and the villains of every James Bond film except *Licence To Kill*. For *Tomorrow Never Dies*, Bapty supplied the villains with everything from the M-79 grenade-launcher with which they assault Bond's BMW to the M-60 machine gun that Stamper uses to murder the British sailors. For the hero, of course, there was a Walther PPK, the legendary German handgun that has become virtually synonymous with 007. This phenomenally popular pistol, along with its slightly bigger brother, the PP, has been in production since 1929 (not 1931, as traditionally claimed) and is still regarded as one of the finest handguns ever made. Ian Fleming first learned of Walther's *Polizeipistole Kriminal*, or "Police Pistol, Detective model", from Scottish gun enthusiast Geoffrey Boothroyd. Boothroyd deplored Fleming's choice of a small-calibre Beretta for Bond and, in a May 1956 letter to the author, suggested several more powerful replacements. Fleming duly exchanged Bond's 6.35mm/.25 ACP Beretta for the 7.65mm/.32 ACP Walther PPK in the opening of *Doctor No*, going on to blame the smaller gun for the near-fatal accident which had closed the previous novel, *From Russia, With Love*. Eon Productions faithfully recreated this exchange for the film version of the story (although without the reference to *From Russia, With Love*, since that novel had yet to be filmed!), apparently taking great pains to get the new gun right. Yet, sharp-eyed gun buffs will notice that what Boothroyd *really* gives Bond is not the famous PPK, but rather the slightly larger PP model. (Although somewhat obscured in the initial briefing scene, the gun is plainly identifiable as a PP, not a PPK, when Leiter gets the drop on Bond at Puss-Feller's.) What's more, when Bond kills Professor Dent at Miss Taro's apartment, his "PPK" has inexplicably switched to an FN Browning Model 1910, and when he takes on Dr. No's "dragon" in the Crab Key swamp, the gun changes yet again, this time to a Colt Model 1911. (The former switch may have been prompted by the need for a silencer, although PPKs can certainly be fitted with silencers.) From the second film on, however, Bond generally carries an actual PPK, occasionally supplementing it with larger, more powerful weapons like the Walther P.38 for the *Goldfinger* car chase shoot-out and the Smith & Wesson Model 66 Combat Magnum revolver for the *Live and Let Die* Voodoo sacrifice. (In *The Spy Who Loved Me*, there is a brief "hiccup" during the scene where Bond shadows Fekkesh at the Pyramids. His gun "magically" switches from a PPK to a Beretta Model 70, then back to a PPK. Moore also used the Beretta in a series of publicity photos taken in Cairo.) For *Octopussy*, Bapty temporarily replaced the seven-shot PPK (not *six*, as Bond says in *The Man With The Golden Gun*, nor *eight* as Brad Whitaker says in *The Living Daylights*) with Walther's 9mm P5, an eight-shot weapon that first hit the market in 1979. Coincidentally (?), the firm had also equipped Sean Connery's "rival" Bond with a P5 earlier in 1982. However, in neither film is the new model mentioned by name. In fact, in *Octopussy*, Bond tells Q that he has "mislaid my *PPK*", even though the gun the bad guy had just kicked out of his hand was clearly a P5. In any case, the real PPK was back on the job in *For Your Eyes Only* (earning a nice close-up, in fact, in the hands of "Gonzales") and would remain Bond's preferred weapon through *Tomorrow Never Dies*. For that film, Bapty *supplemented* Bond's trademark weapon with Walther's new polymer-framed P99, a gun which the Walther firm itself hailed as the "police pistol of the third generation" (the PP/PPK and P5 representing the first and second generations, respectively). Why the switch? According to Bapty general manager Andrew Fletcher, the reason was "to update the character, to provide him with a weapon that would allow him to compete on a more even basis with the villains. The PPK is still a fine weapon, but at the end of the day it's only 7.65mm, with a seven-shot capacity, versus the P99, which is 9mm and will hold 16 rounds [in the high-capacity model]." For *The World Is Not Enough*, Bapty urged the elimination of the smaller gun altogether. "It took us a long time to convince [Eon]," Andrew explained, "because of the long association between Bond and the PPK. But in the end they agreed to make the change." So, Bond would appear to have made one more concession to this ever-changing world, one that many gun buffs will likely applaud, but one that this particular

Bond buff greatly regrets. For *TWINE*, Bapty also supplied the compact, new FN P90 submachine guns used by Renard and his men (this marks the UK film debut of the Belgian-made gun); the laser-sighted Heckler & Koch G36 carbine (also making its UK film debut) and the HK 21 machine gun that forms part of Cigar Girl's formidable arsenal, as well as the Colt Model 1911 used by Bond himself to kill Elektra. And, yes, while they may be specially modified to fire blanks, the vast majority of these weapons are *real*. Rubber copies are only used for stunt work, as when a person is "hit" over the head with a gun. Incidentally, Bapty does *not* make the new black leather holster which Bond uses to harness his P99. That particular piece of equipment (which is never shown in the finished film) was farmed out to a bespoke holster-maker who prefers to remain anonymous. The problem with mass-produced holsters, according to Fletcher, is that they leave a lump in the jacket—and that would never do for an immaculate dresser like Bond. "We therefore had to have something made out of very thin leather—more of a glove than a holster, really," Andrew explained. Even so, the holster still proved to be something of an encumbrance for actor Pierce Brosnan. As supervising armourer Charlie Bodycomb told me: "When Pierce is actually carrying the gun, he finds it more comfortable just tucking it in his trousers!"

Station: Kensal Green (BA) Exit the station to Harrow Road, then turn R. Bapty, which is not open to the public, is ahead on the L.

Trivia Challenge 48: In which film(s), apart from *Octopussy* and *TWINE*, does James Bond *not* use a Walther PPK?

43. KEW

43:1

Royal Botanic Gardens, Kew
Kew Road
Richmond, TW9

Kew Gardens has served as a research center for the scientific study of plants since the 1840s. Today, its 300 acres of landscaped park, mansions, museums and hothouses contain over 30,000 species of trees, flowers, ferns, shrubs and other plants from every part of the globe. Among its most famous and distinctive buildings are the two magnificent glass palaces, Palm House and Temperate House, designed by the renowned Victorian architect Decimus Burton. While you're here, be sure to check out the wild English orchids, which, according to M in Chapter 20 of *OHMSS*, are looked after by "a chap called Summerhayes who's the orchid king at Kew." You may also wish to view the tropical and subtropical species generously donated by a certain "Dr. Guntram Shatterhand". His valuable contributions to Kew, as well as to a "Disneyland of Death" in southern Japan, are detailed in Chapter 7 of *You Only Live Twice*.

Station: Kew Gardens (DI) From the main exit of the station, take the right fork of the road, then turn R into Kew Garden Road and R again into Kew Road; the Gardens are ahead on the L, at the turning for Kew Green. **Hours:** Daily 9:30am-3:30pm (in summer until 6:30pm; 7:30pm on weekends)

44. LEAMOUTH

44:1

Trinity Buoy Wharf
64 Orchard Place, E16

Once owned by Trinity House (the English lighthouse authority mentioned in the novel *Moonraker*), Trinity Buoy Wharf not only contains London's only lighthouse (built for experimental purposes in the 19th century), but also marks the spot where Bond reenters the **Thames** (24:1) in *The World Is Not Enough* boat chase. Here, adjacent to the Chainstore, a refurbished Victorian-era warehouse, the *TWINE* crew recreated the marquee portion of "Viktor's" restaurant (an homage to second unit director Vic Armstrong) through which Bond steers the Q Craft during the land leg of the chase. The first part of the restaurant sequence was filmed at the **Historic Dockyard** (*JBB*) in Chatham, Kent; the shots of Bond going through the tent and shooting back out into the Thames, here in Leamouth. See the **Millennium Dome** (35:1) for what happens next, and the locations under Bermondsey, Isle of Dogs and Wapping districts, Greater London, for the sequences preceding this.

Station: Bank (CE); transfer to Docklands Light Railway and exit at East India (to the W) or Royal Victoria (to the E). For all the trouble to get to the pier, which lies between these two points, it would be just as well to view it from the Dome itself.

45. PARSONS GREEN

45:1

ex H. J. Mulliner & Co. Ltd
212 New King's Road, SW6

Mulliner's is a renowned automobile body maker, famous as the specialist coachbuilders for Rolls-Royce and Bentley (see *JBB* for more on all three firms). One of their customers, according to Chapter 7 of *Thunderball*, was James Bond, who, commissioned Mulliner's to saw off the cramped body of the wrecked Continental Bentley he had bought and replace it with a trim, convertible two-seater affair. Understandably proud of his new toy, Bond again relates the story of its conversion to the chief range officer at the **National Rifle Association** (*JBB*) camp in "The Property of a Lady". In 1961, the year of *Thunderball*'s publication, H. J. Mulliner merged with Park Ward, a division of Rolls-Royce, and today, as Mulliner Park Ward, operates from the Rolls premises in Pyms Lane, Crewe, Cheshire.

Station: Putney Bridge (DI) Exit the station to New King's Road and turn L. Mulliner's was at the end of the road, near Fulham High Street.

Trivia Challenge 49: What was the name of Bond's refurbished auto? Bonus point if you know what Bond refused to let any car do to him.

46. PECKHAM

46:1

ex Seat of Sir Thomas Bond
Peckham Manor
Peckham Hill Street
Peckham, SE15

In Chapter 6 of *On Her Majesty's Secret Service*, the Griffon Or of the **College of Arms** (5:11) speculates that our hero may be related to Sir Thomas Bond, Baronet of Peckham, who financed the initial construction of **Bond Street** (13:9). This "most desirable" baronetcy was founded on October 9, 1658 and although the title is now extinct, Griffon Or suggests that James may be able to claim descent either directly or through a collateral branch of the family. Bond, however, claims that he has no connection with Peckham (his father was Scottish, his mother Swiss) and that he has no interest in the fact that a possible ancestor of his "was responsible for the name of one of the most famous streets in the world." Still, the Bond family motto seems rather fitting: "The World Is Not Enough". The motto and a briefer version of this discussion also find their way into the film version of *OHMSS*, as well as the title of the film *The World Is Not Enough*. Regarding the earlier film, *OHMSS* set decorator Peter Lamont recalled that the painting Sir Hilary shows Bond was adapted by a College of Arms scribe from an original illustration of Sir Thomas's coat of arms in *Burke's Extinct and Dormant Baronetcies*. You may recall that the blazon, or description, of Sir Thomas's shield, in both the novel and the film, is: "Argent, on a chevron sable three bezants." In the quasi-French language of heraldry, this means that the field, or background, of the shield is argent (literally, silver, but in printing usually white) and that it bears a sable (black) chevron containing three bezants. A bezant, however, is not a gold *ball*, as both Fleming and the filmmakers would have you believe. Rather, it is a gold *coin* or *disc*, an adaptation of French *besant*, the name of an ancient Byzantine coin. The motto itself is a Latin one and was originally recorded as *Non Sufficit Orbis*—The World Sufficeth Not. Bond family tradition derives this "worldly" motto—to which they gave a more "spiritual" interpretation—from the arms of Spain's Philip II, although according to the **College of Arms** (5:11) there is no record of the king ever having used it. Indeed, mottoes themselves are not an official part of heraldry or coats of arms: they can be adopted, altered or dropped on a whim. Thus, for euphony or appearance, the College chose to reorder *Non Sufficit Orbis* as *Orbis Non Sufficit* for the film itself. In either case, though, the meaning is the same. As for tracing Bond's line back to "Sir Otto Bond" (or "Sir Otho le Bon", as it is rendered in the release script), this appears to be an invention of the filmmakers (it is not in Fleming). The College has no record of any such chap, nor of "the manor of Wickhamsbreux [held] by a knight's fee from the Earl of Thanet, 1387." Actually, there is an earldom of Thanet, as the College's Lancaster Herald was quick to point out, but it wasn't created until 1628. Sounds as if Phidian wasn't doing such a splendid job, after all….

Station: London Bridge (NO); transfer to British Rail and exit at **Peckham Rye**. Walk up Rye Lane to Peckham High Street, where you will turn R then immediately L into Peckham Hill Street. The new Peckham Library, on the L, stands on the southern end of what was once the Manor of Peckham, Surrey. Sir Thomas Bond acquired the manor from his brother-in-law, Sir Thomas Grimes, and, according to the diarist John Evelyn, enjoyed fine views of London, Greenwich and the Thames. He also achieved fame for his beautiful landscaped garden and the fruit trees he imported from France. (Interestingly, *James* Bond also seemed to have an affinity for fruit trees, for which see **Brogdale Orchards** [*JBB*].) Sir Thomas's son and successor, Sir Henry Bond, sold the estate (possibly to pay off debts incurred from his father's financing of Bond Street), and resettled in France. Henry's son Charles died without issue sometime after 1770 and with him the baronetcy of Peckham came to an end. The manor house was pulled down in 1797 and Peckham itself is now part of the Greater London borough of Southwark.

47. PUTNEY

47:1

Pierce Brosnan's First London Home
Chelverton Road, SW15

Having left Ireland some years earlier to study nursing in London, May Brosnan was finally able to send for her 11-year-old son in August 1964. Young Pierce arrived in London on the 12th of the month, ironically, the very day that Ian Fleming died. Mother and son, along with her new husband Bill, took up residence in a comfortable flat here in Chelverton Road, the precise location of which the present occupants would prefer not to have disclosed. Pierce attended Elliott School in Pullman Gardens, Putney, where he was mercilessly teased about his Irish accent.

The future 007 responded by adopting a Cockney accent in order to sound more like his friends. In 1968, the family moved across the river to 5e Vera Road in Fulham.

Station: East Putney (DI) Walk W in Upper Richmond Road, turn R into Putney High Street, then L into Chelverton Road. To see Elliot School, which is still open, walk back down Putney High Street (which becomes Putney Hill), turn R into Westleigh Avenue and look for the school on the L. Just around the corner, at 25 Putney High Street, is the ABC Cinema where, in September 1964, 11-year-old Pierce Brosnan saw his first Technicolor film: *Goldfinger*.

47:2

ex Home of Sean Connery
1 Bristol Gardens
Portsmoth Road, SW15

After his initial success in *Dr. No* (and with a new family to boot), Sean Connery had acquired Acacia House in Acton (see [28:1]), where he would remain until 1966. Lack of privacy (the house is right on the street) and a series of burglaries prompted the actor to list Acacia House for £17,950 (then just over $50,000) in the spring of 1966. The house sold (naturally), and in April, Sean, his actress wife, Diane Cilento, and their two children, Jason and Gigi, moved to this attractive Victorian house on Putney Heath. Long a favorite of actors and other celebrities, Putney Heath afforded much greater privacy and security and would remain Connery's home through the filming of *Diamonds Are Forever*. In the autumn of 1971, the actor separated from Cilento, from whom he would be granted a divorce in October 1973, and moved into a flat overlooking the **Thames** (24:1) at Chelsea Embankment.

Station: East Putney (DI) This is a bit of a hike. Walk W in Upper Richmond Road, turn L into Putney Hill and continue S. Just past Manor Fields on the R (where you can turn to visit Pierce Brosnan's elementary school [see above]), look for Putney Heath on the R and, veering immediately to the L off of this, Wildcroft Road. At the end of Wildcroft Road turn R into Telegraph Road, then immediately L into Portsmouth Road. Bristol Gardens is on the R.

48. ROTHERHITHE

48:1

Harmsworth Quays Printing Ltd Surrey Quays Road, SE16

Doubles as: Press room, Carver Media Group Complex, Hamburg, Germany (interior) in *Tomorrow Never Dies*

Though originally planned for the larger West Ferry works across the river, the scenes of Bond fending off assailants on the press room's overhead crane were filmed here at Harmsworth Quays, printers of the *Daily Mail*, *The Mail on Sunday* and the *Evening Standard*. Thus, while supposedly set in a German building, the entire sequence of Bond's assault on the Carver Media Group Complex (apart from a brief bit on the roof) was, in fact, filmed in Greater London. See also **West Ferry Printers** (41:3) and **IBM** (33:1).

Station: Surrey Quays (EL) Cross Lower Road to Redriff Road. Surrey Quays Road is ahead to the L.

> **Trivia Challenge 50:** "You break it, you bought it." How much is Carver's new satellite worth?

49. RUISLIP

49:1

RAF Northolt West End Road Ruislip

Doubles as: Blue Grass Field, Kentucky, in *Goldfinger*; Unnamed US airport in *Goldfinger*; RAF Boscombe Down, in *Thunderball*; Unnamed Latin American air base in *Octopussy*; Unnamed airstrip, Baku, Azerbaijan in *The World Is Not Enough*

The Royal Air Force Station with the longest continuous operational service (since 1915), RAF Northolt today functions primarily as the VIP air transport terminal for London. In the years immediately following World War II, however, Northolt served as London's principal civil airport and, indeed, was the busiest airport in Europe. Thus, Major Dexter Smythe recalls having smuggled his ill-gotten German gold through Munich and Northolt in the short story "Octopussy". During the 1960s, the aerodrome was home to the Metropolitan Communications Squadron, which, among other things, provided aircraft for **Air Ministry** (23:7) liaison and staff visits in the UK and Europe. Fortunately, they weren't too busy to lend a helping hand when Pussy Galore needed an airfield for her Flying Circus. Keep this in mind the next time you watch the film *Goldfinger*. When Bond and Pussy disembark from Goldfinger's Lockheed 1329 JetStar and 007 comments on the bourbon and branch water "here in Kentucky", the two are actually standing in front of Northolt's Hangar 311, barely 12 miles from the heart of London. This is also the area where Pussy's pilots land after completing their dress rehearsal and where they take off for the raid on Fort Knox. At the end of the film, a triumphant Bond again appears at the air base, this time, outside the massive Hangar 5, where he boards a plane suspiciously similar to Goldfinger's JetStar, and, of course, is promptly hijacked. As the disabled plane plunges into a mysterious sea located somewhere between Louisville, KY and Washington, D.C., Leiter monitors Bond's descent from the old control tower on the western side of the Northolt base. For *Thunderball*, the geographical stretch is not nearly as great—merely substituting the entrance of a London RAF station for that of one near the southern coast (see **RAF Boscombe Down** [*JBB*] in Wiltshire). The Northolt entrance still looks much as it did in 1965, when SPECTRE agent Angelo used François Derval's credentials to gain admittance and hijack a Vulcan bomber. (The shots of the actual bombers were filmed up in Lincolnshire at **RAF Waddington** [*JBB*].) After this, RAF Northolt saw no more action On Her Majesty's Secret Service until Roger Moore's penultimate outing, *Octopussy*. It's amazing what a good production designer and enough imported palm trees can achieve. (In fact, director John Glen told me that the local punters thought the base had been readied for Argentinian POWs [in the aftermath of the Falklands War] and that the palm trees were introduced to make them feel at home!) Once again, as with *Goldfinger*, good old Hangar 311 gets the Bondian treatment, eventually being blown to bits (or at least a model of it is) in one of the best pre-credit sequences of the series. However, even before the pyrotechnics, there is an impressive bit of special effects magic here at Northolt, namely, the sequence where the Acrostar flies—or, rather, *appears* to fly—through the hangar itself. (You may also wish to consult the entry for **ex Worminghall Airfield** [*JBB*] in Buckinghamshire, where the remainder of this sequence is detailed.) As Bond approaches the airbase, with the missile hot on his tail, we cut to his view of the hangar—a nice aerial shot of the actual building. We then cut to a long shot from the interior of the hangar itself, as the plane speeds toward the frightened soldiers. This was not the Acrostar, but, in fact, a Hawker Siddeley 125, one of the executive jets based here at Northolt. As the soldiers scramble to close the hangar doors, we cut to one more shot of Bond, then to shots of the Acrostar entering the hangar, flying through the building, and exiting on the other side. The "entry" and "exit" shots were actually achieved through the use of foreground miniatures, an idea suggested by art director Michael Lamont (Peter's brother). Thus, when the jet "enters" the hangar, you are really seeing two "layers" of action: a portion of the actual building, along with the scrambling extras, in the *background* of the shot; and a one third-scale model of the Acrostar being flown (by wire) behind a miniature hangar door in the *foreground* of the shot. The model is thus flying *between* the real building in the background and the miniature building *section* in the foreground. For the exit, the miniature was flown from behind a similar miniature hangar section in the foreground, with (again) the real hangar and extras in the background. "Using foreground miniatures is an old technique," John Glen recalled, "but it worked very well. I think it's one of our best shots ever." Special effects supervisor John Richardson concurred, adding, "That's something we mastered on the Bond films over many years: utilizing *all* the effects techniques to their best advantage, rather than just saying, 'Oh, we'll do all this digitally or this way or that way'." (For another splendid example of foreground miniatures in action, see **Beckton Gas Works** [29:1].) The exterior shot of the missile entering the hangar was achieved the same way, while the interior shot—where the missile strikes the floor of the hangar and explodes—was actually done at the studio. "We opened the doors at the far end of the 007 Stage at Pinewood," Richardson revealed, "then we flew a missile down a very long wire and through the studio doors and onto the stage, where we did the explosion." An exquisitely-detailed miniature hangar was then blown up at the studio to complete the sequence. The middle part of this amazing sequence—the "flight" through the hangar itself—was achieved by mounting a full-scale replica of the Acrostar (complete with stunt man) onto a 15-foot steel pole arm, attaching this, in turn, to an old Jaguar and then *driving* the jet past the fleeing extras. The problem wasn't that Acrostar pilot Corkey Fornof couldn't really fly through the hangar—he could. The problem was the duration of the flight itself. "John Glen told me he wanted the plane in the hangar about seven or eight seconds," Fornof recalled. "I said, 'John, what do you want me to do, *taxi* it through the hangar?! Because if I fly it through it's only gonna take about a second and a half." John Richardson also noted that it would have been too

dangerous to have any extras inside the hangar during an actual flight. "Doing it our way," he added, "we could draw it out as long as we wanted and we could have as many people as we wanted around [the plane]." Richardson himself drove the Jaguar, while an assistant in the back of the car used hydraulic controls to "bank" the aircraft so that its wing would conceal the pole arm. The rest of the sequence—the forced landing and gas station bit—was done in Utah and the Pinewood backlot (see the Worminghall entry for details). Today, Northolt's Hangar 311 sports a new coat of dark green paint but otherwise looks much as it did in the films, as does the smaller brick hangar, called Building 120, adjacent to it and clearly visible in *Goldfinger* and—if you look fast—in *Octopussy*, as well. Finally, for *The World Is Not Enough*, the filmmakers needed footage of Bond sneaking into an Azerbaijani airbase and boarding a CASA C-212 Aviocar, so where else would they turn: London's own RAF Northolt, of course. The new footage was shot along the access road leading from the "crash gate" down to the disused runway along which Bond drove the Range Rover in *Octopussy*.

Station: Ruislip Gardens (CE) Turn L out of the station, and walk up West End Road; the entrance—recognizable from *Thunderball*—is on the right. Straight back and to the R is Hangar 311, which appears in *Goldfinger* and *Octopussy*. To get the view of the entrance from the film, just cross the street.

50. ST JOHN'S WOOD

50:1

Lord's Cricket Ground
St John's Wood Road, NW8

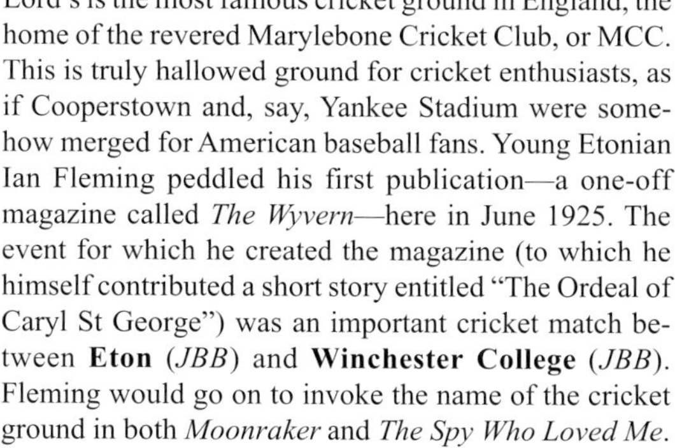

Lord's is the most famous cricket ground in England, the home of the revered Marylebone Cricket Club, or MCC. This is truly hallowed ground for cricket enthusiasts, as if Cooperstown and, say, Yankee Stadium were somehow merged for American baseball fans. Young Etonian Ian Fleming peddled his first publication—a one-off magazine called *The Wyvern*—here in June 1925. The event for which he created the magazine (to which he himself contributed a short story entitled "The Ordeal of Caryl St George") was an important cricket match between **Eton** (*JBB*) and **Winchester College** (*JBB*). Fleming would go on to invoke the name of the cricket ground in both *Moonraker* and *The Spy Who Loved Me*. In the former, it is revealed that Blades (see [16:6]), the most prestigious club in London, maintains one of the finest private boxes here at Lord's. In the latter, we learn that on the day he met our Vivienne, young rogue Derek Mallaby and his parents had gone to see the MCC play Kent here at Lord's. Bond himself champions the game (and the higher level of skill it requires in comparison with American baseball) in Chapter 11 of *You Only Live Twice*, though without reference to a specific club.

Station: St John's Wood (JU) Go L in Wellington Road then R into St John's Wood Road. **Hours:** 10am-5pm on match days; **Guided Tours:** Daily at noon; 2pm and also at 10am on match days.

51. TOTTENHAM

51:1

Vallance Lodge & Co. Ltd
746 High Road, NW17

Horace William Vallance Lodge founded his accounting firm in the North London suburb of Edmonton in 1925. Several years later, he transferred his head office to Tottenham, where it has remained ever since. Of a theatrical bent himself, Vallance Lodge specialized in actors, writers, agents and other "creative" types. For this reason, he always maintained a "West End" office in central London, as well as the suburban head office in Tottenham. During the 1950s and '60s, when Vallance Lodge counted Ian Fleming among his illustrious clients, the central London office was at 4 Bloomsbury Square. In fact, Fleming actually registered his company, **Glidrose Productions** (3:3), at Vallance Lodge's Bloomsbury address. And just for good measure, the author also appropriated the first of his accountant's surnames for that of Assistant Commissioner Ronald Vallance of **Scotland Yard** (27:16) in *Moonraker* and subsequent stories. Mr. Vallance Lodge himself retired in the '60s and died in 1970. His firm continued to serve both Glidrose, then a part of the Booker Group, as well as the *Book Collector*, the high-profile journal once owned by Ian Fleming (see **ex Shenval Press** [19:11]).

Station: Seven Sisters (VI); transfer to British Rail, exit at White Hart Lane. Follow the signs to the Tottenham Hotspur Football Club; Vallance Lodge is in the High Road, adjacent to the clubhouse.

52. WAPPING

52:1

Tobacco Dock Wapping Lane, E1

Doubles as: West India Docks, Isle of Dogs, London in *The World Is Not Enough*

Having been temporarily thwarted by Cigar Girl (see **West India Docks** [41:1]), Bond consults his onboard map and decides to cut across the Isle of Dogs to intercept his prey near the **Millennium Dome** (35:1). The route, as shown on the map, will take him through the West India Docks, which, of course, is precisely where he is sitting as he maps out the interception! To further complicate things, he won't really be traveling through the West India Docks, but rather through Tobacco Dock—some two miles upriver! Confused? Well, don't be. These geographical sleights of hand don't seem to bother Bond in the least. He simply pilots the indestructible Q Boat up Tobacco Dock's Ornamental Canal, crashes through a specially-constructed "London Canoe Club" shed, sails over Wapping Lane, lands on the other side of the road and then continues the chase through the **Historic Dockyard** (*JBB*) in Chatham, Kent, some 30 miles away! Watch for the red double-decker buses in Wapping Lane—they were also used in the Chatham footage to link the two disparate sequences. The cut is a clever one and, as supervising art director Neil Lamont justifiably opined, "It works very well indeed."

Station: Wapping (EL) Go L out of the station then R into Wapping Lane; Tobacco Dock is ahead on the L. This area was reclaimed from the famous London Docks during the 1980s, with tiny Tobacco Dock, the former link between the larger basins, giving its name to a shopping and entertainment complex now known as the "Covent Garden of Docklands".

Eyes Only, 007: Bond's other "brush" with Wapping occurs in the pre-credit sequence of *For Your Eyes Only*. Just after the helicopter pilot is electrocuted, and the craft nosedives toward the Thames, the camera briefly catches sight of Wapping Gardens, Wapping High Street and Wapping New Stairs, as well as the Thames Division police station and its boat yard. Interestingly, the "land leg" of the *TWINE* chase, with Bond taking to recreated East End streets in Chatham's **Historic Dockyard** (*JBB*), were originally planned for Wapping High Street, whose historic 18th-century homes and warehouses were deemed a perfect visual compliment to the action. Unfortunately, the logistics of shutting down the High Street proved an insurmountable obstacle. And, as the shots in Chatham demonstrate, ultimately an unnecessary one.

Stunt woman Sarah Donohue surveys the wreckage of the police boat and yachting fuel station - both destroyed by her powerful Sunseeker boat.
See 41:1 (Page 149)

BIBLIOGRAPHY

Adams, James. *The New Spies: Exploring the Frontiers of Espionage*. London: Hutchinson, 1994.
Adams, Will, and Tricia Adams. *London: A Nostalgic Look at the Capital since 1945*. London: Past and Present Publishing, 1997.
Allison, Ronald, and Sarah Riddell, eds. *The Royal Encyclopedia*. London: Macmillan Press, 1991.
Amis, Kingsley. *The James Bond Dossier*. London: Jonathan Cape, 1965.
Amory, Mark, ed. *The Letters of Ann Fleming*. London: Collins Harvill, 1985.
Andrew, Christopher. *Her Majesty's Secret Service: The Making of the British Intelligence Community*. New York: Penguin Books, 1987.
Balio, Tino. *United Artists: The Company That Changed the Film Industry*. Madison, Wisconsin: The University of Wisconsin Press, 1987.
Barkshire, Reg. Telephone interview. 3 Sept. 1999.
Barnes, Alan, and Marcus Hearn. *Kiss Kiss Bang Bang! The Unofficial James Bond Film Companion*. London: Batsford, 1997.
Barry, John. Interview. *Film Score Monthly* 75 November 1996.
Bennett, Tony, and Janet Woollacott. *Bond and Beyond: The Political Career of a Popular Hero*. New York: Methuen, Inc., 1987.
Berkeley, Roy. *A Spy's London*. London: Leo Cooper, 1994.
Bond, Florence Cynthia. *The Bond Family of Newbury and London*. Florence Cynthia Bond, 1957.
Broccoli, Cubby, with Donald Zec. *When the Snow Melts: The Autobiography of Cubby Broccoli*. London: Boxtree, 1998.
Brooke-Little, J.P. *Royal Heraldry: Beasts and Badges of Britain*. [London:] Pilgrim Press, 1994.
Bruce Lockhart, Robin. *Reilly—Ace of Spies*. 2nd ed. London: Futura Publications, 1983.
Bryce, Ivar. *You Only Live Once: Memories of Ian Fleming*. Rev. ed. London: Weidenfeld and Nicolson, 1985.
Bunson, Matthew E. *Encyclopedia Sherlockiana: An A-to-Z Guide to the World of the Great Detective*. New York: Macmillan, 1994.
Cain, Syd. Telephone interview. 9 July 1999.
Callan, Michael Feeney. *Sean Connery, The Untouchable Hero*. London: Virgin Books, 1993.
Cameron, Robert, and Alistair Cooke. *Above London*. San Francisco: Cameron and Company, 1980.
Cave Brown, Anthony. *"C": the Secret Life of Sir Stewart Menzies, Spymaster to Winston Churchill*. New York: Macmillan, 1987.
Central Intelligence Machinery. London: The Stationery Office, 1996.
Cornelius, Marjory. Telephone interview. 19 June 1999.
Darwin, Robin. Letter to Ian Fleming. 24 November 1961. Russell, L. mss. Lilly Library, Bloomington, Indiana.
Deacon, Richard [Donald McCormick]. *A History of the British Secret Service*. London: Panther, 1980.
Dear, I. C. B., gen. ed. *The Oxford Companion to World War II*. Oxford and New York: Oxford University Press, 1995.
Dorril, Stephen. *MI6: Fifty Years of Special Operations*. London: Fourth Estate, 2000.
Drama Centre London. *Drama Centre London Prospectus 1998-1999*. London: Drama Centre London, 1998.
Duncan, Andrew. *Secret London*. London: New Holland, 1998.
—. *Walking London*. 2nd ed. Chicago: Passport Books, 1999.
Duncan, Fiona, Leonie Glass, and Caroline Sharpe. *London Up Close, District by District, Street by Street*. Lincolnwood, Illinois: Passport Books, 1992.
"'For Your Eyes Only'" and its special effects." *American Cinematograher*. August 1981: 764-766; 786-789.
Fleming, Ian. *Casino Royale*. London: Jonathan Cape, 1953.
—. *Casino Royale*. ms. Lilly Library, Bloomington, Indiana
—. *Diamonds Are Forever*. London: Jonathan Cape, 1956.
—. *Diamonds Are Forever*. ms. Lilly Library, Bloomington, Indiana
—. *Doctor No*. London: Jonathan Cape, 1958.
—. *Doctor No*. ms. Lilly Library, Bloomington, Indiana
—. *For Your Eyes Only*. London: Jonathan Cape, 1960.
—. *From Russia, With Love*. London: Jonathan Cape, 1957.
—. *From Russia, With Love*. ms. Lilly Library, Bloomington, Indiana
—. *Goldfinger*. London: Jonathan Cape, 1959.

—. *Goldfinger*. ms. Lilly Library, Bloomington, Indiana
—. "How to Write a Thriller." *Show*. Aug. 1962.
—. *James Bond of the Secret Service*. Unpublished treatment, 1959.
—. *Live and Let Die*. London: Jonathan Cape, 1954.
—. *Live and Let Die*. ms. Lilly Library, Bloomington, Indiana
—. *The Man with the Golden Gun*. London: Jonathan Cape, 1965.
—. *Moonraker*. London: Jonathan Cape, 1955.
—. *Moonraker*. ms. Lilly Library, Bloomington, Indiana
—. *Octopussy and The Living Daylights*. London: Jonathan Cape, 1966.
—. *On Her Majesty's Secret Service*. London: Jonathan Cape, 1963.
—. *On Her Majesty's Secret Service*. ms. Lilly Library, Bloomington, Indiana
—. *The Spy Who Loved Me*. London: Jonathan Cape, 1962.
—. *The Spy Who Loved Me*. ms. Lilly Library, Bloomington, Indiana
—. *Thrilling Cities*.New York: Signet, 1965.
—. *Thunderball*. London: Jonathan Cape, 1961.
—. "Treasure Hunt in Eden: Part One—Pirate Gold." *The Sunday Times*. 17 Aug. 1958.
—. *You Only Live Twice*. London: Jonathan Cape, 1964.
—. *You Only Live Twice*. ms. Lilly Library, Bloomington, Indiana
—. Foreword. *Room 3603: The Story of the British Intelligence Center in New York during World War II*. By H. Montgomery Hyde. New York: Farrar, Straus and Company, 1963.
—. Interview. *Playboy*. December 1964.
—. Letter to Julie Cohen. 18 October 1962. Russell, L. mss. Lilly Library, Bloomington, Indiana
—. Letter to Robert Darwin. 21 November 1961. Russell, L. mss. Lilly Library, Bloomington, Indiana
—. Letter to Eve Fleming. 11 May 1950. Russell, L. mss. Lilly Library, Bloomington, Indiana
—. Letter to Eve Fleming. 15 June 1950. Russell, L. mss. Lilly Library, Bloomington, Indiana
—. Letter to Eve Fleming. 28 August 1950. Russell, L. mss. Lilly Library, Bloomington, Indiana
—. Letter to Eve Fleming. 1 June 1961. Russell, L. mss. Lilly Library, Bloomington, Indiana
—. Letter to Michael Howard. 1 August 1963. Russell, L. mss. Lilly Library, Bloomington, Indiana
—. Letter to Viscount Nuffield. 27 September 1951. Russell, L. mss. Lilly Library, Bloomington, Indiana
—. Letter to Sir William Stephenson. 11 October 1951. Russell, L. mss. Lilly Library, Bloomington, Indiana
—. Letter to Witney Straight, Esq. 23 July, 1957. Russell, L. mss. Lilly Library, Bloomington, Indiana
Fleming, Ian, and Raymond Chandler. *British and American Thrillers*. The Third Programme. BBC Radio. London. July 1958.
Foulkes, Nicholas. *Turnbull & Asser*. London: Brompton Press, 1997.
Gangarosa, Gene, Jr. *The Walther Handgun Story*. Wayne, New Jersey: Stoeger Publishing Company, 1999.
Glen, John. Telephone interview. 23 Aug. 1998.
Godfrey, John. Letter to Ian Fleming. 14 April, 1961. Russell, L. mss. Lilly Library, Bloomington, Indiana
Great Britain. Cabinet Office. *Secret Service Committee Report*. 1 December 1925.
Gudgin, Peter. *Military Intelligence: The British Story*. London: Arms and Armour, 1989.
Grigg, John. *The History of The Times, Vol. 6: The Thomson Years 1966-1981*. London: Times Books, 1984.
Grimond, Kate. Telephone interview. 24 Aug. 1998.
Hardingham, Samantha. *London: A Guide to Recent Architecture*. London: Ellipsis, 1996.
Harwood, Elain, and Andrew Saint. *London*. London: HMSO, 1991.
Hemming, Lindy. Telephone interview. 25 Nov. 1999.
Hiley, Nicholas. "Decoding German Spies: British Spy Fiction 1908-1918". *Spy Fiction, Spy Films and Real Intelligence*. Ed. Wesley K. Wark. London: Frank Cass and Company, Limited, 1991. 55-79.
Hinsley, F. H., and C. A. G. Simkins. *Security and Counter-Intelligence*. London: HMSO, 1990. Vol. 4 of *British Intelligence in the Second World War*. 5 Vols. 1979-1990.
Howard, Michael. *Jonathan Cape, Publisher*. London: Jonathan Cape, 1980.
—. Letter to Ian Fleming. 31 July 1963. Russell, L. mss. Lilly Library, Bloomington, Indiana
Hunt, Peter. Telephone interview. 17 July 1998.
Hunter, John. *Great Scot, the Life of Sean Connery*. London: Bloomsbury Publishing, 1993.
Innes-Smith, Robert. *An Outline of Heraldry in England and Scotland*. Derby: Pilgrim Press, 1990.
James, Ewart. *NTC's Dictionary of the United Kingdom*. Lincolnwood, Illinois: NTC Publishing Group, 1996.

Johnstone, Iain. *The World Is Not Enough: A Companion*. London: Boxtree, 1999.
Jones, Edward, and Christopher Woodward. *A Guide to the Architecture of London*. 2nd ed.
London: Phoenix Illustrated, 1992.
Judd, Alan. *The Quest for C: Sir Mansfield Cumming and the Founding of the British Secret Service*. London: Harper Collins, 1999.
Juroe, Charles. Telephone interview. 1 Sept. 1999.
Knightley, Phillip. *The Second Oldest Profession: Spies and Spying in the Twentieth Century*. New York: Norton, 1986.
Lacey, Robert. *Sotheby's—Bidding for Class*. Boston: Little, Brown and Company, 1998.
Lamont, Neil. Telephone interview. 13 Aug. 1999.
Lamont, Peter. Telephone interviews. 30 June 1999 and 8 November 1999.
Lane, Sheldon, ed. *For Bond Lovers Only*. New York: Dell, 1965.
Lee, Christopher. Telephone interview. 20 Aug. 1999.
Lejeune, Anthony, and Malcolm Lewis. *The Gentlemen's Clubs of London*. London: Bracken Books, 1984.
Levine, Dan, and Richard Jones. *Frommer's Walking Tours: London*. New York: Prentice Hall Travel, 1993.
"The Living Daylights." *007* 16 June 1987: 20-28.
Lister, Eric. *Portal Painters: A Survey of British Idiosyncratic Artists*. London: Alpine Fine Arts, 1982.
Lloyd's. *Some Unusual Risks*. London: Lloyd's, 1998.
London Clubs International. *Les Ambassadeurs Club: A Brief History of No. 5 Hamilton Place*. London [?]
Lord Lichfield, ed. *Courvoisier's Book of the Best*. London: Ebury Press, 1986.
Luxford, Bert. Telephone interview. 8 Sept. 1999.
Lycett, Andrew. *Ian Fleming: The Man Behind James Bond*. London: Weidenfeld and Nicolson, 1995.
—. Telephone interview. 30 July 1998.
McCormick, Donald. *17F The Life of Ian Fleming*. London: Peter Owen, 1993.
McDonald, Iverach. *The History of The Times, Vol. 5: Struggles in War and Peace 1939-1966*. London: Times Books, 1984.
McInerney, Jay, Nick Foulkes, Neil Norman, and Nick Sullivan. *Dressed To Kill, James Bond the Suited Hero*. New York, Paris: Flammarion, 1996.
McLachlan, Donald. *Room 39: Naval Intelligence in Action 1939-1945*. London: Weidenfeld and Nicolson, 1968.
Masters, Anthony. *The Man Who Was M: The Life of Maxwell Knight*. Oxford: Basil Blackwell, 1984.
Membery, York. *Pierce Brosnan, The New Unauthorised Biography*. London: Virgin, 1997.
Menen, Aubrey. *London*. Amsterdam: Time-Life International, 1976.
Michelin. *Michelin Green Guide to London*. London: Michelin Tyre, 1998.
Moore, Roger. *Roger Moore as James Bond 007: Roger Moore's own account of filming Live and Let Die*. London: Pan Books, 1973.
Nash, Jay Robert. *Spies*. New York: M. Evans & Company, 1997.
O'Connor, Áine, ed. *Hollywood Irish In Their Own Words*. Boulder, Colorado: Roberts Rinehart, 1997.
Pearce, Garth. *The Making of GoldenEye*. Boxtree, 1995.
—. *The Making of Tomorrow Never Dies*. Boxtree, 1997.
Pearson, John. *The Life of Ian Fleming the Creator of James Bond*. London: Jonathan Cape, 1966.
—. Interview with Albert R. Broccoli. Pearson, J. mss. Lilly Library, Bloomington, Indiana
—. Interview with Admiral Sir Norman Denning. Pearson, J. mss. Lilly Library, Bloomington, Indiana
—. Interview with Ann Fleming. Pearson, J. mss. Lilly Library, Bloomington, Indiana
—. Interview with Peter Fleming. Pearson, J. mss. Lilly Library, Bloomington, Indiana
—. Interview with Richard Fleming. Pearson, J. mss. Lilly Library, Bloomington, Indiana
—. Interview with Admiral Sir John Godfrey. Pearson, J. mss. Lilly Library, Bloomington, Indiana
—. Interview with Peter Quennell. Pearson, J. mss. Lilly Library, Bloomington, Indiana
—. Interview with Guy Wellby. Pearson, J. mss. Lilly Library, Bloomington, Indiana
—. Interview with Mr. Whitley of Benson, Perry & Whitley. Pearson, J. mss. Lilly Library, Bloomington, Indiana
Porter, David. *The Man Who Was "Q", The Life of Charles Fraser-Smith*. London: Exeter, 1989.
Quelch, Ron. Telephone interviews. 19 July 1999 and 9 November 1999.
Read, Anthony and David Fisher. *Colonel Z: The Secret Life of a Master of Spies*. New York: Viking, 1985.
Richardson, John. Telephone interview. 4 February 2000.
Room, Adrian. *An A to Z of British Life*. Oxford: Oxford University Press, 1990.
Rose, Iris. Telephone interview. 30 June 1999.

Rosenberg, Bruce A. and Ann Harleman Stewart. *Ian Fleming*. Boston: Twayne Publishers, 1989.
Rubin, Steven Jay. *The Complete James Bond Movie Encyclopedia*. Chicago: Contemporary Books, 1995.
Sauerberg, Lars Ole. *Secret Agents in Fiction: Ian Fleming, John le Carré and Len Deighton*. New York: St. Martin's Press, 1984.
Schreuders, Pet, Mark Lewisohn, and Adam Smith. *The Beatles London: The Ultimate Guide to over 400 Beatles Sites in and around London*. New York: St. Martin's Press, 1994.
Scott, J. D. *Vickers: A History*. London: Weidenfeld and Nicolson, 1962.
Smith, Michael. *New Cloak, Old Dagger: How Britain's Spies Came In From The Cold*. London: Victor Gollancz, 1996.
Spoto, Donald. *The Decline and Fall of the House of Windsor*. New York: Simon & Schuster, 1995.
Stears, John. Telephone interview. 9 January 1999.
Tanner, Lt.-Col. William ('Bill'). *The Book of Bond or every man his own 007*. New York: Viking Press, 1965.
Tesche, Siegfried, and Steve Rubin. *James Bond 007*. Hamburg, Germany: Kino, 1995.
Tonks, Paul. "Tomorrow Never Dies, Yesterday Lives Again." *Film Score Monthly* Nov.-Dec. 1997: 16-21.
Turner, Christopher. *London Step by Step*. New York: St. Martin's Press, 1985.
Volkman, Ernest. *Spies: The Secret Agents Who Changed The Course of History*. New York: John Wiley and Sons, 1994.
Walker, Richard. *The Savile Row Story: An Illustrated History*. London: Prion, 1988.
Walker, Alexander. *Hollywood UK: The British Film Industry in the Sixties*. New York: Stein & Day, 1974.
Weinreb, Ben, and Christopher Hibbert, eds. *The London Encyclopaedia*. 2nd ed. London: Macmillan, 1995.
West, Nigel. *MI5: British Security Service Operations 1909-1945*. New York: Stein and Day, 1981.
—. *MI6: British Secret Intelligence Service Operations 1909-1945*. New York: Random House, 1983.
—. *Secret War: The Story of SOE, Britain's Wartime Sabotage Organisation*. London: Hodder & Stoughton, 1992.
—, ed. *The Faber Book of Espionage*. London: Faber and Faber, 1993.
Worrall, Dave. *The Most Famous Car in the World*. Christchurch, England: Solo, 1993.
Wurman, Richard Saul. *Access London*. 6th ed. New York: Access Press, 1998.
Yapp, Nick. *London: The Secrets and the Splendour*. Cologne: Könemann, 1999.
Young, Terence. Interview with Richard Schenkman. *Bondage* 10 (1981): 1-9.

Ian Fleming's office, 4 Old Mitre Court, London. *See Page 34*

PHOTO CREDITS

All photos by Gary Giblin and Chris Gardner, *except:* photos from the James Bond films courtesy of UIP; photo of Broccoli, Saltzman, Fleming, and Connery courtesy of The Lilly Library, Indiana University, Bloomington, Indiana; photo of *OHMSS* set courtesy of Peter Hunt; photos of Desmond Llewelyn and Madame Tussaud's figure by Ed Maggiani; photos of London Pavilion, *Thunderball* premiere party, Sean Connery in London, and *OHMSS* premiere courtesy of PIC; photo of balloon miniature courtesy of John Richardson; photo of the Cathedral of St Sophia courtesy of the cathedral; photos of Peter Hunt, John Stears, Peter Lamont, Pierce Brosnan at the Regent Hotel, and Terence Young at Harefield courtesy of Dave Worrall; and photos of *TWINE* boat chase action and locations, including back cover photo of Pierce Brosnan on location for *The World Is Not Enough*, courtesy of Dave Williams at: www.bondpix.co.uk.

ABOUT THE AUTHOR

A freelance writer and consultant from Indiana, Gary Giblin has worked on a variety of OO7-related projects, including the 1996 James Bond Jamaica Festival, the 1977 Let's Bond in Britain Tour, and the 2001 "Secrets of Spying" television program on The Learning Channel. In 1998, he served as a consultant to MGM/UA, writing the company's in-house reference guide to the James Bond novels and films. He presently serves as editor and head writer of *Secret Intelligence*, a webzine he created with Lee Pfeiffer and Navin Jain. He and his wife, Lisa, live near Cincinnati, Ohio, where she teaches English. His forthcoming books include *James Bond's Britain* and *Alfred Hitchcock's London*, both from Daleon Enterprises.

Below: Author Gary Giblin in Room 39. *See page 126.*

TRIVIA CHALLENGE ANSWERS

1. Xenia
2. Monaco, which would be handy for the Rainiers, not to mention a bit of *GoldenEye* filming in 1995
3. Nine (with Bond seated in the 007th chair, counting L to R)
4. Four (Rodney; Gibson; Hai Fat; Andrea)
5. *You Only Live Twice*; *OHMSS*; *Live and Let Die*; *For Your Eyes Only*; *A View To A Kill*; *Licence To Kill*
6. Bond scans a copy in *The World Is Not Enough* (on-screen, while searching the MI6 Research Archive).
7. If he knew they were investigating Carver
8. 1,000 guineas
9. *Moonraker*, Chapter 19
10. *Tomorrow Never Dies*, as M's motorcade pulls out into Poultry
11. Siberian Separatists
12. *Moonraker*—"Vesti la giubba" from Leoncavallo's *I Pagliacci*
13. Blue-white flawless diamonds
14. The film that inaugurated a new era of Anglo-Soviet cooperation—*The Spy Who Loved Me*. The occasion was the official dedication of the 007 Stage on December 5, 1976, a ceremony also attended by the British Prime Minister, Harold Wilson.
15. "Questionable"
16. Christopher Lee, who later played Holmes himself in a number of European productions, as well as Holmes' brother Mycroft in Billy Wilder's *The Private Life of Sherlock Holmes*
17. *From Russia With Love*, during the punting scene
18. *Licence To Kill*
19. Half a million pounds
20. In "Risico", to Lisl, for info on drug smuggling. (As in the film *For Your Eyes Only*, Bond is posing as a writer doing research on smugglers.)
21. Van Cleef and Arpels
22. The Minister of Defence
23. February 1969
24. Richard Vernon, who played the Governor of the Bank of England in *Goldfinger*
25. The Homer/receiver to track Goldfinger
26. Felix Leiter in *Thunderball*—after Bond alludes to his underwater equipment as "the kitchen sink"
27. The birth of his son Caspar
28. *From Russia, With Love* (it's the scene of his near-fatal encounter with Rosa Klebb)
29. The surname of SPECTRE's head honcho was pinched from Norfolk farmer Tom Blofeld, chairman of the Country Gentlemen's Association, whose name Fleming had spotted on the list of Boodle's members.
30. Francisco Scaramanga
31. Sir Hilary Bray
32. Augustus John not only painted several portraits of Ian's mother Eve, he also sired her daughter Amaryllis.
33. *For Your Eyes Only*
34. Cubby Broccoli's Memorial Service
35. Shirley Eaton
36. Noël Coward
37. "Most Secret"
38. The First Sea Lord is referred to in *The Spy Who Loved Me*, when Captain Benson telephones him regarding the disappearance of the *Ranger*.
39. *The Man With The Golden Gun*
40. *Dr. No* ("When do you sleep, 007?" "Never on the Firm's time, sir."); Fleming himself uses the name in the story "From a View To a Kill"
41. Q stands for Quartermaster.
42. Empire Chemicals
43. M, in the novel *OHMSS*
44. He isn't
45. The Emperor of the Air
46. Quarterdeck
47. Ernö Goldfinger, an acquaintance of Fleming's, (in)famous for his reinforced concrete tower blocks (apartment buildings) and houses. Fleming himself protested in vain the construction of the houses at 1-3 Willow Road, just down from his own childhood home in North End Avenue. Mr. Goldfinger lived in this very row until his death in 1987.
48. *Moonraker*
49. The Locomotive; own him
50. $300 million

Scoring:

100-91 Apply immediately to MI6—you'll soon be running the Secret Service!
90-81 Bond could scarcely have done better—your success as a Double-0 agent seems assured
80-71 Consider yourself best-suited for *Standard Intelligence* duties—at least for now
70-61 Don't buy your Swaine Adeney attaché case any time soon, although with a little study you might still make the grade
60-00 Forget about it—Jerry Lewis would make a better spy than you!

APPENDIX ONE
James Bond's Guide to Good Living
A Ready Reference

His Armourer
- Bapty, Ltd, Kensal Green (42:1)

His Auctioneer
- Sotheby's, Mayfair (13:11)

His Barber
- Geo. F. Trumper, Mayfair (13:25)

His Booksellers
- Hatchard's, St James's (16:15)

His Bootmakers
- John Lobb, St James's (16:7)
- Church's, Mayfair outlet (13:10)

His Car Dealers/Manufacturers
- Jack Barclay, Mayfair (13:22)
- Rolls Motor Cars, Cheshire (*JBB*)
- Aston Martin Lagonda Ltd, Mayfair and Bucks. (13:Q; *JBB*)
- Lotus Cars, Norfolk (*JBB*)

His China Supplier
- Minton's, Staffordshire (*JBB*)

His Clubs
- Crockford's (now of Mayfair) (16:23)
- Les Ambassadeurs Club, Mayfair (13:38)

His Supplier of Gentleman's Accessories
- Alfred Dunhill, St James's (16:12)

His Golf Courses
- Huntercombe, Oxfordshire, among others (*JBB*)
- Royal St George's, Kent (*JBB*)
- Stoke Poges, Bucks. (*JBB*)

His Grocers
- Fortnum & Mason, St James's (16:13)
- Harrods, Knightsbridge (10:2)

His Hatmaker
- James Lock, St James's (16:8)

His Hotel
- The Ritz, St James's (16:1)

His Jewelers
- Wartski, Mayfair (13:16)
- Cartier, Mayfair (13:19)
- David Morris International, Mayfair (13:20)

His Knifemaker
- Wilkinson Sword (now of North Acton) (see 16:24)

His Leather Goods Suppliers
- Swaine Adeney Brigg, St James's (16:14)
- Alfred Dunhill, St James's (16:12)

His Pharmacist
- John Bell & Croyden, Marylebone (12:Q)

His Raincoat Supplier
- Burberry's, Soho (19:4)

His Favorite Restaurant
- Scott's (now of Mayfair) (19:6)

His Scottish Outfitters
- Scotch House, Knightsbridge (10:1)

His Shirtmakers
- Turnbull & Asser, St James's (16:10)

His Sportswear Supplier
- Lillywhite's, Soho (19:3)

His Tailors
- Anderson & Sheppard (presumed), Mayfair (13:14)
- Major's, Fulham (34:1)
- Douglas Hayward, Mayfair (13:5)
- Brioni of Rome, Mayfair outlets (13:40)

His Toiletries Supplier
- J. Floris, St James's (16:17)

Below: The Ritz. *Right:* Bond's sitting room.

APPENDIX TWO
Ian Fleming's
James Bond of the Secret Service (1959)

In 1959, Ian Fleming wrote a screen treatment for a proposed James Bond film to be financed by his friend Ivar Bryce and directed by Kevin McClory. McClory then hired screenwriter Jack Whittingham to pen the actual shooting script, while Fleming, in turn, went on to write his next novel. When *Thunderball* was published in the spring of 1961, McClory sued Fleming and Bryce for copyright infringement, claiming joint authorship of the novel. The pair settled out of court, ceding McClory the film rights to *Thunderball*, as well as to the scripts and other written materials associated with the original project. McClory eventually produced the film *Thunderball* in temporary partnership with Cubby Broccoli, Harry Saltzman and United Artists. Eighteen years later, Warner Bros. released *Never Say Never Again*, which, in turn, McClory intended to succeed with further Bond films. In 1997, Sony announced plans to launch a "rival" James Bond series based on McClory's rights, at which point MGM/UA countered with its own lawsuit against the Japanese entertainment giant. The highly-publicized case was eventually settled out of court to the satisfaction of MGM and Sony, but not Mr. McClory, who continues to press his claims regarding ownership of the cinematic Bond. Largely overlooked in this 40-year imbroglio has been the little-known treatment at the heart of it all, *James Bond of the Secret Service*. As a Fleming Bond story partly set in England, its locations certainly merit inclusion in this book. However, as this "lost" James Bond adventure has never been published, I have included the following synopsis for reference. Those who have seen the treatment, copies of which have been floating around the fan circuit for years, or those who have read the synopsis in the Spring 1994 issue of *Goldeneye* magazine, may skip this section.

The story begins with Bond completing his regular target practice in the Secret Service's underground shooting gallery, a scene borrowed from the opening of the novel *Moonraker*. Bond is lectured about using "a ladies' gun", the Beretta, just as the Armourer had done in Chapter 2 of *Doctor No*. After returning to his office, Bond is summoned to a meeting with M and Assistant Commissioner Ronald Vallance of Scotland Yard, a character who also appears in *Moonraker* and several other stories. The Yard has been monitoring the activities of one Henrico Largo, the top Mafia man in London, and something big has come up. Largo's gang has scheduled a midnight rendezvous at the Shoeburyness rocket site near the mouth of the Thames and the Yard believes that they may try to steal an atomic warhead. In the unlikely event that they succeed, James Bond of the Secret Service will have to go after them. Bond therefore decides to conduct a recce of the villain's local headquarters, a roadhouse called "The Spangled Room" (à la the American mob described in *Diamonds Are Forever* and *Goldfinger*) on the outskirts of Epping Forest. Made up to look like a thug, right down to the prominent gold tooth (cf. the make-up he wears in *Diamonds Are Forever*), Bond drives his *Moonraker*-era Bentley to the roadhouse and meets with Vallance's undercover agent, Domino Smith. Although her given name anticipates that of *Thunderball*'s heroine, Domino clearly echoes the Gala Brand character in *Moonraker*. She tells Bond how he can break into Largo's private quarters, then warns him that the mobsters are nervous tonight. Adopting yet another disguise, this time as a burglar alarm repairman, Bond begins to snoop in earnest, encounters—and disposes of—one of Largo's guards and then makes his way to the big man's office. Largo himself is there, learning to play the organ (!), and wonders how Bond got past the guard. Toni, Largo's bodyguard, discovers the fallen guard, puts two and two together (to make 007) and beats Bond into unconsciousness. Largo orders that Bond be left to melt in the boiler room, assembles his gang and then departs for the rocket site. Domino rescues Bond and together they drive back to London to warn Vallance. (There were apparently no public telephones in the vicinity.) Naturally, they are too late: Largo and his men, disguised as military personnel, have bluffed their way onto the Shoeburyness rocket site (cf. the villain's "Red Cross" assault on Fort Knox in *Goldfinger*), "identified" a warhead that is supposedly leaking lethal radioactive material and carefully removed it in a helicopter. The Air Ministry and Admiralty immediately dispatch search planes and boats, believing that the helicopter has rendezvoused with a ship in the English Channel. Bond joins the search on a motor torpedo boat (MTB) out of Dover, and eventually discovers a suspicious freighter in the Channel. Boarding the ship with members of the MTB crew, Bond quickly surmises that the mobsters landed here, ditched the helicopter, booby-trapped the freighter and flew off in a seaplane. After exploding the booby-trapped freighter, Bond asks the Air Ministry to check on the whereabouts of all seaplanes similar to the one that Largo would have used for his getaway. Some time later, at London Airport, Vallance tells Bond that the seaplane in question has turned up in Nassau and that the "Capo Mafiosi" has sent a ransom demand to the Prime Minister. If the Mafia doesn't receive £100 million worth of gold in carefully arranged drops over Sicily, they will explode the bomb at a vital Western defense installation and thereby shift the balance of power to the Soviets, not to mention killing a hell of a lot of people. Bond has less than two weeks to find the bomb or else. In this, Vallance tells him, he will be aided by Felix Leiter of the CIA and Domino Smith of Scotland Yard.

The action now shifts to Nassau, where Largo's New York counterpart, Mr. Impellitini, arrives to discuss the underwater rehearsal that must be conducted before they plant the bomb. Bond, meanwhile, has liaised with various government officials, Leiter—whom he meets for the first time—and Domino. During a telephone conversation with M, Bond learns that the intended target is most likely the new Anglo-American rocket site on Grand Bahama, just north of Nassau. The focus of the investigation now turns to Impellitini's magnificent yacht, "The Virginia", which Bond decides to investigate. Here, Fleming inserts another trademark setting, the casino, albeit with Leiter and Domino instead of Bond, who is out conducting the underwater recce. At this point, the story clearly foreshadows the future novel (Chapters 16 and 17, in fact), as Bond fights with a sentry underwater, watches as the man is eaten by a shark (a barracuda in the novel) then swims ashore to be interrogated by the local police. Back at the hotel, Bond uses a nylon ladder to descend to Largo's room and plant a microphone. Largo returns shortly thereafter, with Domino in tow, quickly discovers that she is a phony and begins to assault her. Bond, having overheard the struggle, drops back down to Largo's room (similar to the *Diamonds Are Forever* climax aboard the *Queen Elizabeth*), sneaks up behind him and says, "If you must murder your wife, I wish you'd make less noise about it. I sleep just above you and I simply can't get to sleep." This is the Bond of Fleming's most recent novel, *Goldfinger*, a knowing wisecracker whose lines anticipate those of the "She's just dead" variety in the films to come. This is also the setting for what would become the most famous line in the history of cinema. As Bond prepares to escort Domino from the villain's clutches, he turns to Largo and says: "My name's Bond—James Bond. Perhaps we shall meet some time under happier circumstances." Bond and Domino retreat to her room, she professes her attraction to him and, to quote the unusually reticent Fleming, "a love scene follows."

The next day, Largo's men don diving equipment, exit through a concealed underwater hatch in the Virginia and practice with their CO_2 guns. Bond surveys this spectacle while water-skiing (!) behind a fast speedboat driven by Leiter and filled "with a bevy of miscellaneous girls". Largo and his men then sail to the spot where the seaplane dropped the bomb and recover it. The plan is to place the bomb in the harbor of the rocket base, set the timer and await the ransom money. If all goes well, they will return to the base and remove the bomb. Bond, having guessed what the mobsters are up to, arranges to intercept the Virginia in a US submarine and fight an underwater battle with Largo's men, just as he will do in the subsequent novel. Meanwhile, Domino "makes up" with Largo by accepting an invitation to a party he is throwing aboard the yacht. Once again we enter familiar waters: Domino will be carrying a small, portable Geiger counter in order to determine whether the bomb is already aboard the ship. If so, Bond will have the mobsters arrested at once. Unfortunately, she is caught in the act and *nearly* tortured by Toni. (His lighted cigarette foreshadows the cigar and ice of the novel and film.) Thinking fast, Domino claims to have been looking for stolen Swiss watches on behalf of Customs and Largo, incredibly, swallows her tale. Regrettably, though, he cannot put her ashore as he must take his men on an urgent trip for some "fresh air". Later, with the aid of a knife she removed from her dinner tray (as Bond had done in *Doctor No*), Domino slips out of her locked cabin and steals a set of diving equipment, including a CO_2 gun. Meanwhile, Bond and Leiter shadow the Virginia from the submarine, biding their time until they reach the rocket site. In parentheses, Fleming indicates that "this will, in fact, be Cape Canaveral taken from seawards." Come the morning, the yacht arrives at the base, with the sub close behind. The underwater team emerges with its deadly cargo, while Domino Smith, looking "resplendent in her black underwater suit", watches from the sidelines. Fleming tells us that "Bond's underwater army" (a nice touch, that) converges upon Largo's men and "a great pitched battle then ensues…culminating in a life and death struggle between Bond and Largo." To the rescue comes Domino, who saves Bond's life by shooting Largo with her CO_2 gun. This memorable scene will, of course, reappear in the novel and the film and the remake. The pair then swim to the sands, where they rest in the shallow waters. Bond "lifts off his mask then hers and kisses her."

Screenwriter Whittingham would later complain that too much of this story was told in dialogue, that the Mafia was not menacing enough, that they should steal *two* bombs, that Domino gets away with her antics too easily, that the roadhouse scene was unconvincing, that more people than just Bond should be involved, etc. Some of his criticisms were no doubt valid and Fleming certainly incorporated a number of them in his revised treatment. Indeed, he lopped off virtually the entire English "prologue", having Bond called in *after* the bombs have already been stolen. (He would, of course, restore the English prologue, albeit in a different setting, in the novel.) In the subsequent screenplays, called *Longitude 78 West*, Whittingham went even further, his most drastic change being the elimination of the heroine,

Domino Smith. In her place is "Gaby", the villain's mistress, a vulgar, brainless, money-grubbing bimbo. (At one point, she remarks to Bond that if she doesn't get her ass pinched ten times in two minutes, she'll be slipping. Largo himself calls her a "butt-peddler" and later, when Bond explains that her lover could bring about another Hiroshima, she doesn't understand the reference.) Whittingham clearly had no interest in Fleming's noble and capable heroine (yes, for his time, Fleming was something of a "feminist") nor, for that matter, in Bond himself. Indeed, 007 doesn't enter the script until nearly 30 minutes have passed! And when it comes time for the famous trademarks, forget about it. Whittingham's hero replies to Gaby's "Mr....?" with a matter-of-fact "Bond." Period. And it is *she* who orders a vodka martini, not Bond.

That Fleming based the novel *Thunderball* on the hybrid treatments and screenplays is not disputed. But the difference between the Fleming material and the non-Fleming material is seldom less than crystal clear, in theme, tone and approach, if not always in plot points. For his Bond is a true hero, his heroines truly noble and truly capable. And realistically or not, his Bond will always be the focus of the action, his Bond the one called upon to save the day. That's the way Ian Fleming described his protagonist in 12 novels, nine short stories and two screen treatments. And that, I hope, is the way that James Bond will always be remembered in the hearts and minds of everyone who follows his adventures.

Top: MI6's Fleming-era HQ, Broadway Buildings (*see page 134*)
Above: The Old Admiralty building where Fleming worked for Naval Intelligence (*see page 126*)

INDEX

Note:
The two-part numbers refer to entries, not pages.

Espionage/Defence

Films

Boldface numbers indicate actual filming locations, such as Sotheby's (**13:11**), which appears in *Octopussy*.

Fleming, Ian

Novels and Stories

The End, but James Bond will return in *James Bond's Britain*

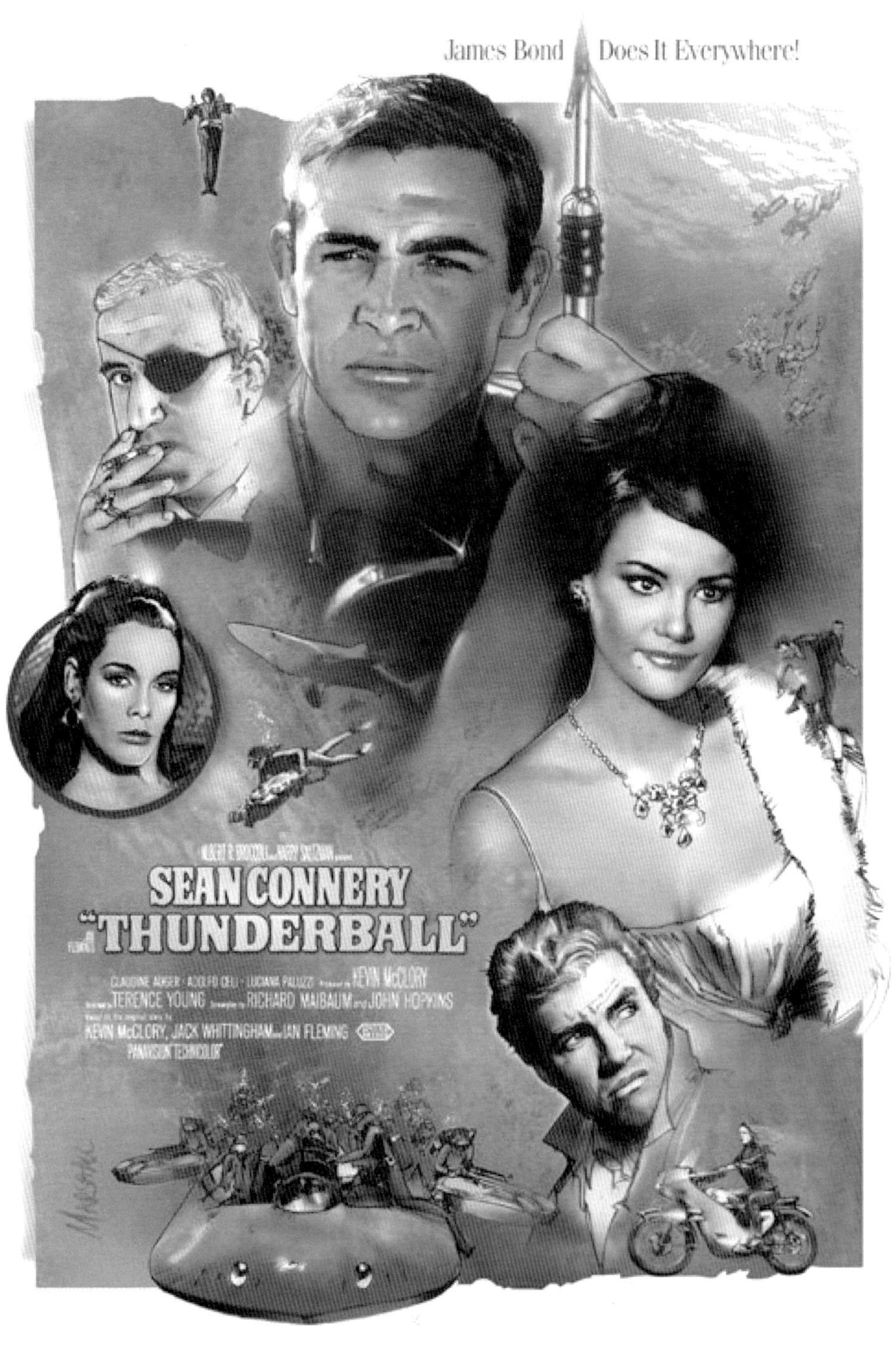
James Bond Does It Everywhere!
SEAN CONNERY
"THUNDERBALL"
CLAUDINE AUGER · ADOLFO CELI · LUCIANA PALUZZI
KEVIN McCLORY
TERENCE YOUNG
RICHARD MAIBAUM
JOHN HOPKINS
KEVIN McCLORY, JACK WHITTINGHAM
IAN FLEMING

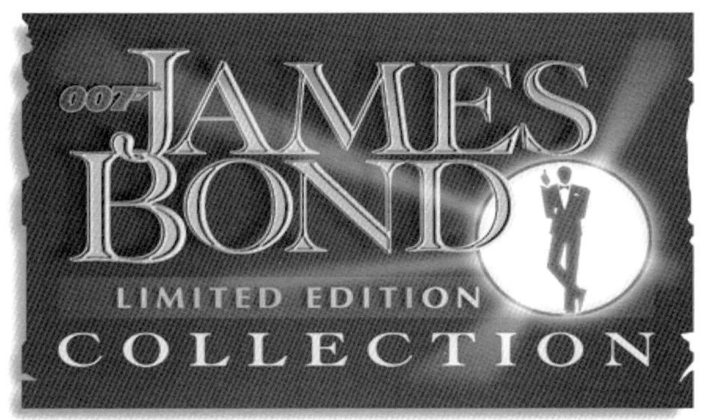
007 JAMES BOND
LIMITED EDITION
COLLECTION

James Bond production designer Syd Cain with the tour party at Pinewood Studios during the 'Let's Bond In Britain Tour' of 1997.

FOR INFORMATION ABOUT TOURS OF LONDON SPY MOVIE LOCATIONS, INCLUDING MANY SITES FROM THIS BOOK, PLEASE VISIT WWW.TWINETOURS.COM OR WRITE TO:

T.W.I.N.E. TOURS
POB 152
DUNELLEN,
NEW JERSEY 08812
USA